The Family Idiot

The Family Idiot

GUSTAVE FLAUBERT, 1821–1857,
AN ABRIDGED EDITION

Jean-Paul Sartre

TRANSLATED BY CAROL COSMAN

ABRIDGED AND INTRODUCED BY JOSEPH S. CATALANO

The University of Chicago Press
Chicago and London

The University of Chicago Press, Chicago 60637
The University of Chicago Press, Ltd., London

Published 2023
Printed in the United States of America

32 31 30 29 28 27 26 25 24 23   1 2 3 4 5

ISBN-13: 978-0-226-82231-0 (cloth)
ISBN-13: 978-0-226-82232-7 (paper)
ISBN-13: 978-0-226-82230-3 (e-book)
DOI: https://doi.org/10.7208/chicago/9780226822303.001.0001

The University of Chicago Press published Jean-Paul Sartre's entire work *The Family Idiot* in five volumes between 1981 and 1994. The present volume is an abridged edition highlighting the Work's main ideas.

Library of Congress Cataloging-in-Publication Data

Names: Sartre, Jean-Paul, 1905–1980, author. | Catalano, Joseph S., editor. | Cosman, Carol, translator.
Title: The family idiot : Gustave Flaubert, 1821–1857, an abridged edition / Jean-Paul Sartre ; translated by Carol Cosman ; abridged and introduced by Joseph S. Catalano.
Other titles: Idiot de la famille. English
Description: Chicago : The University of Chicago Press, 2023. | Includes bibliographical references and index.
Identifiers: LCCN 2022034885 | ISBN 9780226822310 (cloth) | ISBN 9780226822327 (paperback) | ISBN 9780226822303 (ebook)
Subjects: LCSH: Flaubert, Gustave, 1821–1880. | Novelists—Biography. | BISAC: LITERARY CRITICISM / European / French | PHILOSOPHY / Movements / Existentialism
Classification: LCC PQ2247 .S313 2023 | DDC 843/.8—dc23/eng/20220824
LC record available at https://lccn.loc.gov/2022034885

♾ This paper meets the requirements of ANSI/NISO Z39.48-1992 (Permanence of Paper).

Contents

Editor's Introduction

JOSEPH S. CATALANO

When the French philosopher and novelist Jean-Paul Sartre (1905–80) was in his seventies, going blind and aware of his approaching death, he wrote and published a 2,800-page biography of Gustave Flaubert (1821–80). The French publisher Gallimard brought out the work in three volumes from 1971 to 1972. An English translation was made by Carol Cosman and published by the University of Chicago Press in five volumes from 1981 to 1993.

Cosman writes in her translator's note in her first volume:

> *L'Idiot de la famille*, or *The Family Idiot* as I have called it, is Sartre's last major work and a kind of summa of everything in the way of his philosophic, social, and literary thought that had gone before. It is, as Sartre says, an exercise in methodology—a case in point illustrating the procedure formulated in *Search for a Method*. But of course Sartre uses this "exercise" to lead us on an exhaustive search for Flaubert, whose person and persona provide opportunity for the empathetic, imaginative reconstruction of a psyche, for social analysis, for investigations of epistemological and ontological issues, for literary and linguistic speculation.

Granting all the above, we might still rightly ask, "Why all the effort?"

The title of this massive work gives a clue to its importance, *The Family Idiot: Gustave Flaubert, 1821–1857*. Was the French novelist Gustave Flaubert regarded as the idiot of the Flaubert family? Sartre's answer is yes! Was this only when Gustave was young and through some early mistaken judgment about his abilities, and did it change when Gustave became famous? Sartre's answer is no! The idiot scribbles, they said, when Gustave was young, and when Gustave was famous—look, he continues to scribble.

Surely the members of Flaubert family were not idiots themselves. How could they have held such a view of one of their children? The answer, for Sartre, comes in paying attention to the ways these parents viewed their projected family life. The eminent doctor Achille-Cléophas Flaubert and his wife Caroline had plans for their children, and, Sartre observes, when parents have decisive plans, their children have destinies. Clearly there is nothing wrong in parents having some kind of plans for their children. For Sartre, however, all the written evidence points to these particular parents aiming for their children to be reflections of themselves.

For a long time, the family plan seemed to work out. Achille, the firstborn son, was bright, quick to learn the alphabet, and awake to all that went on about him. He fulfilled his destiny by becoming a doctor like his eminent father. Later, after Gustave was born, Caroline, the only daughter, was similarly a quick learner, and she made a good match in marriage like her mother, for whom she was named. From birth, however, Gustave was different. He was slow, backward, appearing always to be in a fog, doing whatever crazy thing his parents might suggest as if words had no real meaning for him. It was as if he suspected what they wanted of him and was unable or unwilling to conform to the family plan.

He paid a price for his resistance. Sartre does not mince words: "Gustave's relationship with his mother deprived him of affirmative power, tainted his relationship to the word and to truth, destined him for sexual perversion; his relationship with his father made him lose his sense of reality" (Cosman 2:69).[1] We might be tempted to put all the blame on the father alone, but Sartre makes a case that the mother refused to put herself on the side of her children, particularly Gustave.

There was also another facet to the family life, one that particularly affected Gustave. The children's destiny was controlled by a return to the older notion of the right of primogeniture—the firstborn son was to be the Flaubert child. Mother Caroline's firstborn was, in fact, a son, Achille. No doubt, she would have dutifully cared for a firstborn daughter, but the expectation of a son would have shadowed this birth. When a daughter, another Caroline, was born, she was the only daughter and thus had her own special place within the family. Gustave, however, was at birth an in-between, a second son who could never surpass the firstborn status of his older brother nor would ever receive the gendered status of his sister.

Finally, there was another consideration that made Gustave's childhood life somewhat ambiguous. The family wanted more children, particularly sons, but there were deaths, one before Gustave was born and one after. As far as sons were concerned, only the first seemed both strong and fully awake to the world: "Big brother Achille became, alone, the fragile hope of a family plagued by death. When Gustave arrived, the chips were already down" (Cosman 1:101).

"The chips are down" recalls the language of *Being and Nothingness*, and the general implication is that reflective decisions about how we should behave frequently follow on more basic earlier attitudes that Sartre refers to as our fundamental project. Not everything we do calls into question our general view of life; this would be burdensome. But now and then we do encounter the ever-present possibility of radical change—conversions. I will return to this idea, but for the present it is sufficient to note that the phrase "the chips are down" refers not only to the precarious position of Gustave as a child who might die but more specifically to his twofold secondary place within the family, second-born son but also fragile in body and slow in mind. Thus, whatever attention was given to Gustave, this attention arose from the lived doubt whether he would survive and, if he did survive, whether he would make the grade as a Flaubert.

But let us return to the theme of Gustave's early resistance to the family plan, which is one of three themes that I see running throughout this massive work. Gustave was misjudged by his family, but, as he grew older, why did he not simply put his family behind him and move on with his life? Strangely, this was not Gustave's choice: "Flaubert lived within the domestic group and never left it. From one end of his life to the other, the younger son regarded himself as an inessential accident: the essential thing for him would always be the family" (Cosman 1:71).

Still, one might call into question whether parents have this much control over their children. Parental presence usually is tempered by the influence of relatives and friends; but when the family structure is tight, as it was with the Flaubert family, the infant can enter the real world only through the family. If the family does not offer the infant a tender love, only one other path beckons: the imaginary. (Later, the child or the adolescent may choose death.) The infant Gustave Flaubert chose the imaginary. Too young to put a bundle of clothes over his shoulder and leave a home in which he felt unwanted, he found a way—as do many others—to keep his fragile body at home while his mind lived elsewhere. In this way, from his earliest years until he was about seven, Flaubert gave himself over to his daydreams and seemed always to be in a stupor. Nevertheless, by ten or eleven years of age, he was already writing with exceptional competence. "Let us not forget," Sartre writes, "that from his thirteenth year the cards were on the table, Gustave wrote books and letters, he had permanent witnesses. It is impossible to take liberties with facts so well known" (Cosman 1:46).

Moving on to the second of the three themes, I now call attention to Sartre's longtime interest in Gustave Flaubert's life. When Sartre was in his midthirties, he had already devoted several pages to Flaubert in *Being and Nothingness*.[2] Sartre there asked why this man wished to write when his family was against it, and why he wrote in the way that he did. Sartre concedes that the answer to these questions would require a kind of "Freud" that did not then exist. *The Family Idiot* is Sartre becoming that kind of Freud.

Still, granting that Sartre could have chosen many individuals to study, we must ask again, "Why Gustave Flaubert?" The most important reason is that critics regard Flaubert as the father of modern realism, but for Sartre, Gustave's realism bespeaks a deep nihilism. Specifically, *Madame Bovary* is regarded by many scholars as the epitome of a modern realist novel; and yet, for Sartre, this work aims to awaken in us despair, hatred of our fellow humans—particularly the weak—and a sense of the uselessness of all human behavior. And yet, most modern readers seem strangely unaware of the negative content of Flaubert's writings.

The third theme I see running through this work is that it is a summary of all Sartre's philosophy, revealing not only the development but also the continuity of Sartre's ideas. From his first major work *Being and Nothingness* to *The Family Idiot*, Sartre's consistent theme is that we are all born to be philosophers; no degree is required as we each spontaneously, at some time in our lives, question what it means to exist. Toward the end of *Being and Nothingness*, part 4, chapter 1, Sartre writes, "My ultimate and initial project—for these are but one—is, we will see, always the outline of a solution of the problem of being." He adds, "But this solution is not first conceived and then realized; we are this solution." We are the solution to the fundamental question of the meaning and use of all things because, first and foremost, it is through us that things are given names. Indeed, in the first volume of *The Family Idiot*, Sartre writes about the linguistic backwardness of the young Gustave, "The question then bears on everything, and this is the stupor: why do names exist?" (Cosman 1:154).

These are the three main themes that I see in *The Family Idiot*: First, a detailed reflection on the vulnerability of infants and children to adults. Second, a detailed reflection on our present notion of what is shadowy and false as opposed to what is real and true. And third, a summary of Sartre's committed philosophy focused on a specific life. As we read this long and at times difficult work, we encounter Sartre's use of the ideas of Karl Marx, Sigmund Freud, and Charles Darwin, always altered and imbued with Sartre's notion of freedom and responsibility, particularly here the freedom of Gustave Flaubert. True, he was not properly loved; still he freely chose to nurse his unwanted status in the family, projecting it onto the world. We witness Flaubert join that strange group of writers, the Knights of Nothingness, the exact opposite of Sartre's notion of the committed writer. For these strange knights, writing refers only to itself, soiled by the very eyes that may run over the pages; and yet through the magic of style, we readers are led to prefer images to what is real and to abandon the meaningfulness of human effort. Fredrick Jameson, in a review in the *New York Times* on December 27, 1981, wrote of our strange preference for images to reality:

> For it should not be thought that the nihilism of the imaginary, as it is elaborately anatomized in *The Family Idiot*, is a mere 19th-century curiosity or a local feature of some specifically French middle-class culture; nor is it a private obsession of Jean-Paul Sartre himself. Turning things into images, abolishing the real world, grasping the world as little more than a text or sign-system—this is notoriously the very logic of our own consumer society, the society of the image or the media event (the Vietnam War as a television series). Flaubert's private solution, his invention of a new "derealizing" esthetic strategy, may seem strange and distant, not because it is archaic, but because it has gradually become the logic of our media society, thereby becoming invisible to us. This is the sense in which *The Family Idiot*—at first glance a cumbersome and forbidding project—may well speak with terrifying immediacy to Americans in the 1980s.

And it speaks beyond the 1980s as well, as we witness how many of our twenty-first-century leaders frequently bask in an empty showmanship in which they alone are important. Still, returning to the life of Gustave Flaubert, Sartre would have us regard with sympathy this poor idiot of the Flaubert family: "Worst of all, he condemns himself in advance—he judges himself according to the norms the Flauberts have adopted" (Cosman 1:337). Gustave Flaubert can never free himself from the influences of his family. Yes, Gustave is free; but he uses his freedom to become the person who strangely regards himself as superior, precisely because he is a Flaubert, and yet he never abandons the family's lowly opinion of him, never really admits to himself that they continue to regard him as the family idiot but always suspects this truth. For Sartre, it is all there in his early writings if you read them carefully: a deep hatred of his parents that later comes out in his false notion of realism. Sartre will devote hundreds of pages to revealing how Gustave develops his personality. It all begins with a "wound" that should never have occurred, and to which I continually return:

> The valorization of the infant through care will touch him more deeply the more this tenderness is manifest. . . . Let a child once in is life—at three months, at six—taste this victory of pride, he is a man, never in all his life will he be able to revive the supreme voluptuousness of this sovereignty or to forget. But he will preserve even in misfortune a kind of religious optimism based on the abstract and calm certainty of his own value. We shall say, in any case, that an adventure begun in this fashion has nothing in common with Flaubert's (Cosman 1:129–30n2).

The specificity of Sartre's analysis accounts for the length and complexity of this study. Nevertheless, universality is also an issue, and it, too, has its own motif in the book, as Sartre makes clear in the first page of his preface:

> For a man is never an individual; it would be more fitting to call him a *universal singular*. Summed up and for this reason universalized by his epoch, he in turn resumes it by reproducing himself in it as singularity. Universal by the singular universality of human history, singular by the universalizing singularity of his projects, he requires simultaneous examination from both ends.

Indeed, no human life begins with a neutral outlook on the world. The infant's clothes, the crib, the crucifix on the wall or the statue of the Buddha on the mantel or the colored objects floating above it as well as the smiles, the frowns, the touches, the feeding and care—all of this comes to the infant as from some heaven, transcending and enveloping its budding freedom, inclining it to develop in this way rather than in another way. This is normal and healthy. Nevertheless, a child who is truly loved will later begin to think for himself or herself, moving forward in life on the memory of the infant's early days in paradise, or carrying the burden of its loss. For Sartre, a great deal depends on the initial glances and touches received by the infant from the mother or guardian. Indeed, if Sartre had neglected to consider the dependence of infants and children on adults in his earlier works, such an omission would have been remedied in great detail in *The Family Idiot*, and yet the work also includes all the major themes of his whole philosophy.

Sartre's Philosophy and *The Family Idiot*

Let us now take a brief look at a few of the central themes of Sartre's philosophy that guide the development of *The Family Idiot*.

In his *Search for a Method*, Sartre writes:

> Recently an essayist, thinking to refute existentialism, wrote: "It is not man who is profound; it is the world." He was perfectly right, and we agree with him without reservations. Only we should add that the world is human, the profundity of man is the world; therefore profundity comes to the world through man.[3]

And, in his study of Jean Genet:

> I have tried to do the following: to indicate the limit of psychoanalytical interpretation and Marxist explanation and to demonstrate that freedom alone can account for a person in his totality.[4]

Freedom accounts for our personality as distinct from our individuality. I understand this to be one of Sartre's greatest contributions to our understanding of ourselves. As an infant and then as a child, I will have all the characteristics of my family heritage, perhaps going back several generations, and thus I do not choose my individuality. My personality, however, arises from the way I unify my individuality, and this subjective totalizing is the result of my freedom. It is in this context that the distinction between prereflective and reflective conscious is important, and I will keep returning to this distinction as it arises in the text. For the present, we may note that our prereflective conscious arises when we do not stop an activity that we may be doing, we do not make it into an object of study, but continue with a fleeting awareness of what we are doing. We may be watching a sunset, enjoying its beauty, and then without interrupting our enjoyment, without saying anything to ourselves or to any companions watching with us, with perhaps only a nod signifying, "Yes, this is beautiful," we continue watching. These fleeting moments of self-awareness are important because in them we experience our freedom. "Yes, this is an amazing sunset, but what am I doing watching it while there are more important things I should be doing?" We have to express this self-awareness in words, which tend to make it seem that we are reflecting upon ourselves as an object; but, in this case, the words do not here reflect the reality.

Sartre continually returns to this distinction between individuality and personality in the hundreds of pages that he devotes to what he terms Gustave's "personalization." What renders our "personalization" complex is that when we do have these privileged glimpses into our freedom, we also encounter the effects of some guardian, friend, someone who was very important to our early life. For Gustave it will always be his father, the eminent doctor Achille-Cléophas, as he looks at his weak son. It is this piercing "look" of his father that gives Gustave his second birth.

THE LOOK

The look signifies our total and absolute dependence on others for our humanity. This is not an exaggeration. Self-confident adults do not "look" at each other in this technical sense of the term. Furthermore, the look is not limited to the eyes; the whole body looks. Even when we use our eyes, the force of their physical presence disappears, and what remains is a dependence that seems to come from another world. This dependence is clearest in the infant-adult relation; for an infant "looks" upon an adult as the fulfillment of all its needs, as a sort of god. In *Being and Nothingness*, part 3, chapter 1, section 4, "The Look"—a particularly long and crucial section that is frequently misunderstood—Sartre consistently calls our attention to our complete dependence on others for the opportunity to become fully human. Yes, we are always free; but, at least initially, we may have to overcome a subhumanity given to us by others, as enslaved American Blacks were frequently viewed by their white masters. Indeed, without some fortuitous outside help, an enslaved person may always see his or her freedom to be that of someone inferior by nature. Sartre writes in the section on "The Look":

> Thus the appearance of the Other's look is not an appearance in the world—neither in "mine" nor in the "Other's"—and the relation which unites me to the Other cannot be a relation of exteriority inside the world. By the Other's look I effect the concrete proof that there is a "beyond the world."

Sartre keeps coming back to our crucial "second birth" throughout his writing. In his study of Genet, Sartre claims that this child conceived of himself as a thief because his foster parents regarded the innocent putting of objects into his pockets as the act of a thief, whereas if he had been truly regarded as their child, they would have seen no guilt in what the child was doing. And, in the same work, reflecting further upon our dependence on others, Sartre writes, "The Indian untouchable thinks he is actually untouchable. He internalizes the prohibition of which he is the object, and makes of it an inner principle which justifies and explains the conduct of the other Hindus toward him."[5]

But let us take a closer look at what Sartre writes about the look in *Being and Nothingness*. Sartre does begin with an example that seems, at first, limited to sight. He invites us to reflect upon how we become aware of our self, if we were caught spying on someone:

> Here I am bent over the keyhole; suddenly I hear a footstep. I shudder as a wave of shame sweeps over me. Somebody has seen me. I straighten up. My eyes run over the deserted corridor. It was a false alarm. I breathe a sigh of relief.

It is interesting to note that even in this example, it is hearing and not sight that is first important. Suppose, however, that I actually saw a blind person approaching. Am I saved from embarrassment? Yes and no. Yes, I realize that I have not actually been seen, but then again I now also realize my fundamental visibility to others: I can be seen. Also, this blind person might bump into me as I am spying. What shall I say? Let us grant that I have a good excuse for my spying: Suppose that a sick person is sleeping in the next room and, having heard a noise, I wanted to see if the person needed help in some way. Whatever I say, I am at that moment of giving my excuse vulnerable to the person who catches me spying. I could attempt to reverse the situation. I might ask the person who catches me spying, "And what are you doing roaming the corridor?" But this implies a self already secure in its worth. Self-confident adults do not "look" at each other in the technical sense of the term, or, to be more exact, when adults attempt such a "look," they usually are attempting at least a temporary superior-inferior relation. Usually it does not work and usually it does not last. But, when we are born, we are all temporally vulnerable. Thus vulnerability is an essential aspect of our primary contact with another.

THE CONTINGENCY OF THE LOOK

The look is a contingent event. The contact may never occur—as with a child abandoned in the wild—and, even if it occurs, it may not be directed toward inducing in the other a true human quality. Again in this same long section of "The Look," Sartre writes, "Thus this relation which I call 'being-seen-by-another' . . . represents an irreducible fact which cannot be deduced either from the essence of the Other-as-object, or from my being-as-a-subject." That is to say, in the abstract, an infant has no specific or general orientation toward other people, even though, in the concrete, the infant needs this contact to be fully human. This claim requires, I believe, a brief clarification.

Both G. W. F. Hegel and Martin Heidegger claim that we have an essential relation to others. Indeed, this seems to be Aristotle's own perspective in calling attention to the social character of our humanity. The general implication is that we are born with a primary and wholesome orientation toward others and the actual contact merely awakens this dormant relation. The problem with this view is that it reduces actual experience to a secondary status—what we actually do to another is not crucial because the other has a primary orientation toward the fully human already within its budding consciousness. For Sartre, our power over others is such that those in a position of relative power can mold the inner consciousnesses of those who are vulnerable away from a true humanity toward subhumanity. Thus Sartre notes that Gustave's father suspects that his son is evading his responsibility to live up to the norms of the family:

> From morning to night, entering at whim, he stares at his son, takes his pulse, casts that "surgical gaze" upon him that detects all lies. . . . But the practitioner's scrutinizing gaze shakes him to the core. Gustave believes he is suspected and hence "receives" the intuition of his deep commitment, the vow he has made to remain forever afflicted. (Cosman 4:119)

And Gustave caries the weight of this look throughout his life:

> Flaubert realizes himself through the gaze and the manipulations of others; beneath the eyes of the Other—who is at once Bismarck and Achille-Cléophas—the great choices of his life are revealed to him as Other. (Cosman 5:555)

OUR EGO AND OUR PERSONALITY

Given the task of trying to understand how our interior reflections are altered by the way people see us, Sartre introduces the distinction between the ego and the personality. What distinguishes our personality from our ego is that the latter is the quasi-frozen image of our freedom that is equally accessible to us and to others. Thus, in Sartre's early monograph *The Transcendence of the Ego*, we read the remarkable words: "My I, in effect, is no more certain for consciousness than the I of other men. It is only more intimate."[6] This intimacy is a special reflective self-awareness. We do not look upon ourselves as an object in the world that can be known by others but as someone who can change at any moment. This is the crucial distinction that occurs frequently in *The Family Idiot*, and to which I will be returning when appropriate. It comes to everyone and to Gustave; but here Gustave meets the ever presence of his father. Frequently when we reflect, we discover within us someone else—an early guardian, or someone who we hope regarded us well. We do not have a pure center that is our self, independent of its relation to others. Although children receive all their initial notions about themselves from others, usually their parents, these notions will normally be given to them in such a way that the children are invited to reexamine them. This possibility is usually made real by other childhood relationships—for example, grandparents, relatives, or young companions. But Gustave is locked within a tight family, and later, when he can break the bond, he chooses not to do so. That is, while conversions are possible—Sartre claims that Genet had at least one; namely, from theft to writing—Gustave Flaubert remains true to his basic outlook on his relation to his family, his strange mixture of hatred and need, what Sartre calls his project.

THE PROJECT

Every life, according to Sartre, is an unfolding of an original project to discover one's place in the world and to give meaning to one's life. "My ultimate and initial project—for these are but one—is . . . always the outline of a solution of the problem of being." He adds, "But this solution is not first conceived and then realized; we are this solution."[7] As we grow older, change or "conversions" are possible; but they are difficult, for they mean reorienting oneself to the world. Elsewhere in *Being and Nothingness*, Sartre had given the example of climbing a mountain, during which he stops to rest while his friend continues to the top. He asks if he could have not also continued to the top, "I could have done otherwise but at what price?"[8] A small personal decision may involve adopting a different relation to all of reality. For one person, fatigue is something to succumb to, whereas for another it may be a challenge. Interestingly, Sartre observes that Flaubert complains of a certain tension between himself and his writings. Sartre refers to a "stress," which is Gustave's continual effort to keep his mind on his work while never admitting to himself that for his family he is a failure. Another person might have simply decided to have nothing to do with his family, but not Gustave, who prefers to suffer as long as he remains in his family:

> Far from touching the child's "human nature" and affecting some so-called universal faculty for suffering, this inferiority assaults the Flaubert in him; in the younger son's Flaubert-being lies his concrete determination, his singularity; as for sufferings, they do exist but they will be Flaubert sufferings. For the excellent reason that a family drama is involved. (Cosman 1:365)

Sartre's Method in *The Family Idiot*

Granting that *The Family Idiot* is a focused elaboration of all of Sartre's philosophy, it is also true that it uniquely expands on a philosophical method that is a refinement of our commonsense understanding of the world. Sartre would never approve of any method that artificially attempts to lead us on the path to truth. He refers to his method very early in his text, and before we clarify the meanings of the terms, let us simply mention them along with Sartre:

> We shall attempt, through description followed by a regressive analysis, to establish what was lacking. And if we succeed, we shall try, through a progressive synthesis, to establish the why of this absence. . . . Since the stubborn naiveté of the future writer is the expression of a poor initial relationship with language, our description will at first aim only to articulate that relationship precisely. (Cosman 1:10)

Sartre explains and elaborates the method as he is using it, aware that he has introduced it in some detail in his monograph *The Search for a Method*. It is important to keep this method in mind for it unites the entire long and difficult work, and I will keep returning to it. But fortunately, as is usually true of Sartre, he gives us a simple example.

I am to imagine that I am in a library with a friend. Suddenly, I see him get up from his chair, go to the window, and open it up. At first, I am not sure what he is doing. Is he going to look out to see someone? No, he returns to his seat, and it is clear to me that he is letting fresh air into the room. Indeed, I become aware that I had been sweating. Sartre writes that if another person had come into the room before my friend had opened the window, he would have called us both "library rats," thereby illuminating "us to the depths of our being."[9]

Sartre states that his method begins with a regressive stage because he takes the initial progressive stage for granted; that is to say, we are concerned with human behavior and not a happening of nature—an earthquake, for example, that might have caused the widow in the library to open. No, I understand my friend's initial behavior of walking to the window and opening it, although at first I may not grasp exactly what is in his mind. Thus, Sartre writes, "immediate experience reveals being at its most concrete, but it takes it at its most superficial level and remains in the realm of abstraction."[10]

And thus, too, we begin here with Gustave in his most abstract conditions, which will be unfolded slowly in great detail. For, example, he is born a second son; but that could mean anything. As we proceed, we also note that he did not choose the family project. There will always be happenings that he did not choose; these are human events, with their own histories. We must get to know through regressive awareness the exact meaning of these human conditions that envelop the infant and then the child. We then note Gustave's free response, the progressive stage.

One of the main difficulties in following Sartre throughout this work is that these stages can continue for hundreds of pages, with subsections. Some readers have been misled to think that Sartre has abandoned his notion of freedom because they have allowed themselves to become lost in an extensive regressive stage. It is here that I think my presence will be useful to the reader as I continually recall where we are and what we are doing in this vast work; elaborating on a regressive stage with subdivisions, each with its own progressive stage, or now finally moving ahead in a broader progressive movement.

In the working out of *The Family Idiot*, the (progressive)-regressive-progressive method is joined to a dialectic—a give-and-take between two phases of freedom—the reciprocal tension that directs Gustave's development within his family, particularly his father. Thus, Gustave's father is watchful, always wondering what this "idiot" will do next. The "idiot" responds by gradually getting his own way, indeed, by truly becoming physically ill. The family agrees that Gustave will never be a doctor, but then they want him to at least be a lawyer, where they judge the strain on him would not be too much to bear. Gustave has no answer, and thus he wears himself out preparing for his law classes. And then, the exhausted Gustave collapses: "Six months later, moreover, in January 1846, the unloved son of Doctor Flaubert began his solitary strike against his father, entering neurosis the way one enters a convent" (Cosman 3:60n48). He has the best doctors, his brother and his watchful father, who "casts his surgical gaze" upon Gustave. The reference to the "gaze" recalls again Sartre's notion of the look in *Being and Nothingness*, and indeed, there is a long section on the look in *The Family Idiot*, which I will include among my readings.[11]

Art for Art's Sake

Following his study of Genet, Sartre also introduces here, in *The Family Idiot*, the imperative "art for art's sake." We should note that this phrase had a healthy and praiseworthy historical birth. It arose from the aim to separate art in all its forms from a dependence on patronage and public opinion, rightly calling attention to the perfection of the work of art itself. As it developed into its final form, however, it implied a "black humanism," without God or people. In this black humanism, there are no true answers to seek concerning the human condition, since all the answers are already part of the furniture of the world and merely have to be discovered by science. We are thus things in a universe of things that move about but have no real freedom or purpose. Recalling explicitly the language of *Being and Nothingness*, Sartre writes of this humanism:

> Man is not a for-itself but fundamentally an in-itself, susceptible to being known in his objectivity and exteriority. This knowledge already acquired, can be exploited, strictly speaking, or developed to practical ends, but there is no more specific problematic of human reality. (Cosman 5:205)

For Sartre, Gustave and the other Knights of Nothingness, such as Stéphane Mallarmé, whose poems aim to "make the world useless," consider us humans to be mere things among other things in the world, with no purpose or value. I am not competent to judge the soundness of Sartre's view of this type of poetry, but what he says about Mallarmé and Charles Baudelaire is clear, namely, even our viewing the world sullies it, for it appears to give the world a witness; but the world has no true witness. There is only Language, the language of the true poets; but this language is for itself, passing over humans as if they did not exist. Sartre writes, "The poets' ambiguous situation lies in taking God's creation in reverse: he puts the Word at the end. To absorb the universe into language is to destroy the universe, but it is to create the poet."[12] And this reversal of our universe and language applies even more strikingly to Gustave Flaubert and his other Knights of Nothingness.

If at times we wonder about the basis for Sartre's analysis, he keeps us informed. "Readers may wonder," Sartre writes, "how I know all this. Well I have read Flaubert; the boy had such lively memories of these lessons [with his father] that he couldn't help sharing them with us" (Cosman 1:355). Thus, *Un Parfum à Sentir* (*A Perfume to Sense*), written at fifteen, tells the story of a father who tries to teach his sons how to dance on a tightrope: "It was Ernesto's turn. He trembled in every limb, and his fear increased when he saw his father take a little rod of white wood" (Cosman 1:356). Continuing, Sartre gives a long quote, which he emphasizes by giving it his own italics:

> *The rod, for its part, followed the dancer's every movement, encouraging him by lowering itself gracefully, threatened him by shaking with fury, showed him the dance by making the measure on the rope, in a word, it was his guardian angel his safeguard, or rather the sword of Damocles suspended over his head by the thought of a false step.*

Sartre concludes, "All of Flaubert is here." Gustave's father would always be there to watch and judge just what this "idiot" would do next, and the idiot would perform for his father. Why? For the infant as for the child Gustave, the family is necessary: how else is he to survive? For the adult and the author, the family is again necessary; but this time by free choice, for Gustave accepts and wishes to live within the mystic of the gift of his election, an election arising from the union of his brilliant father with his socially established mother. As Sartre is reflecting on Gustave's school days, he notes that Gustave joins only the most elite group, as if it were precisely where he belonged: "The hierarchy established among the Flaubert family concerns only them. . . . In other words, a Flaubert idiot is still good enough to make a stir" (Cosman 3:15).

Thus, just as Gustave hated his family and was nevertheless proud of having Flaubert blood, so too, in a more general sense, each budding writer was beckoned to reject the nobles and join the ranks of the bourgeoisie while, nevertheless, strangely convincing himself that, in fact, he had something like aristocratic blood: "Many of Flaubert's contemporaries could claim as their own that sentence he wrote in a letter to Louise: 'We are the Good Lord's aristocracy.' In a bizarre fashion, this sums it all up" (Cosman 4:99). The recipient of the letter was Louise Colet, also referred to by Flaubert as his muse. She was slightly older than Flaubert, a woman of strong passions, who was known to have stabbed an uncomplimentary critic. Flaubert saw her only briefly and at rare intervals. The literary aristocracy to which Flaubert refers, like all aristocracies, views humanity from above; these writers see themselves as the truly privileged ones of society, and they have little regard for humanity as a whole.

Moreover, the notion of "absolute-art" fitted this Second Empire, allowing one to remain asleep in the dream of a beauty that was always elsewhere, seemingly here in the world but more in the imaginary than in the real. Gustave is named Knight of Legion of Honor. Gustave realizes that he is such only as a Knight of Nothingness, but "he rejoices in it" (Cosman 5:534). He and the Empire fit as a glove fits a hand.

And yet, there had always been a different more human path for the writers to follow. Sartre notes that, if they had followed the path of Socrates and were willing to put forth real effort to break from their contradictory relation to their public, "a long movement could have begun, leading to acquired truth. . . . That movement did not occur" (Cosman 5:214).

Without this social revolution, which would have given Gustave Flaubert and his other Knights of Nothingness a new beginning (although I hope we may now in 2022 and beyond have), the simple fact is that Gustave would always regard himself as higher than the rest of humanity. His father had it wrong about greatness, but he would get it right. The members of the Flaubert family were indeed destined; but he, Gustave Flaubert, was their destiny. Toward the end of this long study, after Gustave had achieved international recognition, Sartre writes, "Gustave had wanted to gain glory, to lay it at Achille-Cléophas's feet, and make him weep with remorse" (Cosman 5:556). This father, however, never had regrets or second thoughts; Gustave was, for him, always the idiot of the family, and the idiot will respond with a confused hate-love relation. Still, Sartre recalls his readers and himself to his empathy for Gustave Flaubert:

> He wanted to return to his early childhood, to that nursing baby kneaded, manipulated, made passive by hands that were too expert, not tender enough. (Cosman 5:545)

The Abridgment

There are three large volumes in the original French and five in the English translation. This difference is because Cosman divides the very large second French volume into three. Whether we are in the French or the English, there are twenty-two chapters numbered consecutively across the volumes. I retain at least a brief selection from most of these chapters, noting the continual movement from regressive to progressive understanding of Gustave Flaubert. The original chapters are uneven in length and sometimes very long. My division into seventeen chapters of approximately the same size is, I hope, easier to read than the original. I follow Cosman's translation, with small deviations, such as breaking up very long paragraphs. Moreover, Sartre frequently provides only the last names of persons associated with Flaubert, but I will include the first names together with a very brief description of who they are, using curly brackets { } to indicate my additions. English titles of French works will be provided, although English versions of some smaller works are not easily available. I also have given a brief personal conclusion.

The general structure of the entire work centers around two Problems, one that opens the work and one that begins its conclusion. The Problems clarify the issue to be investigated. The first concerns Gustave's slow initiation into spoken and written language together with the remarkable awakening, when he soon is able to write with clarity beyond his age; and up until he writes *Madame Bovary*, which is, for Sartre, a thoroughly nihilistic work. But this strange work succeeds and is accepted as a model of "realism," both then and now. How and why is this possible? Why is *Madame Bovary* not simply dismissed as a work suited to its author without relevance to its own times and beyond to ours? This is the question that the second Problem examines and continues until the conclusion of the work. I will be considering both Problems at some length with much of the connecting material. The result, I hope, is a cohesive and compelling abridgment, approximately one-tenth the length of a classic text by one of the greatest thinkers of the twentieth century.

CHAPTER ONE

Problem

A FAMILY IDIOT WHO BECAME A GENIUS

Sartre's Preface

The Family Idiot is the sequel to *The Search for a Method*. Its subject: what, at this point in time, can we know about a man? It seemed to me that this question could only be answered by studying a specific case. What do we know, for example, about Gustave Flaubert? Such knowledge would amount to summing up all the data on him at our disposal. We have no assurance at the outset that such a summation is possible and that the truth of a person is not multiple. The fragments of information we have are very different in kind: Flaubert was born in December 1821, in Rouen—that is one kind of information; he writes, much later, to his mistress: "Art terrifies me"—that is another. The first is an objective, social fact, confirmed by official documents; the second, objective too, when one sets some store by what is said, refers in its meaning to a feeling that issues from experience, and we can draw no conclusions about the sense and import of this feeling until we have first established whether Gustave is sincere in general, and in this instance in particular. Do we not then risk ending up with layers of heterogeneous and irreducible meanings? This book attempts to prove that irreducibility is only apparent, and that each piece of data set in its place becomes a portion of the whole, which is constantly being created, and by the same token reveals its profound homogeneity with all the other parts that make up the whole.

For a man is never an individual; it would be more fitting to call him a *universal singular*. Summed up and for this reason universalized by his epoch, he in turn resumes it by reproducing himself in it as singularity. Universal by the singular universality of human history, singular by the universalizing singularity of his projects, he requires simultaneous examination from both ends. We must find an appropriate method. I set out the principles of this method in 1958 and will not repeat what I said; I prefer to demonstrate whenever necessary how this method is created through the very work itself in obedience to the requirements of its object.

A last word. Why Flaubert? For three reasons. The first, very personal, long ago ceased to be as salient as it once was in the origin of this choice. In 1943, rereading his correspondence in the bad edition by Charpentier, I felt I had a score to settle with Flaubert and ought therefore to get to know him better. Since then, my initial antipathy has changed to empathy, the one attitude necessary for understanding. Next, he is objectified in his books. Anyone will tell you, "Gustave Flaubert—he's the author of *Madame Bovary*." What then is the relationship of the man to the work? I have never discussed this until now, nor, to my knowledge, has anyone else. We shall see that this is a double relationship: *Madame Bovary* is defeat and triumph; the man depicted in the defeat is not the same man summoned in its triumph. We must try to understand what this means. Finally, Flaubert's early works and his correspondence (thirteen published volumes) appear, as we shall see, to consist of the strangest, the most easily deciphered revelations. We might imagine we were hearing a neurotic "free associating" on the psychoanalyst's couch. I thought it permissible, for this difficult test case, to choose a compliant subject who yields himself easily and unconsciously. I would add that Flaubert, creator of the "modern" novel, stands at the crossroads of all our literary problems today.

Now we must begin. How, and by what means? It doesn't much matter: a corpse is open to all comers. The essential thing is to set out with a problem. The one I have chosen is hardly ever discussed. Let us read this passage from a letter to Mlle Leroyer de Chantepie: "It is by the sheer force of work that I am able to silence my innate melancholy. But the old nature often reappears, the old nature that no one knows, the deep, always hidden wound."[1] What is the meaning of this? Can a wound be innate? In any event, Flaubert refers us to his prehistory. What we must try to understand is the origin of the wound that is "always hidden" and dates back to his earliest childhood. That will not, I think, be a bad start.

Gustave: The Infant

When, bewildered and still "brutish," little Gustave Flaubert emerges from infancy, skills await him. And roles. Training begins, and apparently not without success—no one tells us, for example, that he had trouble walking. On the other hand, we know that this future writer stumbled when it came to the prime test, his apprenticeship in words. Later we shall try to discover whether, from the very beginning, he had difficulty speaking. What is certain is that he made a poor showing in the other linguistic test—that chief initiation and rite of passage—learning the alphabet. A witness reports that the little boy learned his letters very late and that his family took him for a backward child. Caroline Commanville gives the following account:

> My grandmother had taught her elder son to read. She wanted to do as much for the second and set to work. Little Caroline at Gustave's side learned rapidly; he could not keep up, and after straining to understand these signs that meant nothing to him, he would begin to sob. He was, however, avid for knowledge and his brain was always working. . . . [Since later Papa Mignot read to him,] whenever there were scenes over his difficulty with reading, Gustave's final argument—to his mind irrefutable—was: "What's the use of learning when Papa Mignot reads to me?" But school age was upon him, he had to know at any cost. . . . Gustave applied himself resolutely and in a few months caught up with the children his own age.[2]

We shall see that this poor relationship with words was decisive for his career. Why, it will be asked, should we question the testimony of Flaubert's niece? After all, she lived intimately with her uncle and her grandmother, from whom she received her information. We are prevented, however, from trusting her completely because of the false playfulness of the narrative. Caroline prunes, expurgates, softens; on the other hand, if the incident related does not seem compromising, she polishes it, violating rigor at the expense of truth. One reading is enough to discover the key to these double and contradictory distortions: she aims to please without abandoning the tone of good breeding.

Let us return to the passage just cited. We shall have no trouble glimpsing the truth of Gustave's unhappy childhood. We are told that the child cried bitterly, that he was avid for knowledge, and that his impotence made him miserable. Then, a little further on, we are shown a blustering dunce, stubborn in his refusal to learn—why should I? Papa Mignot reads to me. Is this the same Gustave? Yes, but the first attitude is provoked by an observation he makes himself: the contrariness of things, his own incapacity. The Other is there of course: the witness, the harsh surroundings, necessity. But this is not the source of the child's sorrow, the relation spontaneously established between the lifeless imperatives of the alphabet and his own potential: "I must but I can't." The second attitude implies a combative relationship between the child and his parents. Caroline Commanville tells us, in passing, that there were scenes—this is enough. These scenes did not occur immediately. There was time for patience, then for distress, finally for reproach. At first the family blamed nature, later they accused the child of ill will. He answered belligerently that he didn't need to learn how to read. But he was already defeated, already falsified: by pretending to explain his refusal, he confessed to it. The parents asked no more, and all their impatience was justified.

The defenseless humility, the proud resentment that makes the victim claim as his own the ill will of which he is falsely accused—these two reactions are separated by many years. There was a certain uneasiness in the Flaubert family when Gustave, confronted with his first human tasks, distinguished himself by his failure to perform them. This uneasiness grew from day to day, persisted, rankled. Violence was done to the child. This violence, scarcely evoked but legible, suffices to flaw the benign narrative. An odd confusion of Mme Commanville's increases our discomfort: she informs us that Gustave and Caroline Flaubert learned to read together. But Gustave was four years older than his younger sister. Supposing that Mme Flaubert had begun to teach him at around five years old, the youngest, age twelve or thirteen months, was attending the lessons from her cradle. Of course Achille-Cléophas's three children each in turn received private lessons from Mme Flaubert, the second nine years after the eldest had learned to read, the third four years after the second child had made his first attempt. Nevertheless, here is Mme Commanville, undaunted by these wide intervals, summoning in the same paragraph her two uncles and her mother. Why, when they did not study together? Observe: Mme Flaubert became the teacher of the brilliant Achille; her first success convinced her of her pedagogic gifts—Achille must have been a child prodigy—so she renewed the experiment with Gustave. And Caroline, the last born, mother of the narrator, learned at play. Gustave is squeezed between these two marvels—inferior to both, he doesn't look good.

It is as if Mme Commanville had launched into this comparison—which could have been omitted—in order to remind the public that the inadequacies of the future writer were largely compensated for by the excellence of the two other children. The uncle was already of age when the niece was born; when *Madame Bovary* appeared, she was eleven years old. Never mind; even to Caroline, who saw only what followed, Gustave's first years seem disturbing. There was the slowness, and then the "nervous attack," which she surely must have heard about early on. Nothing further was needed—she would take advantage of his fame but would never be dazzled by it.

Mme Commanville, née Hamard, was a Flaubert on her mother's side; even in the funeral oration for her uncle she made a point of recalling her membership in the most illustrious scientific family of Normandy. To save the Flaubert family honor she flanked a genius bordering on idiocy with two good sorts, two brains, true progeny of the man of science. If this lady herself, half a century after the events, could not resist comparing the three children, it is not difficult to divine what Gustave must have heard between 1827 and 1830. But we shall have occasion to return at length to these comparisons. Our present task is to show that Gustave, by his deficiency, finds himself at the center of a domestic tension that will only increase until he has caught up with "children his own age."

Yet can we be sure that the child did not know his letters before the age of nine? Inclined to believe this, how can we allow that Gustave had learned to write only very recently when he addressed to Ernest Chevalier, on 31 December 1830—at the age of nine years—the astonishing letter to which we shall return many times in the following pages? On rereading, its solidity is impressive: concise, sturdy, and accurate sentences; the spelling is somewhat fanciful, but still within the realm of acceptability. No doubt about it, the author has a mastery of his graphic movements. He proposes, moreover, to his friend Ernest that he will "send him his dramas." The passage is not very clear: are these plays that he has already written or plays that he intends to write when Ernest "writes his dreams"?

In any case the word *writing* already has for him that double meaning which makes it altogether ambiguous. It designates both the common act of tracing words on a sheet of paper and the singular enterprise of composing "writings." We thought to find a former idiot scarcely come out of the fog—and we discover a man of letters. Impossible. True, a change of surroundings, the intelligence of an educator, the advice of a doctor can all help backward children; it is enough to give them a chance. And for many stragglers, entrance into the world of reading comes as a true religious conversion, long and unconsciously cultivated, suddenly achieved. But these abrupt leaps forward compensate the backward child for perhaps one year, or two, to stretch things, but not more. Gustave, if his niece is to be believed, had four or five years to make up.

No, illiterate at nine years old, the child would be too seriously afflicted for his final sprint even to be conceivable. Gustave knew how to read in 1828 or '29, that is, between seven and eight. Earlier, his slowness would not have been so disturbing; later, he would never have caught up. What remains true is that the Flauberts were concerned. For a long while Gustave could not grasp the elementary connections that make letters into a syllable, syllables into a word. These difficulties led to others—how can one count without knowing how to read? How can one retain the most basic elements of history and geography if the instruction remains oral? We don't worry about this today; methods are more solid, predictable; and, above all, we take the student as he is. At that period there was an order to follow, and the child had to bend to it. So Gustave was behind, every step of the way.

Naiveté

Not completely, however. Papa Mignot read to him; the little boy was already broadly cultured, already literary. Novels exercised his imagination, provided new schemata; and he learned the use of the symbol. If a child transforms himself early enough into Don Quixote, he unwittingly incorporates the general principle of all transformations: he knows how to see himself, to find himself, in the life of another, to live his own life as another. Nothing of all this, unfortunately, was visible. The real achievements—new transparencies, the soul's clearings, reflections—were of a kind that only increased the number of his stupors, or at least did not reduce them. Mme Flaubert knew nothing about these exercises. And doubt was born: is Gustave an idiot? We find this alarm again in Mme Commanville's sprightly narrative:

> The child had a calm, meditative nature and a naiveté, traces of which he preserved all his life. My grandmother told me that he would sit for hours, one finger in his mouth, absorbed, looking almost stupid. When he was six, a servant called Pierre, amusing himself with Gustave's innocence, told the boy when he pestered him: "Run to the kitchen . . . and see if I'm there." And the child went off to question the cook, "Pierre told me to come see if he's here." He didn't understand that they wanted to fool him, and in the face of their laughter he remained a dreamer, glimpsing a mystery.[3]

A curious and deceitful text. Beneath the surface of Caroline's good humor the truth breaks through: Gustave was a simple soul, improbably, pathologically credulous; he frequently fell into long stupors—his parents searched his features and feared he was an idiot. It might be thought that these confidences were made lightly, out of a sense of triumphant relief. That would be to misunderstand Gustave's mother; she never believed in her son's genius or even in his talent. In the first place, these words had no meaning for her; as the widow of a brain, brains alone were worthy of her respect. As a practical person, she recognized talent only in capable men who were valued as such, since their capability allowed them to sell their services for a higher price. On this account she must have prized the elder of her sons more than the younger. This is probably what she did, without loving him much. Her heart inclined toward the other, younger son, and then she had difficulties with her daughter-in-law. But she imagined that she remained at Croisset out of duty—Gustave was an invalid, he would die or go mad without maternal care.

So we find this strange ménage: a pair of wounded recluses, each burying himself far from the world in the house at the water's edge and pretending to stay there only to care for the other. But Mme Flaubert's chilling solicitude demonstrates how little respect she had for her son. First there was his idiocy, the father's alarm, calmed for a time, then all at once revived when Gustave was seventeen; the sterile years in Paris; and, to finish up, the attack at Pont-l'Évêque, serious illness, finally voluntary isolation and indolence: all of these misfortunes seem to be connected by a hidden thread. Something in the child's brain was defective, perhaps from birth: epilepsy—this was the name they gave to Flaubert's "disease," in short, chronic idiocy. He spoke, thank God he reasoned, but he was nonetheless incapable of practicing a profession—exactly what they had foreseen from his sixth year.

He wrote, of course, but very little. What was he doing up there in his room? He was dreaming, he would throw himself onto his couch, prostrated by a new attack, or else he would fall into one of his old stupors. He was working, he said, on a new monster he called "la Bovary"; the mother, with a presentiment that he was courting failure, hoped he would never finish his work. Never was there a wiser mother's prayer, as she discovered when she learned that those obscene scribblings were going to dishonor the family and bring their author to the dock of infamy. Little Caroline Hamard was going on twelve years old; the details she reports to us were imparted to her by her grandmother in the years following the scandal. It is clear that the widow felt she was confiding a painful secret, apprehensions unhappily confirmed: "Even as a small boy your uncle gave us plenty of worry." Mme Flaubert was an abusive mother because she was an abused widow. She aggravated her younger son's "irritability" by accepting out of piety all the judgments of her adored spouse. Caroline was her confidante. Gustave was taking a vengeful pleasure in educating his niece: I, the slave of the alphabet, taught by my suffering, I am teaching this child all there is to know without costing her one tear. But the grandmother had prejudiced the niece against him, and the girl remained prejudiced whatever he did; incapable of appreciating her uncle, she knew better how to take advantage of him than to love him.

In order to give the passage cited above its whole meaning, we must view it as a transcription, in an edifying style, of the spiteful babbling of two gossips, one an aging and garrulous woman, the other a petty bourgeois {*sic*} and not very nice girl of twelve or fifteen. They tear the old lady's lodger to pieces, the old woman out of distress and easily wounded vulnerability, the girl out of the malicious conformism of youth. And it must have been the grandmother who said, "a naiveté, traces of which he preserved." Caroline is incapable of making so apt a reflection; besides, she would have had to observe the little boy's innocence for herself in order to recover it from beneath the various masks of the adult Gustave. Coming from Mme Flaubert, supported by the accompanying anecdote, the intention is clear: the novelist who claims to see into the hearts of others is but a fool, a ninny, who has preserved in maturity the exceptional credulity of his childhood.

Furthermore, there is something strange about Gustave's encounter with the servant Pierre. At six years old even "normal" children have difficulty orienting themselves in space and time—they are hesitant about questions of being, of the self; their young minds are perplexed. But it is unlikely they would believe that this old fellow whom they see and touch, who talks to them here and now, is at the same time at the other end of the apartment. Not at six, nor at five, nor even at four. If they should "go look in the kitchen," it is surely because they lack a complete grasp of words and have only half understood or rushed off without listening properly, for the sheer pleasure of running and getting out of breath. The fact is that the oneness of bodies and their spatial perceptions are simple and obvious qualities; it takes mental effort to recognize them, but what will the child do if not internalize the passive synthesis of the outside world? Doubling, on the other hand, or the ubiquity of an individual being, is an abstraction contradicted by everyday experience and something that no mental image can support. In fact these ideas are characterized by their very complexity, and they can be drawn only from the disintegration of the identity; in order to conceptualize this twinning of the identical, one must be an adult and a Theosophist. A backward child may long preserve a confused picture of localized individuality, but the confusion will only take him further from these dichotomies; for just to dream that an individual is doubled requires a knowledge of individualization. Could Gustave be an exception? This would be serious, especially since he goes so far as to question the cook and, even after his disappointment, does not perceive that he has been duped. Happily, the rule is strict, as I have just demonstrated, and does not even tolerate the famous exception that proves it. In other words, the story is an invention, pure and simple.

Explanation through Trust

This instance of naiveté is only a symbol. Caroline found it to be reassuring nonsense and gave it the necessary little push. A symbol of what? Of a multitude of little family happenings, too "private," she thought, to be told. The little boy would have believed the servant, we can be sure, without such mental distortion. For the sake of a joke they could simply have given him false but realistic information: that his playmates had not yet come—when they were waiting behind the door; or that his father had gone "to make his rounds" without taking the boy with him—when the medical director was standing behind him, ready to grab him and whisk him off in the carriage. All parents are jokers; fooled since childhood themselves, they take pleasure in fooling their own youngsters, out of kindness. It never occurs to them that they might be driving their children crazy. The little victims must make do with the false feelings attributed to them, which they internalize, and with the false information that will be denied a moment later or soon afterward. These triflings are not always criminal; the child grows up, frees himself through questioning and refusal, coldly observes grown-ups fooling children.

Yet Gustave remains marked. Mme Flaubert attaches enough importance to his demonstrations of naiveté to pass them on to her granddaughter. The mother would have it that this "innocence" has never entirely disappeared. Is Caroline right when she tells us that love is at its source? Certainly the little boy cannot imagine that adults would deceive through caprice. After all, Descartes finds no other guarantee of human knowledge: God is good, therefore he has no desire to deceive us. A valid reason. For Gustave it is more than a reason, it is a basic right. Trust always involves a calculating generosity: I give it to you, you must deserve it. And the little boy feels, in the transport of his enthusiasm: since you say it, it must be true; you haven't brought me into the world to mock me. But what is the source of this implicit faith? Carried to an extreme, is it not itself a defense? Doesn't it serve, at least, to replace something that has been lost or wanting, to fill a gap?

We must advance cautiously when we are dealing with prehistory and when the witnesses are few and fraudulent. We shall attempt, through a description followed by a regressive analysis, to establish what was lacking. And if we succeed, we shall try, through a progressive synthesis, to discover the why of this absence. This will not be a waste of time. Since the stubborn naiveté of the future writer is the expression of a poor initial relationship with language, our description will at first aim only to articulate that relationship precisely.

Yes, the naiveté is originally just a relationship with speech, for it is through speech that these fabrications are conveyed. Further, since they do not correspond to any reality, one would have to view them only as lexemes. Little Gustave's misfortune is that something inside prevents him from grasping words as simple signs. Of course, even in a "normal" child a long learning period is necessary before he can distinguish the material weight of the vocable, its associations, the intimidating pressure it bears on the "object of locution," in short, the magical power of its pure signifying value. But Gustave's naiveté, because it persists, indicates that he could not fully perform this task; he learns to decode the message, of course, but not to question its contents. A false thought is transmitted to him by the spoken word; soon even he—the little boy—is struck by its absurdity, but he doesn't question it. The meaning becomes substance—it acquires inertia, not by its obviousness but by its density. The idea has thickened, crushing the mind that contains it; it is a stone that can be neither lifted nor thrown off. Still, this enormous mass has remained meaning[ful] all the way through.

Signification—that transcendence which exists only through the project that pursues it—and passivity—pure *En-soi*, material weight of the sign—merge together, a pair of contraries that interpenetrate instead of opposing each other. The most serious consequence is that the child derives no profit from the repeated deceptions. He is told a lie, he is made to believe that his father is gone, the father soon appears amid laughter. But, for the child, this instantly revealed fraud never has the value of an experiment.

It will be understood that I am exposing appearances. To arrive at the truth, the terms must be reversed. It is Gustave's mind that is paralyzed before the spoken word—something is said to him and everything jams, everything comes to a halt. Meaning is not important, it is the verbal materiality that fascinates him. Yet this "paralysis" must be considered only a symbol; the mind is never paralyzed. The symbol can be understood in only one way: from his earliest years, the child is touched by human relationships through the word. Credulity comes to the children of men from those who affect them through language, that is, through the conductive medium of all articulated communications. It surrounds them from the beginning, they are born into it, shaped—for good or ill—to adapt themselves to it. When the sensory-motor apparatus has developed "normally," yet the child's response to the message is "abnormal," this double self originates at the difficult level where all discourse is man, where all of man is discourse; it implies a bad fit in the linguistic universe, that is in the social order, in the family.

To explore this strange credulity further, we should recall certain basic, general facts. First, the language of the speaker generally dissolves at once in the mind of the listener; what remains is a schema, both conceptual and verbal, that controls reconstitution and comprehension. Comprehension will be deeper, the more imprecise the word-for-word reconstitution. Now comprehension is a personal act. If the listener repeats what he has heard, he is merely lending his voice to a transcendent object that is realized through his voice and then flies off toward new tongues. If he comprehends, he reshapes the well-worn path for himself. In the end, the act is completely his own, although the comprehended reality can be a universal notion. Naturally, this is not a matter of thought without words; but intellection—or comprehension—when complete, defines a virtually unlimited series of verbal expressions and creates an a priori rule for choosing among those expressions the one most appropriate in each situation and for each speaker. Thought, then, is neither one nor another part of the series—as if a particular expression ought to be privileged a priori; nor is it a capricious and transcendent option—how can we choose the spoken word unless it is the word itself? Rather, thought is at once the totality of the series—the differential relations that link together various expressions—and a distinct form based on the totalized series of those expressions that seems best adapted to the present situation. An idea that is comprehended is me, and it is all that is not-me—it is my subjectivity, exploding and collapsing, leaving my essence to be absorbed by the object. But am I ever freer and more unconditionally myself than in this "perpetual combustion" that continually expands until it embraces everything?

In the same way, language is me and I am language. An idea, from this point of view, is inside me: the column-sun-drenched capital, pedestal in shadow—of sentences that express it and that define me in time as the reason (hidden to myself) for the words chosen, and at this moment by the sovereign choice of one expression in the infinite tangle of all possible expressions, defining me consequently by my appreciation of men and situations. And in the spiral garland of words must be seen, too, myself in the Other; language expresses human relationship, but it is the relationship of those who seek out the words—to support them, to censure them, to reject them—in each individual. The Other in me makes my language, which is my way of being in the Other. Thus, when man is language and language is human, each word tossed off in passing surpasses us with all its hidden connections to those who are speaking; when we, then, surpass each word in order to grasp the idea it embodies, that is, the infinite series of its possible substitutes, the permeability of consciousness is such that naiveté is no longer conceivable.

To be sure, we lie, we mystify, we deceive everyone all the time. But this is another matter. The mystification of adults reflects alienation—when they invent their lies, they are only concerned with sticking closer to truth. The cleverest liars invent their lies out of small, scarcely perceptible leeches, which they stick onto the skin of a known truth. In other words, language is the means of deception—and of course certain persons are taken in, others not—but language in itself is not deceitful. Certainly there are labyrinths, traps for the unwary; often in the end the word harbors a mirage. Yet quite simply language cannot be separated from the world, from others, and from ourselves. It is not an alien enclave that can outwit me or subvert my purpose; it is me, so that I am nearer to being myself when I am farther away—with others and among things; it is the indissoluble reciprocity of men and their struggles together embodied by the internal relations of this linguistic whole that has neither door nor window, where we can neither go in nor come out, where we are. The homogeneity of the word with all the objective and subjective determinations of man ensures that it cannot come to us as an alien power. For how could this be? Language is within us because we understand it; distant as its source, unforeseen as it may be, it was awaited in the depths of our heart. In sum, it is comprehended only by itself, that is, it is obliterated, invisible; the thing itself remains, sign of the word which is abolished.

Naiveté and Language

I have described, of course, the abstract condition of adults without memory. Through memory, childhood corrupts us from its first words: we believe we have chosen them for their light and airy meanings, when they are actually imposed on us by some obscure sense. But these problems, essential for the analyst, do not yet concern us. The question here is to understand credulity, and after the preceding discussion we can only explain it by an "impact" of the word on consciousness. For little Gustave, everything happens as though the word were at once a meaning comprehended—that is, a determination of his subjectivity—and an objective power. The sentence does not dissolve within him, it is not obliterated in the face of the thing spoken or the speaker who says it. The child understands without the power to integrate. As if the verbal process were only half completed. As if the meaning—seen correctly—instead of becoming a conceptual and practical schema, instead of entering into a relationship with other schemata of the same kind, remained bound to the sign. As if the sign itself, instead of merging with its interior image, retained for the child's consciousness its resonant materiality. As if—in the sense that we talk of stones singing and fountains weeping—language were still, for the child, only noise speaking.

Is this attitude conceivable? It is, if comprehension is arrested before its completion. The idea remains captive of its expression, as much as of the sounds that bear it; for lack of control over the gamut of sentences that might restore it, the content of the signifier remains on the assertoric level—neither possible nor impossible, quite simply it is. The encounter with the signifier-real fact: the child has heard sounds—is not distinguished from this other fact: the real existence of the signified. And more generally, meaning—that strange amalgam of a resonant plenitude and a transcendence aimed at nothing—remains without the determination of modalities. In order to join meaning to hypothetical or apodictical modes, one must detach it from the "mouthful of sound"; but if being is its mode, this pure artifice, for want of definition in relation to the necessary, the possible, remains itself undetermined. It is not surprising, however, that under certain conditions the development of language is arrested, and that, as long as it is incomplete, verbal processes will seem meaningless. We have encountered such imprisoned thought, guaranteed but at the same time crushed by the actual presence of its sign, in magical formulas, in riddles; we find it each night in our dreams.

If Gustave, aged six, confuses sign and meaning to the extent that the material presence of the sign is the evidence that guarantees the truth of the meaning, he must have had a poor initial relationship with the Other. In effect, he believes everything he is told, out of awe before the verbal object, out of devoted love for the adults. But he does not really relate speech to those who have spoken. At first he perceives commands rather than statements; these impose themselves and then he must believe them, since they are a gracious gift made to him by his parents. Besides, lacking the reciprocity—however ephemeral—that establishes complete comprehension with all its forms, the speech of the Other seems to him a word that has been given, in every sense of the term. Speaking is not expressing; the sentence, ample presence, is a material gift—he is offered a music box, imagine, a musical trivet. If the music has meaning, so much the better; the gift is taken, kept, it is a souvenir. What is lacking, we see, is intention. The child adores the object bestowed upon him as evidence of paternal favor, but it is the same generosity that Gustave detects in his father's slightest caress. Speaking to the child or ruffling his hair amounts to the same thing. It might be said that between parents and children the gestures of tenderness—silent, effective, as "brutish" among humans as among the beasts—are the only communication possible. This child, wild and—if we are to believe his first writings—close to the animal state, can love others and believe himself loved only on the level of common subhumanity.

The most striking aspect, indeed, of his niece's narrative is that in the same paragraph she singles out Gustave's trances and his credulity. As though the trances were only repeated attempts to escape his credulity, as though the little boy tried to evade language by allowing himself to drift in silence. He is calm, doesn't breathe a word, lets himself be absorbed by the surroundings, the plants, the pebbles in the small garden, the sky at Yonville, the sea. One could say that he seeks to merge with unnamable nature, fleeing the weight of nomination in the unnamed texture of things, in the irregular, indefinable movements of the foliage, of the waves. I see surprising affinities between these first unconscious ventures beyond the self and the final vow of Saint Antoine—"to be matter." It is too soon, however, to elaborate. Let us limit ourselves to description.

Even when we look at things quite simply, as they are presented, it is striking that the silence of Gustave's trances is quite the opposite of the bronze tones, dull and implacable, that vibrate within him, those of others and his own, suffered, never completely understood. He would sit for hours, a finger in his mouth, looking almost stupid; this calm child who reacts badly when spoken to, feels less than others the need to speak—words, as we say, do not come to him, nor the desire to use them. This means, of course, that he does not communicate willingly. His affections are not in themselves directed toward others, they are not destined for others and do not seek to be expressed. Let us not then conclude that they are intentionally "ego-centric—there is no ego without an alter, without an alter ego; unexpressed to others, his affections remain for Gustave himself inexpressible. They are lived fully and vaguely with no one there to live them, no doubt because their substance is," as {the psychoanalyst Jacques} Lacan would say, "inarticulable." But is not the real cause an early difficulty with articulation, reinforced by a secret preference for the inarticulate? The evident connection between Gustave's inadequacies—as "object of speech" and as "speaker"—is persuasive: in the child, language is a poor conductive medium; through it not only is the relationship with the Other falsified, but also the relationship with the self.

The little boy is badly anchored in the universe of discourse. The word is never his; the trance soon absorbs the word, and by and by the word, fallen from the sky, oppresses him. Finally, in the very depths of his interiority, the word remains external. That is, when it enters the child's ear, the object is not submitted to the classical operations: reception, apprehension, reclassification in a verbal series with respect to the permanent possibility of the subject. These operations occur automatically if the child is already language; or, if you will, to be language is to repeat these operations continually within oneself. Let a word present itself, it is language that receives language. But if the spoken word is alternately absent or deafening, as it is for Gustave, this is because his own disposition, the thread of his "ideas" and affections, is not sufficiently verbalized. At the age when everyone speaks, he is still imitating speakers; and if the sound that rings suddenly in him leaves an impression, it provokes him precisely through this sense of "estrangement."[4] And estrangement has only one explanation: there is no common ground or mediation between Gustave's subjective existence and the universe of meanings; they are two perfectly heterogeneous realities which occasionally meet.

CHAPTER TWO

Quidquid volueris

{Editor's Note: *Quidquid volueris* (*Whatever You Wish*) was written when Gustave was fifteen. Sartre's explanation here is fairly easy to follow, which is not always the case in regard to Gustave's works, in which case I will follow Hazel E. Barnes's interpretation, in her work previously cited in the Editor's Introduction. Here, she notes, "The adjective *bête* means stupid or foolish; as a noun it designates a simpleton or a fool, but also an animal. It has connotations of untamed, natural, innocent. Sartre argues that *bête* and related words held a special significance for Flaubert, one which included all of these meanings" (Barnes, *Sartre & Flaubert*, 19). In this chapter Sartre also draws from the account written by Gustave's niece Caroline Commanville.}

A child of six ordinarily finds himself defined down to his very innermost being by others and by himself, for to live is to produce meanings,[1] to suffer is to speak. The child is receptive to external meanings because he is himself filled with meaning and producer of meanings (I am here—Sartre notes—translating the German word *sinngebend* taken in its phenomenological sense). Gustave does not produce meaning; within himself he is not defined by anything, neither by a proper name nor by the general name of what he feels. He lives, however, he savors his life, he projects himself beyond the boundaries of the self toward the world around him; but life and words are incommensurable. Actually, I am exaggerating. The verbalization of his existence has begun, for lengthy as his silences may be, he speaks, he acquires a vocabulary, he listens and comprehends what is said to him. Very simply, words never really define for him what he experiences, what he feels. Nor, doubtless, his true transcendent relation to the world. The objects that surround him are the things of others.

His parents at times oblige him to define himself through signs that they have chosen: say hello to the lady, tell her your name; where does it hurt? here or here? But, in telling the truth, he realizes that truth is alien to him. This is why he is the most credulous child; since he does not possess truth, since it is a relationship of the others with things and between themselves, since each true utterance, by revealing the shifting ground between existence and the word, is made manifest to him by the discomfort it provokes and never by something obvious, he relies upon the principle of authority.

Let us say he views words from the outside as things, even when they are inside him. Later this turn of mind will be the source of the *Dictionnaire des idées reçues* {*Dictionary of Received Ideas*}. At first, vocables are perceptible realities; then, their connections are effected from the outside—through accident, custom, institution; third comes meaning, the strict result of the first two but in itself arbitrary. Emma and Léon talk about Nature because the situation demands—through social habit—that it be discussed; not that there is any logical reason for it; it is simply that nature is evoked at a certain stage of sexual relations. At the same moment, thousands of couples say the same things in the same terms. The main thing is for all of these still platonic lovers to feel, through these banalities, a "communion of souls" with their future mistresses. In short, the connections of words are physical, they are the modulations of a song.

The established words of lovers are meant to substitute for the caresses that are impossible at this stage, to lay the groundwork for them and, by the exchange of breaths before the kiss, to awaken a feeling of reciprocity. The meaning is there in the vocables, prefabricated; it is not needed for itself, but so that future lovers by sharing a preference create the equivalent of shared desire. In this conception of language—which we shall later discuss at length—we retrieve the child's previous refusals. As an adult, Gustave preserves "traces of his naiveté"; he also preserves, as an essential element of his character, his stubbornness in never entirely entering into the universe of discourse. Outside and inside, he views words inside out; in their sensual strangeness he takes commonplaces for imperatives engraved in the verbal matter that each individual is bound to reproduce by the inflections of his voice; he persists in thinking that the spoken word corrodes and can never completely define. In his case, the difficulty with learning to read comes from a general and earlier trouble, the difficulty with speaking.

Caroline's narrative at least allows us to ascertain all this; it does not give us the tools to examine thoroughly these first impressions. What, precisely, is this radical heterogeneity of Gustave's mental life and language? Merely to demonstrate an apparent incompatibility is not enough; it must be defined with precision. Indeed, no human animal—I will even say no mammal—whether it speaks or not, can live without entering into the dialectical movement of the signifier and the signified. For the simple reason that meaning is born of the project. Therefore Gustave, badly adjusted as he is in the universe of expression, is sign, signified, signifier, signification to the extent that his most basic impulses are made manifest through projects. And he knows it. As he runs, smiling, to throw himself into his father's open arms, he is consciously determined by a sign that embodies a signified relationship between lord and vassal. Better, it is a sign rather than a caress. Why does he crave it if not because it signifies paternal love? Where, then, do the troubles begin, the aversions and the impossibilities? With spoken language? Why?

It is too soon to try to answer these questions. Above all it is important to support this description with other testimony. Let us not forget its fragility: two dubious paragraphs of Mme Commanville's decorous gossip that report, in a sweetened version, the confidences of Mme Flaubert. These confidences, furthermore, concern facts buried in the distant past—a quarter of a century at least separates Gustave's resistance to the alphabet from the moment when Achille-Cléophas's widow confides in her granddaughter. Might not this woman, prematurely aged by successive bereavements, have distorted or simply exaggerated her memories? After all, Gustave reads and writes fluently, well enough, in any case, to have written a masterpiece. His childhood aberrations were either not as marked as his mother pretends, or else they had no serious consequences. Certainly things did not go very well for Flaubert; he hated school life, student life, and as the victim of a "nervous illness"—which his biographer takes care to pass over in silence—he sought isolation at Croisset. But to reconcile this reputedly backward childhood with the troubles of adolescence and maturity, to explain one by the other or simply to use the later difficulties to confirm the statements of Caroline Commanville would be like pulling a rabbit out of a hat if we were not provided with an abundant, detailed testimony that comes only five years after the events in question—the testimony of Gustave himself.

Indeed, his first works deal continually with his childhood. Of course, all of us are constantly discussing the child we were, and are, but at certain periods we are less conscious of it than at others and describe this time past, and impassable, without knowing it. Adolescence in particular is often a point of rupture—we think of the present, of the future, describing what we believe we are today, wanting to know what we will be. In many of his early stories, the fifteen-year-old Gustave speaks knowingly of his early childhood, in particular of his stupors and torments when confronted with the primer. For himself, he has not ceased, nor will he ever cease, being that murdered child. We shall learn the reasons for this fidelity, but not right away. We must allow this life to develop before our eyes and for the moment ask nothing of Flaubert's memoirs but the invalidation or confirmation of Caroline's story.

Quidquid volueris

Let us reread *Quidquid volueris*.[2] It is clear that Djalioh, the ape-man, represents Flaubert himself. At what age? This character is sixteen, a year older than his creator. But he is the product of a monstrous union. A scientist, Monsieur Paul, has in the interests of science had a female slave raped by an orangutan. In the anthropoid issue of this breeding, the simian heritage has arrested the human development. That is, Djalioh is arrested in childhood, just beyond the point at which man and animal are—according to Gustave—still indistinguishable. Does this mean that the young schoolboy wants to define himself as he is now, at his desk? Yes, and no. Gustave is not a "brilliant fellow," we shall see, but he is rather a good student; he reads, he writes, goes around with boys his own age, is elated by discussions of metaphysics with Alfred {Lengline}. He can allude to himself through Djalioh only if he holds his childhood to be the consummate truth of his fifteen years. It is this childhood—unforgettable, unforgotten—that made him what he has become; it remains within him, always in the present. But it is not so much the lived reality of his present as a universal axis of reference, an immediate explanation of everything he does, of everything he feels. The child is not the adolescent; he is the calamity that produced the other and limits his horizons. In this way, childhood is permanent, he touches it; if he thinks of himself, he always refers eight years back to that time between two times when his troubles began.{Sartre has a long note that any of Gustave's writings at this time would reveal similar identifications of science with apelike stupidity and with his father.}

We will not admit Gustave's testimony uncritically. At fifteen the young boy has passed—we shall see why—from flexible defense to counterattack. He begins by accepting the judgment of other people, by pushing it to an extreme: I was backward, worse still, an anthropoid.

But he does this only to effect a sudden reversal of values and hurl the accusation back on his accusers. Ape-man—why not? Be animals if you can, strictly subhuman, anything rather than human beings. We are advised that Djalioh is somewhat unsuited to making logical connections; relations escape him. This is attributed to the peculiarity of his cerebral lobes, and the studious author describes the monster's cranial box: "As for his head, it was narrow and compressed in front, but at the back it showed prodigious development." Atrophy of the frontal lobes, hence of the intelligence; hypertrophy of the occipital lobes, hence of the sensibility. Did the young phrenologist read Gall {Franz Joseph Gall, founder of phrenology}? I rather imagine he took this foolishness from his father. It doesn't matter; what counts is that Djalioh, as the author will tell us when his creature has already gained our sympathy, is illiterate:

> "And so what does he do? . . . Does he like cigars?"
>
> "Not at all, my dear fellow, he can't stand them."
>
> "Does he hunt?"
>
> "Hardly, the shots frighten him."
>
> "Surely he works, he reads; he writes all day?"
>
> "To do that he would have to know how to read and write."

These questions are posed by some foolish libertines and the answers provided by the infamous Monsieur Paul. The author reports the dialogue without any commentary, but he is convinced that we will accept it at face value. Briefly, the question at hand is to situate Djalioh in society. These gentlemen inquire if he is one of them. No—no women, no cigars, no horses, no guns. Then he is suspect, he is probably an intellectual. Monsieur Paul has anticipated such a surmise. Intellectual? Not even that—he is unlettered. The scientist reveals the origin of the monster to the astounded guests. Unlettered, so be it. But why? Was his education neglected? Flaubert doesn't say. But he repeatedly stresses the scientists' interest in the most exciting experiment of the century, and in its happy result. Are we to believe that not even one enthusiastic biologist could be found to teach Djalioh his letters? Science demanded that he be put to the test, so we must assume an attempt was made. In vain. If Djalioh knows nothing, only his constitutional inaptitude is to blame.

He cannot make connections between syllables. Nor, a fortiori, between concepts. Here is confirmation of Mme Flaubert's disclosures—*Quidquid volueris* testifies to a bitter and powerful memory resting on childhood failure. To be a Flaubert, to be seven years old and not know how to read, was what Gustave could not tolerate eight years earlier. At fifteen, this failure remains an intolerable reminder; it is misery and disaster, the origin of what he is, the humiliation for which he compensates by perpetual scrutiny—it is himself.

But Gustave goes further, and behind Djalioh's inability to comprehend the written language we are given a glimpse of his poor relationship with the spoken language. The author does not say expressly that Djalioh cannot speak, although he finds people who condemn his muteness. Let us say that in general Djalioh keeps quiet, and if he tries to speak, the words do not get past his lips and are, in any case, never heard. On one occasion his lips move but nothing comes out. Another time, "Djalioh . . . wanted to say something but it was so low, so timorous, that it was taken for a sigh." We remark that he catches his breath in fear. Yet the anthropoid, apparently docile and calm, does not seem to be particularly fearful of men; it is language itself that disturbs him. Caught halfway between the simian imitation of human speech and the conscious production of signs, poor Djalioh dares not make a sound, ignorant of what he is about, in terror of making a mistake. The same deeper cause constrains him to muteness and prevents him from learning his letters. A defect of intelligence? No doubt, but not only this; he has nothing to say to all these men who are not his own kind. The young storyteller, however, does not deny his character a vague need for expression. But, as Mme de Stael said of one of the lovers who were too young for her, "Speech is not his language." On one occasion, the ape-man comes upon a violin. He turns it over in his hands without really knowing what to do with it, he barely escapes breaking the bow; then, imitating musicians who have just parted from their pupils, "he draws [the instrument] to his chin." At first he plays "a false, strange, incoherent music . . . sounds soft and slow." Then he amuses himself: the bow "skips on the strings." The music "is lurching, filled with shrill notes, with rending cries . . . and then there are bold arpeggios . . . notes that run together and soar like a gothic spire . . . all without tempo, without song, without rhythm, no melody, vague and swift thoughts . . . dreams that pass by and escape, pushed by others in a restless whirlwind."

Yet it must be remarked that this improvisation is not intended to represent poetic ecstasy but rather the earthly passions of the poet. It is clearly stated, besides, that the anthropoid does not dream of attempting to communicate with his audience: "He looked with wonder at all these men, all these women—who at first laugh at the improvisation—he did not understand all this laughter.[3] He continued." He does not play for others . . . he plays and the others are there. However, let us remember this attempt; Djalioh is transformed through the music, he expresses himself through music, but he will not agree to define himself through spoken language.

The Idiot Child

Here is the monster, the idiot child: "fantastic according to some, melancholy according to others, stupid, mad and mute, added the wisest observers . . ." The wisest observers, to be sure, are Madame and Doctor Flaubert, whose blind intelligence cannot distinguish between Djalioh's sighs and his efforts—rare, it is true—to pronounce a word: "Whether it was a word or a sigh," Gustave remarks, "was of little consequence, but inside him there was a complete soul." A complete soul: that is, the backward child was easily superior to the members of our species with regard to the depth of his tender feelings. The motif of the stupors, then, provides a counterpoint to the motif of language. Djalioh's life is cut in two by a catastrophe: Monsieur Paul takes him to France, there the ape-man meets Adele, his master's fiancée, and conceives a violent passion for her; he is tortured to death by jealousy. But what concerns Gustave is that before, before his keepers took it upon themselves to teach him to read, Djalioh experienced a golden age: "Often in the presence of forests, of high mountains, of the ocean, his soul expanded. . . . He trembled all over with the weight of an inner voluptuousness and, with his head between his hands, he would fall into a lethargic melancholy . . ." The author is careful to stress that the passions are not yet unleashed. Even at this age, however, if we are to believe him, the stupor seems to be a familiar outlet: "Nature possessed him in all its forms, the soul's delights, violent passions;[4] gluttonous appetites. . . . His heart . . . was vast like the sea, immense and empty like his solitude."

The symbol is precise: the ape-man, monstrous product of nature and man, must be both the pure object of man and natural subject par excellence. His most intimate relations are with nature and not with men—nature is within him, it is his pure existence; outside him, it is his own potential. His only potential; he can surpass himself only in the direction of nature, making himself so much more nature—that is, spontaneity without a subject—that he loses himself in the unmaned, uncultivated virgin vastness of the ocean or forest. Nature is the meaning and end of his basic project elaborated in a thousand particular appetites; he comes back to himself from the horizons, he is a being from the natural distances. Between immanence and transcendence there is, in Djalioh, reciprocity; therefore, the author insists, it could be said, according to the circumstances, either that he is diluted in nature or that the whole of nature enters him. Although this seems to be a matter of inverse modes, they are actually the same with a different emphasis—sometimes the soul appears as an infinite gap and the world is swallowed up in it, and sometimes it is a finite mode of substance; thus imprisoned within the limits of its determination, it annihilates itself so that it can flow beyond its borders and realize its participation in the indivisible All, in the very movement that dissolves its particularity.

Most important, the basic intention never varies—the goal in both cases is summation. Reciprocal summation of the microcosm by the macrocosm, and vice versa. When this double simultaneous belonging of the soul to the world, the world to the soul, is the object of a concrete and lived experience, Flaubert calls it quite simply poetry. When it is actualized by gathering together all of being and all of man in an intentional synthesis that proceeds from the negation of any analytic determination, it might equally be called metaphysical attitude. Indeed, before ecstasy there is little Gustave, the waves of the sea, the dark sand where the waves subside, the clear dry sand they cannot reach, the remains of a boat stranded on the beach, a cabana, etc.; as soon as the metaphysical attitude is imposed, these objects are annihilated in favor of general determinations: place, time, the infinite, etc.

The reader will have observed that this attitude, while intentional and spontaneous, is suffered by the anthropoid and the child; they do not determine it themselves, they are determined by it. Poetry befalls the subman, as is sufficiently indicated by the word *lethargy* that Gustave uses to designate a certain phase of Djalioh's ecstasy—and even more by the irrepressible shudderings that accompany it most of the time. Poetry is suffered; we must add that it is inborn. What is given to the son of ape and woman cannot be given to the son of man, for intelligence and logic kill pantheistic intuition. The young boy is proud of his trances because he sees his animality continually revived in them. He knows very well that others think he looks stupid at these times. He writes about it unmistakably and at length in *Quidquid volueris*. Mad with jealousy, the monster scratches Adele with his nails. She escapes, he remains alone: "He was as pale as a wedding dress, his thick lips cracked by fever and covered with blisters moved quickly like someone speaking very fast, his eyelids blinked and his eyeball rolled slowly in its socket, like an idiot."

"Brutish—The Best of Me"

This last, terribly violent passage strikes us by a double inaccuracy, or rather by the same one repeated twice: "like someone speaking very fast," "like an idiot." We must pause a moment. Flaubert intentionally revives one of the stupors of his childhood; he shows his behavior from the outside, as it appeared to others, and he does not hesitate to qualify it by the words that were applied to him then—"like an idiot." Yes! I looked like an idiot, I mumbled, I rolled my distracted eyes, I was as pale as death! Why these smug admissions? In order to denounce the criminal thoughtlessness of his former judges who interpreted his dazed gestures only as signs of external weakness and did not understand that they screened the most violent storms. Imagine the passions that rage in Djalioh's soul: love and jealousy, remorse and savagery, gales, gushings, cyclones—a single one would suffice to shatter everything. But they are unleashed all together, with equal force and opposite meaning—they collide, ravaging the soul but mutually contained. The fragile simian body that anchors them, immobile and overwhelmed, is destroyed without a sign. Flaubert triumphs: here is what took place inside me! To put it differently, the adults viewed the stupors as negative behavior—absences, lacks, gaps in attention, a failure of adaptation. Actually, they were signs of "brutishness" in all its plenitude.

All his life, Flaubert attached a particular value to the adjective *brutish*. "The best of me," he was to write years later to Louise, "is poetry, is the brute." Beginning with *Quidquid volueris*, he clearly contrasts Djalioh, "that monstrous freak of nature, [to] Monsieur Paul, that other monster, or rather that marvel of civilization bearing all its symbols, breadth of mind, a withered heart." Language, analysis, commonplaces—this is man. From the moment the human animal begins to speak, even before he can read, he abdicates his native poetry, he passes from nature to culture. We will note the consistency of the Flaubertian vocabulary, how many times Gustave repeats in his correspondence: animals, idiots, fools, children come to me because they know that "I am one of them." Not from any deficiency, but from a dark, rich telluric power that he preserved, thanks to the bad beginning that prevented him from ever becoming fully integrated into the world of culture. The adult speaks in the present: I am one of them. At thirty he believes that his childhood—frustrated, silent, sedentary, and mad—is still with him; the company of other adults, the claims of his mistress pull him momentarily away, out of it, but he falls back as soon as he finds himself alone again. This very rumination on the past reveals in

Gustave the recriminator who progresses backward. But in the early years recrimination did not yet exist.

I only want to indicate that Gustave always valued in himself above all else not the speaking animal, but the nonspeaking animal. By advertising their inability to understand the poet, Monsieur Paul and his friends merely bring the judgment down on their own heads—on the one hand this creature of silence, folded in on himself, and on the other the men of letters, the men of science who use language to go from one table to another repeating the same commonplaces issued from the same paltry wisdom; the literate man is the one disqualified by this comparison. Anyone who has studied Flaubert for some time will have no difficulty reading between the lines Gustave's venomous revenge on Achille: "Yes, at seven I did not know my letters and you, from the age of four, you read fluently. Afterward? I was a brute, meaning a poet, and you, you were a little doctor, meaning a robot, and you remained one."

The Silence of Poetry

In the period these early stories were written, Flaubert is categorical: poetry is a silent adventure of the soul, a lived event that has nothing in common with language; more precisely, poetry takes place against language. If this position is still only implicit in *Quidquid volueris*, it is fully developed a year later in *Mémoires d'un fou* {*Memoirs of a Madman*}. This time we are dealing with an autobiographical sketch. The author says I. Suddenly the symbol has changed: the monster is a madman. And the madman's first transports—the very same kind that Djalioh experienced in his golden age—are expressly linked to Gustave's early childhood: "As a child, I loved what I could see. . . . I dreamed of love. . . . I looked at the vastness, space, the infinite, and my soul fell away before this unlimited horizon." Here, there is no more virgin forest, but "the ocean" recurs a number of times in the first pages. From the time of his first vacations, the child felt bound to the sea. There is an inner relationship between the little boy and this vastness rolling back on itself which, in his eyes, always represents nature without men. In the passage quoted—to which we shall return—this ecstatic relationship is clearly translated into passivity: the soul falls away; this collapse—like an attempt to conquer the plenitude of nature by abandoning oneself to it—is Gustave's childhood stupor, here represented as a voluntary act performed for the purpose of possessing the perceptible infinite.

Yet for the first time Gustave clearly poses the question of how to bind the undifferentiated intuitions of the poet to the language that must convey them: "I had an infinity more vast, if that is possible, than God's . . . and then I had to descend from these sublime regions toward words. . . . How to render through speech the harmony that arises in the heart of the poet? . . . To what extent can poetry humble itself without shattering?" It is a question, of course, of poetic writing, and this problem concerns the adolescent himself. The future writer in him dreams of glory, he tells us about his professional preoccupations; the contradiction that makes any transcription of his ecstasies impossible worries him, here; how will he make himself known as the brilliant poet that he is? But these worries are only the echo of older and deeper preoccupations. There was the undifferentiated plenitude, the child lived in it joyfully, and then all at once the descent again into the fire, the summoning, the forcible return to the words of others: "Gustave, where are you? Take your finger out of your mouth, you look stupid." It can be felt still more a little further on in the same *Mémoires* when Gustave declares that by this necessary descent toward verbal expression, the poet humbles himself, humbles poetry. He does not give his theoretical reasons—Flaubert never gives his reasons—but it is not difficult to give them in his place.

Language—Its Own Object

Since the poetic act is produced outside of language and without it, since it is not necessarily in itself bound to the word, therefore its transcription is not of itself poetic—it can neither capture nor communicate the all-embracing experience. Contrary to what Joë Busquet will say later, one can translate "nothing from silence." Later, when the source of the poetic ecstasies has dried up, this total insufficiency of words to what ought to be their primary object will be a powerful reason for Flaubert to consider language as a separate order of things, which is self-sufficient and its own object. For the moment, let us see in it nothing more than the supremacy of silence reaffirmed. And the condemnation of the word: for the word, a product of culture, pretends to render the natural, intimate movement of the soul and yet expresses only cultural, that is, external, determinations. To analyze—and language for Flaubert is analysis—is to kill. Words decompose. If the poet speaks, what more does he give us than the articulation of the words themselves? A practical joker borrows a watch, takes it all apart; at least he returns the actual mechanism, and if nothing is missing it can be put together again.

The fugitive poet who coins his experiences is worse; he takes the watch and gives in return separate words, which designate the parts of the object. The word *mechanism* and the word *ecstasy*—what are they? Things distinct in their very substance from the objects they pretend to designate. Cumbersome things that occupy center stage and obstruct the view, juxtaposed solitary objects more adjoined than articulated, in short, molecules of language. Whether reality is syncretism or synthesis, existence lived from day to day or the sudden apprehension of the self and the world in a mystic appropriation, it is situated on one or the other side of verbal analysis. In any event, it is life in the present; syncretism, "multiplicity of interpenetration," synthesis—reality is the animality that cannot be decomposed, it keeps its silence.

This is what Gustave thinks at fifteen years old. With a surprising strength of conviction. And of course it is all false. No doubt the sentence is analysis, but it is synthesis as well. The Ideologues had eyes only for the analytic function; they themselves had cut clauses into words and words into syllables in order to apply, first, their principles and methods to their own tools. Thus we see only molecules in the articulated discourse, to such a degree that this individualistic dissociation was at the basis of bourgeois ideology. It could be that the fifteen-year-old Gustave's fables are a distant echo of these "ideas"—through his father he knew Cabanis and Destutt de Tracy {Pierre Jean Georges Cabanis, French materialist philosopher; Antoine Destutt de Tracy, French philosopher who coined the term *ideology*}. Half a century later the questions became more complicated; with the dialectic, the problem of synthesis again becomes the first priority. No one doubts today that a sentence occurs against a background which is nothing more than all of language; no one doubts that the whole of language is needed in it for the sentence to define its own being and its meaning, which is nothing but differentiation. No one doubts that anything can and must be given a name and is even named by all the rest of language, uncovering and defining it, by all other terms, as a certain vacuum which is already, negatively, a name.

As for totalities (ecstasies or long, somnolent vistas of passion), they are never designated, meaning that they always involve new experiences which escape previous nomination and do not necessarily—or even very often—produce the word or sentence that best suits them. But if we know that we are at once natural culture and cultivated nature, if we remember that lived reality rolls its words along, loses one, takes it up again, that the actual, in short, is already verbal—but simply incomplete—we will understand that the role of the word is not to translate the silence of nature into an articulated language. For everyone, speaking is an immediate and spontaneously lived experience, to the extent that speech is a behavior; inversely, what is fully lived is never untouched by words and often revives dated designations which allude to it without really being altogether appropriate.

Thus the verbal act can in no instance be defined as the passage from one order of things to another. How could this be possible, since the reality of man living and speaking is created from moment to moment by the mingling of these two orders? Speaking is nothing more than adapting and enriching a behavior which is already verbal, that is, already expressive in itself. And this means to rework and correct our spontaneous babblings by living more deeply the passions that produce them; to live the original passion with fewer constraints and more radically through the liberating effort that clarifies it by naming it; and sometimes too, through a double error, to pervert the nomination by falsifying the passional movement, to disorder impulse by an error of nomination. The word is not given, it is. There are no words for what I feel, sentences are needed; and these disparate remarks represent simply my attitude toward myself.

The word, if I am content with myself, is always given; the word *love*, old as it is, can suffice for a long while, its lightning bolts still dazzling lovers who were formerly ignorant of each other. And if we want to refine it, there are infinite subdivisions: passionate love, respectful love, and the like, all these cases can be anticipated provided we accept—and who doesn't?—being predictable. And then, if the occasion demands, it will have to be recognized that the love which is lived cannot be named without being reinvented. One will be changed by the other, discourse and lived experience. Or rather, the claims of feeling and of expression are mutually heightened; there is nothing surprising about this since both issue from the same source and interpenetrate from the beginning. It may be that I am irritated today because the word *love* or any other does not do justice to such a feeling. But what does this mean? First, my affection declares that it is not a passive silence but a silent expectation, even an invention; otherwise what is the source of its claims, the urgency to find it a proper qualification? Briefly, on the level that I accept it along with its requirements, it is named and given a false name, and being provoked by this it requires not so much the studied redress of language as the deepening, clarifying, of its reality. The deepening, moreover, is required to perform a creative function, grasping my affection in its synthetic unity and, merely by doing so, inventing the verbal designation of this unity. Meaning that nothing exists that does not require a name, that cannot be given one and cannot even be negatively named by the bankruptcy of language. And at the same time, that nomination from its very origin is an art—nothing is given if not this claim. "We are guaranteed nothing," says Alain. Not even that we will find adequate phrases. Feeling speaks: it says that it exists, that it has been named falsely, that it has developed badly and askew, that it requires another sign or, lacking this, a symbol that might be incorporated and will correct its internal deviation.

One must search; language says only that everything can be invented in it, that expression is always possible, even if indirect, because the verbal totality, instead of reducing itself, as one might think, to the finite number of words to be found in the dictionary, is composed of infinite distinctions—between them, in each of them—which alone make them actual. This means that invention characterizes speech—we will invent if the conditions are favorable; if not, we will have badly named experiences and live them badly. No, nothing is guaranteed; but it can be said in any event that there can be no a priori radical disjunction of language from referent for the simple reason that feeling is discourse and discourse is feeling.

Gustave: The Writer

At fifteen, Gustave declared the contrary. The influences of the father and the century do not sufficiently account for this stubborn ill humor. From this period on he was a writer—with great power and ingenuity, a graceful style. Words obeyed him, they crowded under his pen; his eloquence suffered none of the difficulties that would create the grandeur and austerity of *Madame Bovary*, it flowed naturally. And yet, what purpose does it serve? To write that one mustn't write, that speech is a degraded silence. In his surliness, which the success at hand renders unjustifiable, we shall thus see a survival. It survives, and will survive, in and through an unforgettable childhood that conditions Flaubert's entire subsequent development. Later we shall see the complex reasons why the adolescent has turned himself into a man of letters. He is one, in any event, as we already perceive; at the age of nine Gustave decided to write because at seven he didn't know how to read.

We have proof: Flaubert's adolescent writings entirely corroborate his mother's memories, they allow us to catch a glimpse of the early experience such as it was lived from within. His writings hint that this experience—enriched and magnified through pride and resentment—was often repeated afterward and that the adolescent, like the child before him, never stopped suffering from a linguistic malaise or compensating for it by inexpressible ecstasies. Gustave, with a profound sense of his true problems—which should not be confused with lucidity—immediately puts his finger on the fundamental event in his prehistory; everything began with this poor insertion into the universe of language which is then translated into a dialectical exchange of silence and scrutiny. If we strip it of its hyperbole, *Quidquid volueris* confirms our hypothesis: the child keenly felt the incompatibility of affective syntheses with their conventional signs. The word was for him, first of all, the tool and product of the analytic operations that the adults, from outside, thrust upon him. Through words they communicated conclusions to him which he did not recognize. Not that he had other words with which to counter theirs—he seemed to escape from language through nature. Culture, for him, is theft: it reduces the vague and vast natural consciousness to its being-other, to what it is for others. The word is thing; introduced into a soul, it reabsorbs the soul in its own generality—a veritable metamorphosis. Analysis replaces internal links with purely external bonds. It severs, isolates, replaces interpenetration with continuity; universality does away with subjective singularity for the sake of collective objectivity. The soul, that cosmic and particular fever, becomes a commonplace.

We have shown that this doctrine is false. The abrupt split in Flaubert of the subjective life and language, of the intuitive and the discursive, of nature and culture, cannot be explained by the disjunction, in each of these pairs, of the first term from the second. It must be viewed not as a precocious grasp of the truth, but rather as the singular adventure of a child; various elements, external and internal, are interposed in order to attack what will slowly become his bête noire as well as the material of his art, the word. The doctrine he articulates in *Quidquid volueris* must be read solely as an effort to justify himself and to overcompensate for humiliations he could not forget. If we reject the falsifications, we shall be able to approach his first silences. And first we shall understand that they were not truly silences. Let us consider, for example, Djalioh's pantheistic ecstasies or those of the madman who writes his *Mémoires*—do we accept the notion that these ecstasies lack all verbal content? Impossible, since the flood tide of experience continually tosses up words and carries them along, pell-mell, sometimes on the surface and sometimes engulfing them so as to transport them invisibly underwater. Impossible above all because silence is itself a verbal act, a hole dug in language and which, as such, can be maintained only as a virtual nomination whose sense is defined by the totality of the word.

CHAPTER THREE

Gustave at Fifteen

At fifteen, Gustave wants not to see the words that haunt his poetry. Proof of this is that each time he comes to speak about his intuitions, he employs a rather impoverished and stereotyped vocabulary, always the same terms in the same order. Sometimes, of course, he evokes a simple infinite and sometimes an infinite "vaster than God's"; but these slight variations serve only to accentuate the invariability of the verbal theme. These devices will be found again and again until around 1857; traces of them remain in his correspondence until his death. Fluid, always novel, inexpressible, the ecstasies could be made the referent of allusions more nebulous, more capricious. Instead, everything is devised to last, to repeat itself without flagging. And then, take a look at the terms: *world*, *creation*, *infinite*. All these suggest an endless movement of the mind, a passage to the limit by surpassing all that is given. But Gustave did not discover these terms after the fact in order to designate a process that would have happened without them during the ecstasy; as the process remained virtual, this germ of recurrence had to be sustained and consolidated in each case by a word which was more or less submerged—one or another of the three we have cited—and which, in its materiality as a signpost, substitutes for the impossibility of putting his experience into words. The word *infinite*, for example, is at the heart of Gustave's poetic project. He never had poetic flights without utterance—whether spoken or seen is of little consequence. But known. And we must admit that the "original" silence is intentionally obtained not by abolishing language but by passing it by in silence.

These observations do not probe the nature of his first stupors; at five, he did not know, I imagine, the word *infinite*, certainly not its meaning. No matter; at fifteen, through his drama of silence, he intends to reconstruct his childhood as pride alone has exalted and transformed it. The connections are preserved, big words have penetrated the adolescent's revery; but in the childish ecstasies a cruder language was disguised beneath a vaguer poetry that he refined in secret. By casting a veil everywhere over the works of man, the child produced within himself a nature without human beings. He refused to slip into the mold of sentences, protecting within his own deepest nature an incommunicable essence whose texture is the fabric of the world and which will always escape the adults. This is not at all the suppression of language but making use of it for another purpose. Gustave does not use words to speak; he employs certain of them in solitude without appearing to draw on their suggestive power.

His Strange Use of Words

What we must understand here is that Gustave makes use of words, yet doesn't speak. Speaking is, in one way or another, an act; the sense occurs to the speaker, linguistic structures are imposed but he can adapt them to his advantage, affirming, denying, presuming to communicate this and suppress that. During his ecstasies, Gustave—who is haunted by speech—does not appropriate the "holophrastic" names and phrases that present themselves. It is not that he refuses to use them—this would still be an act; let us say rather that he abandons himself to the forces of inertia. Note how he speaks about his poetic intuitions after the fact: he receives them, he tells us. The "sublime"—in the strictly Kantian sense of the term—attacks him; and what can Gustave do in the face of that aggression? He swoons. A passage from *Mémoires d'un fou* tells us he is "swallowed up." I will cite twenty others further on. These ecstasies, it seems, consist of two moments. First, the moment of ravishment. The soul of the young Ganymede is swept up by an eagle, it feels itself borne up to the sublime height from which the world—everything—can be seen. But "ravishment" implies "abduction"; Gustave ignores the ascent, he plays only with unforeseen assumptions. For someone perched on a summit who claims to see, at last, the undifferentiated unity of the multiple, this universal substance without detail and without aspect is also nothingness, the passage from being into nonbeing and its equivalent. In this moment, if the soul of the little boy feels bound by an internal connection to this utter abolition of the cosmos, it is insofar as the soul wants nothing, feels nothing, desires nothing. Pushed to the limit, it would have to lose consciousness of itself. After the ravishment, the possession.

In *Quidquid volueris* Gustave clearly marks these two moments of ecstasy. In the presence of the sublime (ocean, forest, etc.), "Djalioh's soul expanded. . . . He trembled under the weight of an inner voluptuousness . . . and fell into a lethargic melancholy." The second moment is more important; one might say that the first occurs only in preparation for the second, and that the little boy is looking for a way to take his leave, to slip away unnoticed, sheepishly, down the drain. Briefly, the aim is not even quietism, it is stupefaction, the presence of the soul in the body, which is so muddled that it could well be called absence. Still, this surrender—is it out of pride?—can be produced only on the heights. At least this is what he says. Is this altogether true?

The ravishment—"child, I loved what I could see"—is provoked by the visible world; his gaze must have run to the horizon; the amplitude and recurrence of the thing seen must have evoked place and time for this child so compromised by his family. He invests his gaze with the power to make his escape for him; in fact, the object is not seen for itself, or rather it is apprehended only for the immensity of which it becomes the plastic symbol. And in the beginning, this is only the movement of the gaze touching the sea, astonished to lose itself so easily, encountering no obstacles. Caught unawares by the low resistance of things, Gustave lets himself go in some kind of release of pressure; the slippery evasion that is suffered, that happens passively, transforms perceptible qualities into abstract supports for the flight toward the horizon; across the visible world he pursues the most universal structures of experience. Dilation, relaxation, expansion—but suddenly, impoverishment through dispersal. Perception becomes the systematic negation of all real substance in order to attain the void, a category resembling being and nothingness, internal absenteeism and external lack of differentiation. It is this first moment of ecstasy that the adolescent will christen "elevation" or a "ravishment"; that is, he gently falsifies its meaning. Gustave's original feeling—witness *Quidquid volueris*—was that his being expanded its limits horizontally, losing in precision and clarity what it gained in amplitude; other factors, which we shall mention later, intervene and change the horizontal movement into a vertical translation.

In order to see things as a whole, mustn't they be considered from above? This new interpretation is only a substitution of image. A crucial substitution, certainly—since it introduces the theme of height and depth, assumption and fall, so important in Gustave's writings—but which does not modify the primary structure of the stupors. If we insist on it, this substitution prevents us from grasping the true nature of the release of pressure and the profound homogeneity of the two moments of ecstasy. Indeed, the assumption and the swoon are in opposition, rising up in order to drop down; later, Gustave will derive a whole mythology from this. But to be expanded and diluted are two processes so close to each other that the second seems to be a consequence of the first and perhaps its aim. A captive, incapable of rebellion, mimics an escape on the spot, and his rancor effaces all the determinations of his being, abolishing in the same gesture all his soul's wounds. The rush toward the infinite, in short, works, as in a dream, an infinite destruction for which the child is careful to thrust responsibility upon the external world; it is the world that has dilated or ravished him and destroys itself under his vacant eyes. Thus the swoon begins at the very first moments of the ecstasy, the dilation is a path toward lethargy, better still the lethargy itself finding a pretext for existing in time. We see that the abduction is only an embellishment.

The little boy is not simple. One might say that he unites within him the permanent temptation to disappear and the pride, serious ambition, and jealousy of the Flauberts. The refuge in the infinite, in pantheistic ecstasy, the poetry of silence, the superb vindication of his animality—all this we now understand was added later on, I would imagine from the age of seven. More precisely, from the time the young boy became conscious of his inadequacy, from the time he internalized this objective humiliation in order to make it a permanent structure of his subjectivity. He fools himself, and since the stupor is his temptation he valorizes it, he transforms it under the guise of poetry into a noble annihilation, which might be called, to parody Marx's term, the "becoming-world" of Gustave Flaubert.

Seeking Himself

Is he fooling himself completely? No: this cheap finery rather poorly screens some sort of weariness with living, an immediate and permanent temptation to abandon life. Gustave is convinced that in an extreme instance—under the influence of an unbearable vexation, for example—the swoon might occur without ecstasy or ravishment, in all its naked negativity. Proof of this is that he himself says it, at the age of fifteen, in *La Peste à Florence* [*The Plague in Florence*]: the jealous Garcia witnesses the triumph of François, his older brother; he experiences such chagrin that he falls unconscious in the ballroom and has to be swept out early in the morning like garbage. If someone protests to me that this is a fable and that the author is free to invent what he likes, I shall ask, why this invention rather than another? I recall, indeed, the virulent madness of Garcia's passions—hatred and rage, the scorching coals of envy. Everything seems about to explode and, furthermore, everything does explode—Garcia ends by killing his brother. But the murder is scarcely convincing, and it is Garcia's self-punishing character that interests us most (we shall return to this overdetermined act). In any event, adolescent authors are rare who would not end the ball at the Medicis' palace and the suffering of the young Garcia with some burst of drama. What could he do? He could rip a gown, bloody a beautiful neck with his nails, as he dreams of doing. Or else he could insult a general and provoke him to a duel. Not that these acts of violence would flow directly from his passion; quite to the contrary, they would spring full blown from the pen because they are required by the most banal convention, and most authors, young or old, dare not cast aside the conventional.

It seems natural that such volcanic feelings be externalized, that hatred be manifest as internal suffering, external aggression. In other terms, the active emotions—especially in the case of male characters—are abundantly described in our literature; there is scarcely any place, on the other hand, for passive sorrows, for blue funks, for white rage. They exist, nevertheless, hobbling legs, paralyzing tongues, releasing bowels; pushed to the limit, a person loses his head, falling like a log at the feet of the sworn enemy he would have liked to murder. When Gustave gives his victim Garcia a passive anger that results in the swoon and false death, he avoids convention without even thinking about it, simply because he invents his own truth. At this pitch of hatred, everything must be smashed or burst—he bursts. This manner of leave-taking is one of the two solutions intended to release his inner tension. Why choose this solution and not the other? Because he is defined by it in the very depths of his body and his memory.

We are bound to recall Garcia's fainting fit when we see Gustave at twenty do a nosedive in the carriage and collapse under the eyes of his brother Achille in the course of the famous crisis that finally turns him into Gustave Flaubert. Quite often the younger son of the philosopher-physician boasts that he has powers of prophecy, and for good reason, as we shall discover. It is impossible not to see that in the inanimate body of Garcia he prefigures the terrible passive violence to which he will subject his own body. Moreover, he will declare that in this crisis he discerns a strict culmination of his past life. That is, we must recognize in this crisis the effect of the offenses he suffered and the behavior which in itself resumes, radicalizes, and makes absolute all previous reactions. By his "nervous attack" Gustave takes a decisive step, finding a refuge in helplessness; but at the same time he establishes the continuity of his life, illuminates the past by the present, recognizes himself in Garcia's white rage, in his swoon, in the earliest stupors of the younger Flaubert.

Inertia and Productivity

Inertia, laziness, inner torments, lethargies—we encounter these features from one end of his existence to the other. Taken together they define a strategy that we shall meet again later under the name of passive activity, a kind of nervous weakness in the depths of his physical organism that makes surrender easier. In the beginning, the stupor is a combination of seemingly disparate conditions: frayed nervous pathways in the body, a vocation for apathy always seeking surrender, malaise, a bitter weariness with living and, in certain instances, the intentional use of these facilities to provoke the absence of the soul, the flight into living death. This surrender in itself implies a weariness· that dates back to his first years. Living is too exhausting for him; he forces himself to pass from one moment to the next, but behind his desires, his pleasures, there is a permanent vertigo. Imagine a wounded soldier being pursued. He marches beside his comrades, they encourage him—if he hurries, they will escape from the enemy. He does what they tell him to do but he suffers, and above all fatigue, less tolerable hour by hour, extinguishes the desires he shares with his comrades. To join up with the regiment, to outwit fierce pursuers, to be nursed, healed—he wanted all that, but little by little he loses interest; if these incitements are reawakened, it is in the manner of imperatives and through the mediation of others. Cunning, then violent, finally irresistible, desire rises in him to give up, to leave his comrades, to let himself fall, and to lie passively awaiting disaster and death. He will succumb unless he is carried. But in the delicate moment when weariness and the desire for death poison his humble project of survival, when each step he takes, far from marshaling subsequent efforts, is made to live in him—"I can't hang on much longer"—as one of the last, this soldier resembles Gustave, marching the way the young boy lives, with the same repugnance and the same determination, out of obedience rather than the instinct for self-preservation.

One difference, however. If the wounded soldier lies down, if his comrades abandon him, he will die for good, he will reenter the great silence of inanimate matter. Gustave, like insects that become paralyzed when they are threatened, seeks a "false death." One might say that he scents danger or that he feels his wounds and tries to die while living in order to survive his own death, to make it an event that is lived and surpassed in the midst of his own life, and which is absorbed in his memory along with the danger that provoked it. We shall never again lose sight of this "false death"; at all crossroads, on all great occasions, Gustave will repeat this attempt at flight, which is always spontaneous but increasingly costly—he will be ruined by it. We shall observe how the process, without ever achieving lucidity, gathers meaning as it goes and becomes the basis for a defensive strategy. But it must be added that the "false death" itself, the momentary loss of the senses, is intended but never entirely achieved. As creator, the adolescent Flaubert allows Garcia to revel in it for several hours. But the character only makes manifest the unsatisfied desires of the author he incarnates. The young boy loses consciousness within him for lack of the capacity in itself to suspend even for an instant the faculties of the soul. The stupors never achieve the loss of consciousness which is their end and, as such, their justification; proof is that Gustave at fifteen can present them as poetic ecstasies. As for the false death at Pont-l'Évêque and the attacks that followed, he often repeated that these were marked by a paralysis of his body which rendered him unable to speak or move—and by the incredible visions of his overcharged consciousness. We shall return at length to the content of the ecstasies and the "attacks."

What is noteworthy for the moment is that from the first, the child—even before his exile from the golden age—bears life like a burden. We do not yet have the means to shed light on the source of his malaise. But it is to this, without doubt, that he is alluding when he writes to Mlle Leroyer de Chantepie: "It is by the sheer force of work that I am able to silence my innate melancholy. But the old nature often reappears, the old nature that no one knows, the deep, always hidden wound." A curious text whose apparent contradiction issues—as always with Gustave—from its richness. Indeed, one would be tempted to oppose the "innate melancholy," an inborn or constitutional aspect of character, to the "deep wound," an injury or trauma which by definition must be an event of his prehistory.

But we must take a closer look; one might in fact say that the wound is an injury suffered, hence an accident of his temporality, and at the same time that it has a share a priori in his nontemporal being. And this is just what he means—it is our job to sort things out in order to understand. We shall try our hand at this later. Let us observe for the moment that this "nature"—which is perhaps only a first disguise—turns out to be his malady and at the same time the means, if not to cure it, at least to avoid it by brief, continually repeated escapes. For the deep wound that they have inflicted—this vertigo, this disgust with life, this impossibility of undertaking anything, this difficulty denying and affirming which bars his way into the universe of discourse—must be called, I believe, his passive constitution. It is this, in fact, that he denounces when he concludes that Djalioh "was the epitome of great moral and physical weakness with the full range of emotional vehemence." He does not even hide the extreme fragility of his fits of violence: it is the lightning, he says, "that burns palaces and is extinguished in a puddle of water." And we must try to find out whether his constitution has not in fact been given to him. But when he suffers from it, when he sees his fundamental indisposition as the consequence of a wound inflicted by others, he can momentarily set a limit to his misfortune by improving upon his passivity.

Such is the origin of the stupors: each of them is an attempt to live to the fullest this ordinance decreed by inert materiality. And let us not view these attempts as full-scale undertakings—Gustave the child is not made to act; rather, he makes dizzying surrenders to that established nature which he feels in himself as the product of Others. Dizzying and spiteful: I escape from you by becoming, to spite you, what you wanted me to be. At five years old, of course, nothing is said, for the child would need to have a self-conscious lucidity that does not belong to this age. And above all, he does not say anything, even to himself, since he does not speak. Must we therefore conclude that these surrenders are not experienced? Certainly not, nor should we conclude that they have no intentional structure. But this will be our task when we approach the progressive synthesis, to establish the nature of a "passive activity." Let it suffice at this point to note that from early childhood Gustave can neither surface comfortably in the medium of human praxis nor let himself sink completely into the unconsciousness of the inanimate world. His domain is pathos, the emotions insofar as they are suffered without being assumed, and which ravage him, then vanish, having neither denied nor affirmed anything, lacking the power to assert themselves.

Such is the reason—on the level of pure phenomenological description—for his difficulties in speaking and reading. Ordinarily from the time he cracks that ultimate nut, the soundtrack, a child emerges into the world of discourse. The synthesis of signs, already begun, accomplishes by itself the analysis of the signified. Syllables approach each other, stick together, the child's first faltering efforts produce a totality; from the vague background of the external world a form detaches itself, dispensing the elements that compose it. Since speech can be mute and muteness babbling, since nature and culture are not distinguishable and encounter each other again in the unity of the signifier, the signified, and signification, insofar as we have our origins in our prehistories it is clear that nothing precedes language and that we have passed effortlessly, through our simple, practical affirmation of ourselves, from the spoken soul to the speaking soul.

Gustave's passive constitution long detains him at the stage of the spoken soul; meanings come to him, like tastes and smells, he understands them—but not completely, since he cannot make them his own; what he grasps of them, in any event, is given to him by others. Unable to accomplish the act that is intellection—definite evidence on which to base our certainties—he is reduced to belief. The sentences of others are affirmed in him but not by him. This is what they call his credulity; indeed, he believes everything, and this is to believe nothing, it is only to believe. His credulity is merged with what he will later call his "belief in nothing." He pronounces sentences, nevertheless, he repeats words or puts them together like flowers in a bouquet—he is affected by their vague, lingering sense. As long as no one thinks of giving him a primer, no one perceives that he doesn't speak, rather, that he is spoken. But from the moment he must learn to read, language transforms itself before his eyes—he has to decompose, recompose according to the rules, affirm, deny, communicate; what he must be taught is not only the alphabet but the praxis for which nothing has prepared him. The pathic child approaches practice and discovers he is not suited for it. Or, rather, he does not understand what is required of him. Previously, of course, he was docile and obedient. But this was bending himself to the will of the adults—*perinde ac cadaver*. Now he is commanded to act. But the act, even under orders, is sovereignty, that is, it bears in itself an implicit negation of obedience. For Gustave, reading will not only be an operation that the others demand of him without giving him the proper tools; it will be, above all, an exile. Faced with the primer, he feels he will be routed from the gentle, servile world of childhood.

He will learn his letters, certainly—we shall see at what price. Passivity is his lot, but he is a child of man, not an idiot, not even a wild child; like all men, he is a surpassing, a project; he can act. Only he has more difficulties than others, and more disgust. And then, he does not recognize himself when his docility forces him to become an agent; he loses himself, goes astray in an undertaking that provokes within him the creation of an I that is himself and yet is not at all his ego—the ego solicited by the adults but which, by its very function, escapes them. Action is the unknown, it is anguish; everything vanishes beneath him because he surpasses everything toward a goal that has been set for him. He will read, he will write, but language will always remain in his eyes a double, suspect creature that talks to itself all alone inside him, filling him with incommunicable impressions, a creature that makes itself speak, requiring that Gustave communicate with others when he has literally nothing to communicate. Or, rather, when the very notion and the need for communication are certainly present in him from his prehistory, but are strangers to the extent that the words inside him belong to others and cannot designate his own experience. We shall see that starting with this, we can establish the particular meaning of style in Flaubert, that is, his future practice in relation to the word. For the moment we have only managed to locate the trouble: the child discovers that he is passive in the active universe of discourse. Our description stops there; our present task is to review the course of this history and seek in the depths of the first years the reasons for his passivity.

Is his body responsible for it? To tell the truth, it escapes us. We recognize at the outset that we cannot know the vicissitudes of his intrauterine life. If, at least, the medical opinions on the adult Flaubert had come down to us, if some recorded "checkup" could provide us with information on the condition of the fifty-year-old, we might then enlist the aid of contemporary specialists in tracing our way back in time, step-by-step, to the original propensities of the soma. This would be merely conjecture, of course. It would be useful, however, to learn that Gustave at fifty had low blood pressure, that he was found to show traces of very early decalcification, etc. There is nothing of this kind; medical knowledge in 1875 remained rather crude in spite of the enormous progress that had been made. Even if such diagnoses had been preserved, there would be no hope of extracting anything that would be of help to us. His parents took him for weak in the head and said more than enough about that; but the organism? The weariness with living is there, it would never leave him. He will disguise it with much clamor and commotion, but not convincingly; until the end, his contemporaries would remark upon his crushing torpors, the drowsiness that overtook him at midday. No doubt there "was a hidden correspondence between the apathy of this great strapping fellow—who appears to dismiss his organic constitution—and his lethargies, which entail intentional structures." But what proves that these biological dispositions, supposing they exist, are primary? These questions, when they are posed as generalities, still have no answers. What will happen if we particularize them? If we examine one among the dead—and not the most loquacious—as to the origins of these primary psychosomatic structures?

Transition to Progressive Synthesis

{Editor's Note: To recall briefly the regressive-progressive method that unites this whole work: the regressive stage is simply what happens to one's life, with little reflective judgment of what it means to us. These happenings are sometimes given to us by our own memory, but often they are the testimonies of family, friends, and acquaintances. That Gustave Flaubert is a second son, that his parents wished him to be a doctor or at least a lawyer, and that they had no regard for one who merely writes are all happenings to Gustave. On the other hand, Gustave will have some response to them without, at first, incorporating them deeply within his own personality. This incorporation is the progressive stage of the method, and it continues throughout the whole work. At our present stage, we are just beginning this progressive movement.}

Our difficulty here warns us that regressive analysis has taken us as far as it could, to the phenomenological description of an infantile sensibility. Now the movement must be reversed. Let us proceed backward to the beginnings of this life, to Gustave's birth, and see if we are equipped with sufficient information concerning this prehistory to lure it to the surface; let us proceed, then, with the progressive synthesis that will retrace the genesis of this sensibility. Step-by-step, from the degree zero of this individual accident until the sixth year.

We are going to encounter on the way, one after the other, the various structures we have just made explicit. This is as it should be, since they will serve us as controlling indicators; if the movement of the synthesis is not derailed, we ought to succeed in reconstructing as the products of a history the stupors, the passivity, the weariness with living that we have discovered and demonstrated to be the structures of a certain life lived at a certain moment in time. But let us not be afraid of repetition—the material is the same, the insights are new; the child's qualities are going to shift from the structural to the historical.

We must try to understand this scandalous occurrence: an idiot who becomes a genius. We must, if we don't want to brazen it out with nonsense and turn these first stupors into a mark of election. We must do it for another reason as well, which is that we don't know anyone we love among the dead of former times. Gide, yes—but that was yesterday. The day before yesterday, there is nothing. The nursing, the digestive and excretory functions of the infant, the earliest efforts at toilet training, the relationship with the mother—about these fundamental givens, nothing. Whoever the great man may be, he declines as an adult, like Gérard de Nerval, to venture beyond a marvelous and tragic childhood, and we do not have a single detail. The mothers accomplished their tasks sleepwalking, diligent, often loving, more from habit than from awareness. They have said nothing.

When one tries to reconstruct a life of the last century, one is often tempted to make its fundamental determinants correspond to the first conspicuous facts mentioned by witnesses. I know this only too well, since I committed this error some years ago when I first came in contact with Flaubert. I tried to comprehend his "passive activity" in terms of the seamless unity of his family group. And I was not altogether wrong—we shall see how the little boy, inessential mode of the Flaubert substance, is acquiescent in the depths of his being, and that this acquiescence embodies the arrogant self-approbation of the family through the mediation of each individual member. But this explanation comes much too late in his development; the child has already been penetrated by the proud, dour ambition that the medical director communicated earlier to his elder son.

Gustave too did his apprenticeship in the family structures; his inertia comes from his acceptance of the Flaubert hierarchy and at the same time his inability to tolerate being on the lowest rung. Envy is already born, resentment can become a paralyzing conflict; as an individual he has no value, while as an embodiment of the social unit, he shares with his neighbors an absolute but common value. This modest observation (which we shall soon explore more fully) suffices for the moment to demonstrate that at this point Gustave's intelligence is in the process of full development. In other words, we are at the end of a long evolution; he is nine or perhaps ten years old, and new factors must be introduced for the process of maturation to continue. So highly developed an affective nature will already be passive or will reject passivity.

Such was my mistake. But I exaggerate it purposely; if things were so clear-cut, the explanation of inertia by acquiescence would be superfluous. We shall see that it is not. For this reason precisely, passivity does not simply exist; it must continually create itself or little by little lose its force. The role of new experience is to maintain or destroy it. During all of the early years, passivity is constituted on that deep level where what is experienced, the signifier, and the signified are indistinguishable. In the course of the following years, this basic character of the sensibility no doubt curbed the child's general development, though it could not altogether arrest it since it was an integral part of the whole. The consequence is a hiatus, a disparity; the affective inertia rooted in Gustave's memory, as second nature and first habit, is out of phase, falls behind the general development. The child is taught practical behavior, he is—perhaps in spite of himself—active in a hundred different ways, running, playing, talking, listening, and watching all the other six-year-old boys; and this infantile passivity, a habit carried from the cradle, paralyzes his feelings. He experiences as pathic what would better be given over, perhaps, to a more masterful emotional state. Once experienced, everything takes on inside him some sort of profound, vaguely inappropriate obscurity; the paralysis indicates his inadequacy. At this more conscious and rational stage of development, paralysis is a poor designation for his being-in-the-world, which is not simply an "openness of being"—this would correspond to the passive feelings—but also, for some time now, a certain practical way of plunging into things, of conscious self-assertion through the reach of his aspirations.

This is not a question of what is acquired but of what is made explicit. No matter; the little boy experiences his history with feelings formed in his prehistory. The displacement prompts him to make a modification—either smash everything or restore it. But this obligation is projected onto a shackled sensibility and can be felt only in terms of fate; the child finds himself at an intersection of fatalities. One might imagine that such interactions, the influence of an educator, of the family circle, of tasks so forcibly imposed that what is experienced, crossed by a current of expressive generosity, would partially destroy the introverted avarice that characterizes the child—who would discover that the fullness of "feeling" demands communication. In a certain way this is everyone's history. But not Gustave's. His family is a well, he is at the bottom; age and education slowly hoist him up—the bucket is raised, but how could the inner surface surrounding it be altered? Intelligence is established, behavior learned, there is always more abundant exploration, ample means for discovering the reality of the family situation but not for modifying it. Moreover, he finds that the family does not modify itself; the social unit is too integrated—a last, gratuitous turn of the screw.

The result is that Gustave's "awakening to the world" is only an awakening to the omnipresent and omnivorous family; he will do nothing else in growing up but live out, at different stages, the same family constellation. New factors are former influences illuminated, reconsidered, effective through the mediation of an understanding which elaborates and amplifies them. In certain cases one might imagine that the act of making things explicit in this way might provoke a radical transformation of attitudes—this would be the case in a misunderstanding. No misunderstanding among the Flauberts; new determinations are only the old ones consolidated and aggravated, adapted to the ever-richer relations being formed between the maturing child and the world around him. Thus apathy is first of all the family as it is experienced by a protected organism on the most elementary psychosomatic level—the level of breathing, suction, the digestive functions, the sphincter muscles. After the transformations that we shall try to glimpse, Gustave assumes this apathy in order to make it a more developed behavior and to assign it a new function—passive action becomes a tactical, flexible defense against a danger better understood, pure blind sentience becomes resentment.

We will soon see this, but what is important here is to reject idealism—fundamental attitudes are not adopted unless they first exist.

What is taken is what is at hand, limiting means; poles can be fashioned into spears, nothing more. Those pointed weapons, whatever one does with them, will remain pieces of wood, and their linear materiality does not depend on their new function but on the distant operations which produced that function and are preserved within it. So with emotional inertia. We have seen that it calls forth a stricter integration of the system as it evolves, but this isn't all; by the simple fact of being there, as pure receptivity, the inertia becomes visible, it is transformed into a means and suggests to the child how it can be used to advantage. Finally, when the inertia is entirely absorbed by the resulting praxis and is recomposed as the union of endured feeling and passive action, it will still preserve its archaic sense, just as the spear preserves the substance of the pole it once was. Preserved, surpassed, scored with new and complex meanings, this original sense cannot help being modified. But its modification must be inclusive; indeed, it involves reproducing a new whole out of the internal contradictions of a previous totality and the project that was born of them.

A Review

To repeat briefly: I had previously interpreted Gustave's passivity as a product of his internal relationship with the family, and the interpretation is not invalid; between five and nine years old, that is how things happened. But without the reconstruction of the archaic substructure of his sensibility, that interpretation remains a wild, unsupported guess, its limits set from the outside; the very sense of the determination is concealed in the description. I have said that in the earliest years the organic and the voluntary are confused; thus, sense is material substance and material substance is sense. In a way, if every person in the singular contains in himself the structure of the sign, and if the totaled whole of his possibilities and his projects is assigned to him as its meaning, the hard, dark core of this meaning is early childhood. The apathy received, lived, consolidated in the first two years of life sustains the child's inner passive activity and all the corresponding outlets for feeling; apathy is at once the substance of the sign, the opacity of the signified (a mysterious bypassing of clarity in the direction of more obscure meanings) and the interior delimitation of the signifier. Restrictive truth and plenitude condensed from memory, the prehistoric past returns to the child like fate; it is the source of permanent impossibilities which subsequent determinations—and, for example, the little boy's sense of being-in-the-family at nine years old—would be inadequate to explain. And the past is also, through an original syncretism, the matrix of the most singular inventions, the inextricable confusion which these illuminate and which makes them better understood. Either we shall find the asphalt core around which meaning is formed in its singularity, or we shall find the underlying origins of Gustave Flaubert, and as a consequence the course of his idiosyncrasy will forever escape us.

Without early childhood, it is obvious that the biographer is building on sand—he is constructing his edifice on mist, out of fog. The dialectical understanding can certainly build closer and closer to the last moments of a life; but it begins arbitrarily with the first date mentioned in the records, that is, it is based on the incomprehensible. And that obscurity, surpassed but preserved, remains its permanent limit and internal negation. If the dialectical movement does not find its true point of departure, it will never reach its goal. I can certainly invent highly ingenious conjunctions, no doubt I can anticipate the past that was the future of my great man, yet I understand that I do not understand and, consequently, that I do not understand what I understand.

This ignorance is fairly serious. There are men who have been created more by their histories than by their prehistories, mercilessly crushing within them the child they once were. They are no longer altogether singular, either—we find them at the intersection of the individual and the universal. But Gustave! From the time he begins to write, we have direct experience of the singular. In him at all times, whatever he does, sense becomes evident; it is the unity of the non-sense that defers or becomes a rational and practical signification. And hence childhood. Gustave, we know, is haunted by it; childhood is within him, he sees it, touches it continuously, the least of his gestures expresses it. It is therefore present for us as well, we discover it through the movements of his pen; but basically it escapes us, it is a chasm, and we can see only the edges of it. When we open at random a volume of his correspondence, his childhood leaps from the page but we do not see it.

The whole question is contained in these few words: Gustave never left childhood behind him. He says it, we know it; the adult is possessed by the miserable monster he was. On the other hand, when we try to amass testimony on his first years, we run up against a conspiracy of silence. First, no one took it into his head to observe youngsters and their mothers; and then, the backward little child didn't do credit to his parents; his entrance into life has thus remained hidden—a family secret.

Under these conditions, a choice must be made: to abandon the search or to glean clues from everything, examine documents from another perspective, see them in another light and wrest from them another kind of data. Of the two alternatives, I choose the second. I know the harvest will be meager. If, however, we may learn some of the details or discover the importance of certain facts that we have neglected, we should attempt the progressive synthesis, make conjectures about these six missing years, in short, forge a comprehensive hypothesis which by a continuous movement relates the new facts to the difficulties of the sixth year.

The truth of this reconstruction cannot be proved; its likelihood is not measurable. To be sure, with a bit of luck we shall account for all that we know; but this "all" is so little—almost nothing. Must we take such trouble to achieve, in the final analysis, only this hypothesis riddled with uncertainties and ignorance, without definite probability?

We must. Without a moment's hesitation. I will give my reasons at once, at the risk of coming back to the same thing in conclusion. A life—a life is a childhood with all the stops pulled out, as we know. Therefore our conjectural understanding will be required by all of Flaubert's subsequent conduct; we shall have to introduce the hypothetical reconstruction of the earliest years into all the manifestations of his idiosyncrasies, fill up the voids we have described with those vanished and re-created years, be prepared to restore to this sensibility that shadowy core where the lived body and consciousness merge, that lack of differentiation felt as the carnal stuff of passions. Briefly, we shall be required to do this not once but at every step of the way—comprehensive synthesis stops only at death. If our reconstruction is not rigorous, you can be sure it will be instantly ridiculed. Let us go further; required on all sides, given, submitted to the strongest pressures, it must disintegrate or contain some truth.

The Search for Truth

Indeed, let us not forget that from his thirteenth year the cards were on the table; Gustave wrote books and letters, he had permanent witnesses. It is impossible to take liberties with facts so well known, usually reported by several witnesses at a time or with the interpretations of Flaubert himself; on even slight acquaintance, the reality of this life and work imposes itself. Its density and sharpness are continual proof of its truth. Attempting to illuminate the life as it was lived by the black light of the first years, however, we shall see whether the gradual experience of the adolescent, of the young man, and of the adult is allergic to our hypothesis, tolerates it, or incorporates it and is thereby changed. Flaubert's adventure, then, as it draws near its end, will be the test of that rediscovered childhood and will determine in retrospect its resemblance to reality. This hope is enough for me—I shall give it a try.

CHAPTER FOUR

A Rediscovered Childhood

We have established and described the distinctive features of the six-year-old child. These can be reduced to two basic determinations: one is the pathic character of his sensibility, the other is a certain "difficulty with being" which translates as a psychosomatic unease. If these tendencies were formed in the course of his prehistory, they must indicate a problem in the original relationship that binds the child, flesh in the process of blossoming, to the progenitrix, woman making herself flesh in order to nourish, nurture, and caress the flesh of her flesh. Therefore we must trace back along the course of this life to the first moment when a woman makes herself flesh so that flesh can be made man.

I shall review here the generalities. When a mother nurses or cleans an infant, she expresses, like everyone, her integrity of self, which naturally sums up her entire life from birth; at the same time she achieves a relationship that is variable according to circumstances and individuals—of which she is the subject and which can be called maternal love. I say that it is a relationship and not a feeling; indeed affection, properly speaking, translates itself into actions and is measured by them. But at the same time, by this love and through it, through the very person of the mother—skillful or clumsy, brutal or tender, such as her history has made her—the child is made manifest to himself. That is, he does not discover himself only through his own self-exploration and through his "double-sensations," but he learns his flesh through the pressures, the foreign contacts, the grazings, the bruisings that jostle him, or through a skillful gentleness. He will know his bodily parts, violent, gentle, beaten, constrained, or free through the violence or gentleness of the hands that awaken them. Through his flesh he also knows another flesh, but a bit later. To begin with, he internalizes the maternal rhythms and labors as qualities lived with his own body.

What is this exactly? The handled body discovering itself in its passivity through a strange discovery; if, for example, he is abruptly turned on his back, on his stomach, taken too soon from the breast, how will he discover himself? Brutal or brutalized? Will the dissonance, the shocks become the bruised rhythm of his life or quite simply a constant irritability of the flesh, the promise of great future furies, a violent fatality? Nothing is fixed in advance; it is the total situation that is decisive since it is the whole mother who is projected in the flesh of her flesh. Her violence is perhaps only clumsiness, perhaps while her hands bruise him she sings continually to the child who cannot yet speak, and perhaps when he can see, he learns his own corporal unity from his mother's smiles; or perhaps, on the contrary, she does what is necessary, neither more nor less, without unclenching her teeth, too absorbed in an unpleasant job. The consequences will be very different in the two cases. But in either, the infant, wrought each day by the care bestowed upon him, is penetrated by his passive "being-there," that is, he internalizes the maternal activity as the passivity which conditions all the drives and inner appetite—rhythms, promptings, and accumulated storms, schemes revealing at once organic constants and inexpressible desires—briefly, his own mother, absorbed into his body's innermost depths, becomes the pathic structure of his affective nature.

That doesn't tell the whole story, however. Margaret Mead has demonstrated how in certain societies the adult's aggressiveness depends upon the way he was fed in the cradle. That can be governed by custom—in one place they gorge, in another they feed grudgingly after letting the child cry. In our bourgeois society feeding is no longer regulated by mores but rationalized by medical prescriptions; in any case it depends upon family groups and individuals. At the age when hunger cannot be distinguished from sexual desire, feeding and hygiene condition the first aggressive modes of behavior, which means that need draws the infant to passive violence and pathic swoons; the child's first negation and first project, aggression represents transcendence in its most basic aspect, the primary relationship with the other and the primitive form of action. Thus we can understand that according to his nature and his intensity—that is, according to maternal behavior—the child subsequently becomes more or less passive with respect to his essential activities, more or less active with respect to the simple unleashing of his passions. Beyond properly organic functions, it is the mother who will dispose the baby to hot or cold fury, to fears that are fleeting or that attack or paralyze; in short, to the predominance of the pathic (emotion suffered, internal) or the practical (externalized violence, inner turmoil surpassed through an act of aggression).

The role of the body as given, preexisting, is itself variable; the organism under the influence of purely physiological factors can "be open," or "open itself" to passive emotionality; the pathways of nervous input—in combination with the "temperament"—can facilitate or even elicit the passive feelings and states of transport. This rightful priority (without need of sanction) will perhaps allow passivity to impose itself more often in ambiguous cases, when maternal actions are not in themselves of a kind that deprive the child of aggressiveness. Inversely, if the somatic givens are not favorable, the mother could excite pathic violence in the child only by specific and radical actions; this means that there are thresholds to cross and doors to force.

And occasionally the door resists, the threshold is impassable. Thus in certain cases organic predispositions might elicit from the baby an attitude that maternal behavior, muddled and contradictory, would have trouble etching into his body. And in other cases maternal behavior might be so severe, its meaning might imprint itself so easily in the flesh that the induced reactions would be—in form and nature—highly dependent (these reactions would reexternalize the internalized behavior), if not in spite of the physical makeup at least by means of corporal neutrality. There are infinite gradations from one extreme to the other. Ordinary behavior is like gossip; neither the mother nor nature has fixed anything, so a person is only most frequently inclined in one direction or, at times, in another; in each behavior one catches a glimpse of the blurred outlines that determine it before a spontaneous reorganization goes beyond them toward new objectives. And without any doubt the combining in a single child of certain somatic predispositions and definite incitements—the internalized behavior of the mother—can be attributed at the outset to chance.

On Chance

But when the human being is at issue, chance itself is a producer of meaning; that is, in general existence assumes an artificiality without managing to create it, and in each particular case each individual must seem like a man of chance (insignificant)[1] or the result of a particular chance (oversignifying). This is what Mallarmé explains to us in *Un coup de dès*. The toss of the dice will never do away with chance, for it is contained in its practical essence; and yet the player acts, he casts his dice in a certain way, he reacts in one fashion or another to the numbers that turn up and afterward tries to parlay his good or bad fortune. This is to deny chance and, more profoundly, to integrate it into praxis as its indelible mark. Thus the work of art is accident and artifice combined, and the more carefully constructed the more fortuitous it is; Nicolas de Stäel killed himself because, among other reasons, he understood this inevitable curse of the artist and could neither refuse nor accept contingency. One solution: to take the original contingency for the final goal of the constructive effort. Few creators are resolved to that.[2] In contrast, the dialectic of accident and necessity is freely manifest without discomfiting anyone in each person's pure existence (that is, in experience surpassing itself as praxis and in praxis as it bathes continually in the life-giving medium of experience). I apprehend myself as a man of chance and at the same time as the son of my works. And soon I make my acts, my possibilities, into my most immediate truth; soon the truth of my praxis appears to me in the obscurity of the accidents that make me what I must be to live.

But in neither of these extreme attitudes are fortune and enterprise separated. We see this in lovers: for them, the object of their love is chance itself; they try to reduce it to their first chance encounter and at the same time claim that this product of an encounter was always theirs. What all of us, we too, seek here is the lucky child, the meeting of a certain body and a certain mother, an incomprehensible relationship since it involves two products united for no reason; and at the same time, this relationship is the primary comprehension, the comprehensible foundation of all comprehension. Indeed, these basic determinations, far from joining or affecting each other externally, are immediately etched into the synthetic field of a living totality; they are inseparable, presenting themselves from the moment they appear as parts of a whole: that is, each one is in the other, at least insofar as the part is an embodiment of the whole.

We have at last traced the course of Gustave's life to its beginning; we shall now examine the first chance event that was surpassed in that life, the fundamental feature of its fate. Yet, as we have seen, the inquiry leads us to the persona of the mother. What the child internalizes in the first two years of his life is the progenitrix as a whole; this does not mean that he will resemble her but that he will be fashioned in his irreducible singularity by what she is. In order to understand the passivity by which Gustave is affected, we now turn back to the personal history of Caroline Flaubert. And not only to that but to the relations she maintained with her husband, with her first son, with her later children who died.

It follows, naturally, that we first examine the chief features of

Achille-Cléophas, of big brother Achille and, since this family is a social unit that expresses in its manner and through its singular history the institutions of the society that produced it, at the same time establish the basic structures of this solidly integrated little group, beginning with the general history it reflects. For it is in this setting woven by the trinity of father–mother–older brother that Gustave is going to emerge, and it is the being-itself of the small group that he must internalize first through the mother and the care she gives him. An internalization that is confused, opaque, since Caroline too expresses in her way, through her prehistory, the familial determinations with which she is going to imbue him. In other words, our only possibility of understanding the primary relationship of the infant to the world and to himself is to reconstruct objectively the history and the structures of the Flaubert family unit.

We are going to attempt a first progressive synthesis, and we shall pass, if possible, from the objective characteristics of this unit, namely its contradictions, to Gustave's original determination—he being nothing more at the start than the internalization of the familial environment in an objective situation that externally conditions in advance his conception as singularity.[3]

The Father

When Gustave came into the world in 1821, Louis XVIII had reigned for six years and the class of great landowners had been largely reconstituted. For the fifteen years of the Restoration it would keep industrial development in check; this, during the first half of the century, remained noticeably slower than that of England. Nevertheless, the bourgeoisie maintained and frequently improved its position. The rival classes achieved an apparent accord and found an entirely provisional equilibrium, thanks to the customhouse politics they were both eager to impose on the government, ensuring that certain manufacturers (of iron, textiles, steel) and all agrarian interests would be protected against foreign competition. The rising bourgeoisie and the declining class of landowners could meet only on the ground of compromise, but this compromise was necessary to the bourgeoisie, which was handicapped by its numerical weakness and by the equally meager numbers of the proletariat. In the census of 1826, of a total of thirty-two million inhabitants we find about twenty-two million Frenchmen living directly or indirectly off the land.

For what we might consider to be the "middle" classes, however, the situation was different. They deeply resented the defects of the regime; they suffered at once from the high cost of living, the electoral system that kept them out of public affairs, and the competition of big industry. From their ranks the most violent enemies of the legitimate regime were to be recruited, and later the republicans. Lawyers, doctors, generally all those who practiced a "liberal" profession—and were therefore called "les capacités"—could be ranked in the upper levels of the middle classes. Most of them, educated under the Empire, received a scientific and positivist training that set them against the ideology of the ruling class. They were marked by the current of dechristianization that issued from the monied bourgeoisie around 1789; they had nothing to gain from the compromise that masked the fundamental opposition between the upper classes, which were, moreover, in collusion precisely to deprive them of any access to power. In the beginning, however, they put up little resistance to the masters whose servants and accomplices they were. First of all, they lived off the income of the landowners and the profit of the bourgeoisie; furthermore—and even more important—the "middle class," whose numerical growth was so recent, was caught in its own internal contradictions.

The example, Achille-Cléophas, Flaubert's father, is sufficiently convincing. Indeed, nothing illustrates the contradiction between the ideology of the Flaubert family and its semipatriarchal practice better than the morality of its paterfamilias. Portraying his father under the name of Larivière, Gustave informs us that he practiced virtue without believing in it. Some years earlier, speaking this time about his mother, Gustave wrote to Louise Colet that she was "virtuous without believing in virtue." This was evidently an attitude both parents shared. It bears a trademark, that of La Rochefoucauld {François Alexandre Frédéric, Duc de La Rochefoucauld-Liancourt, a social reformer}, reinvented and popularized in the eighteenth century under the influence of English businessmen and the empiricists, their hired thinkers, of Cabanis, finally of Destutt de Tracy and all the "Ideologues" who resurrected the theory to serve the needs of the Empire.

We shall return to this. The essential thing for the moment is to note the principle: whatever the act, the sole motive is interest. Depending on the milieu and the period, this gives rise to a kind of skeptical and playful hedonism or to the more lugubrious kind of utilitarianism. The Flauberts had chosen utilitarianism—a serious couple, they did not believe in noble sentiments. How was it, in this case, that they were pricked by virtue? The fact is that they preferred the common interest of the family to their particular interests. Each was devoted to his task. The father was concerned only with caring for the sick and making the fortune of his line; the mother, rigid, cold, raised the children and managed the household. Austere, frugal, and quite frankly miserly, the Flauberts, carried along by the sweep of history, practiced a veritable puritanism of utility. They conceived of their family as a private enterprise, its workers connected by blood; and their goal was to accede by stages, through merit and the accumulation of wealth, to the highest levels of Rouen society. The virtue they practiced and imposed on their children was the strict surrender of the individual to the family group. A collective instrument ruled by mutual constraints, virtue was identified, in reality, with the work of social climbing to the extent that this hard labor was performed by everyone without being made explicit.

We could go on, but for our purposes, our first picture is finally complete: passivity, stupors, credulousness, poor relations to language and truth, dramas, intentionally erected beliefs, and, at the end of the road, the possibility—already a likelihood—of the ditch, the tumble into hysteria. It all forms an embryonic system governed by a double denial—love escapes, and its flight is internalized by the child as his own vegetative inertia; valorization by the mother has not taken place, and Gustave lives this deficiency of the Other as his own purposeless, causeless flow, as the stupefying contingency of an inferior being. His astonishment will be explained later in his works. The character in *La Dernière Heure* {*The Final Hour*}, for example—who is Gustave himself at fifteen—writes: "Often when looking at myself, I have wondered: why do you exist?" With these words he reconstructs for us the vague meaning of his dazes—there is no metaphysical question here. And the child never asked himself, "Why is there being rather than nothingness? Why is this being precisely myself?" but much more simply, "I was born unwanted, now who will tell me what the hell I'm doing here."

We are not at the end of our difficulties. Indeed, if it is true that the first two years, which are decisive for development, shaped Gustave for suffering, it is no less true that he knew happiness, beginning when he was three or four years old and for a period we shall have to determine later. And then, however they are understood, neglect, maternal aridity engendered the stupor and the malaise. But as I have said, the child needs love without having the specific desire to be loved; therefore he feels—in the sense that gaslight can be called poor—his poverty of being. Sometimes to the point of ennui. I grant that much, to the point of anguish, but not rage. Yet we shall see later that he never conquered his anger from the time he entered school and in all probability well before that—until his voyage to the Orient; other factors must have intervened and he must have been thoroughly worked over.

In other words, after the earliest period we record a few happy years—but how could this suffering flesh suddenly expand and know joy?—then, abruptly, rage and anguish burst upon him and the whirlpools of ink flow unabated. But what new conflict unleashed the horror in this inert soul? It is possible, indeed, to explain these two successive transformations by the simple development of objective factors, which we have seen internalized. But looking at the dates, we quickly understand: Gustave—at first to his greater happiness and then to his greater pain—has been put into contact with the social world by a new personage clamorously introduced into his life, his father.

Return to Regressive Analysis: Father and Son

{Editor's Note: As the work proceeds, we gradually see Gustave incorporating into his personality the ways he interiorized happenings and choices, and we shall soon see the work pivot about the section called "Personalization," first in a regressive stage and then in a progressive one. This requires some explanation, for it would seem that the issue of personalization should belong only to the progressive stage in which the individual interiorized what is happening to him and the choices that he has. But when a stage has been reached in which the individual has already made a choice for the general course of his life—that is, his project—it is now necessary to return and take a closer look at the happenings that made this possible, before considering how the person interiorized them, and thus, a new regressive stage before a new progressive one. Also, despite all he has said about the importance of a mother, Sartre considers Gustave's father first and in greater depth because he blames the mother, Caroline, for not standing up for Gustave.}

It was his mother's pious and glacial zeal that constituted Gustave a passive agent; Mme Flaubert was the source of this "nature" and the malaise through which it was expressed. She was the one who welcomed him as an undesirable—that is, as the little importunate male who took the place of a daughter; she was the one who could not help seeing in him a future victim of infant mortality and who constrained him to internalize this maternal prejudice in the form of a death wish or, more precisely, an inability to live. And if the overprotection—which first made him the object of excessive attention—originated in Achille-Cléophas's anxieties, the fact is that the child was subjected to it in his earliest years through the attentions Caroline bestowed upon him with a lukewarm alacrity.

However, in his first works, restless and raging, it is striking that he never accuses his mother. He was made monstrous, he tells us bitterly; and he never refrains from denouncing the passivity which is his "nature" and his disease. But when he mentions his "anomaly" he seems to find it more complex than simple constitutional inertia; doubtless the inertia contains the "anomaly," yet it might be said to go beyond it, a complex edifice of which passivity is only the foundation. In any event, the progenitrix is not directly referred to; if Caroline is sometimes embodied—in a secondary character—it is as a victim, and she can be reproached only for being an involuntary accomplice. To whom? This is precisely what we must establish. In order to understand the reasons obliging the young author to rage on, or at least to follow the thread of his anger from one tale to another, we must come back to those first stories. No longer, as we did in the first chapter, to fish for confirmations of detail, but to consider each story as a whole, namely to examine them one after the other for their meaning.

We have remarked that every time Gustave writes in the first person he is insincere; we must therefore put aside for the moment the autobiographical cycle which begins with that first sketch, *Le Dernier jour à Novembre* {*The Last Day of November*, a novella first completed in 1842 and later published in English as simply *November*}, and includes *Agonies* and *Mémoires d'un fou*. Later, when we know him better and have the necessary keys to decipher them, these works will yield us precious information. For the time being, to take them literally would only mislead us. On the other hand, Gustave reveals himself the moment he invents. And from his first known work to the writings of his fifteenth year he can do nothing else. It is here, therefore, that he must be sought, here that he waits for us. He will not tell us the objective truth about his prehistory, but we shall learn from him that other irrefutable truth, the way he felt the movement of his young life.

Yet if we are attempting a truly regressive analysis, it will not do merely to observe rigorously chronological order; his life will have to be followed in reverse. In every investigation concerning interiority, it is a methodological principle to begin the inquiry at the ultimate stage of the experience being studied, namely, when it is present to the subject himself in the fullness of its development—whatever may happen subsequently—that is, as a summation which, though perhaps not complete, may no longer be continued.[4] First of all there is this to be gained: the richer the meaning, the more it approaches an impossible fulfillment, the more comprehensible it is. And here is the other advantage: the oldest intuitions, worn and stunted growths, not only do not contain the indication of future developments—although the subject may experience them as presentiments—but for lack of being grasped through their future vicissitudes, they do not even provide information about the archaic sense which possesses them and which they obscure by condensing it.

On the contrary, if we lay the path in reverse by retracing our steps from 1838 to 1835, this regressive study, which is a systematic interpretation of the present in the light of the achieved future, will permit us to discover in Flaubert the subjective evolution of experience, that is, the perception he has of his own life in its dialectical movement of summation. When the inquiry comes to a halt for lack of documents, it will be time to find out what the writer intends us to understand; from the first signals, difficult but profound, to the rationalized but more superficial constructions of the last tales, something turned on itself endlessly and snowballed, an experience that sought expression a hundred times. What Flaubert thinks of his life, what we must reconstitute, is the time-bound unity of these multiple significations and the meaning discovered in them.

But it must be added that this retrospective method imposes itself where Gustave is concerned more than in other cases. Because of that peculiar quality which belongs to him and which I shall call prophetic anteriority, in each of these first works one keeps finding the same symbols and the same themes—ennui, sorrow, resentment, misanthropy, old age, and death—but each time under these rubrics new experiences are expressed in such a way that the motif always seems adapted to the present situation and always anterior to itself, constituted from the depths of the future like the premonition of a deeper and richer future experience which is outlined through the present, and from the depths of the past like a habit entrenched through repetition, and like an obscure conatus, immemorial in origin, in order to give a meaning to what is experienced. In sum, everything we find in these first works simultaneously foretells future ills and is foretold by former griefs.

He lives, however; he cannot prevent himself from living nor can he prevent obscure, almost animal thoughts from forming in him all the time. These profound significations, which are scarcely disengaged from perception, from emotion, from dream, are untouched by analytic rigor: they are syntheses—hesitant, timid, irreducible. But they are not like accepted ideas either, for they are formed without the concurrence of language—"soft" and fluid thoughts that run close to life and matter and are often merged in dreams. In them we might see nature without man, for man is absent from them, contracted in his negation, in his willful absence; in any case, they express the deepest solitude, the solitude of the beast; such thoughts are what give *Madame Bovary* its incomparable richness.

We shall have to describe them. For the moment we must note their double character. They are rigorously motivated by negativism and by Flaubert's abstention, that is to say, by his complex relations to his class; in this sense he produces such thoughts by his very way of being bourgeois while refusing to be, and this entire system blocked by passivity serves to frame their lawless proliferation. If Gustave had gone beyond the commonplace and beyond analytic decomposition by means of an intellectual act, these thoughts would have disappeared or would have lost their softness; their contingency would have given way to order, a systematic exploitation would have risked distorting them by regularizing their course. But contemporary ideology did not provide Flaubert with the instrument he required—it all comes down to this. He sensed that he was lacking the practical notion of synthesis;[5] he found and rejected it in superstitions, and he sought it in vain in scientific rationalism. In effect, stupidity is decapitated reason, it is the intellectual, operation deprived of its unity, in other words, of its power of unification. Thus Flaubert's absenteeism was merely the expression of his class consciousness, and this is what made possible the swarming of untamed thought inside him. But on the other hand, this untamed thought, through its contents, escaped social determinations; not that it was above social particularities and on the level of a universal humanism—such humanism does not exist and Flaubert did not care to invent it; on the contrary, these obscure significations touch us profoundly to the extent that they express man's universal animality.

Again, we must be precise: this is not a reflection of need or physical violence; rather it is the expression of that "pure boredom with living" which seems especially to be the lot of domestic animals. Such as it is, this cunning proliferation, born of an absence, represented for Flaubert the only possible form of spontaneity. And let us be careful not to read into it some kind of immediate and irreducible subjectivity—the object is present at all levels; I would call it, rather, the animal consciousness of the world.

We have come to the end of part 1. We have tried to establish the larger outlines of Gustave's constitution. But as yet we have only uncovered an abstract conditioning, and no one can be alive without creating himself, that is, without going beyond what others have made of him in the direction of the concrete. We are now going to explore what I have called his personalization.

Personalization: The Imaginary Child

Thus, while our previous descriptions attempted to leave nothing obscure, we never arrived at little Gustave's personalization, an effort made through passive activity to unify the internalized family structures. Indeed, while the two are inseparable, we had decided to limit ourselves, for purposes of clarity, to examining his constitution by means of a collection of testimonies. But the paradox arose from the fact that most of these testimonies about Gustave were offered by the child himself in his first written stories. We were therefore led to search for constituting determinations through a totalizing reaction that preserved them, to be sure, but only by surpassing them, and this we left unexamined. Yet it is obvious that any reader around 1860, if asked the question, Who is Gustave Flaubert?—even if that reader were miraculously privy to certain confidences—would not have replied (or not at first) that he was a frustrated and jealous younger brother or an unloved child or a passive agent (albeit an agent who had lost none of these characteristics);[6] rather, the reply would surely have been "He is a novelist," or "He is the author of *Madame Bovary*." In other words, what was then taken for Flaubert's being was his writer-being, and if one wanted to particularize this designation, which is still too general, one would have had recourse to his particular work.

In the eyes of the public, he was personalized by the novel he published. Clearly, general opinion held him first to be a creator and established an intimate though ineffable link between the pure gratuitousness of the work, an end in itself to the extent that, for the time being, beauty was an absolute end, and the author's labor; but in spite of the impersonality attached to the novelist, the public also felt that he had objectified in his work the complex of his personalized determinations. With the exception of Sainte-Beuve {Charles Augustin de Sainte-Beuve, French literary critic} and his imitators, no one at that time would have thought of making a spectral analysis of a text or of interpreting a work in the light of the writer's life, or vice versa; but through a style and a particular meaning in each book, readers recognized Flaubert the writer in what was incomparably his.

In the movement of sympathy, empathy, or antipathy that draws him to, or distances him from, *Madame Bovary*, the reader places himself in relation to a man, that is, to a style of life infinitely condensed in the swiftness of a sentence, in its resonance, in the succession of paragraphs, or in their breaks. The reader does not yet understand this man but already tastes him and divines that he is understandable; in any event, the flavor, which is sensed immediately, should be reconstituted by the end of a long acquaintance or a biographical study. Yet objectification in the work is a moment of personalization: Gustave's contradictions and disharmonies are all in his novel, but they are integrated in an imaginary way into the unreal object he presents and are simultaneously integrated into reality through his work as the means of creation. Finally, by a sudden reverse movement, the reader's response ("He is the author of *Madame Bovary*") indicates that the writer must have subsequently reinternalized the external and social consequences of his external totalization—"infamous" glory, the trial, etc.

And above all, Gustave must have internalized the necessity of being the man who wrote *Madame Bovary*, hence who has already written it, and who, being summed up, surpassed, objectified in a product of his labor, is rediscovered whole, after publication, with the same conflicts to integrate in another work by a personalizing revolution which must also embrace and assimilate the fact that these conflicts have already served as means in the production of an imaginary object. Thus Flaubert's reader reaches him in his being on the level of personalization and discovers his constitution only through the totalizing intention that made it the tool or the material used to elaborate the man through the work and the work through the man.

Becoming the Writer

We are saying that in order to resolve his inner conflicts, Gustave made himself into a writer. Yet from his earliest correspondence we learn that he wants to write. Was he then constituted as a writer? No, but little by little the meaning of that term becomes more precise and enriched: we raise ourselves from one revolution to the next on the totalizing spiral. I will be a writer. This is the true answer the adolescent made to his inner disharmony, this is his commitment, his fundamental option: to envelop his malady and integrate it as a means of objectifying himself through writing. We are here on the level of stress, since Gustave's malady (namely, his constitution) in turn transforms this totalizing project by thoroughly infecting it, and since the totalizing answer to this generalized infection can be furnished only by a new revolution, that is, by a new metamorphosis of personalization, etc., etc. In the first part of this work we described the malady, not the stress, because mediations were not yet given. Now we must reconstitute in all its phases the dialectical movement by which Flaubert progressively made himself into "the-author-of-*Madame Bovary*." Gustave's answer to his illness, between 1835 and 1839, was to turn it into the means of an enterprise aimed at producing certain objects in the world. He personalizes himself in an enterprise in order to integrate what would otherwise be resistant to integration. The enterprise, in effect, is the reexternalization of the internalized, and such indeed will be Gustave's person, a permanent mediation between the subjective and the objective. More precisely and according to his own testimony, he is retotalized as the man who must achieve glory by creating centers of derealization out of certain combinations of graphemes. This definition is applied to the young Flaubert and not to all the future writers he will become—it suits him at fifteen but not at thirty-five. However, even in this limited way it is not original. At thirty-five, these three notions—glory, unreality, and language—structure a basic option, but, as often happens, before being totalized they are sometimes experienced as separate.

As a child, Gustave wanted to be a great actor. He renounced that ambition—and with very bad grace—only after entering school. At seventeen, he still writes: "I dreamed of glory when I was just a child. . . . If I had been guided, I would have made an excellent actor—I felt the power within me." Thus his totalizing option was at first appreciably different from what it later became. If we wish to understand its dynamics, we must try to answer the following questions: In what way did Gustave's choosing to incarnate imaginary characters represent a totalizing surpassing of his constituted determinations? Why was this the first moment of his personalization? What did glory mean to him? Why did he abandon the stage for literature, and what remained of his first "vocation" in his second? These questions are all the more complex in that they bear on the internal temporalization of a project. But especially to the extent that they concern a totalization that is endlessly detotalized and permanently retotalized by enveloping new determinations, they bring into play Gustave's relations to everything, not only to his family and his friends but to his fellow students, his teachers, the culture he was taught, the institutions of which he gradually gained experience, the social environment, his own class and other classes. We must therefore follow Flaubert's evolution step-by-step in his human relations as well as in his relations to art, since the former condition the latter, which in turn condition the former by subsuming them. But what we must ask ourselves before anything else—since this element remains in each revolution of the spiral and is found from the first—is what is meant by the choice of the unreal.

Sensible children dream of their future: they will plant the flag in new territory, they will save their fellow citizens by the thousands during a cholera epidemic, they will be rich, powerful, honored. Nothing could be more reassuring: these good little citizens please themselves by thinking that they will make their mark in the world. Their desire rests on being, and never for a moment do they lose sight of what is real and true. In fact, things are not so simple. Even among the most realistic children, the desire does not entirely correspond to the wish-fulfilling dream, or to any other. This complex option, totalizing the earliest determinations—familial ones—through a surge of enthusiasm which they condition and which envelops them, cannot be precisely expressed by any image or discourse; in this sense, these primary imaginings harbor the allusive goal of an unreality posed as such and, occasionally, the painful pleasure of unfulfillment. Still, it is no less true that the imaginary is here experienced on the surface as heralding the real, and unfulfillment as promising future fulfillment: the child really will be that heroic doctor, the idol of his native city—as though it were already accomplished. In this sense the fiction is perceived as a postponement of what is true and as permission to enjoy it in advance. Thus, at least explicitly, the imagined future presents itself for what it is on the level of praxis: a mediation that is not to be found at the end of the enterprise—since it is abolished by its own realization—and that is subordinate to real goals, a systematic and interested exploration of the range of possibilities, a passage from being toward being.

CHAPTER FIVE

To Act or To Write

But what if the dream turns into a dream of a future dream? What if the child were imagining a future in which he were someone unreal? What a worry for the parents! They discover that their offspring spends the greater part of his time telling himself that he will be a false physician. Not for the pleasure of imagining himself a true future charlatan (besides, charlatans are never true, even as such), but wholly in order to be false, that is, both not to be what he is and to be what he is not. Worse still, he feels a suspect, pervasive pleasure in the production of an appearance, that is, in mobilizing reality in order to produce something unreal that turns back on reality and totalizes it, in essence reversing the "normal," "healthy," practical order of things by making the real the means to unreality. Here is a suspicious character, the dismayed family will think, whose first move is to place himself outside humanity: he is prepared to let his prey go for the sake of a mere shadow; he prefers nonbeing to being, not having to having, an oneiric quietism. Even more serious, it is not pure nothingness he loves but the nothingness that endows being with a kind of unhealthy appearance of reality. This is the devil, lord of the trompe-l'oeil of illusion and false appearances.

From childhood on, this is Gustave Flaubert. At the age of seven he wanted to be a great actor. Other children about that age, whether or not they might succeed in their ambition, have opted for literature. This does not mean that they were better suited to write than he, simply that they were other, and literary art was other for them, through them. It is therefore of some importance that Gustave's initial project should have been so removed from his definitive project. But if, on the other hand, the truth is in becoming, the writer in him must have preserved the principal features of the actor and his writing style something of his style of acting. And no one can act dramatically without letting himself be completely and publicly consumed by the imaginary.

To Imagine: On Acting

The act of imagining, taken generally, is an act of consciousness that seeks an absent or nonexistent object through a kind of reality that elsewhere I have called an analogue, which functions not as a sign but as a symbol, that is, as the materialization of the sought-after object. To materialize here does not mean to realize but, on the contrary, to unrealize the material through the function assigned to it. When I look at a portrait, the canvas, the spots of dried color, the frame itself constitute the analogue of the object, that is, of the man now dead who served as model for the painter, and at the same time, in an unbreakable unity, the analogue of the work, that is, of the intentional totalization of appearances massed around this famous face. With respect to what are incorrectly termed "mental images," the image-making intention treats as analogue the partial determinations of my body (phosphenes, movement of eyes, fingers, the sound of my breath), and in this way I am partially unrealized: my organism remains an existing body which disengages from being at a single point.[1]

It is quite different for an actor, who seeks to manifest an absent or fictive object through the totality of himself as an individual; he treats himself the way the painter treats his canvas and palette. {The famous British Shakespearean actor Edmund} Kean walking onto the stage at Drury Lane lends his walk to Hamlet; his actual movement when off-stage disappears, no one notices it anymore;[2] in themselves, the comings and goings of this nervous little man have no meaning and no other conceivable purpose than to wear out his shoes. But the comings and goings are absorbed for the public, and for Kean himself, by the Prince of Denmark strolling back and forth and soliloquizing. This also holds for the actor's gestures, voice, and physique. The spectator's perception is unrealized in imagination: he does not observe Kean's tics, his bearing, his "style"; rather, he imagines he is observing those of the imaginary Hamlet. Diderot was right: the actor does not really experience the feelings of his character; but it would be wrong to suppose that he expresses those feelings in cold blood; the truth is that he experiences them unreally.

We must understand that his real affects—stage fright, for example: an actor "acts on his stage fright"—serve him as analogues, and through them he aims at the passions he must express. The actor's technique does not depend on an exact knowledge of his body and the muscles that must be contracted in order to express this or that emotion; it depends above all more complex and less conceptualized—on the utilization of this analogue in terms of the imaginary emotion he must fictively experience. To feel within the context of the unreal, in effect, is not to feel nothing but to trick oneself deliberately as to the meaning of what is felt. The actor preserves the suppressed certainty of not being Hamlet at the very moment he publicly displays himself as Hamlet and, in order to display his character, has to convince himself that he is Hamlet. The spectators' approbation gives him an ambiguous confirmation: on the one hand it consolidates the materialization of the unreal by socializing it ("What is going to happen? What will the prince do after this new turn of fate?"); on the other hand, it refers the actor back to himself: he keeps the audience in suspense and knows he will soon be applauded. But from this very ambiguity he draws a new enthusiasm which serves him in turn as affective analogue.[3]

Besides, a role always involves automatic gestures (habits acquired during rehearsals) controlled by a faultless vigilance; however expected or unexpected, these are released just in time, surprising the actor himself, and are easily unrealized as an imaginary spontaneity, provided he knows how to manipulate his gestures while abandoning himself to them. This kind of vigilance allows him to say as the curtain is lowered, "I was bad tonight" or "I was good"; but such judgments are applied at once to Kean, the individual of flesh and blood whose function is to entertain, and to a Hamlet who consumes him and who, from one day to the next, will be profound, or mediocre, or anywhere between. Thus, for the true actor, every new character becomes a provisional imago, a parasite that even outside his performances lives in symbiosis with him and sometimes, even in the course of his daily activities, dictates his attitudes.[4] What protects him most effectively from madness is less his innermost certainty—he is not very reflective, and if his role demands that he raise himself to the level of reflection, his real ego also serves him as analogue to the imaginary being he incarnates—than the desperate conviction that the character takes everything out of him and gives him nothing. Kean can offer his being to Hamlet, who will never do the same in return; Kean is Hamlet, frenziedly, utterly, desperately, but there is no reciprocity—Hamlet is not Kean. This means that the actor sacrifices himself so that an appearance can exist and makes himself by choice into the support of nonbeing.

We cannot say a priori that the actor has chosen unreality for itself. He may have wanted to lie in order to be true, like the actors trained by Stanislavsky and his followers, yet this desire itself is suspect. In any case, without knowing the details of his life, we cannot say anything decisive about his basic option. However, even for a "realist," his choice, much more clearly than that of the writer or artist, implies a certain preference for total unrealization. The sculptor's raw material is outside him, in the world, it is the block of marble that is unrealized by his chisel; the raw material of the novelist is language, those signs he traces on a sheet of paper; both sculptor and writer can claim that they work without ceasing to be themselves.[5] The actor cannot; his raw material is his own person, his purpose is to be unreally another. Of course, everyone plays at being what he is. But Kean plays at being what he is not and what he knows he cannot be. Thus, every evening he knowingly reenters a metamorphosis that will always be halted at the same point. And it is in this very incompletion that he takes pride: how should people admire him "being" the character so well if no one, beginning with himself, knows that he is not that character in reality? Therefore, not everyone can make a career in the theater; the fundamental qualification is not talent or disposition but a certain constituted relationship between reality and unreality, without which the actor would never even take it into his head to subordinate being to nonbeing.

This relationship undoubtedly made up part of Gustave's constitution at least after the Fall, for he went onstage at the age of eight and did not want to leave. It may be said that his desire rested on something real, the actor's glory. But this would be to reverse the correct order: the desire for glory comes afterward; indeed, he did not think it was due to any special prowess on his part but rather to the good use of a technique of derealization. This can mean only one thing: discovering in himself, as a failure of experience, as his anomaly, the reversal of the "normal" hierarchy that makes the imaginary a means of realization; he tried to become personalized in the enveloping project of turning this deficiency to his advantage and transforming his shame into glory. But for someone to choose to endow the dream itself with inherent value, he must himself be constituted as a dream. Only an imaginary child can contemplate insuring in his person the triumph of the image over reality because he is constituted in his own eyes as pure appearance. Being unhappy is not enough to prompt the choice of the imaginary.

Quite the contrary, the imaginary must choose you and be the source of your unhappiness. Gustave at eight years old suffers his unreality as an elusive lack of being. In order to understand how his personalization first manifests itself as a consuming integration of the unreal to the enterprise of existing, and how unreality figures in his stress under the name of a malady and as a means of escaping that malady, we shall ask ourselves, returning to the conclusions of part 1, what factors affected him in the beginning with an unreality that he was condemned to produce to the exact degree that he submitted to it. I see three such factors, each corresponding to a moment of temporalization but with effects that would make themselves felt at all levels of the totalizing spiral: his relationship with his mother (action, language, sexuality), his relationship with his father (being looked at by the other), and his relationship with his sister (specter of the epic performance).

Inaction and Language

The passive constitution that his mother's ministrations gave him entails the joint diminution of Gustave's reality and of reality itself. In effect, the unveiling of the real is a moment of action: it is revealed in the project that surpasses it as both practical field and permanent threat (the coefficient of adversity); its being is resistance and possibility. When perception is no longer practical, it turns to the imagination. Or, if you will, the difference is diminished between that which is the analogue of an absent object—hence a neutralized and derealized object—and that which seems to subsist as a simple being-there with no connection of any sort to our existence. In this sense, we can say that contemplative quietism makes imaginary what is contemplated. But Gustave is so constituted that, with his needs satisfied even before they are evident, desire is perceived in him not as a demand for satisfaction through the practical but as the oneiric expectation of a satisfaction that may or may not come, over which he has no power in any case. This means not that the impulse is without violence but that for lack of affirming itself it is without right and, indeed, its very being is in doubt—in other words, it is not instituted.

Gustave does not know how to respond to the external world (for loved children, that world is the mother, an always vigilant mediation between their desire and its object); so the impulse goes—by itself and fully awake—toward its imaginary satisfaction. For a desire that is violent but does not believe in itself there is not much difference between a chance satisfaction that is always unforeseen, never obtained, and an imaginary satisfaction. Inversely, the overprotected infant finds himself safe from ordinary dangers and does not need to provide against them. A little later, when they are revealed, he unrealizes himself by becoming derealized. It is a general phenomenon that when it is impossible for us to respond through action to the demands of the world, the world suddenly loses its reality. In a gondola one night in the middle of a Venetian lagoon, threatened by gondoliers who were deliberating whether to take his wallet and perhaps his life, Gide fell into a mood of detached, amused perplexity: nothing was real, everyone was pretending. I recall having experienced the same state of mind in June 1940, when I crossed the central square of a village under the threat of German rifles, while the French, from the top of the church, were taking potshots at the enemy and ourselves. It was a joke, it wasn't real. In truth, I understood then that I was the one who had become imaginary, being unable to find a response adapted to specific and dangerous stimulus. And at once I drew my surroundings into unreality as well. A defensive reaction? No doubt; but one that only serves to underscore a derealization whose source is to be found elsewhere. The salvation of my person no longer depending on myself,[6] I felt my acts reduced to gestures: I was playing a role; others were giving me my cue. Pushed to the limit, this feeling can lead to sleep—I have been told of soldiers under severe bombardment sleeping in the trenches they had dug. In this case, as in those I have just cited, we are dealing with a defensive reflex which can function only if powerlessness transforms mortal danger into a waking nightmare.

In order to pass over into the imaginary, Gustave does not need such hazardous circumstances; his powerlessness is permanent, and the least demand from the external world, the least disequilibrium, plunges him into a daze; on this level, his translation to the imaginary and the unrealization of the world are accomplished together: the daze is understood as an analogue of ecstasy, the sea as analogue of the infinite. Let us not imagine, however, that at bottom the child was not, like everyone else, a "computer of being":[7] on the level of anchorage and of internalization, the reality of the world penetrated him and became his reality. Except that at all levels he escaped from himself—the absence of the power to affirm and to deny reduced him to believing, to believing in himself. And we know that belief and nonbelief are the same thing: to believe is only to believe. The object of the belief is therefore perceived as an unstable being that can at any moment pass from the real to the illusory, so that its reality is exposed by its very presence as a virtual illusion; inversely, illusion, for lack of being denied, is always present in his eyes as capable of being believed and thus containing, to whatever degree, a virtual reality. Gustave does not always have the means to establish a clear-cut difference between the two.

This general lack of differentiation easily leads him from an insufficiently real world to a waking dream whose lack of substance is inadequately felt and which can always be believed if it is pleasing or reassuring. This alone, however, does not allow us to understand why the child dreamer chose to unrealize himself publicly—that is, for others—by playing dramatic roles. Here we should recall that Gustave's passive constitution has had deplorable effects on his entrance into the universe of language.

The cold overprotection that prevailed during his first years prevented his needs from being constituted as aggression against the other; he was never sovereign, never had the chance to bawl out his hunger angrily or manifest it as an imperative; he did not feel maternal love, and as the pure object of maternal care, he did not know that first communication, the reciprocity of tenderness. A little later, after weaning, when he had to express his desires in the hope that they would be satisfied, he was incapable of truly signifying them: the order of experience—which in him was vegetative and pathic—was incommensurate with the order of signs.

"Suffer in silence." This ancient axiom means—among other things—that we are grateful to our friends for telling us in a matter-of-fact way that they have a headache or a stomachache, without dramatizing and in a neutral voice; by keeping their distance with respect to illness, they invite us to do the same. But everyone does what he can, and there are always people who "lay it on"—their voice breaking, or faint, or falsely neutral—who identify with their suffering or refuse to retreat from it and thus make it impossible for us to distance ourselves; this is the appeal of love, of course, and we are right to say that such people want to be pitied, but wrong to be irritated by it. It is this way with Gustave. For him, language remains the principal instrument, but since he has not been initiated from birth in the myriad forms of exchange, an infinitesimal and unbridgeable distance will always separate him from his interlocutors. He thinks his pathos cannot be communicated, and above all he is unaware that every word is a right over the Other; that every sentence, even a purely informative one, is imposed as a question, a solicitation, a command, an acceptance, a refusal, etc., in the interminable conversation men have pursued over the centuries; that every question is answered, even by silence; that any two persons, different as they may be, when placed in each other's presence, carry on a dialogue, though fully intending to keep quiet, because even in the most complete immobility they are necessarily seeing and visible, totally signifying and totally signified.

For the child Gustave—and later for the man—dialogue is not the actualization of reciprocity through the Word, it is an alternation of monologues. And when it is his turn to monologue, he is certain to fail before he even begins. Others can reach him through speech; they affirm in him alien phrases that designate him from the outside and implant themselves in his head; he cannot make them his own because of the weakness of his affirmative power and he feels, when he recites them, that they have lost their power—he will not reach his interlocutor by simple speech. To repeat the words "suffering," "love," "desire" is not enough—he must make them heard; he has no chance of convincing others unless he presents his passion to them quite naked, just as he lives it. In other words, pathos will be manifest in and through sound and gesture, but with no right, no authority; it can only represent his state.

But for this display to elicit the Other's confirmation, it must not be aimed at him. Or at anyone. It is the opposite of information. Outdoing his passivity, the child must suffer the externalization of his pathos: the poor boy had no intention of speaking with a voice altered by emotion; as for the mimicry accompanying his statements, it imposes itself involuntarily, as though his interlocutor had surprised him in his solitude and saw him living his irrepressible suffering. Thus Kean playing Hamlet resolves to ignore his audience; it is the sight of the ghost that tears those stuttering words from him, that recoiling movement—and not the public's expectation. Kean and Gustave, however, through such noncommunication, aim to communicate—indirectly and without reciprocity—a pathic state; both offer themselves, propose themselves to impassive masters, not knowing the welcome they will receive. Will they be believed? Will they move their audience? Will they get what they are asking for? This does not depend on them—yesterday the hall was covered with gold, today, perhaps, it will be only boards. They put themselves in the hands of their judges: the groundlings are free to let themselves be convinced (or not); Gustave's parents are free to believe or not to believe, to let themselves be moved or not.

In sum, the child and the actor share the same helplessness and the same goals, with the difference that Kean does not really feel the fear he represents, while Gustave is convinced he is expressing what he feels. When we look more closely, however, the distance that separates them is notably reduced. Kean experiences Hamlet's terror, as we have seen, unreally. At first the little boy really does experience something. The unreality resides, in his case, in the expression: pain or desire pretend to escape him and provide their own testimony uninvited. At its extreme, this takes the form of the cry, the cry let loose in order to be convincing, which represents itself as torn out of suffering or joy. But can we prescribe the boundaries of unrealization? The emotion Gustave expresses is not identical to the one he believes he is expressing, for his mimicry is necessarily hyperbolic: if he were submitting to it as he pretends instead of making it, it would correspond to an affective confusion of quite another intensity. In this sense we can say that the experienced affect, whatever it is, serves as analogue to the simulated affect.

Helpless before the Other

Can we say that he is lying? Not at all. He wants to be convincing. Unable to affirm, he exaggerates. Insincere—no doubt; but only if we add that he is affected by insincerity—he makes too much of it because he is not capable of asking enough of it. Unable to discover, construct, and affirm his subjective truth all at the same time, he is certain of what he feels only after making a show of it and after receiving the approbation of others, which he internalizes and preserves within him as a hysterical imitation of an affirmation (the judicial act transformed into a verbal gesture). This means that his emotions, waiting to be instituted by his life's witnesses, escape him without being entirely destroyed and seem to be felt in order to be represented. All at once, pathos, instead of being the absolute consciousness of self, becomes the means of offering-oneself-in-a-state-of-emotion-to-the-instituting-eye. Thus the experienced affect is permeated by an impalpable nothingness, which becomes the very flavor of experience but remains inexplicable for the child because, the moment he feels he is being insincere, he feels the sincerity of what he is experiencing and trying to express.

The insincerity here arises from the fact that the sincerity is clandestine. Certainly, the self-consciousness of experience—hence the permanent possibility of a reflective cogito—is undeniable, but Gustave does not consider it an index sui: the sentiment, projecting beyond the simple presence of the felt emotion, always entails a retrospective involvement (a decision colored by the interpretation of the past) and a vow (an involvement with the future); this is the way it escapes consciousness and becomes its quasi object at the core of the psyche, a quasi object whose likelihood increases in proportion to the subject's affirmative power, that is, to his capacity for action, hence to his constitution. But Gustave cannot make a vow or a decision for himself; he receives his vow from others; it is up to them to decide according to his present actions what he ought to have felt and what he will feel.

The others, however, must be persuaded. If Gustave wishes to influence their influence their judgment, he must convince them; and it is fitting as well, while awaiting institution, that he should if not convince himself, at least become disposed to believe in what he is doing. For this reason he struggles with the constant sense of disequilibrium that torments him by intensifying the external manifestations of his state: he throws himself on his knees in order to believe, cries out to be touched by the pain expressed. If he could die of sorrow in front of his family—we know he dreamed of it more than once—this mad excess would be equal, all things considered, to the calm, assertoric judgment I am suffering, which is permitted only to practical agents. It would be proof and who could doubt it? No one, least of all the unhappy younger son, whose last breath would be a sigh of contentment: convinced at last!

In sum, unable to affirm his pathos, he tries to give it the strength to affirm itself through the ravages it provokes. In vain; he fights against constituted unrealization by derealizing himself even more. The gap grows between the intensity of experience and that of its manifestations; he cannot help feeling an emotional inflation—not much gold, lots of paper money. He is irritated: whatever he does sounds false; he will soon accuse himself of hyperbole.[8] Later he dubs himself the Excessive, a name with double meanings related at once to his real "hindddignations" ("I know, I shouldn't. . . . It isn't worth it, but what do you expect, it is stronger than I am") and to the big words, the outbursts, the gesticulations that express them ("I know, I exaggerate, I recognize it, but what do you expect, I'm a mountebank by nature").

At a deeper level, when the child unrealizes himself in order to propose the image of his real state, he plays with his helplessness in order to force the Other to give him a straightforward answer: "It's your ball. I have no right to your help and besides, I am not even appealing to you; if you help me out, it will be pure generosity on your part, you will be my good lord; if you decide to abandon me, you are free to do so, but you will have chosen freedom-to-do-evil and handed the world over to Satan." To playact one's feelings is to pretend to deliver oneself to others and, in actuality, to attempt to blackmail them. But of course this violence must remain hidden, even for the one who commits it; so the unrealization grows, since Gustave seeks to conceal his project from himself at the very moment he achieves it: with all eyes upon him, he deludes himself and imagines he is suffering in solitude when in fact he is acting on himself in order to prompt others to commiserate with him. To act on himself in order to act on others, to make a spectacle of himself in order to move them—this is the prototype of passive action but it is nonetheless action: stage actors do it every night, and they too must forget their true motives if they want to convince their judges.[9] On this level, language itself becomes imaginary. We should understand that the spoken phrases "I am ill" or "I am dying of envy" do not contain real information and are limited to commenting on the presented image, like the title of a work of art. When {Paul} Klee reviewed his new works at the end of the month in order to invent names for them, a kind of osmosis was produced between the word and the painted object; the former structured the latter by pushing unrealization to an extreme, and the latter, by appealing to the former from the depths of the unreal, communicated to it its unreality at the very moment of verbal invention. Words burst forth that had never been yoked together before—for example, "Frog Ventriloquizes in the Swamp"—which have meaning only in relation to the singular image that called them forth. For Gustave, at least in childhood, the derealization of language was not so acute. Yet the fact remains that language appears as a verbal gesture, the integral part of a more general gesture that was intended to show hyperbolically what he was feeling.

The process of derealization does not stop there. The little boy, a slow flow of passive syntheses crushed by the weight of strange phrases that designate him, is informed by these phrases that in the eyes of others he has an other reality, which they take for his true reality. For them he is a person with fixed characteristics. He tries—docilely at first, then after the Fall angrily—to be this person, that is, to act it out; he guides himself by accidental successes, by his intuition, by the intentions manifested by others, expressing his desires and his pain in a certain style he thinks is expected from him. We should not imagine any duplicity on his part; he is not cynically trying to turn himself into what they want in order to please; rather, in the object he is for others he recognizes, as we have seen, an ontological primacy over the subject he is for himself. Gustave thinks he really is this unknown being his parents have discovered; and to the degree he thinks he has divined its features, he tries to represent it, not only to flatter them but to open himself to his objective reality so that this reality, evoked by his miming and beseeching gestures, should slip into him and fill him with its density.

In sum, he tries to incarnate his other self, to lend his living and suffering body to this collection of abstract determinations. But at every ceremony of incarnation he recognizes that he will never be for himself what he is, perhaps, for others. In other words, he wants to seduce his reality—which is in the hands of others—in order to be it, in itself and for itself; but as it never coincides with experience, the incarnation is perceived as at once necessary and impossible, and the child feels that he is in some fundamental way unreal. In one respect, indeed, insofar as he is his own actor, he perceives himself as a character and not as a person; in another, what he experiences for itself is disqualified, seems to be a lesser being, inessential, and somehow without reality. For what is felt—ipseity in its pure contingency—is perceived as a raw and insubstantial material that has no other function than to aid the public display of his character in an elaborated form. There is one standard test, however: this character will be the true one if it convinces others. But what does that prove? That Kean is really Hamlet? Or that he has played his role "well"? Yet applause is the sanction he claims.

If Gustave displays himself convincingly, he receives no applause; he is treated as Gustave, that is, as just the person he does not feel he is. The belief of others is a prize for insincerity; it becomes constitutive in the sense that it prompts his devotion in principle to the representation of his being that gives him the double and contradictory impression of having played well, blindly, according to norms fixed in advance but unknown to him, and of having reached outside himself in the dimension of otherness to the objective being he is but that he cannot realize for himself. To be real, for him, is to be believed. Yet this is the thing he is never sure of; the behavior of others is obscure, unpredictable, and ambiguous. At best he will believe that they believe him; what is more, the child is never more alienated, never more unreal than when he says: "Me, I . . ." Me: the union of the innumerable profiles he unconsciously offers to others. I: the subject of praxis and all affirmation.

Gustave's defective rapport with words will end by thrusting him into an adventure that concludes only with his life: the future writer is fixed from early childhood at the oral stage of discourse. This means that he is alienated from his own voice, not insofar as it is the vehicle of meanings, but to the extent that it testifies, by its own modulations, to a hyperbolic pathos.

The Look:
The Mirror and Laughter

Filial love can be sincere, that is, felt. Filial piety, by contrast, is a "show." The child lends himself to it willingly, he says what the parents expect of him, repeats the gestures that please them—he makes a representation of himself. In this sense, all bourgeois children are more or less actors. But when the parents respond to this "show" with another "show" and cover the little ham with kisses, the role tends to disappear—everything takes place in the context of the intersubjective truth of familial experience. For the truth of my love is the love the other bears me. Warmly welcomed, the childish mimicry is unconscious; it goes beyond itself toward its goal, which is the response of the loved one: he must take the little boy on his knees, in his arms, and institute him as his parents' beloved son. In this response the child's playacted transports find their truth, for they were only the means to obtain that paternal smile by which love returns and is confirmed; the imposed role becomes a sacred rite, insincerity tends to disappear. In early childhood Gustave knew the daily ceremony of love; his displays of emotion were solicited so that they could be responded to. The love he then had for his parents was a passion bound to an imperative. This structure is common to most of our affections: being is duty-being, and vice versa.[10] Nothing could be more reassuring; before the Fall, the younger Flaubert son lived in security, feeling what he should feel because he was what he should be. Yet, the little boy unrealizes himself in the manifestations of his passion. Doesn't he love his father? On the contrary, he adores him. He was made in such a way that he has to "lay it on." And we know why.

He mimes too much what he feels, but he also mimes what he does not feel. Or at least what he does not yet feel. This is easily understandable, and in this respect Gustave is not so different from other children and even adults. Emotion is not separable from the actions that express it, and in daily relations with the "love object," actions often precede emotion and engender it. A child who is bored suddenly takes it into his head to throw himself into his parents' arms; it is not the overflowing feeling of tenderness that pushes him to it, but the future joy he will experience with their kisses. With lovers, too, amorous transports are provoked more often than we like to admit by dryness and emptiness. Love is there, however—past and to come; the memory of it is a measure and a promise: if the momentarily absent but manifested tenderness of one of the lovers answers the real but provoked tenderness of the other, an event—fundamentally dual in structure—is realized.

Of course, even if tenderness is merely produced in one lover by the other, it is reciprocal in each of them; by provoking in his beloved a true surge of emotion that overwhelms him, the lover himself feels his feigned transport transformed into the fullness of love. Gustave runs toward his father: if the father lifts him up high in the air and sets him on his lap, the insincerity is officially eliminated; what the child then happily feels is not at first his own feeling but a feeling that his lord has the goodness to nurture him; plenitude is born here from the passive internalization of paternal kisses, the externalizations of an active love. It seems to him, moreover, that in responding to his transports, his sovereign recognizes the truth of the vassal's love and devotion.

As long as the paterfamilias was disposed to accept his younger son's demonstrations—though hyperbolic—he validated them. The little boy believed he was raised from nothingness purposely to witness the glory of his creator, and the daily ceremony of adoration that seemed to him constitutive of his creatural being. He was not altogether mistaken: Dr. Flaubert, patriarchal bourgeois, did not deign to solicit love, but he would have been astonished not to be adored. This golden age, as we know, did not last long; gloomy, nervous, skeptical, Achille-Cléophas put an early end to the whole drama. This was his ruling contradiction: to claim the homage of his vassals on the strength of his mere existence as head of the family, and at the same time to condemn as a scientist all feudal behavior in the name of psychosocial atomism. For Gustave, this was a catastrophe. He derived his truth from the Other, having none of his own; when the father withdrew his credit, this second weaning created a breach in the sweet immediate confusion of intersubjective life, and such an abrupt disconnection threw the child back onto the solitude of the inexpressible, even as it made him unbearably visible.

The child was still expressly invited to the ceremony of love—if only by his mother, whose statements must have confirmed his feeling for his vocation—but scarcely did he begin than he was exposed by a cold look, a hand that pushed him away, an obvious indifference, or, worse, a nasty crack, a gibe. Ham! Thrust back on himself, that is, on nontruth, Gustave was amazed to discover his unreality; unreality, indeed, which characterized his being, had been developed in order to escape the insipidness of his facticity (as we saw in part 1) and to endow himself with a being-for-adoration, which could be seen from our new perspective as the dawning of personalization. But it is this very being that paternal rejection throws into question. Is he devoted? He would like to believe it with all his heart; his mother tells him so, his father denies the child's vocation without diminishing his demands. Is he doing badly what he is being asked to do well? Or is nothing at all being asked of him? Where is the proof of his mission? It must be felt tenderness; every time he dramatizes—which is more and more often—his transports are revealed to him in their nakedness, their insincerity is unmasked.

He throws himself on his father to find in his father's arms the warmth of which he is deprived; in the absence of a loving response, he discovers that he himself has "acted coldly," that a futile desire to please was made manifest by an ineffectual display. Wouldn't it be the same for any child, formerly loved, whose father one day turned away from him? It all depends on the "mothering"; if the child is a practical agent to even the slightest degree, he will undoubtedly be familiar with the daze and distress, but he will break out of it—for good or ill—by playing the mother against the father, that is, by endeavoring to become his own truth. When challenged, he will affirm that he loves, that he has never merely playacted love (which will be partly false), and that he has been betrayed. This experiment cannot be performed, of course, without provoking deep wounds, but because the trauma is not the same the stress will also be different.

Gustave's misfortune is that he hasn't the means to be his own truth and thereby to affirm himself against his lord and accuse him of felony.

The acts of grace, consequently, remain in his eyes his constituted duty-being, which is separate from being; the little boy feels constrained to act endlessly in a drama in which he no longer believes. The memory of endured disgust, the terror of failure—daily reinforced by new failures—is enough to purge him of any tender emotion; he offers himself frozen to the warmth that is refused, he solicits it with increasingly hyperbolic actions in the name of a love he feels less and less frequently.

In brief, it is his reality itself that the father's refusal derealizes; Achille-Cléophas has eyes only for the imaginary (what is not true, not felt, but only acted), and suddenly the child feels imaginary himself under the father's gaze. Dr. Flaubert was a highly nervous man and therefore occasionally nasty; when irritated, he managed, with a few sarcastic words, to reduce his son's "lies" to "fragments." For Gustave, called upon to weld himself to the being-he-must-be, it was as though he had stopped midway and, mobilizing his entire body in order to make it the analogue of a displayed but never felt pathos, he had merely succeeded in transforming himself into an image of love. He certainly does not think he is playing the lucidity game, which would perhaps have freed him, but believes he is affected by permanent nonbeing.

He has two ways of existing: either he sinks into the quagmire of contingency, the wretched slough where nothing is false and nothing is true; or else he unrealizes himself as a distraught lover, and experience vampirized by nonbeing serves only to lend this minimum of being to the nothingness that allows it to appear at all. He loves, nonetheless; but love, being a duality, falls when it is not shared into the domain of doxa, which is in the last analysis the realm of imagination. Thus, since his sincerity, such as it is, is rejected, and since he does not recognize his own right to feel anything until adults have given their consent, he is condemned by his father's capricious mistrust never to determine whether he is feeling or just imagining his feelings. The deeper meaning of this personalizing revolution is that the child no longer knows whether he exists or is just pretending to exist. Given this option, Gustave unconsciously chooses anti-Cartesianism and, more obscurely, irrationality. If he manages only to produce images, isn't he an image himself? This might be the key to the paradox. And, if so, what follows from such an assumption is his defense: if all Gustave's feelings are imaginary (that is, true in their essence but experienced as unreal), he will be able to explore and reclaim as his own all the feelings he took pleasure in imagining. This paradoxical level, which he will later be able to use to such good effect, is intimated now without being explicit, but its very presence leads him astray.

The truth exists for him, he believes in it; it's merely that it belongs to others; he has lost his truth, assuming he ever had one, but the others have kept theirs. When he compares himself to those solid persons, determined and impenetrable, he feels with terror that he is made of a diaphanous, proteiform substance that can imitate everything because it is never anything. All his life he will be haunted by the anguish that there might be people who love and suffer absolutely for real. We must see him at eighteen, mad with jealousy because his friend Hamard (who has just lost a brother) is overcome with grief: that cretin is suffering, and in reality I shall never reach that degree of suffering except through imagination! We are familiar with his defensive reaction: beginning in childhood and throughout his life he played the role of the unhappiest man alive. After the defeat of Sedan and the fall of the Second Empire, he would write—a disarmingly naive confession—that there are surely men in France who have more reason than he to suffer, but there is no one who suffers more. The fact is, Gustave suffered an extremely violent identity crisis after his fall from favor, because his being was stolen from him and he was no longer anyone.

For others, however, he is quite real; they see him, they know him, they have information about him that he is unaware of and that allows them to judge him. They withhold his truth and hide it from him. Since he cannot convince them to institute him as he would like to be, if he could at least see himself through their eyes and experience as a subject the object he is for them, he would lose himself to that being-for-others, fleeting, abstract, that is both held out to him and withheld, designated in him by words he cannot comprehend. He will be what they want, provided that he is something and someone for himself; passivity, failure, and despair lead him to submission. In his impatience to accept himself, he tries to see himself from the outside. This is less an effort to know himself than an irrational and passionate attempt; the unreal child wants to coincide with his reality.

For this reason, as he says a hundred times, mirrors fascinate him. If he surprises himself in the mirror, he will be for himself the object he is for everyone else; if in the unity of a similar enterprise, he felt he were a subject outside and an object inside himself, he would recover himself entirely and would act his truth. There in the mirror, he would have the same consistency as others, the same materiality. In fact, Gustave's relation to his reflection is originally only a particular aspect of his relation to his father. At the age of five he runs to his mirror when he cries. Is this so that he can "see what kind of face he's making"? Yes and no. The grimacing itself doesn't interest him. But having shed his tears in the absence of witnesses, he is convinced—wrongly—of his sincerity. Since this is what is at issue, he longs to observe himself in action—the way his father would if he were present—the spontaneous manifestations of an undeniable unhappiness. He has so little confidence in himself, this unfortunate child, that he does not ask himself, “How do I look when I cry?” but, “How do I look when I am innocent?”

CHAPTER SIX

Being Seen

His misfortune is that he immediately becomes guilty and is aware of it. How do we know? He tells us himself: no sooner is he standing before his image than he starts to make faces at himself, forcing his tears or his laughter, just as the young Charles Baudelaire did at the same period and for similar reasons. Gustave is waiting for proof, and for this very reason he is disappointed: the spontaneous mimicry that ought to bear the marks of sincerity is not convincing. The image in the mirror is only the vague and banal illustration of that suffering which ought to reveal to him his being-in-itself. He expected to surprise himself in *real* pain, an impervious lump outside him which is offered *to others only* as a "particular and affirmative essence," of which his inner affect can only be an internalization.

In sum, he has reversed the terms and invested being in appearance—the mirror reestablishes the true order; it is the interior, so difficult, never convincing enough, that commands the visible and communicates its uncertainty to its external manifestations. And then, the child is no longer the same: he watches himself cry the way we listen to ourselves talk; indeed, he cries just to watch himself cry the way we talk to hear ourselves talk. Is he crying again? And, if it can be determined, are these the same sobs that are distorting his features? He views himself through Dr. Flaubert's eyes and observes—incredulous, scornful—the child gesticulating in the mirror in order to persuade him. Moreover, the unreality grows: the object seen is *his image*, it is not him; the reflection serves as analogue to his visible body, which eludes him; and he himself is unrealized without knowing it: a haughty observer of himself, he plays the role of the medical director. As a reaction against his disappointment and also because he is consumed—false witness to a false appearance—by the cold flames of the imaginary, he catches himself breaking through his mimicry in order to invite his own assent, which means his father's.

In brief, he reverts to the only tactic he has left: convincing by performance. In this respect he is like an actor standing in front of his mirror in order to study the "impression" he makes. To tell the truth, he thought of it in the first place: when he claimed he wanted only to observe his spontaneous mimicry, he was concealing from himself his intention to learn it in order to reproduce it. How could he *see himself as innocent* without wishing to *show* himself as such to his family? He is like someone on trial working with a tape recorder so that he can let out a "cry of innocence" at just the right moment.

When he runs toward his reflection, Gustave does not so much imagine he will see himself as that he will *see himself seen* so as to adjust his image *in the sight of others*. But this is what he is forbidden to do; man's relation to his reflection resembles what the psychologists call the *double sensation*: if my thumb touches my index finger, neither of the fingers is truly an object for the other since each of them is at once seeking and sought, feeling and felt, active and passive; in the same way, I can see myself smile or raise my eyebrows when looking in the mirror and at the same time I am conscious of willing these actions and producing them as a function of the reflection of my face. As a consequence, I never see *a man smiling at me* but only the image that results from the muscular contractions I have intentionally effected. Nevertheless, there is something to be learned from a reflection; we observe in it, in a certain sense, what is related to being-in-the-midst-of-the-world (relations to the environment), but never being-in-the-world.[1] The character we *see* who docilely complies with our decisions and reproduces our movements as we make them is taken in its unity as a whole, a *quasi object*, predictable and not totalizable at least insofar as it appears as an agent.

Therefore the failure is total, and suddenly the little boy explicitly grasps his intentions: hamming! What shall he do? Cry with shame? Lose his temper? Not at all—he bursts out laughing. This is the second phase of the operation: unable to force others to institute him in his being as he would like, the child tries to identify with the being they would like to give him. In Flaubert's correspondence, from the first letters to the last, the mirror is linked to two different themes: laughter and femininity. Both express his submission.[2]

Gustave claims that he cannot shave in front of his mirror without bursting out laughing. To Ernest {Chevalier}, who has become a deputy prosecutor and whom he suspects of taking himself seriously, he writes, "Look at yourself in the mirror right now and tell me if you aren't greatly tempted to laugh. So much the worse for you if you aren't,"[3] and so forth. But laughter is a collective reaction, a point we shall return to later, by which a group threatened with some danger withdraws solidarity from the man in whom the danger is incarnate. This does not mean that one cannot truly laugh alone in one's room; it simply means that the person laughing, even in isolation, actualizes through his hilarity his membership in some community ("I'll tell them about this and they'll have a good laugh," or, "How Pierre and Marc would laugh if they were here," etc.). This behavior is not necessarily unrealizing, or we would have to believe that a priest, an officer, or a communist stop being priest, officer, or communist when they are alone. The act of withdrawing solidarity, however, is intended to break the nondifferentiation of intersubjectivity in order to constitute the compromising *other* as an object and the event as spectacle. If this is so, can one laugh at oneself?

For someone *truly* capable of it, laughing at oneself would be a way of affirming oneself as an integrated member of a *current* group and of withdrawing solidarity from one's singularity insofar as singularity is perceived as a vestige of revolt against integration. At the very least it involves combating in oneself a certain integration with another—this is what Gustave expects of Ernest. He invites him to draw upon his membership in the "free-masonry" of ex-schoolboy creators of the "Garçon" {discussed further in chapter 8} in order to reject the spirit of seriousness, that is, membership in the magistrature. In front of his own reflection, let him recover the collective eye of his adolescence, and behind the magistrate he will discover the naked ape. If he is still conscious of the absurdity of this hairless beast who busies himself with judging other beasts of the same species, it will be proof that he preserves a real bond with his scattered comrades, in spite of the distance between them; if not, it is proof that he belongs fully to the constituted body of which he is a member.

According to Flaubert, then, one can laugh at one's image—as a protest, a sign of youthful spirits, of moral health. The trouble is, he has long felt that Ernest is lost. He *pretends* to believe that his friend is still capable of following his advice in order to present him with an alternative (either you make fun of yourself, you great triviality, or you are a filthy bourgeois), of which the first term is annulled in advance and the second is a judgment without appeal.

And Gustave? Does he really laugh when he shaves? I do not doubt that he sometimes erupts in peals of laughter; this monster who posts himself in front of his reflection is capable of imitating Father Couillères or reproducing the laughter of the "Garçon." Does this mean that he is the victim of his hilarity, that he cannot hold it in? Certainly not; for the simple reason that it is not sincere. In fact, when he presents the "Garçon" to the Goncourt brothers {Edmond Huot de Goncourt and Jules Huot de Goncourt, French writers working on aesthetic problems related to those examined by Flaubert}, he specifies that "his laughter was not laughter" and consequently resumes his exercises in front of his full-length mirror, at the same time denouncing their vanity. Certainly the persistence of the man shaving himself can appear comic—such an explosive mixture of nature and culture—especially if we take Flaubert's point of view and judge it absurd that an ambulatory corpse should concern himself daily with mowing the grass growing on his bones. But this is comic in the realm of *ideas*; it does not incite laughter and is aimed at the species in general, not at Gustave in particular.

Besides, laughter results from surprise, and our reflection does not surprise us when it illustrates the daily and deliberate actions of which it is the indispensable instrument; let us say that the young man tries to find himself laughable by making use of the other's look in order to withdraw solidarity from his own image. But all this is imaginary—the recourse to the other and the withdrawal of solidarity; indeed, Gustave reverses the terms: for him, denunciation of the self is only a means of identifying with those who denounce him. And this is his goal, pursued from childhood and later rationalized: he looks at his tears and then, disappointed, turns them into sobs in order *to be Pain*; he forgets his lines in front of himself, becomes conscious of his imposture, and quickly exaggerates his mimicry *in order to make himself laugh*; that is, he now accepts being the imposter he seems. He is judged as such, he recognizes himself as such—anything but this dreamlike lack of substance; what is unbearable to him is to remain on the border between unreality and the real.

In order to become his own object, he must begin by withdrawing solidarity from himself; he will borrow *from others* the hilarious mistrust provoked by his insincere efforts to recover sincerity. He will transform the discomfort he feels before the rather unconvincing reflection of his tears into *their* derision. Now he plays the clown so that *their* laughter should come to his aid and reveal his *visible-being*; but the laughter does not come, the faces he makes do not amuse him any more than his sobs made him sad; so he laughs *to make himself* laugh—just the way he cried to make himself cry. Standing in front of his full-length mirror, then, he *plays the role of someone laughing*, hoping that the imitation will be so perfect that it will be indistinguishable from its model, just as when we want to yawn, a few pretended yawns invariably provoke a true one.

What does he want? To laugh, or to become the other who is laughing at him? Both: to see himself as he is seen (therefore, according to him, as he is) and to disarm the laughter by appropriating it.

For it exists elsewhere, that cosmic and sacred hilarity, that negation which *institutes him as laughable*. It is of course his father's laughter, the laughter of that sarcastic demon whose irony, by derealizing the child's behavior, made him forever an imposter, that is, other than what he claimed to be, without revealing to him what he was. If Gustave agrees to surprise his ludicrous side in the mirror, he may discover the secret of his singular essence.

What is more, to put himself on the side of the scoffers is to put them on his side. By mocking his sorrow, his agonies of lost love, his fruitless, grotesque efforts to communicate, he is identifying with the aggressor, with the paterfamilias, claiming as his own the terrible *surgical look* that never swerves away from him since the other is already inside him, observing him; in a sense he is perching above himself and *mocking* his object, the poor contemptible thing that is nevertheless necessary to his *becoming-mocker*. Briefly, despair pushes him to this harrowing and contradictory attempt: to be his being in total submission and to escape from it by becoming his executioners' accomplice; he knows the tune and sees life as a conjuror's bag of tricks. Gustave is going to become the man-who-laughs, like Gwynplaine—in other words, a man who never laughs. Obviously this new effort merely enlarges the area of unreality within him by making it part of the reflection itself. The laughter inside him is *induced*: it comes from the outside and, even internalized, preserves its transcendence; he does everything possible to give it the concrete immanence of experience, but lacking the power of suffering, he only succeeds in playacting. All his life, Flaubert's laughter *was a role he played*.

Flaubert's Style

Later we shall see that the secret of style in Flaubert's great works is eloquence *rejected*. And rejected *by the other*. Gustave wrote *Madame Bovary* in a state of oratorical abandon, then cut and trimmed under Bouilhet's influence. {Louis Bouilhet was a poet and dramatist respected by Flaubert.} The orator is there, everywhere, but censored, rejected, painful; he is hounded, compromised, but he returns *in the very compression* of the prose to lend a strange, sonorous vibration to even the most stripped-down sentences. All we need to indicate here—

and we shall take it up at greater length later—is that the *voice* remains to the end *the completion of the writing*. Not that the style of the great works is oral—quite the contrary. Rather, the writing itself is double-faced and becomes an audiovisual means of communication—otherwise how are we to understand that he "needs to shout out" all the sentences he writes?[4]

The true conclusion of his works is surely the moment when he reads them before a chosen circle of friends or colleagues. It is at this moment that the word takes its fullness and borrows its singularity from the particular timbre of the voice that forms it. Public readings were certainly the fashion; in the salons of the Arsenal, people were always declaiming their works. But usually these were poems or plays. Gustave, on the other hand, invited Maxime and Louis to Croisset to subject them to *thirty-six hours* of performance, *interpreting* his first *Saint Antoine* for them. Even more distressing, he sought their judgment on the basis of this single, tedious audition. As if the words pronounced by him, articulated into sentences by his breathing, should instantly acquire complete intelligibility, as if it were possible to judge a large work full of paradoxes, each of which should be the object of lengthy reflection, on the basis of a single test run.

Naturally the listeners' verdict was negative: the work should be put in the closet. Was he not conscious that he had done himself a disservice? He was and he wasn't: he had a vague presentiment of it but he persevered in his error. Not only because he loved to be unrealized in his voice but because he could not conceive of the beauty of a paragraph without its musical organization. Or without its meaning, which, according to him, becomes clearer to an audience through the articulation of intelligible mouthfuls of sound.

The ideal thing, then, would be written words spoken with his voice in the heads of unknown readers. And since that cannot be, the real celebration must be the public reading; the moment of publication—even if the book were to be read by every Frenchman—must be something of a letdown. Testimony to these complex and contradictory sentiments is found in a note he sent to the Goncourts to invite them to hear *Salammbô*, which was to be declaimed before his friends "from 4 to 7 o'clock and after coffee until the listeners croak." You might say he does everything to ensure his failure and that he is aware of it but cannot prevent himself; he knows very well that he will make his public "croak." Not, of course, from cardiac arrest but from boredom, by demanding of them an almost intolerable effort of attention which will end, sooner or later, in a sort of tetanus of the mind. He knows this but goes ahead anyway: he is the good giant, the giver (this is a new myth, which we shall explore in a subsequent chapter), and so much the worse for the recipient if he is crushed by the bounty of this Pantagruel.

The Writer/Actor

The essential thing is the *giving* of his work and its transformation into a performance in which Gustave is the only actor. Here we find him, then, in this last phase of creation, become once more the author/actor inhabited by the imperatives he has given to himself as other. Still, this return to dramatic interpretation is quite rare: to give himself one evening's pleasure he must put himself out for several years. And he knows very well that reading aloud—which *for him* is the conclusion of a thankless labor—represents only one inessential moment of the literacy process.

The book will be read by thousands of *eyes*; for these readers, the sonority of the text, if it exists in some dim way, is only a pleasant remnant—silence is its essential quality. Not only the silence of the study, but, even more important, the meaning beyond language which is the mute totalization of the written work, that is, of everything that is expressed through words. Put differently, while the audiovisual aspect of the word is always present for him, it is merely a rather futile attempt at recuperation; thrown back on graphemes, Gustave submits to a net loss for which he will never sufficiently compensate.

Can we say he is aware of this loss? Absolutely. From the age of fourteen, he is quite explicit about his dissatisfaction with the written word—a dissatisfaction that will persist at least until the crisis of 1844; the written word is clearly inadequate as it can render neither feelings, sensations, nor ecstasies. This denunciation is his recurrent subject, and, as we know, the deepest reasons for it lie elsewhere; but if he slips it into most of his early works from the age of fourteen on, it is as an occasional yet crucial motif. He was forbidden the career of actor; hence, words were deprived of their ordinary accompanying gestures, mimicry, and intonation; they were suddenly mutilated, became little more than inert scaffolding—how could he give them back their former fullness? Deprived of his old sound tools, he had to replace them by crude, mute instruments which, because they were not heated by his breath, would never express his animating pathos. Of course, he would read his text aloud, interpret it, giving a singular aspect to the universal vocable through the *timbre* of his voice, and hence would be able—on rare occasions—to preserve the illusion that he *was giving birth* to it by expectoration. But he knew very well that reading is not acting. Even the ludic aspect of literature has nothing to do with acting.[5]

Above all, *writing* for unknown readers is an attempt to captivate and seduce them by defenseless graphemes, which they interpret as they like. He is vulnerable—nothing in his hands, nothing in his pockets; the writer traces his scrawl and goes away, leaving it to the most malevolent inspection. It is one of Flaubert the *stylist's* deepest intentions to find a written equivalent to oral seduction. As an actor he could have fascinated, he thinks; therefore, he must find a *trick* for fascinating by writing. But this search will come later, after a great deal of anger, and will involve sacrificing the already precarious health of his mind. For the moment, he is thrown into a contradiction from which he cannot escape: while writing, he keeps within him the dream of an oral conclusion to his literary work, but at the same time he discovers what would have remained hidden to the author/actor: *that we do not write the way we speak*. I do not claim that this banality is true.

But neither is it completely false. Certainly an apprentice writer is often unequipped; I have known some, among my old friends, whose conversation was seductive and whom we never tired of listening to—their physical and intellectual charm was communicated in words that issued from them and came to us as their image in sound, whereas in writing, much to our surprise, they faded before our eyes. If they made progress, it wasn't by bringing their works into relation to their oral discourse but—as Gustave would do—by making *some other use* of language and by inventing *written* equivalents for their gestures, their voice, their style of life, directed to the eyes of their readers. We do not write the way we speak, and yet we write, at least in the course of life, when we cannot speak. This is the antinomy the child ran up against. What is writing, then? He will give an answer to that question and we will eventually learn what it is. For the moment, disgruntled and anxious as he is, writing strikes him as an austere last resort.

In any case, his desire for glory fades and gradually turns into a refusal of all notoriety. As an actor he would have brought honor to his century—he was certain of it; the vicious circle of sadomasochism could function only on the basis of this certainty. Now he no longer knows what to do: How is he to play this inferior instrument with half the strings broken? And when others know how to use it, they are simply demonstrating that they had a vocation to write. Despite his pride, Gustave cannot convince himself that he is dedicated to writing, for he is sure that his genius disposed him to dramatic art; he imagines he is exercising an inferior activity for which he has no gift. And so he is plunged into doubt and rage; his mental state is revealed to us in a letter—no doubt a little tardy—that he wrote to Ernest on 23 July 1839, parts of which I have already cited: "I might have been . . . an excellent actor, I felt the inner strength, and now I declaim more pitifully than the worst bungler because I have gratuitously killed my zeal. . . . As for writing, I have completely renounced it and I am sure that you will never see my name in print; I have no more strength, I no longer feel capable of it." Later we shall see the incidental causes of these complaints. But the text is revealing; he speaks *first* of his talent as an actor, a talent botched by others' rejection and his own self-destructive tendency. Yet his talent is himself. And from the way literature is introduced into the paragraph, we understand that it is only a secondary activity, a last resort that hardly concerns him. He *might have been* an actor, but he has not tried, according to him, to *be* a writer; he has written, that's all, no doubt to conceal from himself the loss to which he was subjected when others refused to sanction his true vocation. The prepositional phrase "as for" indicates clearly that the information following is of marginal importance, inessential; it merely completes the picture and answers Ernest's possible objection in advance: "You declaim like a bungler, all right. But what about your writing?" For Gustave, the important information is given in the first sentence: from the moment I could not become what I am and study drama, I gratuitously killed my zeal. My heart is ravaged by a mass of artificial things and endless clowning—and nothing will come of it! So much the better! As for writing, etc. The essential thing is said, the totalization done: I am cold and dry, I read nothing, I write nothing, I am nothing because I have destroyed myself with my own hands to finish the work of the executioners who have deprived me of myself. I had the "inner strength" of a great actor: others did not want to recognize my inclination, and suddenly I lost it, I am a shorn Samson.

The word *strength* is repeated when there is a need to explain why Gustave *also* renounced writing: "I *no longer* have the strength for it." So he had it in the past? Certainly he believes he did, but he does not claim to have possessed at any moment of his former life a special gift for literature or any mandate. He quite simply refers to that zeal, that inner strength which dedicated him to the theater; even after he was forbidden access to it, he retained enough of the old fire, he thought, to throw himself into eloquence and writing. It is true that artistic choice is often polyvalent in the early years. Yet a hierarchy exists in each individual case, conditioned by familial structures and early history.

{Maurice} Ravel might *also* have been able to write and paint in his youth, but he became a musician. Let us imagine the impossible: no sooner had he caught a glimpse of his principal vocation than he was forbidden to compose; he would have painted, no doubt, or written. But we can imagine his rages, his regrets, and his bitter conviction—without any real basis—of being inferior as a plastic artist to the musician he might have been, and of persisting in doing something for which he was not entirely suited.[6] Gustave had similar frustrations in his adolescence. {Franz} Kafka said, "I have a mandate but I don't know who gave it to me." As a writer, Flaubert did not have this good fortune. We shall see him haunted all his life by the disturbing question, Do I even have a mandate? Aren't I "a bourgeois who lives in the country and busies himself with literature"? If we want to understand the reasons for the insistence with which he repeats {Georges-Louis Leclerc, Comte de} Buffon's saying, "Genius is but extended patience," we must remember that he did not "enter literature" by the king's highway but by the narrow gate, and that, not being one of the *chosen* in this domain, he was compelled quite early, from the age of fifteen, to find a replacement for inspiration—those sure of their election have only to abandon themselves to it. In others it is a trick, a malicious joke played by the devil; they think they are singing and are merely braying—by *labor improbus* {work conquers all}. We shall return to this.

Certainly we should not push this interpretation too far. Indeed, the letter of 23 July 1839 can be understood quite differently: if Gustave decides to give up writing—quite provisionally since a month later, in August, he produces *Les Funérailles du docteur Mathurin*—it is because he is unhappy with *Smarh*, which he finished in April; we shall see in a subsequent chapter what great hopes he attached to this work when he conceived it. Rereading it one year later, he would be highly disappointed: "It is all right to turn out drivel, but not this sort." And we know that from April on, afraid to reopen his manuscript, he was troubled, sensing that "the famous mystery is bereft of ideas."[7] So he should have reversed the exposition of his motifs as he presented them to Ernest: a *literary* failure is the basis of his decision to renounce literature. If he mentions his thwarted vocation, it is in order to blame others for that failure: it wouldn't have happened if they had encouraged me to go onto the stage. And it is also to escape the temptation to deny his own worth: better to be a comic genius stifled from birth by his family than a nothing, pure and simple, without vocation or mandate, "an imbecile," someone merely "taking up space in society." In the same letter he prophesies that he will be "a respectable man, dutiful and all that. . . . I will be like the next man, proper, like everyone else." But while he is thinking that others have misunderstood and broken his "inner strength," and that his literary failure results from the fact that *his mission was different*, he remains superior to the mediocrity they inflict on him. The center of his preoccupations, then, the *essential* thing, is literature; and in his usual fashion he invokes his first choice only in order to conceal from Ernest and from himself the true direction of his thoughts.

To Act or To Write? Both

{Editor's Note: The phrase used in this section, "scripta manent," is an abbreviation of the Latin expression *verba volant, scripta manent*—words fly, written words remain. For Gustave, however, this obvious saying means that the shape and beauty of the word are what is important, and this beauty is beyond human value.}

This interpretation is quite valid, and I believe it is as true as the other. What is more, while the two seem incompatible at first sight, I am convinced we must adopt both. At seventeen, Gustave accommodated to the substitution that was imposed on him. At first he was merely resigned to writing, but he eventually became *invested* in the enterprise: he understood, no doubt, that the glory of Molière crowned the creator rather than the actor.

In the hierarchy of his personal options, the actor precedes the writer, there is no doubt of that; in the social hierarchy—on which he is more dependent than others—the situation is reversed. He would be greater as a novelist than if he limited himself to playing Sganarelle. Tension is established between these two scales of values, both of which are internalized: troubled, he is going to attempt to write, *scripta manent*; he will mark his century, and his work, less ephemeral than the *flatus vocis* {sounds without meaning} of the actor, will long outlive him. He thus accepts doing what he likes least. *On condition that he excels in his art*: if he takes pen in hand, he must become at the very least the leading writer of his time. When he is able to believe, to convince himself—at the moment of conception—that the scope, the richness, the beauty of his projected work will equal the greatest of the classics, he takes on writing with enthusiasm. At this moment he is not concerned with the path that leads to celebrity; *renown* is what counts, this alone will satisfy his pride and his resentment. But as soon as he attempts to realize his work, he is disgusted with what he writes.

Obviously; he has only one subject, the world, and his art is not yet equal to his ambitions. Suddenly he rediscovers his folly: what need did he have to impose this *pensum* of writing on himself when in his heart he felt the zeal, the inner strength, of a comic actor; he is punished for listening to others and betraying his vocation. *Pensum* is what he will later call his novel about la Bovary. But he must rise even higher and convince himself that this word—except when he abandons himself to eloquence—designates in his eyes the whole of literature, that abstract and sustained work he does so joylessly. For this reason we are not surprised by his confession in his letter of 23 July, "By wanting to climb so high, I have torn my feet on the rocks." He played *Poursôgnac* happily, abandoning himself to his "nature"; in order to produce *Smarh*, he toils and misses his mark ("I could have made myself miserable, I could have made everyone around me suffer," 23 July); so he furnishes himself with proof that he was not made to write. Later he will talk once again about glory. But never as he did before. First, he is convinced that it will forever elude him, and besides, intangible literary renown, lifeless and diffuse, has nothing in common with his childhood dream, the intoxicating pleasure of immediate success, an entire audience on its feet, applauding and shouting "bravo."

There is more. As a comic actor, Gustave gives himself to everyone sadistically, masochistically; in the billiard room he plays the buffoon and bares his bottom for an enema—he is not afraid of suffering as "annominious" martyr and of provoking laughter. He could well be called an exhibitionist. On the other hand, he hides his writings. Aside from Alfred and Ernest—who is still not always admitted to the private readings—no one knows anything about them. Until the publication of *Madame Bovary*, writing seemed to him like *sinning alone*.[8] At the beginning or the end of a story, he often challenges unknown readers who might try to open his manuscript: *"Do not read me!"* Look at the beginning of *Agonies*—he is sixteen: "The author has written without pretention to style, without desire for glory, the way one weeps without affectation. . . . He never wrote with the aim of publishing later; his belief in nothing was too real to him, too devout, to be told to men. He wrote for one or two people at most. . . . If by chance some unfortunate hand should discover these lines, let it beware of touching them! For they will burn the hand that touches them, exhaust the eyes that read them, murder the soul that understands them." We could cite many such warnings.

Furthermore, he "dedicated and gave" *Mémoires d'un fou* to Alfred, which means that he wrote for him alone and arranged that he alone should read the work. He repeats a hundred times in his correspondence that he will never publish. To Louise, in the epicoratorial style he is fond of employing in the early years of their liaison, he declares that he will be buried with his manuscripts unviolated, like a warrior with his horse. And this vow is continually repeated: to leave no trace of himself on earth, to erase his footsteps, to be forgotten, twice dead, as if he had never existed. Thus the passage from dramatic art to literary art seems to be similar to the passage from *social* being to secret singularity.

Let us not, however, jump to the conclusion that he breaks the hold others have over him; as an actor he delivers himself, as a creator he writes in fear and resentment, he disguises himself; but in both cases he continues to be dominated by the Other—isn't hiding oneself an implicit recognition of the primacy of the person one is hiding from? What is the difference, then, between the two attitudes? First, as always, it is the material conditions that surpass and structure the praxis. To play comedy *implies*, whatever the actor's feelings, that he is *representing* a character to an audience: theater is collective. To write the role one is going to play—as does the author/actor—already entails a certain isolation; while he is composing a role or inventing dialogue, the author/actor must physically or mentally retreat, distance himself in order to have the leisure to envisage the dramatic situation as a whole.

But this retreat is *passed over in silence*, and the author/actor is only half aware of this because he is writing for performance and for the actors in his troupe; he is therefore *in the midst of the crowd*, even in the silence of his study, imagining the reactions of the public and trying to utilize his comrades to the best of their abilities. If, on the other hand, the work being written is destined for a purely *optic* reading, the retreat is fully conscious; it becomes the object of a formal intention. And certainly an author is in the midst of his characters, he is always wondering what reactions best suit their natures—"can I push this blonde's passions to their extreme? After what I've said about her already, can she have such strong feelings?" Which amounts to asking: "Is she a well-made character?" But this is living with the *author's* creatures, remaining in *his* imaginary universe. In this case there is no longer that osmosis which makes the author/actor continually compare his fantasies with the capacities of living persons, inventing—sometimes improvising on stage, in the course of rehearsals—dialogue suggested by the actors' particular way of interpreting their roles, or revising a couplet the actor cannot manage to "get out" the right way.

In this sense the writer, even when he envisages one or another of his characters *objectively*, remains alone with himself. Not that it would be impossible—as bourgeois subjectivism has too often claimed—for him to speak of someone other than himself, or that his creatures are necessarily projections of himself in the milieu of otherness; the question is more complex and we can answer it only by a dialectical treatment of its primary data—in this chapter we shall have occasion to study the crude and archaic aspects of Gustave's first creations. In any event, to the extent that the author invents, he ultimately deals only with himself:

his fictions are not always himself as other, but they are always *his*; *he* always smells, as he creates, the "bad odor" of his imagination.[9]

{Editor's Note: Sartre will here refer to his notion of a group-in-fusion; briefly: I act alone and yet not alone, for I know that, if and when you can, you will be here to support me. I thus know that what I am doing here, you are also doing in your place in support of our common intention. There is no mystery or unconscious motivation in a group-in-fusion. Each member comprehends that they are bonded to each other through the mediation of every other. In a true group-in-fusion—Sartre uses the example of the storming of the Bastille—there is no outside leader or particular chosen leader. Rather, everyone comprehends what is to be done, and each depends on every other as a possible "regulatory third" who can unite and direct the group for a time.}

By the same token, we don't mean to deny that in writing he preserved a direct bond with his public. But this bond, at *that* time and in *that* society, could only confirm him in his solitude. Not only, as we shall see, because he was doing his work at the time of an unreachable public. But also because the reader, while reading, was—as the custom of the time dictated—as alone as the writer was while writing. I have shown elsewhere that certain works break the barrier of seriality and create, even in the most complete isolation, a kind of appeal to the solidarity of the group. In that postromantic period, however, reading obviously serialized the reader and returned him to his serial individuality. Thus, even though an author might have his public constantly in mind and attempt to foresee its reactions to every word he wrote, he would have only a confused impression of juxtaposed solitudes, which would necessarily confirm him in his own.

Thus, the literary relationship between members of the creating couple at this point in time can be qualified as *nocturnal*: Gustave falls back on masturbation because this relationship seems to him like onanism for two. He reacts against it by imposing on his friends those sessions of reading aloud which were "more noisy than agreeable." But his attempt at socialization merely increased his loneliness: by reserving his work for two, or rather only one *listener*, he forced himself to reject all the unknown readers who might have liked what he produced. Anyway, how can you write without wanting to be read? The consequence of these contradictory postulations is that Gustave established his rapport with the public beyond its radical negation.

This is marked by the naiveté evidenced at the end of *Un Parfum*, when Gustave pretends to discourage from reading his work those who, by necessity, have already read it from beginning to end. He is aware of it, and tries to correct his false candor by an ironic "if it isn't too late." In *Agonies* he guards against making the same mistake and this time begs the reader at the outset to put down this "book" whose lines "burn one's eyes." But why? Isn't it already a *book*? Isn't it already "in circulation"? Can Gustave help wanting to be published? The last words of his first chapter prove that "when he is in despair, he is still hoping" to find an unknown alter ego who, despite his prodigious warnings, will go past them and "thank him . . . for having brought together in a few pages an enormous abyss of skepticism and despair."

We can now understand the clandestine aspect of writing for the young Flaubert. As an actor he wanted to make people laugh and so was not afraid of ridicule. From its conception to its realization, comedy is entirely a social enterprise: it is born of a collective fact, laughter, and results in the comic, a proposition to the audience of the laughable thing *reworked*. The child makes himself comic because he discovers that he is laughable; in this sense the flight toward the role is ambiguous: he yields to it, certainly, when he plays the buffoon, but at the same time he controls the laughter; and then, too, the character he interprets is, in spite of everything, other than himself. In short, he reveals nothing to the honorable company other than what they knowingly made of him. Socialized by derision, he attempts to institute himself as the qualified representative of all who are laughable. The *social* aspect of the enterprise protects him against any temptation to reveal himself in his solitary truth; on the level of the comic, such truths have no currency; no one can even conceive of them, since the actor makes people laugh only by breaking solidarity with himself. From start to finish, everything is public.

It begins with the others' "impact" on Gustave and ought to end with Gustave's "impact" on them. An ignominious triumph, certainly, but one in which the child has nothing to lose. Suddenly the enterprise is *denied*: the little boy is still laughable, but they deny him the right to make himself comic, which casts him back into his solitary truth—or, rather, reveals to him his *nonsocialized* subjectivity. In fact, as we have seen, even his interiority at its most profound has been shaped by others, and the awareness he now has of his anomaly was triggered by the fact that others have refused to allow him to elaborate socially the risibility they have given him. Since literature, for the child, is primarily dramatic art *denied*, it seems to him to embody his unsociability—his exile in himself. The denial circumscribes and sanctions his *anomaly*: he is already laughable—hence the object of a minor disgrace—but by forbidding him to exploit his social character, the others force him to defend himself *by taking himself seriously*. He was expecting comedy to institute his other-being, meaning his being-for-others; this denied, he expects literature—against his social dimension, which remains but which he is forbidden to exploit and must suffer in humility—to institute his being-for-himself, which until now he was living in the whirl of the immediate. The result: set against laughter, he weeps through his writing. His early works, with few exceptions, are grim. It will be pointed out that they were written under the influence of romanticism, of his unhappy life at school; and, in a sense that we shall explore later, this is not incorrect. But let us not forget that the author of *L'Amant avare* [Molière] had already read tragedies and dramas and was not particularly happy; at that time, however, he wrote only comedies.

His relations at school could not have been so unpleasant for him at first since he invited school friends to the billiard room so as to clown for them. The main reason for his change in outlook is that he was thrown back on his interiority, which appeared to him for the first time in his life as it really was: a nest of vipers. What he surpassed in the comic parade now becomes impassable; not that interiority is self-affirmed—it is the outward rejection that reduces Flaubert to a state of thankless misery and resentment. If chance had at least made him a narcissist. But he scarcely likes himself. His "written cries," in the service of the impassable, can only be cries of hatred against others and proclaimed disgust for himself. At the same time the sentences he writes satisfy strange, dark desires he knows nothing about firsthand. Perhaps the most striking texts from this point of view are not those we interpreted in part 1 but the plans for "melodramas" that he conceived without ever giving them finished form. Through the fabulations of his despair we glimpse the "family romance" of which I spoke earlier: his mother is raped or seduced and abandoned. In any case, deflowered in duplicity or horror, the wretched woman gives birth to him, the child is taken away, and she wallows in the gutter. In the end, Gustave has her for a hundred sous at the brothel. Having recognized—too late—her lover as her son, the infamous creature throws herself beneath the wheels of the hearse that carries him to his grave.

Who is this weeping woman, this victim, this creature whose most sublime feelings are brutally mocked? As we have seen, she is both Mme Flaubert and Flaubert himself. But how could the child move from light comedy to these perverse and morose lucubrations? Quite simply because he does not give himself a role in the plays he aspires to write. The author/actor could do only farces, since he had to reserve the "starring roles" for himself; the actor having taken leave, the author dreams of writing for the theater, but since he is no longer constrained to do comedy, there is a change of perspective and the plays in hand take a definitively dark turn. They are no longer—to the same degree that his other writings were—a social means of visually presenting his executioners with the monster they made him, but rather a nocturnal and masturbatory effort to give substance to his rancorous dreams, his forbidden desires, his moods, by *setting them down* on paper.

CHAPTER SEVEN

Ambivalent

For this reason his attitude toward his new state is ambivalent: he wants to be there and at the same time he doesn't. Let someone else masturbate at night if he should chance to find one of Gustave's manuscripts and read it by candlelight, hiding from his family, finding there the confirmation of his terrors and the disturbing satisfaction of his desires. The writer-in-spite-of-himself certainly wants this, and indeed such a reader is by definition the opposite of a mocker—he is disarmed by solitude. Yet the young Flaubert has only a minimum of sympathy for this alter ego: too close, during his nocturnal orgies, to confer a true *objective-being* upon his creations, he is liable from one moment to the next to join his comrades and deride the fool who moments earlier moved him to tears. The best thing would be to kill himself, as was the fashion after the publication of *Werther*.

In any event, the danger of literature is here: by expressing his inner feelings in written words, Gustave the laughable gives laughers new occasion to laugh. If he spoke to them, his presence, his force, his conviction, his voice might restrain their hilarity; but he has slipped into the inert graphemes that are only what they are. Here he is quite the opposite, completely naked, defenseless, the prisoner of these soiled pages, which readers can interpret as they like, a cold surgical eye can size up, or a group of young jokers can read aloud for their amusement. Later, Gustave will try to provide against these things by his stance of "impersonalism," a set of operations aimed less at suppressing the author's *presence-in-person* than at concealing it from the suckers who read his books. In the meantime, throughout his adolescence he writes only to unburden himself and is terrified lest someone make fun of his complaints.[1]

This is the source of his double writing, aggressive and disagreeable: he abandons himself and takes himself seriously only to turn around and be *the first* to mock himself. He who breaks solidarity with himself first, as we have seen, has some hope of escaping collective laughter or, at least, of getting the laughers on his side. But if it isn't a matter of chance, of an unexpected circumstance that made him momentarily laughable, what a painful position to be in! He is constantly being waylaid, analyzed, his speech is scrutinized, his unintended puns and involuntary and unfortunate allusions to well-known events are exposed, etc., etc. He is like the school scapegoat: forbidden to laugh at others though they are free to laugh at him, arousing in the pharisees around him the contempt a respectable man feels for a fellow who makes himself absurd—"in order to seem interesting," say these fine pricks, while for such unfortunates the only issue is to avoid the grinding scorn that would isolate them and compensate for it by denouncing it when it manifests itself.

Still Acting?

This is Gustave's state as author during his adolescence. He abandons himself to his complaints and hastens to break solidarity with those complaints by declaring them laughable. In short, his writings are clandestine from the beginning: he protects them from the Other by locking them away in his drawer and, in the text itself, by recourse to laughter. This new avatar will provide a better understanding of the evolution of the comic for the adolescent, and of the way he moves from being a laughable object to the subject of laughter (no longer controlling the laughter of others but appropriating it in order to transform it into a trap, enticing others to laugh at him so that they may be constituted as laughable by their very laughter and revealed as the pure objects of his derision)—in a word, the way he passes from *Poursôgnac* to the god Yuk. At the present moment he borrows the laughter of others to forestall intolerable mockery, to proclaim before and after his complaints: readers, these are jeremiads; don't worry about making fun of them, I transcribed them for your amusement and I don't take myself seriously.

But *he does take himself seriously*; his irony is only a precaution—it clenches its teeth or, rather, it is acted. In this way it reveals to him that it is otherness, the others' view of him, and that somehow he stole it from them, that he knows their motives and turns their hilarity against them. From Gustave's point of view, the procedure is the chief thing. But we can also see in it—we shall return to this soon—the *purposely worked* transformation of the primary comic (the buffoon offers himself to men who take him for a subman) into one of its secondary forms (by laughing at himself the comedian laughs at his human nature, and the laughter he deliberately provokes in others throws into derision, by them and through them, the whole human race). In this period, the combination of candid abandon and black humor is unique to Gustave.

We must still explain the nature of the passionate and grim interiority into which he was plunged in his thirteenth year by a sovereign rejection. Does he discover it or create it? Both. In truth, it already existed implicitly as what he tried to surpass in the being of the actor, as the deep but unknowable humus from which he drew, through confident inspiration, his most comic effects; in other words, as what *he should not have taken seriously*. He wanted, we know, to flee his derealization by *realizing himself as actor*. A rejected actor, he finds himself again in his *constituted dereality* as imaginary child. But since his games with {his sister} Caroline, this imaginary child has been enriched with negative content; in the beginning this was merely love refused, pathos lived but denounced by the outside world as a lie. Now the original castration is twice repeated: there was the Fall, then the opposed vocation; resentment raises its head and does its work, all the lived experience we described in part 1 [*The Problem*, chapter 1, 2, 3, etc.] becomes explicit, affirms itself—wasn't it by reading his early works that we were able to decipher the underlying intentions of this sundered heart? Jealousy, envy, bitterness, misanthropy, fatalism, skepticism, the conflict of two opposed ideologies, it's all there; at the age of thirteen, "the worst is always certain," he won't give that up again. But this induced pathos, developed and made more openly explicit, remains nonetheless *derealized*. He suffers, he despises, he is enraged, certainly, but he never manages to convince himself fully that he feels his passions *for real*. First of all, they do not contain affirmative power; they run rampant and carry him away like natural forces, but his constituted passivity deprives him of any possibility of assuming them or combating them. By this means—and by the surgical look that disarms them—he submits to their violence as in a dream, without being able to recognize them or ordain their reality. Here we have the primary insincerity: he is incapable of knowing whether he is suffering for real or playing at suffering, and at the same time he crams this felt but unvalidated pathos with imagined feelings—such as the Great Desire we spoke of earlier—by which he is affected but to which he does not submit, or, more precisely, with feelings he isn't certain are his own or someone else's and which he is only attempting to experience properly in all their phases, but *in imagination*.

In other words, after this new banishment, thrown back on an *autistic* solitude in which his thoughts develop without any reducing agent, the social buffoon, far from finding himself in these thoughts as a *person*, sees himself plunged into the pitiless, dark world of the imagination; this world, interior and exterior, subjective and objective, consists of the shifting relations of an illusory macrocosm with an illusory microcosm where everything is experienced "between the lines" by a *He* and an *I* indistinct from each other. Formerly, I have said, this muddy business was submerged in dramatic *interpretation*; now that is forbidden. Certainly he will not stop *playing roles* before his peers or showing himself to his intimates by means of what I have earlier called *epic performance*. But pride prevents him from giving himself to others in all his dereality: as vassal, he displays the lord's *epic performance*; at school he plays the *role* of the Gargantuan naughty boy. For the rest of his life he has but one means to express all his misery and shame: the word. His insubstantial emotions will take on substance only when he puts them down on paper; the pen alone transforms his dereality into unrealization. Reduced to monologue, speaking alone and knowing neither *who* is *speaking* in him nor *to whom*, nor what this *in him* means, he will escape total disintegration only by personalizing himself as *at least* the one whose duty is to transcribe the voices he hears.

Here we find a new option; we can say it was developed under the pressures of constraint and urgency. Thrown back on derealization, the child is concerned not with *expressing himself* but with personalizing himself through words. He will be an *author*, fine. But this choice of an imposed mutilation must surely present the *literary thing* to him as a confused jumble of contradictions. Objectively, an author has higher standing than an actor; for Gustave, subjectively, it is the other way around. These two axiological systems are purely and simply incompatible. But their antagonism is not experienced openly. In the first place, the Other is sovereign; he is the one, in the child's eyes, who holds the keys to reality; if the move from dramatic to literary art is held to be progress, it must be so; *true* glory is the glory of Hugo, not of Kean. This affirmation of the Other in him is all the more striking as it is deep down and surreptitiously denied by experience: Gustave *falls from above* into literature, he suffers it, he harbors a secret resentment against words. In consequence, the literary object first appears to him as ambiguous, or as singularly deceptive. Gustave's ambivalence concerning his new enterprise is marked by alternating moments of enthusiasm and disgust. He glimpses a subject that seems to him grandiose and is nothing less, as we know, than totalization. On this level of abstraction, it matters very little whether the totalizing enterprise is undertaken by the author/actor or the writer; whatever the approach, the work—this is the essential thing—will be nothing less than the All caught in a trap. He is burning, with his cheeks on fire he throws himself into writing, and the disillusionment comes with the very movement of his pen. This isn't what he wanted; he had hoped to cry out, to faint, and what does he have to do with these silent daubs drying on the paper? It is at this point that he abandons the work.

Un Parfum

{Editor's Note: To repeat from my Editor's Introduction, *Un Parfum à Sentir* (*A Perfume to Sense*), written at fifteen, tells the story of a father who tries to teach his sons how to dance on a tightrope: "It was Ernesto's turn. He trembled in every limb, and his fear increased when he saw his father take a little rod of white wood." Sartre gives a long quote which he emphasizes by giving it his own italics: *"The rod, for its part, followed the dancer's every movement, encouraging him by lowering itself gracefully, threatened him by shaking with fury, showed him the dance by making the measure on the rope, in a word, it was his guardian angel, his safeguard, or rather the sword of Damocles suspended over his head by the thought of a false step."* Sartre concludes, "All of Flaubert is here." Here, I note that Gustave's father would always be there to watch and judge just what this "idiot" would do next, and the idiot would perform for his father. Why? For the infant as for the child Gustave, the family is necessary: how else is he to survive? For the adult and the author, the family is again necessary; but this time by free choice, for Gustave accepts and wishes to live within the mystic of the gift of his election, an election arising from the union of his brilliant father with his socially established mother.}

Let us recall *Un Parfum*, taken up, dropped, taken up again: one day of work, a month without opening his notebook, a week for the five subsequent chapters, and then, after a new silence of undetermined duration, two days for writing the last seven chapters and the conclusion—rushing at the end, it seems, in order to be rid of a disheartening task. This is not entirely the case; let us say that he abandons himself to inspiration to the extent that it is oratorical and that words disappoint him to the degree that they detach themselves from his interior monologue and become—by a transubstantiation that never fails to surprise him—the black shells of dead insects. We know the reasons for this ambiguity. He gets pleasure from pushing his eloquence to an extreme *even as* disillusionment invades him, and he takes the bit in his teeth in order *to have done with it* sooner, before he is overtaken by ennui and forced to throw in the towel, leaving the work unfinished. It is not a question of dissatisfaction stemming from the author's inadequacies; the disgust comes afterward, when he rereads his work. What he feels deeply, without ever articulating it, is the inadequacy of written language: on paper every sentence seems to be an impoverishment of what he imagines he conceives or feels, which is in fact only the sonorous—and imagined—richness of his eloquence. Upon rereading, he verifies his defects; it is as though, while working, he were somehow thinking: this instrument is not made for me; and later, avidly rereading his work in order to find traces of his talent, as though he had concluded: I am not made to play this instrument. Let us not imagine that he hated writing; on the contrary, he took pleasure in listening to the words bubbling up in his head; rather, his pleasure is continually spoiled by the necessity of *transcribing*. And he preserved, at the time, a secret animosity toward his own enterprise. Animosity, a malaise hidden beneath the exuberance of inspiration—this is how he first *lived* his relationship to literature.

There is another contradiction which, like the last one and for the same reasons, is by no means a confrontation of opposed principles but manifests itself as an objective ambiguity: his style *roars*; in other words, his sentences have persistent sonority. We have enumerated above the chief consequences of this *superaudibility*; but at the same time he is not unaware that his task as a writer is to favor the *visible* in order to compensate for the disappearance of sonority and its accompaniments in the way of gesture. There is more: the primacy of the phoneme is maintained on the sly, muted as it were, with all the immediate sociability it implies for Gustave—it is his rejected *public-being*—while the structure of the grapheme necessarily sends the young author back to a solitude he cannot assume—in effect, the solitude of dereality and not a *real* isolation. On this level we might say without exaggeration that the ambivalence of his enterprise is translated by what fascinates him (the vertigo of the soliloquy or of masturbation; a perpetual temptation to leave the "Rabelaisian laughter," his new public role, for the dismal and sordid comforts of sadness and to push his anomaly to the extreme in the imaginary), and what frightens him (just as onanism and sinking into a narcissistic bog can frighten a bourgeois child stuffed with prohibitions).

The Father: Again

What further contributes to veil these antinomies is that the paterfamilias has scarcely more indulgence for men of letters than he does for actors. Certainly the profession of writer is not dishonorable, but it is nonetheless unworthy of a Flaubert. On this point Achille-Cléophas's thought was probably more complex: he admired Montaigne, I suppose, since he cites him in a letter to Gustave. And Voltaire. If by some supernatural premonition he had known that his younger son would later equal either of these great men, he might have softened. But he was only too certain of the contrary: his son didn't have much of a brain, he would never rise to the level of these moralists. The philosophical practitioner, who prided himself on writing well, as the applied elegances of his thesis demonstrate, judged both that literature is within everyone's reach (a good mind, cultivated and with a solid knowledge of its mother tongue, is always capable of dispatching a missive or spinning out an argument) and that one must have a powerful mind and keen intelligence, be a brilliant observer of human mores, to dare to be a specialist in it without seeming ridiculous.

Gustave was perfectly informed on this point. His father was not unaware that he wrote and did not see any harm in it, provided the young man's studies did not suffer. He would undoubtedly have accepted the idea that this son, having become a physician, subprefect, prosecutor, or notary, might publish at his own expense a slim volume of verse written at idle moments, but for him it was inconceivable that anyone could devote his life to so futile an occupation. Thus the prohibition remained, and the child, who was conscious of it, felt clearly that by writing he remained on the level of the imaginary, that he was merely playing at being a writer; the ludic aspect of this activity deterred him from examining its contradictory nature. As he did not encounter the same inflexible denial to which his family had subjected his true vocation, Gustave felt neither the passion nor the sadomasochistic emotions that had earlier tormented him; he no longer dreamed of affirming himself against them through the "glory of the good-for-nothing." At first, in any case, he confined himself to living with literature without deciding whether he was made for it or whether, as he would soon say, Art is the most sublime and the most disappointing of illusions; nor was he much afraid that he would one day be forbidden from consecrating this union. In any case, if there is a prohibition, it will not have the character of an anathema; it will be possible to combat it or get around it (later we shall see Gustave pitted mercilessly against his father, the passive activity of the former against the voluntarist activism of the latter).

Less threatened, this new occupation lacks the rending fragility of the earlier one; he is less tempted to cling to it in desperation. For these reasons he is in no hurry to throw his second challenge in the face of his family—*"I will be a writer"*—and to commit his whole future with a precipitous vow. He writes between parentheses, casually, without being much concerned with why he does it or with forcing his immediate intentions. Literature is a dreary and solitary game, he plays at it *faute de mieux*, without true pleasure but with the awareness that while he merely pretends to write, someone or something deep inside him takes it seriously—which gives him no joy but profound anxiety.

Here we have a child, then, who launched himself into a formidable enterprise to which he believed he was destined. It was dismissed, and he was forced to specialize in an activity that corresponded, according to him, to an inessential phase of the earlier one; he wrote the way he hammered the boards of his theater together: in order to go onstage. This means of a means becomes his unsurpassable end; the shock would scarcely have been greater if, for having hammered nails before playing *Poursôgnac*, he suddenly turned out to be a carpenter. The metamorphosis is more radical in any case, for he is sent from sociability to autism and discovers in himself, without knowing very clearly *who* is thinking them, a confused swarm of thoughts that horrify him. At the same time his essential problem seems to lose any chance of being resolved: he must have himself instituted by others as a center of derealization *in his body*. Finished: the body is rendered to its animal reality, the unreality remains in his soul.

He is stripped of his comic voice, of his clownish gestures; he feels his frustration in the disgust of every word he writes. Discontented, anxious, he keeps thinking they made him drop his substance for his shadow. If this is how it is, one question arises: Why does he persist in writing? Why all that labor? All those passionately scribbled pages? If literature is an imposition, why does he do it with such avidity? Others, no doubt, would have dropped it, or else have gone mad. By what sublime or stupid heroism does Gustave persist in following a path he thinks will lead him nowhere? How, in the same work, can he clearly express his disgust as a writer and suddenly cry out: "Maybe you don't know what a pleasure it is to compose! To write, oh, to write is to seize the world, its prejudices, its virtues, and to sum them up in a book; it is to feel your thought being born, growing, living, standing on a pedestal, and remaining there for ever!"[2] This cannot be understood unless the second castration was the source of a progressive *conversion.*

The Conversion

By incorporating Alfred's being, however, Gustave internalizes his gratuitousness. As a child, he felt himself to be superfluous; this was an obsession from which he could escape only by throwing himself into the rarely open arms of Achille-Cléophas; rejected, he retained the feeling of being *de trop* {too much} in his family and in the world—he led a life without a visa, he existed without an existence permit. By giving himself the mission of instituting Alfred, would he not have a chance to transform this *being-de-trop* into *being-de-luxe* {from superfluous to luxurious}? We shall soon see him reinstate in himself as principal virtues his dead friend's emptiness and boredom. Wasn't he himself bored, in former times? Yes, but like a plebeian: the boredom that made him "swollen" was the very taste of his contingency. Now he sees it as his passport to nobility: it is proof that his pride places him above men. But the "good worker" will not abandon his task: this emptiness is the sign of his election by the absolute end. He can think, according to his desire of the moment, that his lacunary gratuitousness is the internalization of the artistic imperative, or that it is what designates him as being a "worker" in art.

We shall be struck by his newfound pride if we reread his letter to his mother of 15 December 1850: "If a man, whether of high or low degree, wishes to meddle with God's works, he must begin, if only as a healthy precaution, by putting himself in a position in which he cannot be made a fool of. You can depict wine, love, women, and glory on condition that you are not a drunkard, a lover, a husband, or a foot soldier. Meddle actively with life and you don't see it clearly: you suffer from it too much or enjoy it too much. The artist, to my way of thinking, is a monstrosity, something outside of nature."[3] Which this arrogant claim very well sums up: "We artists are God's aristocrats." This hired laborer in letters takes himself for a prince when he has a mind to. He is nothing of the sort, thank God. But there are moments when he must believe it or die. Alfred, *incorporated*, encourages his illusions: it is *the Other* in Flaubert who is princely.

Gustave's dominant personalization therefore integrates Alfred in three distinct dimensions, of which two are imaginary: the dead youth is the source of Great Desire or infinite privation; he is instituted by his friend and within him as the *being* of the artist—that is, as his inert and noble gratuitousness of the art object. The third dimension, real or at least in the process of realization, is determined the gratuitousness of the *work to be done*. Deprived of everything, superfluous by birth, and disdainful of the necessary, Gustave *is nothing* else, in truth, but a worker of the imaginary, that is, the means of an inhuman end. It is as though at his friend's death he had decided to remain as two men in one, a couple with only one life, in short, Gustave and Alfred simultaneously. This is made easier for him by the perpetual doubling of his ego, that is, by the constant movement in him from *I* to *he*, and vice versa. Yet the disparity of the couple is undeniable, and it results from the disparity of social conditions. The path upward remains closed to the man of the necessary: Gustave knew this from 1848 on, although he hardly says so. We shall see in the third part of this work that he could escape from his class only by dropping *below it*, that is, having himself completely disqualified and discarded as an *unusable* means. He learned, then, that the path to the "superhuman" first runs below, in the realm of the submen. Be that as it may. For Gustave, the institution of Alfred makes Alfred the tutor of his pride. The survivor never stops inflating the merits of the deceased in order to inflate himself, Alfred's peer in the eyes of the world, in the esteem of others and in his own.

Structure

Gustave, by his own admission, saw the "society of children" as prefiguring the society of men: the same injustice of the crowd, the same tyranny of prejudice and force, the same egotism. Are we to believe that the scholarly community is the model of every possible society? Hasn't he, without knowing it, moved from one type of society to *one* other? He says he was "thwarted" in his "penchant for solitary unsociability." Was he then so unsociable before 1832? He sometimes escaped, of course, took refuge in stupors in order to extricate himself from the pressures of his surroundings. But can we call him solitary—the boy who until the age of ten didn't leave Caroline's side, who called Ernest "his friend for life" or "till death," who liked to spend long hours at Alfred and Laure's house, who amused himself in the company of the Vasse children and others, sons and daughters of his parents' friends?

Moreover, the first contact with his schoolmates could not have been so bad, since he wrote to Ernest, 3 April 1832: "When you come, Amedee, Edmond, Madame Chevalier, mama, 2 servants and perhaps some students will come to see us act." *Perhaps some students*: his aversion for his comrades was not immediate. He had ties to certain of them; he invited them to the famous performance at Easter 1832 which marked the peak and the end of his dramatic career. They may not have come, they may have laughed at him, but it was neither their absence nor their offensive remarks that determined Gustave's general relations with his fellow students. Before going to school, and even in his first year as a boarder, the boy was not unsociable; he *became* unsociable after leaving the society of the family. With his earliest friends, those he met at their fathers' homes or his own, he had the intersubjective relations of feudalism. The families had mutual ties, these children knew each other through their parents; the bond of vassal to lord, spilling beyond the family network, structured the entire little society. When the kids romped under the maternal eye (interchangeable mothers, unvarying eye, the same in all of them, charged with the same vigilance and the same authority of paternal origin), they were all vavasors surveyed by the great vassals, delegates from the council of lords. Relations that were falsified but overprotected by the parents, who were omnipresent even in their absence—the children anticipated them when they wrote to each other, felt compelled to add a line now and then in which the fathers greet the fathers through the sons' pens. To cite only one example, we shall not find a single letter from the years 1831–33 that does not contain allusions to the relationship between the Flauberts and the Chevaliers: "Heartfelt greetings to your dear family from me" (31 December 1830). "Your dear father is always the same" (4 February). "I beg you to give me news of your dear aunt as well as of your fine family"[4] (11 February). "Your dear papa is a little better, the remedy papa gave him made him more comfortable and we hope that he will soon be cured" (15 January 1832). "My father and mother and I offer our respects to your dear parents" (23 August 1832), etc. In becoming friends, Ernest and Gustave merely *perpetuated* the courtly relations between their lords; they felt encouraged in them, their ties were *sacred*.

This is not all. In that interfamilial hierarchy, Gustave was convinced that his family held first place: he shared with Achille and Caroline the certainty that a Flaubert was *wellborn*. It is true that through their mother they preserved distant links with the Normandy gentry, but to their mind these links had only symbolic value: their blue blood guaranteed—neither more nor less than their Canadian ancestors' "Indian blood"—the aristocracy of fact which was transmitted by Achille-Cléophas to his progeny. There is a *Flaubert honor*, a collective and instituted pride, that each of the children must uphold wherever he goes. To measure the extent to which Gustave was heir to this pride, we have only to read the letters he writes in 1857 to his brother Achille at the time of his trial:

> Information on the influential position my father and you had and have in Rouen are all to the good; they thought they were attacking a poor nobody, and when they first saw that I had means, they began to open their eyes. They should know at the Ministry of the Interior that in Rouen we are what is called *a family*, meaning that we have deep roots in the country, and that by attacking me, especially for immorality, many people will be offended. Try using your skill to have it said that there will be a certain danger in attacking me, in attacking us, because of the coming elections.[5]

Two days later, the same thing:

> The only really influential thing will be Father's name and the fear that a condemnation will prejudice the people of Rouen in the future elections. . . . In short, the prefect, Monsieur Leroy, and Monsieur Franck-Carré must write directly to the director of the Sûreté Générale telling them what influence we have and how much this would outrage the morality of the region. This is purely a political affair. . . . What will stop it is making them see the *political inconvenience* of the thing.[6]

With what fatuousness he writes on 30 January: "Maitre Sénard's speech was splendid. . . . He began by talking about Father, then you, and finally me. . . . 'Ah! You are attacking the second son of Monsieur Flaubert! . . . No one, Monsieur l'avocat général, and not even you, can give him lessons in morality."[7] This last passage is all the more piquant as Gustave, we shall see later, had deliberately written a *demoralizing* work. But who would dare attack the morality of Monsieur Flaubert's son? Attacked *as an individual*, Gustave's first reaction is to defend himself as *son of the family*, as a member of a familial community. "We are a family!" Nothing in common with those animal colonies that congregate around the couple who engendered them; for Flaubert, a "family" is characterized by the inheritance of responsibilities and virtues, which is why he even takes pride in the fact that Achille-Cléophas's office should have come to Achille rather than falling into strange hands. The Messieurs de Flaubert have this in common with the nobility of the sword, that they give inexhaustibly of their person. The inhabitants of Rouen are obligated to them; the proof: a bumbling functionary need merely attack the younger son of the philosophical practitioner and he will lose the government elections. Hence that wonderful line, "this would outrage the morality of the region." Do we see the people of Rouen, enraged by this insult, staying away from the polls or voting for the opposition candidate? In 1857 Achille-Cléophas had been dead for ten years; his eldest son was far from his caliber, and his clientele was well aware of it, while his younger son buried himself in the country with an old woman and a child; relations between the two brothers were not the best, and the elder preferred to pay visits to his mother and younger brother on Sundays rather than invite them to his home, especially to his exclusive dinners. Be that as it may, dominated even in solitude by his high and noble lineage, the scandalous writer—whom Rouen would not adopt before his death—could calmly write: "There could be some danger in attacking me." He immediately adds, it is true, "in attacking *us*." But this is politeness or calculated flattery; the "attacking me" says it all, since Gustave was convinced from his earliest years that every Flaubert child, whatever his place and circumstance, was the qualified representative of the entire family.

This was how the little boy imagined his future as a schoolboy even before entering the *collège*. He was not beginning his studies in complete ignorance: the royal *collège* of Rouen was an integral part of the Flaubert saga—Achille had excelled there until 1830. For a very young child, things have the impenetrable density of what has always been there: a hundred-year-old forest, animals who were there when he was born, a monument, they are all part of the same thing; the world presented, transmitted, given by his parents seems to him *instituted* rather than natural. Better, institution seems to be nature and nature institution. As far back as Gustave can remember, his older brother has been a *collégien*; it is his instituted nature. On weekdays, Achille is absent. On holidays he shows up in uniform, he has the right to talk to his heart's content; he recounts his life, his successes, and the philosophical practitioner's eyes brighten. Gustave knows from hearsay the curriculum, the gardens, the classrooms, the long corridors of the school; he has heard them telling about the great collective ceremonies, which scare him a little: going to bed in the dormitories, waking up to the bells, group meals in the refectory. There are the actors as well—he can already call them by name: the masters, who are judged worthy of respect, friendly, or despicable according to criteria that elude him; the fellow students, good boys of an inferior species, certainly not all stupid, who get out of breath in their vain attempts to catch up with the agile Achille.

Before the Fall, Gustave did not view his brother's laurels with a jaundiced eye. He could not conceive that they were the reward of assiduous effort; rather he imagined them to be an *honor* conferred upon the Flaubert son from the first day. His older brother had the right to praise and prizes—by blood. What is more, the adults did not refrain from announcing to the younger child that he would gather the same laurels when his turn came. Thus, as a developing society sees its future image in a more advanced one, Gustave seized upon the present Achille as his own future. An instituted future: he would be that same schoolboy who spoke in such a reasonable way, he would at once be given the same honor, he would dress in the same uniform, and in every subject, every year, he would garner all the prizes. First place would come to him by right because it was the only thing worthy of a Flaubert: it awaited him, he knew in advance the words the masters would use to assure him of their admiration.

Doctor Flaubert must at times have tried to make him understand that he would not triumph without effort; he would have insisted on the moral aspect of the enterprise: it was Gustave's *duty* to show himself worthy of an exceptional father and brother. Until he was eight years old, the little boy viewed his mission calmly: good blood cannot lie. From birth he held a power which—he willingly admitted—contained the obligation to vanquish but also the right and the means. What was involved was merely a ritual: represented by their children, the respectable fathers of Rouen would come to bow before the chief surgeon, who had begun his third childhood in Gustave's person.

After the Fall, this calm certainty thickened, darkened, was suffused with anguish, but the misunderstanding remained. Relegated to the lowest rung of the family, Gustave thought it would kill him. But the hierarchy established among the Flauberts concerns only them; the lowest member of the Hôtel-Dieu is still first in the town. In other words, a Flaubert idiot is still good enough to make a stir at the *collège* and sweep away all the prizes. However, something has changed: he was earlier in the father's good graces, but no longer is. In order to restore this original relationship, would it be enough to excel in everything from the fourth year to the sixth? No; bent beneath those trophies, what would he have proved? That he is a Flaubert goes without saying, but not the greatest of the future Flauberts, the only one worthy of the eponymous hero. When the little boy begins his studies, Achille has been out of school ten years, but the old place still echoes with his name. What can Gustave do that his older brother has not already done? He will equal him, that's all. And so the perspective changes: he will not be able to defeat the usurper and regain paternal favor on this ground; it's simply a matter of *not losing*. And when he has shown himself a worthy successor in every way to Achille-Cléophas and Achille, the paterfamilias's judgment will still not be challenged: as he cannot help winning, these triumphs—which he owes to his blood—cannot compensate for his past faults.

All the little adept of this gloomy pietism can hope for is an act of perfectly gratuitous generosity by which his lord will decide to reinstate him in paradise. Thus for the Roundheads, all men are lost, but God in his infinite love will perform that veritable miracle of according salvation to a few of these hell-bound victims. Religious consciousness consists, then, of knowing oneself to be damned in all justice and of never despairing of divine charity: no action can procure salvation, but some acts can discourage God from offering it to us. We know what deadly boredom characterizes the thread of these lives. It is that same boredom which Gustave expects to encounter at school. A single command: not to contravene the law. One certainty: he will not contravene. And another: he runs no risk of losing but has nothing to gain. Eight years, eight new terms, each one similar to the one before, everything foreseen, everything lived over again, and every July the same gathering of tired laurels begins again, always the same. At most, a viper may sometimes lurk beneath these dull leaves: and what if the younger boy's performance in school should confirm that he is by nature inferior to Achille? First in all things, he will *in any case* have only feudal relations with his fellow students: in class they will be his unfortunate rivals; in play, his vassals. Therefore, they don't count. But what if the school year were to turn out badly? In that case, Gustave would risk remaining at the head of the class with a lower average than Achille had obtained in the same year; the paternal judgment would be confirmed and maintained forever. This infuriating thought pricks him and vanishes; we cannot say it torments him, but it is enough to conceal from him the true nature of scholarly competition.

Few children have been farther from understanding the reality of bourgeois education and less adapted to the social demand that conditions it. Bound to Achille's past by his own Fall, aspiring to shape the present in the image of the past, he enters school haunted. Committing the disastrous blunder of taking his classmates for a simple plural mediation between himself and his brother, he approaches the competitive "little society" that incorporates him as if it were a hierarchically structured community and prepares eight years of hell for himself. What the "society of children" does offer the little vassal is not the image of society in general—this does not exist, nor does man—but quite simply that of French society under Louis-Philippe, or rather of triumphant bourgeois society at the stage of primitive accumulation.

"Anyone who puts a grade on a paper *is* an asshole." —On the Walls of May

Gustave enters unsuspiciously into the serial circularity of a heated competition produced and established by the real competitive system that intends it as an "introduction to bourgeois life." This means that the little vassal will be made to swallow his blue-blooded pride by a certain practico-inert "collective." Apparently, he is asked to reproduce the taught "material" or to make something of it through what is called *his* work. It is all very personal, it seems: "Do you know *your* lesson? Conjugate *your* Latin verbs for me!" In fact, nothing is his. Nor is it anyone's. In this circular system, an ungraspable centrifugal force determines the value of each student, not only—nor especially—in relation to his own work but in relation to that of others. He is judged not by what *he* does, understands, and knows but rather by what the others understand, know, and do or have not done, known, or understood. Not in relation to the real knowledge of the time but deliberately in relation to the meager information and uncultivated intelligence of the companions tossed him by chance. To value each one in relation to all the others makes him other than himself, compels him *as other* to condition all the others. In order to initiate them into the society of adults, children are pushed willy-nilly into the abstractly fabricated universe of pure otherness.

The Jesuits started it; it was they, of course, who built the *collège* at Rouen—we know that they wanted to win over a resentful bourgeoisie from the Jansenists and Protestants. The victors of July replaced them and made "humanism" an instrument of dehumanization. Since man—meaning bourgeois man—defined himself under Louis-Philippe as competitor, the "humanities" had to be structured competitively. To begin with, the principle of egalitarianism was introduced into teaching. It was the systematic dismantling of the last bastions of feudalism; the sons of the ruling class all had the same opportunities at the outset. It was the end of the gracious gift, of homage and blood ties; in this way the bourgeoisie thought to crush in embryo any compliance with tyranny. The new gentlemen wanted to do business in peace; they did not want their children falling into the hands of the "Warlords" at a time when the citizen-king aspired to deserve the epithet "Napoleon of Peace." Since this liquidation was not followed by any reevaluation of human relations, schoolboys would be saved from feudal ideology only at the price of a "reification" imposed by the system. Two types of relations were admitted among them: if they took the same courses, competition; in all other cases, simple coexistence. Individuals would no longer assert themselves in the name of mysterious powers passed on to them by their families—this was undeniable progress. On the other hand, the new class system was still worse than the hierarchy of the Old Regime, since *real* property was reflected in the competitive order of the *collège*. In the former, as in the latter, nothing was offered and nothing was received.

The new class system substituted exchange value for use value, transforming property into merchandise: payment effaced the mark of human effort and that of the former owner; a *thing* was all that remained. There is the same relation between the schoolboy and his product: the bond of interiority that unites this young worker with his work is broken by paying him for it with a *grade*. In fact, the number set down on an essay is equivalent, all things being equal, to the price of a piece of merchandise. And just as the merchant or manufacturer is threatened in his property—which has become his objective reality or his "interest"—by other reified property owners, so the student is *endangered* in the quantified object that has ceased to be his product in order to become his objective reality.

His class ranking becomes his *interest* to the extent that the scholarly system is intentionally structured in the image of competitive society. In the France of 1830, where practically no monopolies existed and the economy remained protected by high customs duties, competition revealed to the bourgeois his true underpinnings: it was a selective system based on scarcity, and its result, if not its purpose, was the concentration of goods. The iron laws of bourgeois economics necessarily have the effect of facilitating necessary liquidations—social, judicial, and even physical[8]—that is, of suppressing superfluous candidates. In this indirect but pitiless form of the "struggle for life," every man in the ruling classes is a millionaire in hope but equally a potential bankrupt. The Rouen manufacturer who makes an effort to lower his costs feels his interest threatened *everywhere*, never directly or in a standoff with his rivals but, to the contrary, by a seriality that may depreciate it without ever attacking it, by the machines—to take up a previously cited example—that his competitors, unbeknownst to him, have imported from England.

In the closed circle of the "little scholarly society," his son experiences the same tension to the degree that scholarly competition serves the purpose of eliminating the greatest number of candidates possible before "starting out in life." He is threatened directly (constituted character, illnesses, personal relations with the teacher) and, even more, indirectly, as he has been thrust into a collective where the forces and events that can raise or lower his grade and instantly change his class ranking are in great part outside his field of action and frequently manifest themselves as unforeseeable accidents, at least in relation to him.[9] In this sense, in a competitive field, accident and the luck of others are an integral part of my own objective reality, which I must cling to, though I lack the means to preserve it intact.

Obviously, scholastic competition is not fatal—at least in principle—

and for many children it assumes a ludic aspect, for apparently money has been replaced with dry beans. The school years, however, will not end without some memorable shipwrecks: adolescents are withdrawn from school under the pretext that they could not "keep up." What class doesn't have its dropouts, victims of a system so fashioned that it had decided their fate in advance and awaited them *in order to eliminate them*? The *collège* works a triple *Verdinglichung* [making social relations into things]: it identifies the schoolboy with his *quantified* product; it substitutes for human relations of interiority the inert relations between things in order to dispose of those who cannot adapt themselves to the law of exteriority. Teaching petrifies the content of granted knowledge in such a way that, having itself become a thing, it is homogeneous with the *interest* of the competitors and allows them to be evaluated according to the quantity of their accumulated knowledge. However, the selectionist intention did not appear clearly at this period, either to parents or to children; indeed, in 1830, not all the families that sent their sons to secondary establishments were rich—far from it.[10] And Bouilhet, for example, who was without a fortune, combined a real taste for learning with the determination to rise to the upper levels of society. Nonetheless, rare as the students were whose fathers paid the electoral tax, the majority of these sons of the professional class lived in comfort and could even count on their parents' leaving them property. In other words, the future professionals were recruited among the sons of professionals, that is, from the highest stratum of the middle classes. It would take more than half a century and the promotion of the petite bourgeoisie—which began with the Third Republic and radicalism—for the state apparatus, faced with an increase in both volume and number of candidates for culture, to think of implementing the arrangement devised in the eighteenth century and to transform—in conformity with the will of the founding fathers—virtual eliminatory measures into a real process of elimination. The criminal absurdity of the system became manifest to schoolboys themselves only in those last years, following the steadily climbing percentage of children educated at the secondary level.[11] Between 1830 and 1880, selection operated elsewhere and otherwise: the viscosity of class was such that very few families among the unprivileged would have taken it into their heads to send their children to the establishments of the bourgeois university. A first sorting was accomplished, then, on the level of primary instruction: rural France—from 1830 to 1850, in any case—knew how to pray but not how to read.

As a consequence, the young gentlemen from the sixth to the final year were authorized to feel "at home." The competitions, for the most part, had scarcely any practical significance—the students knew they were taken care of in advance. In the meantime, they had to "do their humanities." After seven or eight years of studies, these young people would sit for the baccalaureate, a simple review of acquired knowledge. The certainty that indulgent teachers would accord the title of bachelor to all candidates who reached the mean level, and would "fish out" a good number of those who did not, contributed to give the jousts of the school year a sufficiently academic character. These adolescents were hardly excited at the prospect of being awarded a certificate of membership in the bourgeoisie at the end of their secondary studies, since they knew they were bourgeois by birth.

CHAPTER EIGHT

Birth of the Garçon

The first time Flaubert refers to him in his correspondence is on 24 March 1837: "When I think of the proctor's mug, caught in the act . . . I cry out, I laugh, I drink, I chant, ha! ha! ha! ha! ha! and I let the Garçon's laughter ring out." Yet the letter immediately preceding this one is dated 24 August 1835; his silence of eighteen months remains unexplained, but whatever the reason for it—letters Chevalier lost or burned, etc.—it is clear that the character made his appearance during this period at a date we can determine very approximately by rereading the previous letters.

Until the summer holidays of 1834, these letters have the naiveté, the seriousness of childhood.[1] Gustave scarcely smiles and willingly moves from righteous indignation to commonplace and sometimes elegiac sententiousness.[2] From 29 August 1834 on, he gives evidence of the most vivid and brutal frenzies; if he didn't have "a queen of France at the end of his pen" (he is writing a novel about Isabeau de Bavière), a bullet would long since have delivered him from this farcical joke called life. The first totalization through laughter: life is a farce; there are only two ways out, suicide or literature. Yuk does not yet exist, but he is very close to being born and dethroning Satan. The change is emphasized with the letter from the following 28 September: until now, Gustave has used the proper phrases of a well-bred child. Yet here he raises his voice, the language becomes coarser: "derision" makes its entrance. The publisher—unless it was Ernest—has taken it upon himself to delete two passages (this is the first time but not the last); happily, what remains gives us the measure of what was removed: "Here's the start of school again *r'arriving* with its bloody affected air. . . . Well, dogshit on it." From this point on, his writing will alternate between the clownish and the serious, and he will ever more frequently express the nastiness of resentment (we know what *that* means) by laughter: "You will be pleased to learn that our friend Delhomme has a black eye, his right one, but in a strange way, so weird and brutal that the whole side of his face is swollen as a result. . . . He was in the infirmary, they put ten leeches on the shiner. Ah, poor Livarot, a damned good joke! That'll give us something to laugh about for two or three days at least."[3] And it is striking that Gustave's reaction is so close to the one he will have nineteen months later upon learning, on 24 March 1837, that the proctor has been caught in a brothel. In '35: "You will be pleased to learn . . ." In '37: "I have a pleasant bit of news to tell you . . ." In both cases the account of the event follows, laced with exclamation marks, with insults to the victim. Then comes the jubilation; in 1835: "a damned good joke!"; in 1837: "Now there's a good trick!" Each of the two paragraphs ends with a burst of laughter; in 1835, Gustave promises to "laugh about it for two or three days at least"; in 1837, the description is more epic: "I am rolling on the ground, tearing my hair out, it's so good," etc. But of course the news is much funnier: a broken jaw is an ordinary occurrence; a proctor caught at a brothel—that's a rare treat.

The only notable difference between the two texts is that in the first one the *Garçon* is not named. From this we can conclude that he was not yet born in July 1835: since the two attitudes are basically identical, why wouldn't Flaubert have mentioned him? But by the same token we must recognize that everything is in place and everyone is waiting just for him: the *persona* is being gestated through whom cosmic laughter will have the means to become a singular universal. Other signs announce the appearance of the persona: it is at this period, indeed, that Gustave's tendency to clothe himself in pseudonyms so as to maintain his inner experience between the "I" and the "He" is manifest for the first time in his correspondence. In the same letter he writes: "I forgot to tell you a new bit of news, that my poetic incognito is 'Gustave Koclott.' I hope this will suffice to baffle the most cunning and vicious tongue in our good town of Rouen." And he signs: "Gustave Antuoskothi Koclott."

2 July: The schoolboys are about to leave on vacation; it seems unlikely that in the last days of the school year the students of the upper seventh term would have taken the time to forge a myth. We must suppose that the creation took place after the "October reunion." Not later, in any case, than the end of autumn 1835 or than the beginning of January 1836. Since the summer, Gustave had been in confinement: he was going on fourteen and knew that he had lost the game, but the flattering encouragement of {French historians Pierre Adolph} Chéruel and {Gaspard} Gourgaud gave him the inner strength to do an about-

face; he remained surrounded, ill, but instead of charging at random, he deliberately marched forward and tried to give as good as he got. Between July and October, he discovered laughter as the disqualification of the finite by the infinite and of being by nothingness. No doubt the shock provoked by the return to school, "*r'arriving* with its bloody affected air," sufficed to induce the birth.

This does not of course mean that one day Gustave could have cried out, "Suddenly, there was the Garçon," as Cocteau would do—"Suddenly, there was Eugene"—in *Le Potomak*. We know that there were "Garçonnades" in which this character did not figure at all. For example, that procession of skeletons for which Flaubert acted as master of ceremonies—the Garçon would have adored this mockery of life by death and death by life; there is no doubt that he would have taken part in the ceremony if not for one major obstacle: he had not yet been born. Gustave made a new beginning, he returned to school determined to assert himself by his "buffoonery"; certain of his classmates made themselves his accomplices, and their buffoonery remained impersonal until they claimed a *collective subject*, the symbol and unity of these desperate pranksters.

Here the question of paternity arises: who created the Garçon? Gustave? His gang? The two together? What share of the responsibility should be given to the group, what to the individual? The Goncourts' text is quite clear: they note on 10 April 1860: "Flaubert . . . spoke to us at length about a creation that deeply occupied his early youth. With several comrades and with one in particular, Le Poittevin, a school friend . . . , they had invented an imaginary character. . . . They took turns putting themselves in his shoes, and their joking spirit into his voice."[4] Unfortunately, these few sentences are swarming with errors: Le Poittevin was not and never had been "Gustave's schoolmate." He left the *collège* in July, 1834, after his year of Rhetoric. Besides, in none of the letters we possess does he claim paternity or copaternity of the Garçon. The rare times that, to my knowledge, he speaks of him, he keeps his distance and seems to regard him as a creature belonging to Flaubert. If at times Alfred behaves in the style of this mythic hero, it is without ever referring to him. We have seen him imitate the cries of "the woman being pleasured." And when he laughs at Lengline, his "strange" laugh, reflexive and secondary, which denounces the foolish cynicism of the young bourgeois's primary and spontaneous laughter, is not without analogy, at least in its meaning, to the laughter of the Garçon, but Alfred is far removed from the frantic violence and the gigantism that characterize the invented persona. He prefers aesthetic detachment, which he no doubt judges more "elegant," and a number of times comes close to faulting the "extravagances" of his comrade.[5] If he "shamelessly" questions passersby and acts out "the woman being pleasured," it is on his own account, for no other reason than his whim and circumstance: this individualist is not at all tempted to escape from himself, to leave his own skin and put himself into the skin of a collective, ritual being. We have seen that he is constitutionally allergic to ceremonies—except those that are celebrated in the family. Moreover, even when he unwinds, he remains cold and lucid: "We have committed, as is reasonable, not a little nonsense." And he adds that he has come home weary of others and of himself. If he was sometimes able, out of complacency, to adopt what the Goncourts call "a heavy, obstinate, enduring joke," I doubt that he ever took much interest in it or could be ranked among its "coauthors." The Thursday conversations, moreover, and Gustave explicitly says so, revolved around "elevated" subjects—"we flew so high"—and if the two friends ridiculed the whole of Creation they claimed, at least, to do it as "philosophers" and not as "buffoons."

Ernest himself "did the Garçon," we can be sure. He bowed at times to the tyranny of the Garçonic "freemasonry"—which allows Gustave to fault the serious young deputy magistrate of Calvi *in the name of his hero*. Ernest's contribution to *Art et Progrès* proves that the future card-carrying bourgeois began, like anyone else, by despising his class of origin; the national guardsman whose cowardice he ridicules in his story is none other than the bourgeoisie under Louis-Philippe, meaning, more or less directly—did he know it?—his father. We are aware, as well, that he carried a knife in his pocket "like Antony." Only the friends were neither in the same year nor in the same class at school. Ernest was beginning the tenth term when Gustave was starting the eighth. Certainly they saw each other often at school; the journal that was the fruit of their collaboration is proof of that. But for them to have collaborated in the collective creation as well, to have spontaneously invented and imposed their inventions on Gustave's comrades, would have required Ernest's being around them every day, which is hardly credible. Gustave himself, in his correspondence, mentions neither Chevalier nor Le Poittevin among the creators. In point of fact, he names only one of them, Pagnerre, in a line that implies that there were others, "one *of the* creators." But the collaboration with Pagnerre seems somehow to exclude the possibility that Gustave's two childhood friends would have contributed much to the invention of the character: Pagnerre, in fact, never counted among Flaubert's "intimates"; he was a good pal, that's all. We must conclude that the Garçon, far from being a hothouse product cultivated in the intimacy of the Hôtel-Dieu by three inseparable friends, first saw the light of day outdoors, in the course of quarrels and practical jokes, and that he was created out in the open (at recess, in the refectories and dormitories) by those same boys who took him as a symbol of universal mockery: a group of "scamps" belonging to the upper half of the eighth-year class.

{Editor's Note: We are continuing with our efforts to understand Gustave's personalization—that is, how he integrated the events of his life to make himself the person that he was, the person who could write *Madame Bovary*, and the nihilism that Sartre attributes to it. Whoever actually invented the Garçon, it became for Gustave a precursor to *Madame Bovary*; but now we continue reflecting on the relation of myth to truth.}

On Truth and the Garçon

What shall we conclude from this first sorting? If Gustave mystifies his comrades, if radical evil is only a fiction, what does he hold to be the truth of man and of the universe? Does he believe that we live in the best of all possible worlds? Or, in any event, that there might be worse ones? Shall we allow that this purveyor of bad jokes is an optimist? We wouldn't know him very well in that case. Under the circumstances, however, we must pose the question of his relations with truth.

The answer is simple, and we have already given it in other chapters apropos of other problems: Flaubert's constituted passivity forbids him any practical relation to truth; to be frank, he cannot even conceive of what a true idea might be. When the word *truth* appears in his discourse, it refers either to the judgments of others—principally to those of scientists and practitioners which he knows are founded on methodical inquiries—or else to a certain subjective state, that is, to a vivid and transitory belief. In the first case, scientific truths are imposed on him by virtue of the principle of authority without ever convincing him completely; in the second, just when his subjective adherence represents the idea to him as true, it denounces itself as a simple belief without revealing to him what certainty might be: "There is no such thing as a true idea or a false idea. At first you eagerly adopt things, then you reflect, then doubt, and there you remain."[6] What is left? Nothing. By raping Truth, Yuk has broken her neck. The real is not *true*, the unreal is not *false*. Then, it will be asked, isn't the Garçon a *false* image of man? Doesn't he mean to deceive his comrades? Let us say that *for Gustave* this character is neither true nor false: he is unreal, that is all. The trap comes into play when his comrades, believing in Truth and Error, take their creation for a myth—a hyperbolic or epic metaphor—that restores man *in his truth*. They are the ones who trap themselves because *in their system of thought* the imaginary is at the service of praxis and, consequently, of truth. When in sound mind, they resort to images only in order to determine, in the course of a mental experiment, the consequences of a possible action. The imaginary child, who takes the image for an end in itself, whatever its relation to the real, is delighted by the vicious circle he has imposed on his comrades by forcing them to interpret through their realistic categories (truth, utility, etc.) their total and veritably mad unrealization. These unfortunates, subjected to a monstrous idol, are sufficiently insane to believe that the "tangle of calumnies" that demoralizes them can *be of use*, that laughter is a means of knowledge, and that the ignoble is the best approach to man. To man *as he should be*, in any case. Gustave enjoys himself immensely: speaking their language, he has put this madness into their heads; the *should-being* of man, what does this mean if God does not exist? If the cosmos is nothing but a great heap of matter, adrift and uncreated? These overexcited schoolboys ought rather to speak of the should-being of God. In the mechanistic universe, fact is king; an absolute nominalism: no eidos; man is what he is, nothing more, nothing less, since no one in heaven demands that he come close to an essence that doesn't even exist.

Such is what I shall call one *attitude* of Gustave's toward his own creature. But there are others that he adopts by turns, according to his whim and the circumstances. For, as we know, he is a materialist out of spite, and two ideologies never cease contesting each other within him. After all, he too has reproached, still reproaches, God for His absence; he too, in his bitter agnosticism, condemns the human race—quite unjustly—because it is without God. He too, in his solitary exultations, has in utter seriousness played the mediator between the infinite negative and our Lilliput. The difference between these ascensions—which originate in rage and shame—and the Garçon, a three-stage strategy, can be summed up in a single word: laughter. While he clowns in public, mocking even his own dolorism, he weeps in secret and draws some consolation from the stories he tells himself: he will be greater than all of them, like the Garçon; he will make heads roll, he will be cruel, merciless, like Yuk; he will demoralize the human race, like the Garçonic trinity. Sobs, forced cries of triumph, hate-filled broodings, dreams of vengeance: this is what we find in the dark and sinister tales he shows to no one but two childhood friends. This is the same adolescent who writes, at several months' interval, the two "formulas," as he calls them: "I believe that humanity has only one purpose, to suffer," and "I love to see humanity debased, this spectacle gives me pleasure when I am weary."[7] Comparing these two maxims, we find the explanation of the Garçonic joke: since that wretched strumpet loves to suffer, since—like me—she draws her dignity from suffering, let's debase her by infecting her with a colossal laughter that will ridicule her pain, let us make the unhappiest and the proudest man unable to look at himself in a mirror without seeing an obscene, grotesque monkey he will be forced to laugh at. Through phantasms, let us compel the entire race to be penetrated by an unreal but tenacious baseness, and let us through various stratagems induce the race to become really ignoble in order to conform to its image. In those moments, as we can see, Gustave does not aim so much to *expose* our baseness to us as to *affect* us with an *artificial* baseness that will end by becoming habitual. Men are not commonly attracted to their excrement; yet rather ordinary illusions will persuade them to regard themselves as turds. In this second attitude, Gustave does not scorn his peers out of hand; he even recognizes that dolorism—of which he is proud—it is a practice common to everyone; he simply hates them and attempts to change them into swine precisely because he does not succeed in finding them sufficiently repugnant. He often takes part in the game himself. Then he goes mad like his comrades; fascinated by his invented character, he bustles around, gesticulates, becomes intoxicated by his own paradoxes, takes pleasure in his gigantic strength as much as in his vileness. If the other actors respond to his attempt, if the spectators laugh, he feels that he is asserting himself and is enclosing, like a gigantic folktale figure, all his comrades in his loins. In those moments, author, actor, and director, he rejoices: he returns to his old passion, the theater; he plays the Garçon as he played Poursôgnac: the malicious intention becomes secondary; the essential thing is to have genius. Conscious of his generosity, he makes a gift of his person, unrealizing himself in order to give his comrades the unity of a group-in-fusion. The intention to do harm is nearly forgotten: he is leading the realists to the superior spheres of unreality, and he feels real sympathy for the scamps he has overwhelmed and who, in return, agree to play the supporting roles so that he can play the main character. In sum, he keeps playacting, now diabolical and now possessed, now mystifier and now simple actor, now sadist, now *heautontimoroumenos*; and what matters to him is that his comrades, as satellites, revolve and playact with him.

Beginning to Know Himself, and Then

The child who looks at himself in the mirror who scrutinizes his eyes, his forehead, looking for a sign of genius, who caresses himself and kisses himself onanistically to compensate for feeling forlorn—we already know that this is Gustave and he alone. In other words: generalizations are possible, but if they take place they will be effectuated *by others* (this will later be psychoanalytic experience), who will compare this "inner life" *to others* from the outside; and the essential thing will no longer be pride but the internalization of protohistory. In this case it would be possible to refer to pessimism but at another level and or entirely other reasons. For him alone, and even if what we today call self-analysis were possible for him, Gustave descending into himself would only enclose himself in the singularity he wants to escape. For this reason he repeats himself: this theoretician of pride, who claims to speak "as a past master," barely advances. He admits, in spite of his personal experience and in the abstract, that other impulses are irreducible *in order to maintain* the irreducibility of pride, that generic given, against all temptation to go deeper. He has frozen his knowledge out of the desire to present every introspective discovery as a two-pronged thought leading on the one hand to the particular and on the other to the universal. He barely consents to note his individual difference, saying either that he is prouder than others or that he is more conscious of his pride—which amounts to the same thing, depending on whether we understand this to mean: if my reflexive consciousness of this motive is more developed, it is because this affect is in me more accentuated; or we construe it to mean: by my very lucidity I become The Proud Man, he who discovers that he is obsessed with Pride and connects everything to this irreducible impulse.

He really feels he is breaking loose: his theory always "embarrasses" him. On 21 May 1841 he writes in his notebook: "Ah! my pride, my pride, no one knows you, neither my family nor my friends nor myself. After all, I refer everything back to it and perhaps I am mistaken." He is no longer even certain that this pride, rooted in darkness, is his basic motivation. And isn't self-knowledge by definition a fraud?

> When I began this, I wanted to make it a faithful record of what I thought, felt, and it has not happened once, to such a degree does man lie to himself; you look at yourself in the mirror but your face is reversed; in short, it is impossible to tell the truth when you write. You make contact, you laugh at yourself, you simper, sometimes it happens that contrary thoughts come to you while you are writing the same sentence. You hurry, you cut things off; you hold yourself back, you overrefine and slacken.

In the vision of oneself there is already a play of reflections; and to know oneself is to *play oneself*: introspection should put an end to the drama but actually develops it, and reflexive sincerity is not possible. Doesn't this throw into question the value of all self-knowledge? What the adolescent tells us is that reflection challenges itself, that the experimenter, with his habits, his desires, and his prejudices, becomes part of the reflexive experiment and must a priori falsify it. In fact, the known is an *object*: how, therefore, could one know *oneself* except as the object that one is for others? But the purpose of Flaubert's *Gnôthi seauton* [know thyself] is precisely to tear the self away from others, to deny the objectivity with which they prematurely affected him, and to play the part of knowing and known *subject*—which is, strictly speaking, impossible. The remarks we have just cited aim at demonstrating once again the impossibility of all reflexive knowledge.

Flaubert's disgust is so great at this period that he incidentally comes to challenge the analytic method: "The sciences proceed by analysis—they believe that this constitutes their glory when it is their shame. Nature is a synthesis, and in order to study it you cut, you separate, you dissect, and when you want to make a whole of all these parts, the whole is artificial, you make the synthesis after having deflowered it, the links no longer exist: yours are imaginary and I daresay hypothetical." Such passages, it must be said, are rare in Flaubert's work. In this one, which deliberately attacks the paterfamilias and contains *Bouvard et Pécuchet* in embryo [Flaubert's "novel in which the ideas themselves destroy each other"; Barnes, *Sartre & Flaubert*, 308], there is undoubtedly an implicit opposition between science and Art, which alone can directly render the living synthesis, the connection between the microcosm and the macrocosm. More striking still is the secret disavowal of the psychology of analysis. An *Erlebnis* is a whole that is not reduced to the sum of its elements. Therefore the work that Gustave claims to do is merely a delusion. His reflection allows him to catch a glimpse of slippery syntheses that escape him when he tries to grasp them, that present themselves and disintegrate when he looks at them, but that seem to him the truth of lived experience. His critique of analysis ends with an incomplete sentence: "The science of the connections between things, the science of the passage from cause to effect, the science of impulse, of embryology, of articulation . . ." The meaning is clear: this discipline is yet to be created; it alone, however, would deserve the name of science, for it would allow us to understand the birth and development of its object. Applied to self-knowledge, this requirement becomes specific: we need a genetic psychology that retraces the dialectical progression of a psychic whole and describes its articulations for us.

He understands so well at this period that knowledge requires an object to know and that the systematic reduction of a whole to its unvarying elements falsifies concrete reality—in short, he is so conscious of the defects of his method and of his position—that he tries twice over to know himself *as other*. He will be other in relation to himself to the extent that time will make his thought of the day before yesterday the object of today's thought. In January 1841, on the advice of Doctor Cloquet, he tries "to put in writing and in the form of aphorisms all my ideas." The aim is to "seal up the paper and open it in fifteen years." What tempts him is the doctor's remark, "You will find another man." The slippage, the changes occurring in that gap of years, will allow him, after he has passed the age of thirty, to conjure up the young man he once was. He will see him as a strange reality, which will reveal itself to him in all its complexity. In this form, however, the attempt is desperate: he himself, today, at nineteen years old, is the one he wants to know; must he wait fifteen years to resolve what he is? He puts himself to the task with some haste, and then we see his zeal abate, and in the end the notebooks of the *Pensées intimes* {*Intimate Notebook*} are abandoned. What will remain of this attempt is a certain concern with observing himself from the outside, looking at himself in the third person as the object of an inquiry, traces of which we will find in *Novembre* with the doubling "I"/"He." But he realizes immediately that he is falsifying all the facts and that the "He" is not really an object (although he had forged a fictive witness—who is still himself). And from the first *Education sentimentale*, he will seek refuge in fictional invention. Jules, once again, is *Gustave to the extent that he is not Gustave.*

In short, Gustave is driven to know himself; but the analytic method deserts him in his enterprise, and the premature passage to the universal is a veritable swindle. As counterpart to an impossible *self-knowledge*, he possesses an exceptional *understanding* of his inner impulses. We need hardly emphasize the abyss that separates the two. Understanding is a silent adjunct to lived experience, a familiarity of the subjective enterprise with itself, a way of putting components and moments in perspective but without explanation; it is an obscure grasp of the meaning of a process beyond its significations. In other words, it is itself lived experience, and I shall call it *prereflexive* (and not unreflected) because it appears as an undistanced redoubling of internalization. Intermediary between nonthetic consciousness and reflexive thematization, it is the dawning of a reflection, but when it surges up with its verbal tools it frequently falsifies what is "understood": other forces come into play (in Flaubert, for example, the denial of the singular), which will divert it or compel it to replace meaning with a network of significations, depths glimpsed through verbal and superficial generalities.

Flaubert at sixteen is perfectly conscious of this difference. In chapter 13 of the *Mémoires* he writes: "How to render in words those things for which there is no language, those impressions of the heart, those mysteries of the soul unknown to the soul itself?"[8] But he does much more than mention it in passing. Between two eloquent flourishes or two fake analyses, strange reflections surge up in his works, which proceed from *understanding* but which, even in full daylight, remain obscure—suggestive allusions to an elusive meaning. I offer as examples only the two dreams he reports in chapter 4 of the *Mémoires*. If the narrative of the two dreams were replaced by "I had terrifying nightmares," the end of chapter 3 would be perfectly joined to chapter 5: "At night, I listened for a long time to the wind blowing heavily . . . I would fall asleep . . . half in dreams, half in tears, and I had terrifying nightmares. This is how I was," etc. At that period the dream as such had no right of entry into literature unless it furthered the complications of plot and integrated itself in the form, for example, of premonitory visions.[9] What, then, compelled Gustave to jot down two obviously selected nightmares without the least concern for breaking the thread of the narrative? No doubt they are related in their somber mood to the sadness of life at the *collège*, to the general pessimism of the *Mémoires*. But this should not have been sufficient because—according to the literary a prioris of the period—they do nothing to advance the story. There is no doubt that the young author must have sensed their secret importance. The one concerns his relations with his mother, the other his relations with his father: this last is incontestably—the comment has often been made—the first dream of castration[10] intentionally told in French literature. It is as if Gustave, neither able nor willing to speak about his family—he does not say a word about them when he tells of his Trouville loves, although all the Flauberts were present—had charged two dreams with expressing his relations with the couple who had engendered him in a form at once unknowable and understandable.

Let us be clear: first of all, the unknowable becomes the object of knowledge when one is in possession of a method of interpretation; *for us* twentieth-century readers, Flaubert's dreams are decipherable. But he leaves no doubt that the unknowable—always provisional—seemed to him definitive. On the other hand, we must not imagine Flaubert choosing with lucid determination to offer us information without the code that would permit us to decode it. He does not know this code himself. The oneiric intention is extended in the author by a vague feeling of the autobiographical *importance* of the two nightmares. We do not know what struck him: perhaps the dreams recurred frequently and he was moved by their repetition. Perhaps one occasion sufficed to give him a glimpse of the "abysses." What matters is the appropriateness of a spontaneous but unintellectual appreciation; the evaluation is not transparent to itself and undoubtedly presents itself as a literary choice or, more probably, as a suffered necessity—he *must* write *this*. Later, when Gustave continually repeats to us that one does not write what one wants, he is alluding to the category of options that are lived as compulsions for not having been recognized as choices. A half-century before the *Interpretation of Dreams*, when psychologists still saw dream life as simply a revival of the impressions of one's waking hours distorted by the organic life of the sleeper, Flaubert demonstrates that he somehow grasped the function of dream life as the route of access to himself by coupling two dreams (the father, the mother) together. Immediately, however, the diver makes a violent effort to rise to the surface again: *Novembre* and the correspondence inform us that his nights, following his years as a boarder and until the "attack," remain highly disturbed, but while the young man signals his nocturnal difficulties, he no longer describes them to us; the oyster has closed up.

The letters and the *Souvenirs*, however, are full of brief indications that Gustave lived his "estrangement" from himself as an understanding that could not and would not be transformed into intellection. If these dreams astound him, it is because he sees them as the echo of *waking* inclinations and thoughts that are equally indecipherable. We know that he will write to Louise that his heart is exhausted by the "visitation of unhealthy things," and that he will voluntarily compare himself to a muddy pond that must not be disturbed for fear that stinking slime will rise to the surface. He therefore has a perception of the psychology of the depths. But well before, in 1841, he writes in the *Souvenirs*:

> If I have delicious desires for love, I have ardent ones, bloody ones, horrible ones. The most virtuous man has in his heart the glimmers of dreadful things. There are thoughts or actions that one admits to no one, not even to one's partner, not even to one's friend, that one does not say aloud to oneself. Have you sometimes blushed at secret, base impulses that rose in you and then abated, leaving you utterly astonished, utterly surprised to have had them?[11]

These secret impulses are his sadism and his masochism; they are his jealous rages, his black relations with the family. We are in the realm of understanding: he *lives* his anomaly, it astonishes him but he adheres to it; yet the moment he is about to open himself and see in depth the father's curse, he snaps shut. He escapes from understanding, as from knowledge, through generalization: "*The most virtuous man* . . . one admits to no one . . . Have *you* sometimes . . . ?" Be that as it may, these thoughts are "glimmers": in other words, they are not only lived for themselves, they vaguely enlighten the person with regard to himself.

CHAPTER NINE

A Review

Let us summarize. Gustave has lived uncomfortably with his idiosyncrasy; for a long time an intimate participation with himself has allowed him to understand himself, to adhere to the impulses of his life and even, to a certain degree, to direct them. The shift to reflection, facilitated by Alfred's influence, leads him to schematize and to generalize certain determinations of lived experience: he will escape the bourgeois curse if his somber moods present themselves to him as the correct and unsophisticated evaluation of the human condition. The young author's primary intention, when he writes *Mémoires d'un fou*, is not to advance in self-knowledge but to realize the death of the soul in general by an interior totalization. The difficulties of the work and finally its total failure make it necessary for him to use reflection in order to know himself.

But the nature of his project—to escape the *self* as anomaly—his will to generalize, and the inadequacy of his tools lead him to challenge any possibility of introspective knowledge. Therefore he will be ignorant of himself. But at the same time, his deepening understanding infuses him with the feeling that in spite of everything there is *someone* in him who must be known. He glimpses this *someone* in flashes but takes fright in the face of what he divines; the flashes of understanding cannot—in the absence of a method or a witness—be converted to intellection. Gustave can *experience himself* but not construct a *model of lived experience*. Moreover, he is fascinated by the "himself" that haunts him, but he dreads it and refuses to *admit himself to himself*. He will therefore live in increased discomfort: never is he more present to his subjective life than at the moment when self-knowledge seems impossible to him. The "glimmers" disturb him, reveal everything to him, and at the same time dazzle him: he sees himself unceasingly and sees nothing at all.

The discomfort arises here from the fact that understanding permanently devalorizes knowledge, even while demanding it in a way. From the moment he ceases to think of it, the monster he does not want to be invades him, and when he finally dares to look at it, the filthy beast has disappeared. We might say that the censoring apparatus, on its usual level, functions poorly, and that repression is accomplished even on the level of reflection. He will explain himself on the matter sometime later in a letter to his sister that seems to be a conclusion to this long adventure. It is 1845; Caroline has married Hamard. They return from their honeymoon and remain in Paris "to find lodgings and furnishings." Flaubert is surprised that he isn't sad and recognizes that he does not know how to anticipate himself. In order not to be jealous, he says hypocritically, "I must love this good Emile." Nothing could be more false and he knows it: he detests and mistrusts his brother-in-law, of whom he wrote in 1840: "He is abysmally stupid."[1]

He gives us the truth unwittingly and in spite of himself—as he often does—with a simple turn of phrase: "If you love me it is only right, for I have loved you." In other words, he perceives or thinks he perceives that he no longer loves Caroline—rancor has stifled or masked love—and he is dumbfounded by it. He concludes:

> I am a strange character, as Chéruel used to say; I thought to know myself for a time, but by dint of analyzing myself, I no longer know at all what I am; also I have lost the silly pretense of wanting to grope about in that obscure chamber of the heart that is lit from time to time by a brief flash that reveals everything, it is true, but in return blinds you for a long time. You tell yourself: I have seen this or that, oh yes, I shall certainly find my way, and you set off and run up against all the corners, you lacerate yourself on all the angles. If I know where this analogy came from, I'll be damned. It has been a very long time since I have written anything, and from time to time I need to exercise a little style.[2]

This text is of capital importance—first of all because it retraces the moments of this evolution. Gustave has analyzed himself *too much*; he has lost the silly pretense of constructing self-knowledge on the silent flashes of understanding. Now he no longer knows himself, does not know what he is, and his reactions always surprise him. The moment he "believed he knew himself" corresponds to the first periods of reflection. At that time—1837–38—he amassed several "introspective" discoveries; he caught himself in the act, his hand in the pot, in his reactions of exasperated pride. He then considers applying the analytic method: it is a failure. Indeed, his purpose is tarnished with moralistic thinking, trying to separate the wheat from the chaff. In this sense, analysis is the movement of disillusionment: I believed I was good (when I was a child), I am not; which can also be expressed—in the light of his resentment—in these terms: I *was* good, they made me mean. But analysis leads him astray to the extent that it must by definition reduce a particular whole to its universal elements.

The presuppositions of the method serve his major aim only too well, which is to universalize himself through reflexive knowledge. Thus what he describes is his anxious quest in the years 1838–42. What he means here by the *abuse* of analysis is really the wrong use made of it. And reading between the lines we discover that he means its *use pure and simple*: psychological atomism falsifies the understanding of self by the universalizing will to reduce irreducibility to invariable elements whose combination alone varies. This analysis fascinates him (it is the father's gaze), horrifies him (dissection), serves him only too well (justification), and finally produces no result. Must it therefore be renounced? The word *too* shows here all the ambiguity of Flaubert's thought. In truth, he cannot condemn analysis entirely since he sees in it the scientific method. Yet the analytic knowledge he claims to possess hides his real *existence* from him; he is aware of it: those abstractions remaining in the bottom of the test tube have nothing in common with the syncretism of lived experience. Is he going to condemn analysis? No. At the last moment he recoils and prefers to condemn the abuse of it. This is slipping from one idea to another and essentially condemning—as does conventional wisdom—the use of reflection: I have too much observed myself living; I should have lived spontaneously. But he knows that this spontaneous life, unreflected or prereflected, which envelops his own understanding, does not by itself offer the tools that would permit knowledge of it.

Therefore, rather than refute analysis as a psychological method, he prefers to declare that self-knowledge is *impossible* because understanding is not reducible to knowledge. But obviously this irreducibility makes the analytic method (in the eighteenth-century sense of the term) perfectly inapplicable.

What is striking in this letter, despite the emphasis—quite commendable—on style, is Flaubert's extraordinary consciousness of self-understanding. Of course, it is primarily intuition as opposed to the discursive, the sudden horrified pleasure in oneself as opposed to methodical research. Where does this perception of the whole person come from? No one can tell us. I suppose that it appears in certain states of *estrangement* in which Flaubert is surprised by his behavior: he tears himself open from top to bottom and sees himself. In general, we lack the facts to support this conjecture: Gustave gives us his experiences allusively; he speaks of thoughts that he is ashamed of, that he would not confide even to Alfred, "not even to yourself." But he hides their contents from us. Two passages of the *Souvenirs*, however, give us a hint as to what might occasion these revelatory flashes.

Here is the first. Flaubert is eighteen years old. Hamard, whose brother is dying, comes "to announce this dying to him": "He squeezed my hand affectionately, and as for me, I let him squeeze it; I left him laughing idiotically, the way I would have smiled in a salon. I didn't like it at all; that man humiliated me. It was because he was full of a feeling and I was empty of it—I saw him again yesterday—yet he is abysmally stupid, but I remember how much I loathed myself and thought myself detestable at that moment." And here is the other: "I am jealous of the life of great artists; the joy of money, the joy of art, the joy of opulence, are theirs," which is completed by this remark: "[If I wrote] a book, it would be on the turpitude of great men—I am glad that great men should have had any."

In both cases, Flaubert astonishes himself. His jealousy of great men makes him ashamed: he catches himself maliciously seeking out their pettiness because he has convinced himself that he is a "great man manqué." But what particularly astounds him is that he should go so far as to envy the great sadness of an imbecile. Obviously he does not reproach himself for not suffering as much as his friend, under the circumstances; no, but he compares this overwhelming unhappiness to his own "emptiness," he senses his coldness and that in a similar case that he would be incapable of a sadness as dense, as profound. He loathes himself: he goes well beyond this particular behavior and takes it for the expression of his inner reality, of his concrete relations with the various members of his family. Undoubtedly it is so: the fact that he takes the trouble to note this particular and *dated* reaction, something so rare for him, is enough to show the importance he attaches to it. I would even say that this reaction is the only one—among many others, perhaps more important but, as he will say later, playing on the word, *unsayable*—that he had dared to put down in writing, and that it stands, in his mind, for all those he had to keep silent about, for fear of being read.

His Inability to Learn about Himself

But did the sudden anguish that no doubt followed teach him something? No. And it is here that Gustave—in the letter to Caroline—shows his penetration: this brief flash "reveals everything, it is true, but in return blinds you for a long time." First of all, it will be noted that this inner truth *invades* Gustave. Intuition is never expected and cannot be reproduced; again we encounter the young man's underlying passivity—these are visitations. He thus underlines the syncretic indivisibility of this totalizing view. But there is more: it is dazzling. Meaning that this view *blinds* understanding. It is not simply irreducible; understanding and knowledge are not only incommensurate in principle, but the *dazzlement* demonstrates that understanding is the *denial of self-knowledge*. Restraints and inhibitions are immediately set in motion—they may even be said to be part of it—which makes understanding indecipherable: everything reveals and conceals itself at the same time. The passive activity of the young man limits itself to denying what is given to him. All the same, when the light is extinguished, it seems to Flaubert that he can profit from the experience. The work he undertakes, against himself, in anguish and in disgust, with the insincere but profound intention of knowing *what he is all about*, curiously resembles self-analysis (in the sense in which present-day analysts use the term). It is not a matter of dissection, this time, but of progressive reconstruction: an attempt to put the disappeared whole into perspective, a desire to discover its articulations and fix them through discourse.

In this dark night, you think you are going forward, you try to remember a road that has never existed and that would have to be invented. You try to guide yourself, as by the stars, by visual impressions that the lightning flash has left in the memory, but which vanish when you use them as landmarks. You knock yourself out, batter yourself: you find within you resistances and indefinable sorrows, *unnamable* asperities, shames whose object cannot be identified. This remarkable text seems to confirm in advance the Freudian cautions against self-analysis. It rejects at once psychological atomism with its dissections and the possibility of retrieving the articulations of that subjective totality which occasionally offers itself, suddenly, in fear and trembling. It is all the more striking that Flaubert, in tracing these lines—as in the most revelatory passages in his correspondence—has only a very confused consciousness of their importance. He is astonished after the fact at having written them, and all at once, by a half-intentional error, explains them by his desire "to exercise a little style." Thus everything is obscured, including the impression of being obscure to himself. Only the conclusion is not obscure: *one must give up the idea of knowing oneself*.

Yet we should not take literally the historical sketch that Gustave has penned for Caroline, which begins with the abuse of analysis only to end in resignation. In general, the direction is correct: around the age of sixteen he tries to know himself; at twenty-four he knows that he will never know himself. But in fact it is all there at the same time, in every moment of the process: knowledge and its negation, analysis and understanding: only the *emphasis* varies. He both wants and does not want to reveal himself to himself. Rather, he is led to want it on the basis of an immutable denial. The acknowledged insincerity of the *Mémoires* prompts him to open a new notebook and to attempt to write down his introspective observations. But he has no sooner turned the first page than he seems to give up. Indeed, after a vengeful tirade against men ("I expect nothing good on [their] part"), he writes: "I have within me all contradictions, all absurdities, all stupidities." He adds, revealing his fears and proving that he does not yet consider himself finished, hence determined: "I do not even rely on myself, I may become a vile creature, mean and cowardly, how do I know?" Only to take himself in hand again immediately with the reassurance, "I believe, however, that I would be more virtuous than others because I have more pride."[3] And this bent toward agnosticism will express itself eight years later *in the same terms* when he tells the Muse: "I am a poor man, very simple and very easy and *very human*, 'all meandering and various,' made of bits and pieces, *full of contradictions and absurdities*. If you understand nothing about me, I do not understand much more myself."[4]

Meanwhile, how does he live this perpetual seesaw from 1838 to 1842? In discomfort. He passively *suffers* his pessimism and at the same time continually finds himself acting it out—which will later lead him to this confession: "My basic nature, whatever anyone says, is that of a mountebank." This perpetual exaggeration disconcerts and irritates him: hence the "deplorable mania for analysis," that morose tendency constantly to spy on himself in order to determine the respective shares of rigamarole and sincerity. But what *does he know* about himself? Nothing, except that he is dangerous and in danger. In vain does he want to flee from himself and look down at himself from above: he is at once the pond's calm surface and its muddy bottom; the least wrinkle on this smooth water has its source in the unseen movements of the slime and conversely perpetuates those deep disturbances. His understanding of himself constantly whispers to him that he is heading toward a great unhappiness, that he is running toward it and in some way seeking it out. What can he do? Turn the headlights on this destination that terrifies him? He would find no one there anymore. Forget that "horrible worker"? But this is letting him take over: God knows what suicide he is preparing.

Gustave has the uncomfortable feeling that he has fallen prey to someone unknown who is leading him to his doom. Someone unknown who is both closer and more distant than a twin brother, who wants the worst, who has already killed his soul by projecting an absurd "thought" into it, a pessimistic truth that devours him and exhausts him in order to justify itself. Gustave, prey to himself, is all the more desperate as he *does not like himself*. The *Souvenirs* are full of bitterness and grinding complaints against himself: "[Despite] an immense pride, I am increasingly in doubt. If you knew what anguish it is! If you knew my vanity. What a savage vulture, eating out my heart—how lonely I am, isolated, mistrustful, base, jealous, egotistical, fierce." We must take his pessimism literally: miserable and mean, he is ashamed of his misery and repelled by his meanness; cynicism, which he deplores and of which he does not want to know the causes, has taken hold in him, and he falls into a stupor when he glimpses the origin of that abstract, desperate repetition, not the objective situation or everyday experience but the secret intention of an invisible enemy who is none other than himself. On the surface, he is disgusted with himself; deep down, he dreads himself.

But let us remind ourselves that the terror of this haunted boy, the incessant battle in him between the determinations of his ipseity—class-being, the ego of basic intention, the alter ego that others denounce, the quasi object of introspection, and the reflexive subject of knowledge—is not separable in 1838 from his literary failure. At the beginning of that autumn, he abandons—provisionally—interior totalization through the work of art and at the same time tries (in boredom and veiled refusal, in short in bad faith) to jot down in a notebook, without preparation, without style, therefore—he believes—without dramatization, the results of his introspective analysis. In literary terms, the result is that the "Artist" loses confidence in himself: to write, he must be sincere; to dissipate the spontaneous insincerity of the mountebank, he must know himself; yet self-knowledge is revealed to him as an impossibility in theory because he does not want it in reality. So he floats, cut off from his roots. But at the same time he gets ready to "bounce back." His reveries, the plans he outlines, the scenes he imagines, all lead him to *Smarh*: in other words, he returns, more decisively than ever, to exterior totalization.

Return to the Infinite

After the failure of the *Mémoires*, Gustave spends a long time dreaming. As usual, he blindly inverts particular scenes, becomes fixed on certain images, which he subsequently varies on a whim; and all at once these disconnected efforts lead him to discover the whole. Boredom then gives way to sudden enthusiasm. He writes to Ernest, 26 December 1938: "Fifteen days ago I was in the best state in the world."[5] Fifteen days ago—at the moment of *conception*: at the beginning of the month there was this brief lightning flash; he was in doubt, and then, all at once, the "Mystery" organized itself. Never has he had such ambition: he wants to write "something extraordinary, gigantic, absurd, unintelligible to me and to others"; this will be a "mad work" in which "[his] mind [will be] extended to its full range" and which will be accomplished "in the highest regions of heaven." The afterword, which he adds in 1840, informs us that he "took himself for a little Goethe." In short, there is every indication that he wants to attempt a great coup.

Let us not treat these aspirations lightly. Since the young man became conscious of the "thought" that devours him, since he took as his goal the communication of this thought through his writings, he has gone from failure to failure. He doubts his genius: nothing will free him from his disgust but a startling act of retaliation that will allow him to consider his previous works as studies—unsatisfying but *preliminary* efforts for a work that has finally "come together." During the autumn of 1838 he was vexed, embittered; his "immense pride" suffered. But this same pride, conscious of itself, is now going to save him. To understand this reversal, we must illuminate the cause by its effect: we shall anticipate and follow the developments of this mental exercise in the following years—we shall see him become more conscious, systematic. We shall then be entitled to come back to the Mystery of 1839 and to shed light on its author's design, to clarify the connection between pride and exterior totalization.

On 23 May 1852 he writes to the Muse: "One saves oneself from everything with pride. One must learn a lesson from every misfortune and *bounce back after falls*." He has indeed just applied the technique of bouncing back. On 20–21 March 1852 having confided the manuscript of *La Bretagne* Flaubert asks her to give it to Theophile Gautier to read: "As for *La Bretagne*, I would not be miffed if Gautier read it now. But if you are entirely involved in your comedy, stay with it, it is more important. . . . In any case, just send *La Bretagne* to Gautier when you have read it, and let me know. I shall send you a little note to enclose in the package." He has been back in Paris for several days, and this is his first mention of Gautier, so we are not certain that Louise did not *first* suggest to him that she should play the role of intermediary. What is certain, in any case, is that he has taken the offer seriously: he admires Gautier and is burning to submit his work to him. The desire is only normal in a young man who has not published anything. But Louise, who in the meantime has become acquainted with the manuscript, flatly refuses to send it to "Theo." On 3 April Flaubert *thanks* her for it; that day, however, he naively acknowledges that he is "in a prodigiously bad humor . . . enraged, without knowing at what." Of course, Louise's judgment, which is that "jokes and vulgarities abound" in *La Bretagne*, has nothing to do with it. He is pleased to tell her, on the contrary: "What you have noticed in *La Bretagne* is also what I like best." And suddenly:

> May I hug you and kiss you on both cheeks and on your breast for something that escaped you and has deeply flattered me. You do not think *La Bretagne* exceptional enough to be shown to Gautier, and you would like his first impression of me to be a violent one. It is better to abstain. You recall me to my pride. Thank you. I have certainly played hard to get, with old Gautier. Here he has been asking me for a long time to show him something, and I keep promising. It is astonishing how modest I am in that respect . . . To wish to please is to stoop. From the moment one publishes, one descends from one's work. The thought of remaining all my life totally unknown does not sadden me in the least . . . It is a shame that I should require an extralarge tomb: I would have [my manuscripts] buried with me, like a savage with his horse.

What a marvelous reversal! It is Gautier who begs and Flaubert who refuses, playing hard to get. And there he goes, meditating on his perhaps overly reserved nature: "It is astonishing how modest I am in that respect." The first impulse was an act of naive faith in his work; he wanted to show it to Gautier so as to impress him. Louise's criticism and her refusal are the fall. The bounce back immediately follows: Gustave internalizes the refusal and presents it as his own decision. Denying his legitimate desire to be read, he takes it for an absurd failing. And since, until now, he has shown his writings only to his close friends, he links this past conduct to Louise's present attitude; it is *his* haughty reserve that is expressed by the Muse's pen: "You recall me to my pride!" That is, to his profound truth. He has taken off now, he glides above Gautier, "old" Gautier, reproaching himself for being barely civil to him. Above Louise, too, to whom he explains the motives of the implacable no she has given *on his command* to Theo's beseechings: "To want to please is to stoop."

But this is not yet sufficient. With renewed effort, Gustave gains height; his negation is universalized; now it is from the human race that he will hide his writings: "From the moment one publishes, one descends from one's work." This passage to the absolute permits him to judge *La Bretagne* harshly and to condemn the miserable failing of his constituted self. Seen from above, Flaubert's empirical ego and those of

Louise and Gautier become confused with one another and disappear into space. The real subject is above them, has escaped from them, and has only a negative connection with the human race. All that remains is to give a subjective value to the work whose objective value has just been challenged. Gustave takes this up in the next paragraph: "These poor pages have indeed helped me to cross the long plain . . . With them I have passed through storms, crying alone into the wind and walking dry-footed through swamps in which ordinary travelers remain mired to their chins." The trick is played: moral greatness is substituted for literary talent: for better or worse, *La Bretagne* is a talisman that allowed Gustave to avoid ambushes and to continue on his way, without stooping, as a solitary pilgrim.[6] Let us note that "these poor pages" were written between September and December 1847. First a misunderstanding with Louise and then the trip to the Orient prevented Gustave from showing them to the Muse. Three months, four at most: and should we not say that this slight work carried him across plains and tides as a steed would have done? There too, Flaubert amplifies and recapitulates: he moves from *La Bretagne* to his entire oeuvre thanks to the simple metaphor of the savage who has himself buried with his horse. The horse is the totality of his manuscripts. Does Gustave perceive that by this comparison he is making art a means of getting through life? Certainly, but this means becomes sacred to the extent that it has protected Flaubert from errors and vices; and above all the young author confers an *ethical* value on his works to the same extent that others argue their aesthetic value: poor pages, so be it; but I owe them my aristocratic dignity.

How, after this example, shall we define the technique of bouncing back? Let us note, first of all, that it is employed after "falls." But the "falls" are wounds of pride—and we can be sure that Flaubert roared with rage when he received Louise's letter. In short, one cures the wounds of passive pride by overdoing active pride. In the first moment, the bouncing back appears to be an intentional shift from the unreflected to the reflexive life: humiliated; Gustave withdraws to a high place and becomes purely a witness to his humiliation. He will use reflexive scissiparity to double himself: abandoning his self-object, as passive victim, to the hands of his tormentors, he makes himself the contemplative subject and watches with indifference as the inner object sinks down at his feet.

Of course he is deceiving himself; the subject of reflection participates, from the time of its appearance, in the intentions of the reflected from which it is born; the moment we wish to see suffering and shame in ourselves, they are *already* in the reflexive consciousness, which grasps them simultaneously as a quasi object, a provisional unity of lived experience. Be that as it may, the shift to reflection is usually motivated by the intention to break with the self, to keep one's distance from affects or inclinations that one denies. Gustave, who aims to break solidarity with the self by perching, a steely witness, above his life, has the same goal as those who, for example, believe in escaping guilt by acknowledging that they are guilty.

Deepening His Personalization

Gustave is really not sure of anything. For a constituted passivity, boredom is above all primary matter: it exists first, it is the taste of lived experience. Yet in order to radicalize it, behaviors must *animate* it: "the boredom that two men have brought to the *boil*," he writes later to Bouilhet. He fully recognizes that they have forced primitive boredom to its limit since he immediately adds: "Beware, when you are amused at being bored, it's a slippery slope." A line that cannot help evoking the six words from *Novembre*.

Thus, Gustave considers that from age fifteen to twenty he sinned through complacency. In the same letter, the metaphor is multiplied: that stagnant liquid which he used to "bring to the boil" and of which he used to "feel the weight" has now become a "slippery slope." But these transformations are quite instructive: the three images, used simultaneously, can render what one might call the three dimensions of boredom. The weight defines it, in effect, in its original inertia, in its being-there; the provoked boilings manifest Gustave's activity, the grand gestures he makes in order to stir up the liquid, but the comparison preserves a ludic and gratuitous character for these enterprises; we are merely at the moment when one is *amused* at being bored. The more banal image of the "slippery slope" has the advantage of indicating the underlying attraction Flaubert feels for the bottom of the precipice where, dizzying as it is, radical boredom awaits him. At the outset, the exercise of boredom seemed merely a means of keeping the world at a distance: one was perched above it all. Now, quite to the contrary, he rolls down to the bottom; the world closes over him, swallowing him up. The amusement was merely an enticement disguising a dangerous fascination, a distant magic charm or perhaps a summons: in any case, this broken metaphor serves to introduce the relation to the Other—even if this Other were merely an alter ego. Some otherness has slipped into the relation of self to self—the boredom that is suffered and is suddenly conjured up as a demand from the depths, as something *to realize*. It has become a habit, and Gustave has lost control of it; invaded, he suffers it.

But he suffers it as he made it: this foreign body inside him carries his label; he must recognize it as *his* (as the result of his exercises), as *other* (as the present heteronomy of his spontaneity), as *his own as other*: you wanted it, Gustave Flaubert.

This, at least, is what the author of *Novembre* says to himself *in order to reassure himself*: the *other* intention would be merely *his* intention, but in the past. Does he fully believe it? What if it were—like the stupefaction that precedes and provokes it—the forewarning or symbol of a deeper and wholly alien intention? Passive activity is no doubt in itself the setting of surrender; like the original boredom, it is what makes the crisis of boredom possible. But if there were nothing to reinforce it, Gustave could combat it and win provisional victories over it. What is the source of its present power? It is as if someone in Flaubert were making use of it in order to attain a monstrous end. We are familiar with this end: we have seen Flaubert imitate the epileptic of Nevers in order to create *in the imaginary* the experience of subhumanity. Unreal as it was and remained from beginning to end, that experience terrorized him. He wonders now if the underlying intention of an unknown ego which he shelters in his depths would not be to make him fall *really* and *permanently* into the state of human rubbish. He tried to fight the bourgeoisie by perching above it: well and good, but that would have taken genius. Lacking genius, didn't he persuade himself that one leaves the bourgeois environment only by falling below it?

The only way out was to become the family idiot—hadn't he already chosen that way? In this case, the failure of August '42 would manifest his underlying intention: to lose everything and constitute himself truly, by means of a slow internal effort, as failed-man. From this moment, Flaubert is afraid. He feels as though he has a suspect and hidden accomplice who executes promptly but *badly* the sentence he has brought against himself, who gives an effective reality to what remained until then on the border between the imaginary and the real.

His Lived Body

And what, then, is this Other inside him whose poisoned compliance risks realizing the unreal? A little later, in Paris, a strange experience enables him to discover it—it is his body. In *Novembre* he goes on at length and repeatedly about his abstinence. He *wills* it. And in the most radical way. An impecunious student goes to bed with grisettes—as Ernest does—or with whores. Gustave means to pass up both. And abstinence is not enough for him, there must be a total absence of desires in him. Making love hastily for four sous is relieving a need—and needs, as we know, horrify him. Early on, plagued by sex, he dreams of cutting off his balls: "[Louis Lambert] wants to castrate himself. At nineteen, in the midst of my Paris boredom, I had this wish as well (I will show you, in the rue Vivienne, a shop where I once stopped, seized by this idea with an imperious intensity)."[7] And then the desire disappears: Flaubert says at the time that the law killed it: "The law puts me in a state of moral castration strange to conceive." *Moral*, certainly: literary impotence, indifference toward everything that formerly moved him, in particular toward books. But the *physical* soon gets into the act. We read in the Goncourts' *Journal*: "Yesterday, Flaubert told me: I did no fucking from the age of twenty to twenty-two because I had promised myself not to fuck."[8] Which is explained and confirmed by a letter to Louise: "I loved a woman . . . until the age of twenty without telling her, without touching [her]; and I was almost three more years without feeling my sex. For a moment I thought that I would die this way."[9] This last text, still quite close to the period in question, insists on the experienced, suffered aspect of this anorexia—Flaubert says clearly to Louise: I thought I had no more desire, you are the one who awakened me. His confidence to the Goncourts emphasizes—a bit too heavy-handedly—the *voluntary* aspect of this abstinence: "I had promised myself not to fuck." Gustave in 1863 is playing a role: he wants to prove that he can control his needs. Be that as it may, when we compare these three citations it seems that his impotence is *intentional*: it corresponds on the sexual level to the stupefaction Gustave intentionally affects when he opens his Code. Furthermore, there is only one intention which—in two different domains—is replayed by the body with similar docility: as passive activity, if Flaubert can't rebel, he wants to *swoon*; through the provoked stupor he refuses the "trivial" condition imposed on him, and through frigidity he refuses the "mean" life he would lead if desire were no more than a need. No more needs, no more intelligence: to be nothing. His body realizes in 1842 what he wished for after the failure of *Smarh*. Indeed, considered on the level of sexuality, the negative enterprise has immediate results, complete and lasting. It is as if the organism, with a slight delay, were penetrated by these castrating intentions, had assumed and realized them spontaneously. Gustave explicitly acknowledges these intentions as his own: yet this docility disturbs him. In 1863, he tries to rationalize the event: he speaks to the Goncourts of voluntary chastity and not of anorexia. But his confidences to Louise still bear traces of his disarray. A surgeon's son, he is—we can believe—highly informed about the anatomy and physiology of sex; he knows how one gets an erection and how one ejaculates, that is, he *also* knows these phenomena *in ex-*

teriority, as the *inhuman, of which man is made*.

These are chain reactions, nothing more; excessive chastity is an accumulation of energy; once beyond the alarming level, this energy will dispense itself in a violent discharge: here we have the need, the nocturnal emissions, and, with a little luck, coitus. And in front of Gustave's eyes this rigorous and nonsignifying process is transformed into discourse. The silence of "that brave genital organ" is a *speech*, the flesh signifies. But the signification, here, is not separable from a real work: in his interior monologue, in his letters, Gustave speaks of castrating himself; he speaks of it *in order not to do it*, disarming the future act by describing it as a *possible*. And the body *does not know possibility*: castration can become a corporal discourse only by realizing itself as a fatality. For this reason it is an oracular language, effective but maliciously indeterminate. The death of sex is a signifying fact; it is said to Gustave: you desired it, here it is. As a result, Gustave thinks that he did not entirely desire it, or not this way. First of all, who will say whether it is provisional or definitive? Limited to a few years, it might have turned out all right. But, he says, "I thought for a moment that I would die this way." To lose his virility forever is to become an invalid, a subman. Besides, he doesn't like the way *they* took him at his word. What should he believe? he asks himself.

Must we see in the body an obscure, confused thought which overflows and harms us because it takes our conscious desires literally and, for lack of understanding them, caricatures them? Or, on the contrary, is it from organic materiality that we learn our true options in their radical form? If the first hypothesis disturbs him, the second terrifies him: if I must read my intentions in the spontaneous comportments of my organism, Gustave says to himself, I must be inhabited by a self-destructive frenzy; when I dreamed of castration in front of the shop in the rue Vivienne, I saw it merely as a gesture appropriate to soothe my rage. Now I perceive that thought is not the mere representation of possibilities but that, through the play of corporal mediations, it is permanently an act. In other words, the body has no imagination, and my little dramas become real in it; my own truth, the flight into the imaginary, is forbidden me, or rather it is an appearance, for sooner or later I am organically conditioned by what I imagined. *I have emasculated myself*: in order to avoid debasing myself with random whores, I have chosen *against myself* to fall still lower through a curse that puts me beneath men. At any event, for Flaubert *corporal speech* bears witness to the existence of a black radicalism that torments him: the process is exactly the one we described just now with regard to boredom: it is the politics of the worst. One tries to escape from desire by rising above it, and one removes oneself from it only by falling below the level of man. One tries to be *nothing*, and precisely because if that one makes oneself into *something*: a failed man, a hominid, a child of man made to accede to the human condition and which a monstrous anomaly retains in a state of quasi animality. In both cases, Flaubert has recourse to Reason to protect himself from the horror: the chastity, he says to the Goncourts, was voluntary; boredom, he writes in *Novembre*, is the result of a reasoned asceticism. But at the same time that he claims through his interpretations to maintain himself in *normality*; he senses that he has lost in advance, that he is not simply anomalous but is becoming truly abnormal.

His experience of 1841–42 leaves a clearly pathological aftertaste: he was playacting brutishness, that's for sure. But it was not only habit that abruptly provoked boredom and "the resulting" apathy: the body produced it spontaneously, like a certain state of being savored, that settled in unexpectedly and disappeared without any explanation. Suddenly, arms, legs, and head *were putting themselves spontaneously* out of commission. And this happened at the very moment he had decided to "slog away" seriously. Similarly, in certain novels we encounter a loyal servant who seems to do nothing but obey. But gently, imperceptibly, out of hatred or perversity, by his way of fulfilling his master's commands with a little too much alacrity, just a little too quickly, or sometimes with a slight lag, carrying out the previous day's orders the moment they have just been repealed—but he has all the excuses, he *cannot* be conscious of his abrupt about-face—this valet leads the young son of the family to ruin, to vice, to irreparable degradation. The procedure is as simple as can be: *signifying* to the master his *ill will* as his truest nature, bringing him a glass of alcohol just as he has given up drinking. Gustave's body has chosen the same procedure. And he is certain that something is not right, for out of intermittent apathy and permanent anorexia it is the soma that signifies and the mind that becomes the signified.

CHAPTER TEN

The Last Spiral

THE EVENT

{Editor's Note: We now continue with our attempt to understand Gustave's personalization, his spiral existence as he continually attempts to continue in his writing, coping with his family's consistent unwillingness to let him be an author, and yet not leaving his family, all with the result that he is molding a passive-active nature within himself. Here then, we encounter the crucial "Fall," the collapse before his brother, that has been referred to previously, which, for Sartre, Gustave had been preparing for throughout most of his life and which "allows" him to be an author while remaining in the family.}

One evening in January 1844, Achille and Gustave were returning from Deauville, where they had been to see the site of the new country house. It was pitch-dark; Gustave was driving the cabriolet himself. Suddenly, in the vicinity of Pont-l'Évêque, as a wagon passed to the right of the carriage, Gustave dropped the reins and fell at his brother's feet as if struck by lightning. Seeing him motionless as a corpse, Achille thought he was dead or dying. In the distance, the lights of a house were visible. The elder son carried his brother to the house and gave him emergency treatment. Gustave remained for a few minutes in this cataleptic state; he had, however, retained full consciousness. When he opened his eyes, he may have had convulsions, but we have no firm evidence. In any case, his brother took him to Rouen that same night.

Before going further, we must determine the *date* of this attack. In a letter from Caroline written *17 January 1844* and addressed to rue de l'Est, we read: "Your letter reached us only at five last evening and we were afraid that you had been ill, so if we had not received news of you, you might well have had a visit from someone from the family." Since the Flauberts were worried on the 17th, Gustave must have departed at least three days before, hence, close to the date he had set in December. On the other hand, he writes to Ernest toward the end of January or the beginning of February: "I nearly popped off in the hands of my family (where I had gone to spend two or three days recovering from the awful scenes I had witnessed at Hamard's)."

Most commentators consider that the letter to Chevalier alludes to the *first* crisis, that is, to the one at Pont-l'Évêque. According to this supposition, Gustave would have left for Paris, nervous but unscathed, around 15 January. At Caroline's entreaty, he would have paid a visit to Hamard, who had just lost his mother, *after* 17 January.[1] Shaken by the "awful scenes," he would have returned to his family around the 20th to calm down a little before getting back to his studies.

The incident at Pont-l'Évêque would have happened during the two days that followed his arrival at Rouen, since he writes that he had "come to spend *two or three days*." We could then safely locate the event between 20 and 25 of January—closer to the 20th if Gustave left Paris without warning, in a sort of retreat; closer to the 25th if he had first wanted to inform his parents—by a note which is now lost.[2]

This commonly accepted thesis is countered by Jean Bruneau, who contends that the crisis of Pont-l'Évêque had taken place *before* the 15th, during Flaubert's first visit to Rouen. It "could not have inordinately worried the two doctors Flaubert," since they allowed him to leave again for Paris. The attack that felled him, which in his letter to Ernest he calls "a miniature apoplexy," would thus be a *second* crisis, more serious than the first, and would probably have occurred in the town itself, perhaps at the Hôtel-Dieu. In other words, the letter to Chevalier describing his "congestion" and that of 2 September '53 in which he recounts to Louise his accident at Pont-l'Évêque would not concern the same event. We would have to accept the following chronology: during the New Year's vacation, a first "apoplexy"; then, from around the 15th to the 20th, Paris; after that, between the 20th and the 25th—approximately—a second attack, of which we know only what Flaubert tells Ernest, that is, almost nothing: indeed, he mentions neither the circumstances, nor the moment, nor the place, nor the singular form of this new accident.

That Gustave *discovered* his illness at Pont-l'Évêque when he suffered the first seizures, no one doubts. The question—an important one, as we shall see—is to determine whether this discovery took place *before* his return to Paris or *during* his second visit to Rouen. We lack precise information on this point. However, unless Bruneau has evidence that he did not provide in his book, his hypothesis of *two* crises seems inadequately supported.

What argues in its favor is that Flaubert "had an epileptic fit" when returning from Deauville, where he had gone with Achille to examine the work the chief surgeon was having done on the recently acquired land. Wouldn't Gustave have wanted to see this "country house," which "was preventing" him "from working," and to see it *right away*? He arrives on New Year's Day. What is the family discussing? The country house. That is enough for him to fix a date with Achille: they will go to inspect the work in three days, or at latest by the end of the week. Therefore, according to Bruneau, probability requires that this unfortunate journey should take place in the first half of January, and as near as possible to New Year's Day. Caroline's letter alone would suggest it; it betrays the family's anxiety: "If you were not to go . . ." This is not her usual way: obviously something has happened. Having searched carefully, I see nothing else to support this conjecture except perhaps the fact that Gustave in '52, recounting the first accident, mentions simply "the house where my brother cared for me"; whereas in the letter of '44 to Ernest he writes that he was given three simultaneous bleedings.

What are we to make of these hypotheses? That they have very little foundation. We know that, on 20 December, Flaubert was delighting in the thought of the country house that his father was going to have built. Let us note in passing that in the two letters where he speaks of it he does not even say that he wishes to see the work in progress. Had it even begun? On 20 December, it seems they were still discussing the architect's plans. There is no evidence that Gustave wanted to go to Deauville, or that there was anything to see there. There is no evidence, either, that he did not go there twice: first before the 15th, and again on his return from Paris. It could even be that around the 20th, Achille-Cléophas, worried by his son's extreme nervousness, had the idea that a journey by cabriolet followed by a brief visit to the seashore would help calm him down. Thus, the attack could very well have taken place after the 15th, in the course of either a first or a second return from Deauville to Rouen.

There remains Caroline's anxiety. But no one doubts that during the New Year's vacation Flaubert appeared tormented, or that certain troubles of previous years recurred during his period at home. Besides, the postscript is curious: "Papa read your letter and said nothing to me about your arm, but here is my prescription: rest and grease." Flaubert was complaining of an arm: had he bruised a muscle? His father takes the letter from Caroline's hands, reads it in silence, and gives it back without a word; so the problem Gustave mentioned was a minor one. In any case, this is not the attitude of a doctor who feared the return of a "miniature apoplexy." Besides, is it conceivable that the two doctors Flaubert would have allowed Gustave to return if Achille had "thought for ten minutes that he was dead"? Maxime tells us that Achille, at Pont-l'Évêque,[3] "hoped, though he didn't really believe it, that the crisis would not be repeated," and that the father "was in despair." Certainly he is a doubtful witness and begins by mistaking the date and the place. But he had seen Flaubert during the winter of '44 and took this information from him. If the two doctors had allowed him to depart after the attack, Gustave's resentment would have prompted him to point out this huge professional error to Maxime, who would have taken pleasure in reporting it to us: Du Camp's testimony, in fact, aims at denigrating Achille-Cléophas by presenting him as a disciple of {the French physician François-Joseph-Victor} Broussais, "who doesn't know how to do anything but bleed people."

And then, if Gustave *had already* suffered his crisis by 17 January, his father's diagnosis would already have been made: cerebral congestion. In this case, the family's anxiety—as it becomes apparent through Caroline's letter—seems rather feeble: if he was in danger of a relapse, if to survive he urgently needed bleeding, it would not have sufficed to send someone to Paris; they should not have let him out of their sight. The words "we were afraid that you had been ill . . . , you might well have had a visit from someone from the family" are justified only in a case of *moderate urgency*. If Flaubert was really subject to bouts of apoplexy, this "someone from the family," at the end of a long journey, was in serious danger of finding a decomposing corpse at rue de l'Est. The sentence becomes clear, on the other hand, if we suppose that Gustave left his family without notable incident but in an alarming mental state. When he arrives at the Hôtel-Dieu, he has just spent a day at Vernon with the Schlesinger family; he is certainly relaxed, happy. But the next day, a change of scene: in Paris, Rouen was hope, happy expectation, escape; now the expectation remains but offers up its true meaning: it is the Parisian prison that he awaits, the dreadful repetition of the already done, the already seen. He wouldn't dream of resisting, but in the inflexible temporalization that leads him toward a future so near and so detested he sees the symbol of his entire life, drawn by that other-future, the *profession*. From one day to the next he grows more nervous, more irritable; he is sometimes depressed, sometimes overexcited, always anxious.

We shall say that the disorders are nonsignifying because they are symptomatic of neither an identifiable illness, nor an enterprise, nor a hidden intention: they simply indicate that Flaubert lives with increasing exasperation a contradiction that can be neither borne nor transcended. If these disorders expressed anything, it would be the structural disarray of an unhappy young man who does not know what to do, who doesn't even take it into his head to devise a solution, who is at once convinced of the fate that awaits him and unable to believe in it; in sum, the disorders present themselves exactly for what they are: meaningless agitations that take the place of an impossible and even inconceivable behavior in a tormenting but unrealizable situation. Overexcitement feeds on itself: he sleeps badly, no doubt, scarcely eats, drinks too much. He flies into a rage over nothing. Maxime claimed that these disturbances were a consequence of his illness—rather quickly assimilated to epilepsy. "At the least incident disturbing the extreme quiet of his existence, he would go off his head. I have seen him shouting and running around his apartment because he couldn't find his penknife."

When Did the Event—the Total Collapse—Happen?

But we have enough familiarity with his youthful works and the correspondence to know that these disorders long preceded the illness: Gustave's impulse to shout, to bellow, to smash everything, his sudden desire to throw himself on passersby and massacre them did not begin just yesterday. It seems certain that these "itchings"—as he himself calls them—or these panics probably grew in frequency and intensity at the beginning of January, to the point that the family finally took notice. For Achille-Cléophas, the tremors have *one* very precise meaning: they remind him of the "illness" which, from '39 to '42, compelled him to keep Gustave near him. Isn't his son cured, then? He lets him depart, nonetheless, but in this hypothesis his behavior is perfectly comprehensible; his paternal obstinacy aside, he does not want to "settle" his son into his illness by taking its vague symptoms too seriously: nothing could be worse for Gustave, he thinks, than to be authorized to interrupt his studies and once more sequester himself in his room. The father promises himself to watch over his son from a distance; after all, isn't Dr. Cloquet keeping an eye on him? For the moment, the paterfamilias intends to make no change of plans. Gustave must have left in a state of extreme despondency; for this reason his mother and sister are worried by his silence; and if it had lasted, one of them would have come to settle in at rue de l'Est; this is the meaning of "someone from the family." A woman to watch over him, to look after his needs while awaiting the father's decisions, and, *especially*, to "boost his morale." What the Flauberts dread, on 17 January, is not the return of a definite attack but the physical effects of solitude and anguish.

In the letter to Ernest of January–February 1844, we find a confirmation of our conjectures. This time *an* attack has taken place, and he says so. Is it the first? The second? What is certain is that the description he gives of it can be applied precisely to the attack at Pont-l'Évêque. For ten minutes Achille thought I was dead, he would write in '52; and in '44: "I almost popped off in the hands of my family." Then I was bled, he tells Louise. And to Ernest he speaks of a triple bleeding. In both letters he says that he "opened his eyes again." Both mention the bad case of nerves that follow the "resurrection," etc. It is not conclusive, of course, that both letters are describing the same attack; the first attacks, in any case, must have closely resembled each other. But if the accident he reports to Chevalier is not the first, why doesn't he tell him that an earlier one preceded it?

To be sure, he is not always sincere with his old friend. But what need does he have to conceal this particular truth from Ernest? Subsequently, between February and June, he readily speaks to him of his attacks, in the plural: "My last major attack," etc. Why not mention the original one? The lie would not jibe with a certain attitude Gustave took toward his ailment, an attitude we shall discuss shortly; it would also be absurd because unmotivated. Forgetfulness? Negligence? Quite the contrary: although he nowhere says, "This was the first time it happened to me," everything suggests that it was. Gustave is still astonished; he tells of his adventure with the importance of someone who has had a brush with death. But the most significant thing is that he unreservedly adopts his father's diagnosis, although within eight days he will radically challenge it.[4] For him to believe he was the victim of a cerebral congestion, he must have been taken by surprise: this can be explained only by his stupefaction at an unfamiliar event, that is, an event which is unrecognizable, unique. In fact, he will very quickly understand, as we shall soon see. And if by the end of January he had undergone *two* experiences of the same kind, separated by an interval of a fortnight, if before the second attack he had been able to spend two weeks thinking about the first and doing some soul-searching, we can be certain that he would have seen the second in the light of the first and interpreted it quite otherwise. To conclude: although firm proof remains impossible for lack of documentation, the strongest probabilities are that one evening at Pont-l'Évêque, between 20 and 25 January, Gustave fell victim to an affliction he had never before experienced. This shall be our working hypothesis. If the attack at Pont-l'Évêque had indeed taken place *before* 15 January, and if the two doctors Flaubert had treated it lightly, they would have found themselves in contradiction with the patient himself. For them, in effect, the second manifestation of illness would have been decisive.

The Event: Unique

But for Gustave, the only one that counted was the first, which he still regarded ten years later as the chief event of his life. It was at Pont-l'Évêque, according to him, that his youth was "concluded," it was there that one man died and another was born {editor's italics}. In the "attacks" that followed he never saw anything but weakened repetitions of this archetypal fulguration. Is such a misunderstanding likely? Is it believable that Achille-Cléophas regarded merely as a negligible incident what his son experienced as the "fatal moment" determining an entire existence? Of course, the good surgeon hardly knew his son. But in this case it was not a question of fathoming a heart: somatic disorders were manifest, and, for Gustave to have kept this terrifying memory of it, their intensity must have been extreme: he fell down, he says, in floods of fire, as if struck by lightning.

To the credit of Achille and Achille-Cléophas, we refuse to believe that they could have been mistaken. For if there were *two* accidents—the first at Pont-l'Évêque before the 15th, the second after the 20th—and if they were similar, the *repetition* would most certainly have prompted them to change their diagnosis. It was after the attack at Pont-1'Évêque that they were able to settle on cerebral congestion. But a "miniature apoplexy" does not repeat itself after eight or ten days without being fatal. If the attack recurs, and if the patient survives it, other interpretations must be considered. This is precisely what Achille-Cléophas did in February: before the cyclical return of the problems, he abandoned apoplexies and congestions for the diagnosis of a "nervous illness" and, perhaps more precisely, epilepsy. He must be given credit for this correct about-face: since it was made between the end of January and the beginning of February, he would have been capable of making it two weeks earlier.

In short, it was perfectly excusable, if the first appearance of illness is situated around the 20th or the 25th, to reach the conclusion of congestion, and then, with its recurrence, of a nervous disorder; on the other hand, if the accident at Pont-l'Évêque had taken place before the 15th, it would have been absurd for him to begin by diagnosing a nervous illness and later, when it recurred, to decide that it was a cerebral congestion. And that is precisely what we cannot accuse Achille-Cléophas of doing: one more reason for situating at Pont-l'Évêque Gustave's first pathological experience and for dating it at the end of January 1844.

Toward the middle of the month, then, the young man once more finds himself in his Paris apartment, deeply shaken but still unscathed.

For the neurosis to become structured, he needed to discover, during the trajectory of the return, the true meaning of passive activity: he does what repels him because he cannot find in himself the will not to do so. No sooner does he return to Paris than his despondence is transformed into a stupor: he *should not* be there, it is absurd since he cannot bear being there; and yet he is there; he came *willingly*, so he *must* be there. No contingency here: the necessary is indeed the impossible—and the reverse is also true. Merely being present between these walls seems at once an objective truth and a nightmare. The denial is total but passive, and conscious of being so; obedience—passive also but subsumed by the appearance of activity—seems convincing to him, like an underlying determination of his life: this is what will determine his future.

Thus posed, the contradiction can find a precise solution within him: his passivity must be charged with depriving him of the means to obey. This scheme is obscurely linked to this temptation to collapse, which will give that abstract, rigorous form its content. Nothing is said, however, nothing is known; and yet nothing is hidden, no choice is made: it is a matter of setting up an arrangement that may facilitate a future choice. At the heart of clear consciousness, by contrast, is resentment on the one hand (he did not find the strength to write immediately to his family that he had arrived—*as if* he wanted to enjoy their anxiety and prolong it awhile, *as if* he wanted to compel them to say to themselves: we were wrong to let him go),[5] and, on the other hand, a passionate desire suddenly to find himself at the Hôtel-Dieu again, in his room, and to stay there forever. But this desire is not only disputed by rancor; it can end only in dream: it poses itself as unrealizable since there is no conceivable means of satisfying it. Gustave said so in his letter of 20 December, and he certainly said the same thing to his father: on 15 January he will start preparing for his February exam. This is what was repeated at their farewells: "Good-bye, see you soon, we shall expect you on the first of March."

The young man knows he will have no excuse to renege on his commitments. But of course—illness. Yet he is not ill, just desperate. Simulation would be revolt and would testify to a cynicism of which this inveterate boaster of vice is quite incapable. Besides, as he knows from experience, it would be merely an expedient. For those few days, between the four walls of his room in Paris, Gustave felt as Baudelaire would feel later, "brushed by the wing of imbecility": the inconceivable realizes and imposes itself but can be neither lived nor thought; one can only fall into the daze or escape into the imaginary. He does not touch his law books: this time he does not even find the strength to push obedience to the point of active complicity. He waits—for *nothing*; he vegetates, oversensitive, a stranger to himself, in the midst of a crisis of depersonalization.

This was the moment Caroline chose to advise him to pay a visit to Hamard: "The news of Madame Hamard's illness made me sorry for her son; in less than two years he will have lost everything he loved, poor Hamard; go see him, for he likes you and has often spoken to me about you."[6] The tone is new; a few years earlier, Gustave, Hamard's friend and Caroline's brother, was their only link. Now it is Caroline who acts as intermediary, informing Flaubert of Hamard's feelings and dictating how he should behave toward his comrade. From the beginning of June '43, Hamard, who shuttles between Rouen and Paris, is charged with transmitting Caroline's letters to Gustave. He sees the girl frequently and regularly. It is true, they will not announce their engagement until November '44, but in this new year there is already something between them that is more than friendship. Gustave, who will feign astonishment when he announces the "big news" to Ernest the following autumn, does not know, perhaps, precisely that they are in love: he cannot be unaware that they now have a personal relationship and that he has no place in it. We are already familiar with his jealous rages, and, as I have shown above in my analysis of one of his letters, he will make a clean break with his sister—without telling her—the day the two young people make known their engagement. It is therefore perfectly clear from this time that he harbored a vigorous personal resentment of Caroline.

Of course, he could not help being jealous, but there is more: the little sister was his vassal; she lived in his dependence and was the object—he thought—of his inexhaustible generosity. Here another man unexpectedly turns up: there is no question of sharing her; Gustave must be everything to her, or she must be nothing to him. A vassal's betrayal is more criminal than that of a friend: it is the denial of *homage*. And above all it casts doubt on the Lord: he perceives that his "man" was his objective truth; without fealty, no longer Lord, just a poor wretch. Vassal to his father and to Alfred, rejected by both, Gustave was sovereign only to Caroline. By breaking her bonds, she leaves him *destitute* and causes him to fall back into a dark, hopeless vassalage; she ravages his memory by sullying the remembrance of their common childhood; beside her he was *himself*, a subject, an agent of history: she has returned him to his other-being, to his relative-being. In short, in this moment of his life when the failures are accumulating, he experiences his sister's love affair as a new failure, more profound, perhaps, than all the others. We shall have no difficulty imagining his mood when he reads the letter in which she enjoins him, kindly but peremptorily, to go to her lover's home. He goes, nonetheless. Out of a masochism born of resentment; it is as if he were saying to his sister: I shall go, nervous and morose as I am; I shall do what you wish; but you will see what a state this visit will put me in.

He has another motive as well. According to him, Hamard is "pitifully stupid." Once, however, when he was telling Gustave about his brother's death throes, he was fascinating. As we have seen, Flaubert observed then: "I didn't like it at all; that man humiliated me. He was full of feeling and I was empty . . . I recall how I hated myself and thought myself loathsome for a moment." This time it will be even worse. No sooner emerged from his first bereavement, Hamard sees his mother die and is about to find himself utterly alone. We know the effect these repeated shocks would produce in this unfortunate man: after Caroline's death, he went quite mad. Beginning in '44, at the bedside of his dying or already dead mother, suffering makes him fall into mental disarray. Gustave suspects it: half-mad himself, he goes to the home of a madman; unfeeling and wretched, he goes to contemplate a despair incommensurate with his own. Not that Hamard's unhappiness is deeper: it is *other*. Gustave's, most of the time, is lived intensely and for short periods: he calls it *ennui*, and at times must *summon* it by gestures in order to establish it inside him. The *other* has entered Hamard by breaking in: it imposes itself and sponges on him.

Here again, Flaubert thinks, is the dichotomy of empty and full. In fact, he is mistaken. Mourning is an unlivable emptiness, and yet it must be lived, no matter how; it is a discourse that cannot cease to address the other; remaining a dialogue, it experiences itself as monologue. Lacking an answer, in these real moments when the living person, amputated, feels the mutilation internalized, there is some phantom of dark comedy that holds in derision the worst suffering. Then comes mental disarray, prompted by the unrealizable fracture of a reciprocal relation whose reciprocity the entire act of mourning maintains in a vacuum. In order to realize an impossible plenitude, one resorts to the craziest gestures or loses oneself in meaningless convulsions. Flaubert is unaware of all that: empty, and ashamed of being empty, he is about to contemplate a horrible void, which he takes for plenitude. He has understood for himself that our misfortune is to be *lacunary*; he has generalized in vain—he is unaware that this lacuna is characteristic of our condition and is to be found in all our feelings.[7]

Of course, the reality surpasses his hopes. Hamard is dazed, convulsive; he probably falls upon Gustave and clings to him; he may even be delirious. Flaubert abhors him and finds *himself* abhorrent. He is cold, stiff, exasperated: he doesn't "go along" with it, and yet this appearance of plenitude fascinates him. He would like to establish it inside himself, this beautiful suffering, this opaque block of unhappiness, in order to fill his emptiness at last, to *realize* hell even as he scorns the man writhing before his eyes. It seems to him, in short—this is what disconcerts him—that Hamard does not deserve his suffering and that he, Gustave, who alone is worthy of it, is condemned not to feel it. At the same time, terror overtakes him: this fascination, already a temptation, may tomorrow be an attempt. He vaguely understands his pithiatism, as we have seen; he is afraid of autosuggestion, of letting himself go in an act of irreparable, fatal violence initiated by envy and self-loathing. Yes, he is transfixed by *his doom*: he wants to die and to survive, to play at once the role of mother and son, because he is sure that he can weep for only one death with that marvelous intensity—his own. He can no longer cut himself off from Hamard; apparently he returns several days in a row to the house of death, for he speaks to Ernest of *some* scenes that took place there.

This will not be surprising if we recall that beginning in April '38, he evoked—out of a generalized prudence—the "natural feeling that impels man to become impassioned by what is hideous and bitterly grotesque." What is hideous, here, is agony and death; what is grotesque is that despair which has mistaken the sufferer and gives itself undeserved to Hamard, defrauding Gustave. Two words make Flaubert's real feelings manifest: "horrible scenes." He is rarely so pathetic where a death is concerned. These scenes, he says, so shook him that he needed to "recover" from them. Yet the word *horrible* betrays him: it implies a certain blame, a repugnance, which is not contained in *terrible*. Hamard's *terrible* suffering *horrifies* Gustave. Precisely because it attracts him, it repels him. He must flee, flee these nightmarish days that he lives now at his friend's and now immured in his own room, trembling with fear. Here he has found the pretext for rejoining his family. But it is already too late. For what he flees is himself, the option that imposes itself on his shattered nerves. In vain: the choice is made.

Barely two or three days after the return to Rouen, he will execute the sentence he has passed on himself. So it must *also* be understood that his haste is motivated by a presentiment: if the worst must happen, let it strike in the midst of his family. First of all because the "survival" will be less painful, and second because it will make his family eyewitnesses to the disaster they have provoked. We might say that he both retreats from this disaster and pursues it. Come tonight to Samarkand. This is what gives all its meaning to that sentence in the letter to Ernest: "I almost popped off *in the hands of my family*."

Beginning to Interpret the Event

Before interpreting the attack at Pont-l'Évêque, we must ask what role it played in that curious neurosis from which Gustave was to suffer for nearly ten years. Was it a warning signal, a symptom, the first appearance of an illness that would run its course, intensifying to a *maximum* point, after which it would begin to abate? Would this first disorder, original and definite, be followed by others, equally definite but of a different nature, which cannot be identified with it because, although they might have been the effect and expression of the same morbid entity, they manifested it at different moments in its evolution? In short, was it the initial stage of a complex and unforeseeable development, or did it embody the entire illness in a flash of lightning? Would this illness grow, overwhelming other aspects of his being, or, to the contrary, would it mark time, be lost in repetitions, in replays? Would there be, at least for a few months, a progression of psychopathic inventiveness, or was the neurotic structure completed at Pont-l'Évêque once and for all? In order to answer these questions, it will suffice to examine the subsequent attacks.

On those that took place from January to June we have little information: Gustave tells us only that they were numerous at first and subsequently became less frequent. On 7 June he writes to Ernest: "As for your servant, he is doing all right without precisely doing well. Not a day passes without my seeing something now and then like bundles of hair or fireworks passing before my eyes. This lasts for quite a long time. Still, my last big attack was milder than the others." In short, the frequency and intensity are diminishing; several years later, Flaubert will write to Louise that his "attacks" are repeated about every four months.

Maxime was not an eyewitness to the attack at Pont-l'Évêque. But he witnessed several of those which followed, and we have no reason to doubt his testimony.

> He grew very pale . . . This state . . . sometimes went on for several minutes . . . He still hoped it was just a scare . . . Then he walked, he ran toward his bed, lay down, as dismal as if he were lying down alive in a coffin . . . He would cry: "Drop the reins; here comes the wagoner, I hear the bells! Ah! I see the lantern of the inn!" Then he would groan . . . and the convulsion would lift his body . . . a paroxysm in which his whole being would shake, [followed] invariably by a deep sleep and a fatigue that lasted several days.

This description calls forth several comments. First of all, the basic character of these attacks is that they are explicitly constituted as references to the first attack. In a way, they resurrect it. But these stereotypical repetitions of the archetypal event are also weakened reproductions. The attack at Pont-l'Évêque had jumped Gustave like a thief: now the young man has a *warning*. An unutterable malaise and the impression of seeing "fireworks" serve as alarms. He waits, *conscious* of the danger that threatens him, and instead of falling as if struck by lightning he has time to go and lie down on his couch. From this point on, the primal scene is relived *in the imaginary* on the basis of a few indices, always the same, provided by memory. "I see the wagoner, the lights," etc. In a sense, it is *played* and, above all, *spoken*: the psychopathic aggression that Flaubert suffered he reconstitutes here as a *role*. The content is, moreover, debased: Flaubert often spoke of the millions of images and ideas that rushed through his consciousness when he fell at his brother's feet; they were "all the ignited rockets of a fireworks display." This incommunicable richness of perception—illusory but experienced—contrasts with the poverty of discourse, and consequently of thoughts, in the referential attacks. The wagoner's noisy cart, the distant lights, etc., make up the meager bunch of auditory and visual images or, rather, the assortment of *words* that monopolize his consciousness. It is like a conjuring trick: the patient *invokes* and *convokes* the false death that felled him one night. But it doesn't come: Achille believed for ten minutes that he was dead.

Maxime doesn't believe it for a moment. Cataleptic immobility is replaced by convulsions; these disordered movements, it seems, are born of the futile quest for a former state and the impossibility of reproducing it. Did the "fireworks" of thoughts light up at that moment in Flaubert's head? It is unlikely. He repeated, of course, that he never lost consciousness on those occasions. But the "catalepsy" at Pont-l'Évêque was favorable to "mentism" [the flight of ideas]. During convulsions, the jerks of the body suffice to occupy the consciousness; it is hard to imagine that they accelerate thought and foster ideas. *Physically* exhausted, the patient falls into a heavy sleep, and this is how it ends until the next time.

These referential attacks occur frequently in certain patients. Janet {Beizer, writer and author of *Thinking through the Mothers*} cites, among others, the case of a young girl who *reproduced* the terrible night she had kept vigil over her dead mother with her dead-drunk father close by. Autonomous systems, constituted *on one occasion*, reappear in progressively weakened form and are finally reduced to a symbolic skeleton, a few stereotypical movements. In Flaubert's case, a single moment seems to have assured the passage from a normal to a pathological state. The morbid creation and the *fiat* (the neurotic consent to the neurosis) are merged into a single moment on a moonless night in January 1844. After that night, the neurosis in Gustave invented nothing more; it seemed out of breath. As a result, no other disorder appended itself to the first ones; the illness did not develop, it had no history, it was maintained in the circular time of repetition: it was an *involution* rather than an evolution. Flaubert feels this; he feels that his illness *consumes him*. In a word, the only moment that counts is that of the archetypal event: in it, the neurosis is chosen, structured, realized; in the depths, a choice has taken place, four years in the making, which has willed itself to be irreversible or, rather, was none other than a consented irreversibility.

Afterward, for nearly ten years, disorders will occur that no longer have the same meaning, precisely because their purpose is merely to reproduce the original choice, maintain it across the temporal flow. The convulsive attacks are suffered yet playacted ceremonies intended to commemorate the irreversible, to confirm the patient in his neurotic option. We shall certainly have to explain the meaning of this eternal return. And, in a sense, the original crisis *aims* to reproduce itself symbolically. Be that as it may, the original crisis is what creates the irreversibility and will consequently be the essential subject of our study: we shall attempt to use it in order to illuminate the entire "illness."

CHAPTER ELEVEN

Hysterical Commitment

NEUROSIS AS RESPONSE

The Fall

If we wish to penetrate further into Gustave's neurosis, a summary of the "event" at Pont-l'Évêque is now in order, and provisionally setting aside the two systems of references, we shall attempt to envisage it in its concrete reality. There was a *fall*, followed by temporary paralysis. It is this fall itself and *as such* that we must now describe. And we affirm that beyond or on this side of madness and death (to die, to go mad, is not necessarily to fall) it presents an immediate meaning that is all its own: to fall is, in the first place, to fall from honor, etc. I hasten to observe that here we have a "popular" metaphor: what I mean is that it has been internalized by Flaubert but is not properly his. Although high and low are principal determinations of his space, he has internalized a social scheme.

What does belong to him is the underlying meaning he gives to the fall. As a common symbol, it marks primarily the passage from a higher echelon of the accepted hierarchy to a lower one. Gustave sees even more in it: to fall is to cede to gravity, therefore to return, at least for a moment, to original passivity. Indeed, a man who falls causes himself to be signified by the world as temporarily dehumanized: he is no more than an inert object on which great physical forces exert themselves, the first being gravity. As long as he has not touched the ground, it is of no use to him to be an organism, he is no more than a mass. Most of the time, accidental falls are due to a loss of equilibrium. For Flaubert in

January '44, the fall—the return to the state of inorganic materiality—is the consequence of a muscular resolution, a sudden weakening of tone in the muscles that support upright posture.

I am pushing ahead a little, and it is not clear whether we are dealing in fact with a generalized loss of tone rather than a sudden tension of the opposing muscles. Was Gustave "betrayed" by his body, or did he fall at his brother's feet in imitation of the *suffered* collapse? In the latter hypothesis, we would find ourselves confronted by a behavior closer in appearance to simulation. It must not be forgotten, however, that in the former hypothesis the muscular resolution in this particular case can result only in a modification of the nervous influx. Thus, in any event, the origin of the phenomenon is central. Similarly, when he is down, the fact that he finds it impossible to move or even to open his eyes can be conceived equally as resulting from a contraction of the striated muscles or from a neural disconnection, such as we experience during sleep when we feel literally incapable of moving a finger. For my part, I lean toward this latter interpretation without entirely excluding the first: fascinated by the cold and polished metal of the night, Gustave may have gradually put himself into a neurovegetative state. As we have seen, the decisive factor was belief and not revolt or affirmation.

In any event, this problem is of only minor interest to us. If Gustave's behavior is the result of sudden muscular contractions (like the spasms in referential attacks), we can easily assure ourselves that although it *seems* to betray some simulation, there is none. Whatever our interpretation, the disorders at Pont-l'Évêque are organized under the direction of a vigorous, autonomous scheme, which we can call psychomotor because it has imposed itself on Flaubert's body and sensibility for many years. From the beginning of this study, we have had occasion to point out that the scheme of verticality conditioned the child, then the adolescent. He raises himself up or throws himself down. Behind the description of his ascents, we have often discovered actual falls. Furthermore, most of the time it is not true that he rises to the heavens unaided: he is lifted, and it is the Devil who kidnaps him, only to let him fall like Smarh into a nothingness where he will twist and turn endlessly. In short, negative verticality, passive descent, yielding to one's own weight is a dominant theme, and the pseudoascents, still passive, spontaneously turn into tumbles. The future tumble is inscribed in advance in these pseudoascents as their underlying meaning and their purpose, signaled from the moment of his takeoff by dizziness and fear. Smarh, clinging to Satan's coattails, is a mass that is terrified to be the object of universal gravity. Nothing like this would be imagined if an actual Assumption were in question.

In the preceding chapters, the theme of negative verticality appeared to us as an organization of the imaginary. And that must be so, for we have discerned it especially in Gustave's fictional works. However, we observed it just now, without any loss of its unreality, in its symbolic function—the fall of Smarh, or reversed ascent, or the false elevation of the schoolboy who ends by *drowning* at the edge of possible worlds—as well as in a more material though still symbolic aspect—the fainting of Garcia, or of the Bibliomane who displays his pain and his impotence by crashing to the ground. This fascination with absolute passivity did not come to Gustave from the outside: it is and always will remain the temptation of a passive activity that tries to resolve its underlying contradiction (the necessity of praxis and constituted passivity of lived experience) by forcing one of the terms, by seeking through it to realize the pathetic element as an absolute. Thus the reclining mortuary figures—whose status he envies—have fallen, overtaken by death, and their perishable flesh has been replaced by stone; this petrification, and not real death, is what the young author of *Novembre* covets. The fall and mineralization are one and the same.

Of course, these are dreams. But the dreams, so often repeated, bear witness to an *exis* of the imagination.[1] Once solicited, the imagination will construct all the concrete images demanded of it within the framework of negative verticality conceived as a return *to* the mineral state. We all have our own guiding schemes, and we surpass them by the singular inventions they structure. But rarely has a writer set down rules so meager and constraining. The ironclad law that compels him to playact his being with the means at hand, to determine himself in the unreal lived according to negative verticality and passivity, can be taken as constitutive of his unreality.

All the evidence suggests that this structure of being overflows the fictions and is lived equally as a real impulse of his ordinary existence. Originally there was the stupor of a wretched boy fascinated by the world, but there were also those very real falls which, as a child, landed him on the floor, headfirst, when he was engrossed in his readings, as if, incapable of the marginal vigilance necessary to remain upright, he no longer reacted as an organism and was transformed into a purely mechanical system. The falls are not *only* imaginary, nor are those vague impulses to suicide that push him to throw himself out the window, to hurl himself from the height of a sea wall into the black waves that "detonate like cannons." This suicidal scheme is so imperious in him that much later, in 1875, when he recounts the life of Saint Julian the Hospitaller, he writes: "He resolved to die. And one day when he found himself at the rim of a fountain, as he leaned over to gauge the depths of the water . . ."[2] One would expect this turbulent captain, this violent and bloody hunter, to fall on his sword. But the author, out of love, chooses for him that most feminine of deaths: drowning. He leans, leans, and if it had not been for an unforeseen event, which we shall discuss later, he would have let himself fall headfirst, dragged down by his weight to be swallowed up in his own reflection.

These remarks indicate that during the crisis of Pont-l'Évêque, and on that level, *morbid invention* counts for very little. True, he has fallen; he has become an inert mass, his brother and neighbors had to carry him like a sack of potatoes to the nearest house and lay him down on the table where Achille was going to treat him. But he had been carrying every aspect of this behavior inside him from his childhood: a dream of abdication, a desire to fall, to be one with earth or water, with the original passivity of matter, with minerality; he knows and acknowledges this primary theme, which is the organizing principle of his life, the immediate flavor of his consciousness, dreaded in real existence and considerably exploited in the imaginary. Beginning in 1838, his neurosis is organized—to the extent that it is organized at all—around this temptation. I'm certain that Flaubert allowed himself to fall like this continually: in Paris, he would fall onto his bed, his eyes open, his boots on; he may even have given himself the pleasure of falling to the floor, like Garcia.

These were solitary celebrations, offered to himself only briefly and behind closed doors. Yet they were implicitly, at least by way of an *anticipatory experiment*, the radical meaning of the attack that would knock him down at Pont-l'Évêque; for this was surely an *abdication* embodied by a loss of equilibrium and a fall into passivity. Even in the crudest way, the fall always signified the denial of the human for Flaubert, a role too difficult to maintain as long as the status of humanity seemed to him to coincide with an upright posture, the symbol of activity. But while this collapse offered a total meaning—and, besides, was consolidated as *exis* and impulse together—Gustave was conscious each time from the outset of being able to recover himself. Once up again, dusted off, unseen, unapprehended, he found human dignity once more. Indeed, if he authorized these descents into the inhuman, it was because he was sure of a return. When he threw himself onto his bed in the rue de l'Est, or when he set about aping the fits of the journalist from Nevers, all four paws in the air, he did not really feel he *was committed.*

Sartre's Dialectical Nominalism

{Editor's Note: Sartre urges us to be careful when we attempt to understand the empirical existence of things. For example, the person who appears to have measles is a person not only with spots but also with *these* spots. True, the spots can be identified as measles and treated as such, but one person may die and another live from the same medical treatment of these spots. Of course, in an epidemic of measles, the universal characteristics will be treated hastily; but this is itself a historical event that calls for a particular application of the universal. Universality is indeed important, but it must come to philosophy through a secondary reflection that is based on the existential awareness of the empirically existing thing as such. This movement to the concrete is the basis for Sartre's continual use of examples; it is an instance of his dialectical nominalism.}

For this reason, the accident at Pont-l'Évêque encourages nominalism. In itself it seems atypical: if we start with the universal, we shall understand nothing about it. By contrast, to anyone who has followed Gustave from early childhood, it is clear that the attack somehow reproduces a singular experience, repeated a hundred times, now sudden and suffered, now playacted, now imagined and attributed to a fictional character. At issue, here, is a protean behavior that mimics itself or lives itself or speaks itself, but gradually becomes a guiding scheme of Flaubertian spontaneity. The sole difference—but it is crucial—is that the January fall bears in it a deliberate intention of irreversibility. So the teleological intention is reversed: ordinarily, he *realizes* the fall (or is unrealized in it, if he takes it as a role) in order to enjoy passivity through it. But another barely decipherable, ambiguous intention is discernible in this abandon: the intention to constitute the fall as a revelation of his true nature, which according to him is absolute inertia. It is this implicit intention that becomes fundamental in the crisis. It is no longer a matter of enjoying a moment of his "nature," either in act or in illusion, but of obeying it; that nature *produces* the fall: it is Flaubert's *truth*, which external influences, ignorant or ill-intended, have vainly tried to mask for more than twenty years by imprinting on him, from the outside, motions that he could not *sustain* and that were perpetuated in him for a time by his very inertia.

On a certain level of meaning, the fall appears, as we have seen, to be provoked by obedience pushed to the limit: Flaubert has been *too obedient*, which presupposes that he admits to himself a certain power of activity that is, however, restrained and characterized by singular ends, that has been broken by being forced, pushed artificially beyond its limits, and deviated by substituting for his own aims objectives that are alien to him. But, underneath, the challenge is much more radical: we are no longer dealing with an illness, an abnormal reaction, but with the abrupt appearance, a sudden, experienced illumination, of the absolute truth. On this level, Gustave enjoys his passivity bitterly and fully, in the midst of total wreckage, passivity being conceived here as a negative power—passive resistance or the force of inertia. Despite the ill will of others and his own illusions—maintained through obedience—the truth is unmasked in a lightning flash and publicly denounces the bad shepherds. Triumphant passivity becomes a fall: and Gustave, who has so often played this role of inert mass, *recognizes himself* in this "thing" that *falls like a mass*, that reveals itself as mere weight, defined by its multiple relations to the great cosmic forces.

Therefore, to the extent that the Fall, as a unique possible response to the singular Destiny he has been assigned, has been in preparation for twenty years through various exercises, it reveals itself in a flash as a return to the truth. Shortly afterward, Gustave proudly states that one must live *according to one's nature*. He adds: circumstances allowed me to do it, but my will also had something to do with it. Which means: the attack was the rebellion of my true nature (I am not made to act, nor above all to enjoy), my merit is in having been able to understand that and in limiting myself henceforth to being only what I am.

Precisely for these reasons the crisis at Pont-l'Évêque, despite its public character, would be more symbolic than efficacious if taken in itself and enclosed in its instantaneousness. To fall, as we have said, is to fall from honor, etc.—so be it. But this is merely a humorous image; the real collapse accommodates itself splendidly to upright posture. One can, of course, measure rank by altitude. But there are other signs (badges, medals, uniforms, etc.) that allow dignitaries to be distinguished from the common people while remaining on an equal footing with the man in the street. Moreover, when Gustave takes a nosedive and crumbles at his brother's feet, two images interfere and become muddled: is he becoming infamous or is he encountering his essence? Neither: to fall is merely a symbol of infamy, decipherable for him alone; and although he is certainly a passive agent, inertia is not his status except metaphorically. I know quite well that he collapses with the conviction of destroying himself or finding that he has turned into an idiot.

But what of it? He will pick himself up exhausted, anxious, his nerves in shreds, *sound of mind*; he will be shaky on his legs but will remain standing and, alone or supported by his brother, will go back to the cabriolet *walking on his own feet*. In short, if it were *merely itself*, the crisis would have to be regarded as a metaphoric, localized totalization by which Gustave has gathered his grievances, his disgusts, his anguish, his resentments in an instant by affecting qualities (mad, dead, inorganic) that he has never really possessed. As such, I have noted, the crisis would have been inefficacious: indeed, as we have seen, Gustave will be a notary or an attorney unless an event independent of his will deprives him of the possibility of obeying his father. And the accident at Pont-l'Évêque cannot suffice to remove him from practical life: if it were not to recur, the young man would remain a few months under observation at the Hôtel-Dieu, then again take the road to Paris. This is the meaning of Maxime's sentence: "[Achille] was hoping, without much assurance, that he had just been witness to an act that would not happen again."

The older brother, who sees the attack *from the outside*, can still suppose that it is an isolated event. The violence and force of the manifestations, however, already trouble him: but he sees them as merely a sign of the possibility—strictly speaking, the probability—that they will be repeated, nothing more, for the brother does not know *what* is at issue. Gustave himself has a certain comprehension of lived experience on the level of nonthetic consciousness: a feeling of déjà-vu, of familiarity, gives him the obscure certainty that the crisis *will not go any further*, that he "will not pop off" in Achille's hands, or become senile. All this would be of no consequence if the fall itself did not present a counterpoint to his acknowledged inefficacy, a neurotic mortgage on the future, the commitment not to go instantly to the worst but to repeat itself indefinitely.

Nothing is as clear as that, of course: let us say that it is lived as a *beginning*. Not at all as an immediate and decisive rupture but as the beginning of an illness *that becomes temporalized*. And what can it forecast, in that atrocious moment when Gustave is incapable of forming a single thought, except *itself*, its eternal return? This unformulated anticipation is in itself merely a certain temporal density of lived experience. Obviously we are dealing with a *hysterical commitment*: the old vow to collapse is present in the midst of these disorders as a teleological intention, but we have seen above what form intentions take in passive agents: they become *prophetic beliefs*. On the surface, Flaubert believes that *in this very crisis* he will go to the end, but *beneath* this belief there is the implicit knowledge of unsurpassable limits (it can neither produce death nor structure itself as insanity), so that his actual pithiatic belief, deep down, is that the symptoms will maintain themselves indefinitely, which is equivalent to the commitment to repeat them as often as he must.

Thus we shall better understand Gustave's terrors and his feeling of sinking into the atrocious: what terrifies him is not really the conviction that *this time* he is going to sink to the bottom, it is his commitment—belief, in short, his conviction that the present disorders are equally more of the future, and that he is in the process of living the totality of his future in anticipation. The fall *had* to bring Gustave to the point of no return, which is just what it did: not in that moment—when it was merely a metaphor—but in signifying to him by some ghastly flavor of lived experience that the point of no return resides in the repetitive structure of the suffered event. The immediate future (I am dying, I am sinking) becomes the symbol of the distant future, believed and dreamed in a terror itself imaginary. Gustave's whole life will be changed from day to day by the intermittent resurgence of disorders that are always similar and whose referential character is present even in the original attack, although veiled by the desperate and sadomasochistic haste to radicalize everything instantly.

In this sense, of the two radicalizing metaphors it is death that will henceforth obsess him: it will appear to Flaubert on the level of metaphoric reflection, and in the light of the referential disorders, as the most appropriate symbol of his state. For after January '44 the young man can no longer doubt it: *he is not mad*; aside from brief attacks he has all his reason, and henceforth he will go around repeating that he has had a brush with madness but that, thank God, he was immunized. The one who is dead—Gustave returns a hundred times to this subject in the letters to Louise and in the first *Education*—is the young man who was still healthy but tormented by the paternal curse. The one who rises from the grave and allows himself to be defined by the repetition of the attacks is the young man with a *nervous* illness whose sensibility, as we shall see, has suffered a radical modification and who must forever renounce the "active and passionate life" of his youth.

Thus the collapse—undeniable *from the point of view of others*—far from realizing itself in a lightning flash as radical irreversibility, will be lived and suffered on a daily basis. The attacks, the affective void they provoke, which is at the same time the very setting in which they can be engendered, the affliction as an objective definition of Gustave's state by the paterfamilias, the sequestration—everything comes from the secret and terrifying commitment to *maintain* this state through symptoms suffered in the measure of the most perspicacious witness, the man who slices through lies with a scalpel and makes them fall to pieces at his feet.

Here the objective of the passive enterprise is manifestly clear to us: what Flaubert could not achieve in 1841-42 because he had not decided to *believe in it*, he now believes, and as a result he achieves it in earnest: by accepting himself as the shame of the family, he manages to remain in it indefinitely, realizing at last the way of life to which he had been aspiring in vain for many years: semisequestration.

Neurosis as Regression

The moment Flaubert felt threatened, as we have seen, he hastily left Paris and took refuge at the Hôtel-Dieu. Not to avoid a disaster he believed inevitable, but so that his mother, his father, his brother, and his sister could be witnesses to it. This reaction shows an explicit and immediately recognizable intention. Many people tear themselves away from solitude and return to die in the midst of their family, if they can. It is not so much that they are seeking physical help, but they don't want "to croak like rats in a hole"; in short, they want to recuperate their death by socializing it as a communal adventure of the group from which they came and which will survive them. Death will no longer be the pure abolition of an existence: recaptured and, if possible, transmitted from generation to generation, it will become a dated event in the family history, a determination of communal life surpassed but preserved, *instituted* as an imperative of the sensibility and as a repetitive ceremonial. The dying person desires to live his death as a passage to eternity by discovering it in the eyes of those near to him as an archetypal event that will henceforth be maintained in the form of a celebrated eternal return. Flaubert feels the weight of a terrible threat, but he hesitates with regard to the nature of the peril; in any case, he rejoins his family. Since he has wanted the group to institute the catastrophe that will crush him, the immediate proximity of the family setting is a direct entreaty: the attack strikes him down *here and now*, in urgency, because soon *there will be no more time*, because he has only two or three days, and once he has passed this ultimate limit he will have to suffer the attack in solitude. In short, he abandons himself to it at Pont-l'Évêque so as not to be its victim in Paris.

Beneath this first intention—so common that it does not permit interpretation of his illness in its singularity—we shall easily discover another, which is more personal to him: he harbors the desire to plunge his family into remorse—they will be seized with horror if they see him struck down at their feet. But, in a way, this negative intention aims at something imaginary: Flaubert is inclined to give himself the (unreal) satisfaction of moving Achille-Cléophas to a repentance that, in any event, the father will not feel. This bitter and insubstantial pleasure can be lived only in the most atrocious solitude, at the price of a difficult *derealization*—at the edge of autism and madness. He will come to it, as I shall show in this chapter. But we know the ambivalence of his filial feelings. Nor should it surprise us first to encounter in him another, more positive intentional level.

Indeed, if we reread the letter to Ernest, one sentence stands out dramatically: there is a kind of felicitous fatuity about it, out of place as it is in the sad enumeration of Gustave's ills: "I nearly popped off in the hands of my family." To communicate the simple news of his "congestion," three words would have sufficed: "I nearly croaked." But—whether or not he is explicitly conscious of it—this dry information could not satisfy Gustave, it would not take account of the concrete event in its synthetic unity, it would be an abstraction. The originality of the crisis is expressed in these strictly inseparable terms, which must be read as a single movement: "pop-off-in-the-hands-of-my-family." His false death is familial, it is a *restoration* of the Flaubert group through the sacrifice of the younger brother. Until then, this student, past his majority and enfranchised, by spending several days with his relations could be said to be living *with* them or even, strictly speaking, to be living off them. But he was about to leave, take his exams, enter a profession that would permit him to reproduce his life through his work. And now the catastrophe has put him back "in their hands." These words at first suggest the anxious solicitude of *all* the Flauberts, gathered at his bedside, clutching his body with their eight pairs of hands to wrench him away from death.

From this point of view, the intention is clear: unloved children injure or burn themselves to reawaken love. So it is with Gustave; we know that he dreams of making his father weep; here is the chance to do it. When Maxime came to pay him a visit, Achille-Cléophas was still tormented, but the family no longer feared for the life of their younger son, nor even for his reason. It was Flaubert himself who informed his friend that the paterfamilias "was desperate." What gives Du Camp's narrative its strange flavor—even if we take no account of this author's malicious intentions—is the juxtaposition of contradictory information obviously furnished by Gustave alone: "He saw no other remedy than bleeding to excess"—that is what satisfied the younger son's *resentment*. In the "father's despair" we have the fulfillment of his frustrated desire as loving vassal. The father weeps, and the patient, immobile and mute, thinks ecstatically: "So he did love me!" The letter to Ernest confirms this, the tone of certain passages does not deceive: "My father wants to keep me here for a long time and to treat me attentively, *although my morale is good*."[3] You have read correctly: Gustave, if it were up to him, would take several weeks of rest and gaily return to Paris. But it is the father who *wants* to keep him: a superfluous precaution, no doubt, but one that Gustave accepts as an act of love.

The slyboots! Look how he has reversed the situation! Now it is his father who orders him to interrupt his studies, and it is Gustave who *agrees, out of obedience*, so as not to plunge the family into anguish, not to return to his beloved room in the rue de l'Est, to interrupt *sine die* his passionate reading of the Civil Code. And the strange thing is that it is true: by the sacrifice at Pont-l'Évêque, he has compelled the head of the family to withdraw him from the world and from active life. With what delight does he submit to the decision of his master!

But what makes his comfort complete is the promise that accompanies this decision: "My father wants . . . to treat me attentively." It is not simply a question of keeping him at home: Achille-Cléophas is constantly engaged in caring for him; here he is, that overworked physician who had eyes only for Big Brother Achille, finding the time to watch over his younger son attentively, to pay *attention* to him. Gustave's triumph—discreet but visible—enlightens us as to one of the chief meanings of his collapse: when he is struck down at his brother's feet, it is not only out of masochism. Death and madness, no doubt, transform him *into an object*. He is *pliable*, and if he "nearly popped off," it was in the hands of his rival, the detested usurper.

But he makes himself an object in order to *become the object of care*. Since he does not go to the end of either death or insanity, the two doctors Flaubert must try to cure him. Certainly he is ashamed to entrust his destiny, his life, to his enemy brother, and his fall is a prostration. On the other hand, he compels Achille-Cléophas's representative to behave as his father would have done, to bend over his younger son, to fear the worst, to try everything to save him. In short, he restores to him his function of benevolent big brother. Adult, married, a father, waiting to inherit the responsibilities of the chief physician, Achille leads *his* life; always bound on the deepest level to Achille-Cléophas, he has taken his distance in relation to the other Flauberts. Gustave compels him, by means of the care required by his condition, to reenter the family circle, of which the younger brother has suddenly become the center through his unforeseen fall. The tormented face of the young Doctor Flaubert at this moment prefigures that of the paterfamilias, until now excessively severe, ironic, and often irritated; that of the mother, austere, a bit distracted, and too often glacial; that of the traitor Caroline, who forgets him for a Hamard—all those faces that in a few hours will be turned toward Gustave, anxious or imploring. An object, certainly, since mute, blind, paralyzed, he mimics the inertia of an object, but an object of love, *at last*, he awaits the gentle murmurings at his bedside, the respectful silences, the looks filled with tenderness. He goes still further, and if he abandons himself to false death it is not in order to "pop off" but to abdicate "in the hands" of his family. He feels a certain self-indulgence in writing: "*They will make me* take the sea air early this year, *they will subject me* to a good deal of exercise and especially to a good deal of calm." This reveals the underlying meaning of his passive option: naked, fragile, defenseless, his powerlessness as patient must restore to him the powerlessness of the nursing infant. Through death and madness, he aspires to *regress* to his protohistory.

He prepares to receive the expected medical care *in the same way that he received the first maternal care*. These practices, conscientious, expert, and without warmth, have affected him, we know, with a constitutional passivity. But, precisely for that reason, he aspires to pure passivity. It is no accident that the crisis took the form of a *fall*, followed by paralysis: he has lost the use of all learned gestures, he can no longer speak, or walk, or even stand upright; Achille is bringing a newborn back to the Hôtel-Dieu. In that "fatal moment," is it out of antagonism to the paterfamilias (who condemned him to activity) that Gustave returns to his first infancy? Is it from his mother that he seeks to retrieve the firm authority that prevailed before the reign of the father by retracing the course of time back to this golden age? No, or rather not only: she had charge of him then, it's true; but now the father alone can give him the care Gustave demands, which is quite as intimate (he is "sodomized by the syringe"). Indeed, one intention of the fall—highly ambivalent, as we shall see, but we are examining here only its positive aspect—is to compel that forgetful and unjust father, that terrible, virile Moses, to become *maternal*, to treat his son manually, as Madame Flaubert did, to reconstitute the collapsed, decomposed body that she had constituted in 1821—in short, to leave his lordly, masculine authority at Gustave's door and to enter his room in skirts, to manipulate or sodomize him with a feminine gentleness.[4] To transform a progenitor into a progenitrix is no small matter: this, however, is what Gustave is set on doing from the moment of his crisis, and it must be acknowledged that the operation, promptly executed, will be crowned with success, at least until the end of the summer of '44. Above all, he attempts to start his protohistory over again by improving it, and to create a tender, intersubjective setting around himself of which he will be the principal purpose and which will make *all decisions* for him, out of love.

Here he is undoubtedly pursuing two complementary ends: to make himself the beloved child he never was by sowing anxiety through a sudden regression; and to palm off onto the Flaubert community all the responsibilities that crush him—including the obligation to wash, shave, defecate, etc. This second objective is perhaps the more important, because it concerns Gustave's mode of *existence*, in other words, his ontological relations to temporalization and localization.

We would be wrong to believe that he aspires to the condition of object as a lesser evil, or only to elicit love. He also seeks it for itself. When in Paris, he suffered his own activity as an alien force that he did not recognize yet had to claim as his own. He made no decisions by himself yet had to internalize the decisions of others and assume them because others needed him to turn himself, in the heteronomy of his spontaneity, into the conscious means of their enterprises. Thus, subjective intimacy was his damnation, for it was reduced to the internalization of instructions, which immediately became his freely accepted responsibilities. It is easy to see how, leaning over the chasm at Pont-l'Évêque, he could be seized by the vertigo of irresponsibility. If he finally fell like a ninepin, it was also to free himself from subjective intimacy and thus from the prison of internalization. Let others decide in his place, as they have always done, but let them execute those decisions themselves. Gustave will remain external to himself, he will have no more self, he will make himself the provisional incarnation of being-in-exteriority; he will receive from the outside the motor impulses that will be prolonged in movement if nothing from the outside comes along to oppose them. But this motive power will no longer have an "inside" to take charge of these impulses.

Let them do with him what they will, let them purge him, let them raise him up or lay him down, set him aside or carry him: Gustave will offer no resistance to them—except that of his weight; he has made himself unable to lend his assistance. What mortuary calm: he loses both the possibility of obeying and the dream of an impossible revolt; the ninepin declines all responsibility. For want of being a ninepin, the cadaverous state will serve his purpose better than insanity. Not only because it represents the return from the For-itself to the In-itself, but also because the theme of the becoming-thing of man has always haunted Gustave: Marguerite ends up on a dissection table, and an autopsy will be done on Charles Bovary. In between, what sullied, profaned deaths: the great man now a carcass manipulated by the gravediggers in front of a crowd; Djalioh is impaled; Mazza is naked, dead, violated by the obscene gaze of the commissioner, etc. This motif has a masochistic meaning that allows him to link the temptation of death to the desire to collapse. But it also contains a meaning from much earlier times, born in the days when Gustave and Caroline, by hoisting themselves up, could surprise Achille-Cléophas at his labors of dissection. The cadaver is an eminently *manipulable* thing; it is undressed, laid out on a table, its belly cut open; this primitive vision surely played its role in the crisis. The intention of death did not aspire so much to the abolition of consciousness as to a cadaveresque survival *in exteriority* during which Gustave, delivered up to his relations, would become the innocent object of all their enterprises. Starting here, the syncretism of the crisis appears clearly, for the madman, the cadaver, and the nursing infant represent in varying degrees a manipulable but *still human* irresponsibility. In death itself, the family tie—Gustave's *constitutive* relationship—is maintained: the body is, at the very least, determined as an object of ceremonies. Things will not go that far, of course; Gustave will survive, he will not fall back into childhood. The essential point is that he has had the radical intention of abdicating his humanity: nothing less was needed for him simply to be *ill* again, for his secondary attacks to be always suffered and never simulated. At the same time, the result he obtains—that incurable illness which defies Achille-Cléophas's diagnosis—while greatly inferior to what he expected, remains homogeneous with it: since the cadaver or the idiot represents *irresponsibility within the family*, his nervous affliction is a way of *living* this irresponsibility. Though not reaching back as far as his protohistory, as he would have liked, this regression is no less effective: it leads him back to his adolescence. This chronic patient is maintained by his illness in a state of extreme dependence; an accident has reduced him to the condition of the eternal minor, in other words, to the female condition.

CHAPTER TWELVE

Approaching Conversion

In this sense, the attack at Pont-l'Évêque is the crucial episode in his battle against temporalization. For several years now we have seen him determined to destroy the future—*his future*—whether by tearing himself away from human duration, turning himself into a panoramic consciousness and establishing himself in the Eternal, or by plunging into the pure present through hedonism ("the future will be black, let us drink") or through stupor. In vain. Eternity is not accessible to him, and even in a drunken state his present is structured by his future condition, his life is implacably oriented; he can *forget* the Future but not suppress it, and when he forgets it for a moment, he merely lets himself be carried blindly toward the ignoble end that awaits him. Made and suffered, temporalization is the woof of lived experience, its law. A sole means remains to him, the one he chose at Pont-l'Évêque: to kill a boy with a future and, by the same stroke, give birth to a man without a future. The man contemplates the boy; indeed, he has no other purpose than contemplation: empty, without passion, without character, without interests, he is merely the beam of light that explores a memory. His own? No; he says expressly: that of another. Nothing will ever happen to him because he has been made in such a way that nothing—except death—can happen to him.

In other words, it is a matter of constituting, by means of the attack, an entire life of passion, hopes, rage, and horror as a *before* so that the other, the survivor committed to contemplating it, may have no other temporal determination than that of being his *after*. And certainly Gustave is compensated for knowing that every moment lived in the present is dialectically constituted as a *before* to the same degree that it is lived as an *after*. But, as he will say later, arrogantly: "We are not made to live." Who is this "we"? And what does he mean by "live"? We shall soon see. Here we should merely note that an *after* without a *before* can be only an abstraction, that Gustave is convinced of this, but that by means of the catastrophe of Pont-l'Évêque he aspires to constitute an absolute *before* (his defunct youth, which will have no more *after* even as he annihilates himself by totalizing it) and, by the same token, a *pure after*, which, reduced to a pure remembering consciousness, can in no case be the *before* of anything of anyone.

This is the dichotomy of *Novembre*, realized by the false death of January '44. For the operation to succeed, he had to believe passionately in dying; and this same belief had to contain the intention to resuscitate the *other*, emptied of his richness and even of his personality, a pure transcendental ego, recording and unifying the debris of an experience totalized in a sudden lightning flash, then scattered by death. But let there be no mistake: it is not the dead young man that interests Gustave, it is the other, his archaeologist; he kills the first in order to save the second. This second, of course, can only be an old man. From the letter of January '44 on, the first in which he mentions his "congestion," the theme of old age, familiar to his adolescence, reappears in all its force: "I must be boring you stiff with the story of my pains. But what do you expect? If I already have the afflictions of old men, I shall surely be allowed to ramble on the way they do." This leitmotif has a multiplicity of functions and meanings in Flaubert. Here it recalls the "I would like to be already old" of *Mémoires d'un fou*, and its principal purpose is to burst the structures of temporalization: an old man is a man who turns toward his past and has no more future. Everything had been prepared; the day after the crisis that must strip him of his future, Gustave already knew the role he had to play to profit from it: he would live his affliction as a precocious senility. That would not be difficult for him; it is commonly said of people who have suffered or will still suffer a physical affliction that they are old before their time. And his other phantasms would accommodate themselves rather well to this new metaphor: an old man falls back into childhood; he is, like children, the irresponsible object of care and concern; everything is decided *for his own good* and without consulting him.

Here he is, then, immovable. In reality. So he has won against the world. We know that this theme is not new for him; he triumphantly takes it up again after the crisis and emphasizes it. "As for your servant, it is always the same story: neither better nor worse, neither worse nor better; as you know him, have known him, and will know him, always that same *kid*, rather boring where others are concerned, and even more so for himself, although he has had some good moments in society, in liberal society, especially, and is hardly prudish."[1] A little later, after losing his father and his sister, he was to repeat to Maxime: "It seems to me that I am in an unalterable state. It is an illusion, no doubt, but I have only that one illusion left, if it be such. When I think of everything that can unexpectedly occur, I do not see what could change me; I mean the basics, life, the ordinary sequence of days."[2] The superficial meaning of this second passage is clear enough: *after these two bereavements*, I have fallen into a lucid and permanent despair which can be neither increased nor diminished. And certainly this is what he wants to convey to Maxime; but we know very well that he truly mourned neither Achille-Cléophas nor Caroline. Besides, at the end of the same sentence he adds: "And then, I am beginning to take up a habit of working, for which I thank heaven." From the time of his adolescence he had desired immutability against his bourgeois destiny, and it was not the death of others that gave it to him but his own death in January '44. From that time on, he no longer changes, and the passing days are all the same: "Each day is like the other. There is not one that stands out in my memory," he writes to Alfred in September '45. He is not complaining, quite the contrary, since he adds: "Isn't that the right way to live?" The whole of the letter is moreover devoted to explaining the reasons for his serenity. Ten years later, returning from a journey to Trouville, he writes with pleasure: "Thus begins again another series of days like other days." And a little further on: "Nothing more effectively proves the *limited character* of our human life than *displacement*. The more our life is shaken, the hollower it sounds. Because we must rest after moving about, because our activity, however diversified it may seem, is merely a continual repetition, we are never more convinced of the narrowness of our soul than when our body sallies forth."[3]

This remark takes on its full value when we realize that it was made *after* his journey to the Orient. It is striking that, returning in the middle of the night to Pont-l'Évêque ten years after the crisis, he said to himself: ten years ago, I was there. "And one is there, and one thinks the same things, and the interval between is forgotten. Then this interval seems to you like an immense precipice with nothingness whirling below. Something indefinite separates you from your own person."[4] Indefinite because empty: one same, solitary day, colorless, endlessly begun anew. What separates him from himself is pure time, stripped of all content. Neither his bereavements nor Alfred's betrayal nor the meeting with Louise nor his journey have filled *his* duration. Everything has slid by without altering that "limited character" he gave himself in January '44.

He is referring explicitly to the night at Pont-l'Évêque, for that is where he gave himself immutability. Beginning in '44, he is conscious of it. To be convinced of it we have only to reread the end of *L'Education sentimentale*, which he started writing in July. Jules, of course, has had no crisis. However, without our knowing exactly the reason, a break has taken place in him: "The calm in which he wanted to live . . . distanced him . . . abruptly from his youth. . . . His heart [was] almost petrified." Turning back to his past, to the life he led *before* the break, he is "frightened by the vividness of his memories, rendered more vivid still by the presence of those places where they had been facts and feelings; he wonders if all of them belong to the same man, if a single life could be sufficient for them." Then he was not the "skeleton" he has now become: at that time, he *was changing*." "He looked at himself with astonishment, thinking of all those different ideas that had come to him." But a little further on—several years have passed—speaking of the present life of his hero, Flaubert writes: "His life is obscure. On the surface, sadly for others and for himself, it runs on in the monotony of the same labors and the same contemplations, nothing re-creates it or sustains it."[5]

Immutability—desired, proclaimed since adolescence, realized at Pont-l'Évêque—is, in a sense, the irruption of eternity in time, and as a result the bursting of temporalization. Gustave has chosen: to be *merely that*, but to be it *forever*; to define himself—in great part by negation—but to give himself through this minimum of distinctive traits a rough carapace, so crude that it resists everything. As we see it, Gustave's effort is to *change time*, at least insofar as it concerns him personally. If he is no longer anything but a mechanical system given once and for all, if he assumes the being-in-itself of things and of the past, then the irreversibility of temporalization made and suffered gives way to the homogeneous milieu of succession, that is, to the time of Newtonian mechanics. The time of history is abolished; the time of mathematics replaces it, a simple, indefinitely divisible recipient that possesses no efficacy in itself, that can exercise no action on its contents.

Reliving the Past of the Event

From this perspective, the future, the present, the past are not differently structured "existential" elements: we already know that the future moment—considered in its temporal *form*—will be identical to the present moment and to moments gone by. Flaubert goes still further: immutable, he claims that, for him, the future content will be nothing but the present content itself. Death and inertia constitute the sole means of destroying the primacy of the future and of affirming the perfect homogeneity of the temporal "container." Gustave has understood that time was *himself*; it crumbles, congeals, and thus deinternalizes temporality. He dehumanizes it as well, since it is no more than a universal and totally inert setting. To choose the moment, that infinitesimal suspense when the before and the after neutralize each other, the temporal image of Eternity—this choice is to cling to the present, to affirm that beyond the lived moment there will be nothing other than the restitution of that same moment. It is to deny his life the atrocious yet human meaning that he gave it under the name of Destiny. Destiny is dead: that dreamed destiny of the Artist-Genius as well as that destiny, so dreaded, of the great man manqué, the notary in Yvetot. Flaubert's existence is no longer *vectoral*, it has irreversibly lost its irreversibility. Better, it is a succession of empty presents, for the surviving old man can only be defined in himself as an inert lacuna. What characterizes him is the contemplation of the dead young man that *he* is *not*. Thus, since he is *nothing*, nothing can reach him; and as for the deceased, despite all his richness, time is without power over him since indeed he no longer is, or, which amounts to the same thing, since he *is-in-himself*. This choice of the moment could only be realized as the choice of *a* moment: a *fatal moment* had to manifest the madness of all human activities, destroying by its instantaneous lightning flash all the Flaubert son's projects; Eternity, by its sudden irruption, had to cause an instantaneous disconnection from our wretched duration. Indeed, if temporalization is the very woof of praxis, instantaneous options are by definition destructive.

Thus Gustave, at Pont-l'Évêque, chose to privilege a moment, the intratemporal negation of temporality: *something happens to him* (the moment is also the suffered time of the event) *so that nothing more will ever happen to him*. The crisis is born during that night, at that hour, out of Gustave's pithiatic fascination with the moment: he has stretched autosuggestion to the point of detemporalizing himself, that is, to the point of no longer even comprehending the reasons for that perpetual *postponement* which belongs to human reality, and to the point of finding the absolute in the demands of the immediate.

This passive option does not aspire so much to death as to death's view of life. Be that as it may, to achieve his purpose, Flaubert would really have had to die. He accommodates himself to survival because, behind that radical goal of the impossible, there is another one, more modest but realizable: to substitute for the vectoral time of history the rural and domestic time of circularity. Indeed, repetition too is a fine image of eternity—as the myth of eternal return demonstrates well enough; that which returns indefinitely at a fixed date is a temporal equivalent of immutability. And by mutilating himself in order to become petrified in the family setting, Flaubert was plunging into the universe of repetition (meals taken in common at set hours, ritual pleasantries, collective customs, holidays, birthdays, etc.). And this repetition—with the ambivalence we have underscored—was the deepest object of his desire, as it represented his return to childhood.

For this reason, as we have seen, the first attack bore in it, as an essential structure of its *meaning*, the intimate, *organic* commitment to repeat itself. Indeed, the subsequent attacks are exact replicas of it. Each is a reproduction of eternity or, if you will, of the fragmentation of practical time lived as instantaneous. Their unpredictable but frequent returns[6] somehow maintain the predominance of cyclical time, of reversibility, and of permanence over the oriented time of the Act. The subsequent attacks recur, always similar, like calendrical holidays, and finally they *are* holidays. Dreadful holidays, certainly—although less and less terrifying—but celebrating them has the purpose of maintaining Flaubert in the setting of repetition and *symbolizing* familial repetition. Indeed, since he suffers family practices in dependence and inactivity, the intermittent reappearance of a collective practice *affects* him—whether he takes pleasure in it or not—as would an attack. Conversely, these referential attacks, "under the aspect of memory," have meaning for him only if they take place in a cyclical setting.

When Achille-Cléophas is somewhat reassured, when they know—or believe they know—what must be done to remedy them, the attacks themselves become collective habits mobilizing the entire family, they punctuate Flaubert's slow vegetative life and that of his parents, as do birthdays and public holidays. Gustave understands very well that cyclical time is the degraded image of eternity, for he writes to Louise, in a letter I have already cited, that "our activity is merely a continual repetition, however diversified it may seem," which amounts, this time, to laying the blame directly on acts, denouncing them as illusions and showing beneath their claim to *invent* solutions to new problems the old circularity of routines and habits.

It is true, he will never change again. This choice of the immutable, in January '44, was not dreamed: it produced a real metamorphosis, a definitive blockage in Gustave of all living forces. Maxime, in his *Souvenirs littéraires*, writes: "As I found him in February '43 [*sic*] at the Hôtel-Dieu in Rouen, so he was to be all his life. Ten, twenty years later, he admired the same verse, sought the same comic effects, admired the same things, and, despite the true chastity of his life, enjoyed readings of obscene stupidity which never managed to disgust him . . . He seems to have had all 'his conceptions around twenty years of age and to have spent his whole life fleshing them out.'" The author's purpose is clear: he appears to pity Gustave, and all he does is disparage him, concluding: "My conviction is unshakable: Gustave Flaubert was a writer of rare talent; without the nervous illness that had him in its grip, he would have been a man of genius." Or, as he says elsewhere: his friend's "creative faculties" were "knotted up."

On the other hand, he sees Gustave's immobilism as the rigorous and nonsignifying effect of an affliction suffered totally by the nervous system—hence external to Flaubert's *person*. On these two points he is mistaken. If Gustave has congealed, it was intentionally, as we have just seen; and his refusal to change exists only on the level of daily life: the same readings, the same jokes, etc. From her early childhood, his niece felt the life of Croisset to be a return governed by the same daily rituals. But it should not be concluded that Gustave's creative faculties suffered from this; we shall see in the next chapter that it was quite the contrary. It is true that he showed evidence of a rare precociousness; yet he did not possess "all his conceptions" at the age of twenty but, rather, at fifteen. And the illness did not in the least *arrest* him, since its purpose was not to discover other conceptions but to utilize those he already had to produce *beautiful* works; if one could say of Hugo that he was a form in search of content, Gustave, from '41 on, might be called content in search of a form. Moreover, Du Camp's testimony, biased as it is, confirms the evidence Flaubert has given us in his correspondence. For many years he rejected maturity and its obligations, desiring a prolonged childhood or sudden senility: time was running on, however, carrying him toward the adult he did not want to be. In '44, he works things so that he can remain eternally what he is, and his false death symbolizes and realizes, at one and the same time, his passive choice of *living minimally* in order to change as little as possible.

This denial of temporality must be lived simultaneously as the choice of a new localization or as the restoration of a former *situs*: in effect, inertia is a spatiotemporal determination. The choice of *being-in-itself* is a passive refusal to realize life as an adventure, lest it become a destiny; so it must manifest itself as a pithiatic attempt to substitute for "being-in-the-world," which defines transcendence, being-in-the-midst-of-the-world, which is the characteristic of things. Facticity—anchorage—a contingency perpetually surpassed and preserved by the project, must, if the project tends to negate itself, become degraded as a material *being-situated*. To tell the truth, the object is never situated by itself: *it* is *the project* that a situation confers on it in our practical field.[7] But when transcendence is inverted and seeks to make facticity into inertia,[8] it must define it by an unlimited *situs*. The result is double confusion: interiority will be lived as exteriority, and vice versa.

This is precisely the *spatial* meaning of the passive choice we are examining. The collapse and the illness are aimed at integrating Gustave into the family setting. On one level, his motivations are to be sought in his relations to his father and to his older brother: Achille, the preferred son, is no longer *in* the family; he has started a family of his own and is earning his living. Gustave takes his revenge against the usurper by choosing for his *situs* the secret center of the temple; through his weakness, his fragility, his dependence, he claims a prominent place *inside* the group and thus avenges himself on the future heir, who, through his intelligence, his strength of character, etc., is outside it. On another level, however, the process of integration takes on a more profound and radical meaning: it can be lived to the end only in the form of *sequestration*. Not only because Gustave, upon reentering the bosom of the family by means of the spectacular crisis of '44, is tacitly committed to *never leaving it again*, but also because the collapse, once accepted, exacerbates his misanthropy and makes any dealings with others, with the exception of the family, intolerable to him. In this sense, not only does he seek refuge at the Hôtel-Dieu in order to ask his family to care for him and to protect him against new attacks, but he *hides there*.

Thenceforth, *place* takes on a crucial importance: walls must be built against men; certainly, it is primarily the family that *acts as his ramparts*; but walls, authentic and inert ramparts, become the objectivization of the family and, above all the objectivation of Gustave—his shell. Later, he will often lay emphasis on what a bourgeois tradition calls the "impenetrability of others," which he compares—as many others have done before or will do later—to the insularity of a group of archipelagoes. But an island can even more effectively symbolize the *domain* and the high walls that encircle it. Neither man nor things are impenetrable, but the impenetrability comes through things to man when he uses their exteriority to create for himself an interiority from which he excludes other men. By the act of appropriation of a house and a piece of land, the property owner unites, in a magical relationship of belonging, a set of material elements whose actual relationship is one of reciprocal exteriority; by an equivalent act, he presses these particles together, pushes other men out, and encloses himself in his thus delimited bit of space. In this way, man particularizes the thing possessed; but conversely, the singularity reverts from the thing to the man. By realizing *through gestures* the synthetic unification of the room and the house as the unity of his property, Gustave transforms himself into the *proprietor of that thing*; which means that his essence is outside him, in the possessed object. By conferring interiority on matter (each part of the house, insofar as the act of appropriation transforms it into a human whole, is *interior* to everything), he confers exteriority on himself; and that house becomes his exterior, through it he gives himself interiority as internalization of that exteriority. He has an "interior" which is simply the interior face of the exterior; he has an "interior life" which does not take place inside his head but in his interior, by synthetic connection with objects possessed.

Flaubert's life of the interior will become the basis and the reality of his inner life. It will be defined by its singularity, that is, by the singularity of the "interior" in which it takes place; walls will shield it from sight; light will come in through apertures opened by design; the present, as for {the French philosopher Henri} Bergson, will be merely the extreme point of an upended cone that is totally occupied by memories because the object possessed emerges from the familial and historic past in order to be seen at the level of the present.

This interior life will have its "depth," its "mystery," which represent purely and simply the opacity of its "contents" (namely, rooms and furnishings). Alienated from his room, Flaubert chooses to *be* rather than to *exist*, and to *have* rather than to *do*. At the same time he demands that a familial pact and a social contract acknowledge that in his room he is "at home," that others take responsibility for the impenetrability of the walls—the symbol of his own impenetrability, and, reciprocally, his desire for eternity. His passive choice of inertia, his choice of *being*, manifests itself not only by the decomposition of time into identical molecules, it is *materialized* by the lived assimilation of his existence with the *inert-being* of the thing. So the extreme solitude of the failed man, realized through illness, is merely the realization pushed to the extreme of *appropriation*, grasped as the movement of isolation that engenders solipsism, its most radical ideological manifestation.

The false death at Pont-l'Évêque is Flaubert's transformation into *domus* (at once into grave and into domain); it is the proprioceptive act (or rather its imitation) insofar as it realizes property as an enchanted thing becoming the objectivization of a man. The appropriation of the domain is what constitutes the infrastructure of the dream in *Novembre*: when Gustave envies the reclining mortuary figures, and when he wishes to be nothing but matter while remaining conscious of no longer being, he defines the condition of the property owner whose life, reproduced by the work of others and punctuated by the eternal return of income from properties, falls outside of praxis and makes clear what it has become through the real property that it unifies synthetically. In other words, the desire of the proprietor is ultimately to become the pure synthetic consciousness of his properties (of their internal-external *limits*, the inorganic inertia of the terrain, the vegetative life of the grain, the cyclical temporality of seasons and labors). We have recognized Gustave's old desire: he withdraws from the world of activity and of production in order to reconnect with the feudal form of society, where the emphasis is put on consumption and where work is disqualified or passed over in silence. He agrees to become a great man manqué and, worse, a *failed bourgeois* so that he may be transformed into a member of the landed gentry. His affliction will become identified, over time, with the house at Croisset; when it erupts, it is the conversion of a bourgeois to feudal parasitism within the framework of bourgeois property. Indeed, Achille-Cléophas does *not* live off the income from his properties—although it is rather considerable; he lives primarily by his work. When he buys lands or decides to build houses, he is merely following the general current of investments. If he "rounds out" his domain, it is neither through inheritance nor through marriage nor through seigneurial gift: he buys land with money that he earns by practicing his profession. As soon as it is spent, the money effaces even the memory of the former owners, and nothing remains of the complex relations of family or vassalage which from a certain point of view "humanized" feudal appropriation. This shrewd man is making investments, that's all. His fixed goods are his *real* property: the bond that unites him with the thing possessed—*jus utendi et abutendi*—is immediate and absolute.

For Gustave, everything is different: as a sick man he lives not off his own properties but off those of another; his attack forces his lord and father to support him indefinitely; he has the joy—at Achille's expense—of inheriting by anticipation; by supporting him, his father gives him an advance on the inheritance. The young man is a property owner by procurance, by *gift*, which restores the human relation of vassalage between him and the goods he uses. Moreover, he knows he will not keep that room in the Hôtel-Dieu where he wants to sequester himself. One day, on his father's death, Achille Flaubert's household will come and settle there. Thus the movement of appropriation is an effort of petrification that knows its own futility. Certainly, as early as June '44 the chief surgeon acquired Croisset—where the family was definitively to settle only a year later. But when Gustave moves in, he must already know he will not inherit it: it will be his sister Caroline's portion and after her death will revert to her daughter. Thus, from one end of his life to the other, he will have never been *at home*.

This does not mean he did not appropriate *his* room at the Hôtel-Dieu, or, even more important, the one at Croisset. What it does mean is that his possessing goods owned by others, goods whose use is conceded to him—provisionally or until the end of his life—will facilitate through its ambiguity the wide oscillation that makes this bourgeois now an aristocrat, now a saint. We shall have occasion to return to this point. For the moment, it is sufficient to observe that when Flaubert feels himself kept between the four walls of his voluntary prison by the express intentions of other members of his family ("my father *wants* to keep me near him"—later his mother's last wishes will be that they allow Gustave the use of Croisset until his death), he lives this actual nonproperty as a feudal proprietor and identifies with the *thing* insofar as it is already humanized and familial. In this way he can feel he is a lord in the essentially bourgeois moment of his reification. The room is *his* room insofar as it proclaims the seigneurial will of his father and the depths of a collective past. He sequesters himself in it, but all *his* world is already contained in it. By contrast, when he does emphasize the fact that he does not really possess his *situs*—and this happens frequently—he experiences the bitter pleasure of poverty.[9] Its walls and furnishings refer him to his image; long years have structured the hodological space of his study and of the house in such a way that his gestures and thoughts are stirred up in an order defined by the innumerable bonds he has forged between his armchair, his work table, his divan, etc. At Croisset, the room he has chosen on the first floor materializes the impulse of "rebound," the vertical ascent that must perch him above the world. And the "point of view of the absolute"—which will be style—has as its infrastructure the plunging perspective he has to take, from above, onto the garden, the Seine, and the opposite bank. But this objectivization of his person, even while imposing itself as his inert or repetitive being-in-itself and directing his very dreams, preserves some kind of slippery inconsistency, does not adhere entirely to the rooms, to the objects that surround him, simply because nothing belongs to him completely, and because the *situs* that characterizes him so deeply in his very interiority is at the same time outside him, in the hands of others, and on loan to him out of tolerance. Hence Gustave, carried away, can persuade himself that he has definitively broken with the bourgeoisie—defined in his eyes by real property—because he lives in a cell, conceded to him by the goodwill of a community, which could at any moment be taken from him; in short, that he is a monk, a saint, and has cut the last bonds that held him to our world.

CHAPTER THIRTEEN

Conversion

Thus the attack at Pont-l'Évêque has all the characteristics of a conversion: instantaneous, shocking, and long in the making, it renders Flaubert an heir, a vassal, a monk, even as it ties him to his room and leads him to objectify himself—a cadaver under a spell—in a real property, scarcely disguised, which will become the inert infrastructure of his immutability. *To be*, for him, means announcing what he is through his permanent possessions and hiding from himself the bourgeois character of this appropriation while compelling himself, at the cost of the worst collapse, to *receive as a gift* what he was being required to earn by work. And, of course, Gustave is also tempted metaphysically, for reasons we are familiar with, to abandon the dimension of the For-itself and to sink into the unlimited In-itself. In this pantheistic form the boundaries of property are suppressed. But this aspiration can be realized, according to his belief, only as a surpassing of appropriation. Appropriation must turn Flaubert into *this* matter so that he may accede thence to the material condition, hoping to surpass it subsequently toward infinite materiality, not by a real act but by a *mental disposition*—that is, ideally.

Indeed, the nonreal, nonpractical character of the appropriation—since what is involved at the Hôtel-Dieu, as at Croisset, is the property of others—will permit the proprioceptive act to slide toward pantheistic ecstasy. Work is objectivization; joy is internalization. The moment when Flaubert, in order to interrupt an odious labor, falls headfirst and hits the floor, he abandons himself to passivity, and that passivity is given him as the sign of his deepest being, of his constitutional inertia. But this negation of activity, despite itself, involves a *surpassing*: it is proposed as a capturing and internalization of the inorganic—in other words, as possession or, better, as the reciprocity of possession (property possesses its owner at least as much as he possesses it; the only difference is that the possession of man by thing is demonic, something we have elsewhere called *an inverse possession*).

The choice of being nothing more than a house in the midst of a domain bounded by walls could not even be conceived if this inert whole did not already present a multiplicity of human meanings: work—crystallized in its products—and especially *patria potestas*, the authority and glory of the progenitor. But these meanings, which assert themselves and demand to be internalized, are themselves fixed: inert demands, they put their stamp on material inertia; Gustave is penetrated by them insofar as they are the inhuman reverse of human significations. In January '44, when Gustave abandons himself to his constitutional passivity, he falls headlong into property.

I may be accused of going too far, of giving the crisis at Pont-l'Évêque economic motivations which—in whatever form—did not exist for Flaubert at the time. To which I respond simply: in the course of this book, haven't we seen Gustave dream a hundred times of *inherited* wealth? From '39 on, wasn't he calculating the income from properties his father would leave him, and didn't he see himself living off them in Naples, where life is less expensive than in Paris, *without doing anything*? If the situation of the Flaubert family had been different, if the paterfamilias, while disinheriting his younger son *morally* to the advantage of the older son, had not had the means to support him even after his own death, can we believe that the cursed child would have become a one-hundred-percent permanent invalid? The frustrations would have remained, and the despair and the constitutional passivity, but the neurosis would have taken another course. We shall understand nothing of the illness that struck the young student failing his exams unless we interpret it primarily as the "stress" of a *son of good family* for whom money *earned* is necessarily vulgar and who can accept only *bequeathed* wealth. It is not so surprising, then, if by means of a collapse that bears in itself a commitment to sequestration he resolves to live his condition of legatee in advance.

Through the atomization of time and the identification of his person with the *situs* that conditions it, has he really escaped temporalization? No, for what is involved is an existential structure. He will live it beneath a mask, however, as an *exterior* determination of his life which he must suffer and is powerless to influence. In other words, oriented time has not disappeared, and the cyclical time of repetition is merely its superficial representation. This underlying duration is now defined as the time of degradation and involution. In a sense, none of this is very new: Gustave, turning toward the lost paradise of childish loves, has never seen in temporality anything but its negative power: it distances, separates, exploits. And his passivity forbids him, of course, to instrumentalize it. But until the crisis, vectoral duration was *in him* like an enemy force, it was confused with the authority of the symbolic father, and even while reducing him through fatigue to a precocious senility, it carried him swiftly toward that other-being that was awaiting him and that he dreaded: his Destiny as bourgeois, as mediocrity.

In '44 it becomes a slow stream that bears him *toward ruin*. The immutable, by dint of being tossed about by the currents, suffers passively the slow deformations that are imposed on it from the outside: inert, external forces destroy it without its having any power to resist them. Or, if you will, he foresees that by their very return, the repetitions of cyclical time are going to harden, to ossify. Ruin is the thing that haunts the landowner: having made the exterior his interiority, he finds himself threatened by universal exteriority, even in his interior life. It is also the thing that haunts Gustave: his letters bear witness to it—as do his novels, whose heroes die ruined. Later, we shall demonstrate more effectively the meaning of this long sliding of things and beings toward decadence, and the course that the author will take in *Madame Bovary*. Here we need only show that he tries, beginning in '44, to duplicate temporalization and to replace Destiny (concurrence with his being) with Ruin (progressive deterioration of an inert motor by friction and deceleration).

Flaubert's Illness as "Murder of the Father"

If we wish to restore the fundamental unity of these multiple intentions and see all the attacks in their true light, we must understand that they represent above all a crucial moment in Gustave's relations with the paterfamilias. All the rest—whether the masochistic impulse that throws Gustave at the feet of his triumphant brother or the underlying connection between sequestration and income property—necessarily refers to the "object relation" that both binds Gustave to the chief surgeon and sets him against him. Indeed, until '44, in the very measure that Gustave has been constituted a relative-being, that constitutive relationship is established in relation to a double personage who is—simultaneously or by turns—the symbolic Father (at first positive, then negative) and the empirical father, a little too nervous, choleric, sometimes whining, often "lead-assed." In this relationship, Moses is the independent variable, the absolute being; dependence and relativity are on Gustave's side. Hence, the essence of lived experience for the child, then for the young man, must be envisaged as a discourse with the Father that can never take place.[1] A negative but unreal discourse, since the locutor has no affirmative power at his disposal and consequently no power of negation. A dialogue of the deaf that has been going on for twenty years; even through Alfred, Gustave is still addressing himself to the father. In vain; the definitive heart-to-heart talk will never take place, the fault lying as much with Gustave, a mute who wants to speak, as with Achille-Cléophas, who understands nothing about his son and does not care to understand him.

In other words, Gustave's neurosis is the Father himself, that absolute Other, that Superego inside him who has constituted him as impotent negativity (this negativity cannot be changed into negation and is inclined only to *positive* behavior—obedience, respect, haste—to achieve its ends, that is, to *deny* imposed Destiny). It is easy to conclude that Gustave's body takes charge, in its fashion, in the form of suffered disorders, words that cannot be pronounced: the fall at Pont-l'Évêque *says something* to the Progenitor. By mutely denouncing the vanity of activism, it symbolically condemns the activist in charge, first of all by forcing him to assume the consequences of a voluntarist education—this is what you've made me—and then, more profoundly, by challenging the virtues of any activity. What the agent takes to be acts is merely superficial fidgeting; one makes a fool of oneself believing that one is autonomous, hard reality takes on the job of disabusing us: we are matter, therefore incapable of spontaneity, and the impulses that animate us come from the outside and disappear while being communicated from the outside to other bodies.

In short, there are two levels of meanings. One is restricted: I *am* passivity, I cannot act. The other generalized: and as for you, you are merely an inert mass, buffeted by external impulses. Without being opposed, the two meanings, if expressed simultaneously through discourse, would merely serve to undermine each other. For the first meaning aspires to specify Gustave's singularity, as it was fashioned; it does not put the sources of activity in others in question and simply shows that Gustave—is it an anomaly?—is not made to act, that he has tried loyally, as a conscious subject, and that his "nature" has reduced his efforts to nothingness. By contrast, the second meaning, aimed directly against the father and rejecting the very idea that a man can be an agent, risks conceding the argument to Achille-Cléophas by affirming that under any circumstances one is *acted upon*: if we are all equal, you are not anomalous, and despite our universal passivity you can, like me, win over the animating cosmic forces. But Gustave, who in his writings is not embarrassed to expound two ideas simultaneously,[2] is careful not to express them together here. He uses all the means at his disposal against the progenitor: he tells him simultaneously, you are torturing me, I am not made for the destiny you impose on me—and, like me, you are merely a puppet; with action denied to man, activism is a ridiculous frenzy. Thus the fall as the offensive return of passivity aims at nothing less than destroying the very authority of the father; we shall understand this better by examining these two "languages" one by one.

We shall pass over the former quickly: his "death" at Pont-l'Évêque proves that he was not made for the future that had been imposed on him. Error or cruelty, the paterfamilias bears full responsibility for it; in a word, this is the discourse of resentment. The point here is to plunge Moses into remorse, and so Gustave must survive to enjoy his pain. The second intention is more complex. We have seen Gustave set against the empirical father who destines him to that minor hell, mediocrity, the ferocious Progenitor who has sworn him to abjection, death. The crisis called him from the former to the latter. But at the same time, it has another objective: to kill Moses after using him, and to allow a pathetic, highly excessive, and rather grotesque fellow to survive. As we have seen, the *maternalization* of Achille-Cléophas already betrays the ambivalence of Gustave's feelings: it signals the unloved young man's deep need for tenderness, but there is obviously a malicious intention as well, to ridicule his Lord by feminizing him. He goes much further, though, and gives himself the bitter and triumphant pleasure of being *badly treated*: "[I am doing] very badly, [I am] following a stupid regimen; as for the illness itself, [I] don't give a damn."[3] I have observed above that Gustave was contesting not so much the regimen as the diagnosis. Certainly he complains of being uselessly tortured, deprived of wine and tobacco, immobilized by a seton. But this is not the essential thing: he is being treated for a miniapoplexy—by multiple bleedings, which weaken him—when he is suffering from nerves. To tell the truth, Achille-Cléophas's mistake is imposed on him by the illness itself, which at the time can only elicit a false diagnosis since the nature of hysterical diseases is to look like what they are not. Gustave rejoices in being more in the know about what is happening to him than the illustrious surgeon of Rouen. Not that he is amusing himself by tricking his father—we know he is not simulating illness. But his affliction implies a certain understanding of itself, whose consequence is to demonstrate the incompetence of medicine—something beyond Flaubert's wildest hopes, which will be manifest *in action* through his daily martyrdom: in short, it is *as if* the patient were fooling his doctor.

"Art Terrifies Me" (The Real Meaning of "Loser Wins")

We have seen Gustave's distress when, at the end of *L'Education*, he attempts to answer for the work of art as he understands it—vampirization of being by nonbeing, center of unrealization, triumph of appearance as such, concrete identification of Evil and Beauty—sometimes by the Evil One and sometimes by the Almighty, which leads him to invert their roles, or rather to radicalize the inversion we encounter in his work, beginning with *Le Voyage en enfer* {*The Trip through Hell*}. This is what led us to assume the existence of a cruder and more profound "Loser wins," which regressive analysis allowed us to establish. In this version, it seems at first that the principle of Evil and the principle of Good are in place and correctly exercise their powers: Satan does only harm, so nothing is asked of him, he is made a fool of, that's all; it is God one implores, it is God that one seeks, groaning, it is from Him that one awaits grace. But if we reflect on it, don't we rediscover the same confusion in this terribly crude wager as in its rational elaboration? Not entirely the same, since the Devil is practically eliminated; but the Almighty multiplies his functions: all by Himself He plays the God of Light and the Prince of Darkness. Is it indeed the *good* Lord that Gustave invokes and seeks to tempt by his stoically borne sufferings?

Let Him hide himself, well and good. We have known since the sixteenth century that He has moved out: the laicization of all sectors of human activity left Him—from the beginning of merchant capitalism—no more place in space or time. Let Him take pleasure in torturing his creatures, well and good. After all, it is rather in keeping with the ways of the Christian God. And Gustave did not invent salutary trials or preach that pain should be put to good use. But he asks Him to guarantee the nonbeing of being, and it is not rightly His business: man can have access to appearance by virtue of his own nothingness, but the absolute Being is excluded from it by his very plenitude. How can Flaubert want the Creator of all *reality* to introduce it into the dark universe of succubus and incubus, which is the realm of Satan? And if the greatest geniuses are those "who laughed in the face of Humanity," if the Artist's purpose is to demoralize, if Gustave's desire is to write like an angel to turn his readers into beasts—even into beasts in heat—in short, if Beauty is Evil, is he quite certain of knocking at the right door? Has he changed since *Smarh*? Everything suggests the opposite: in the first *Saint Antoine*, as in the "Mystery Play" of 1839, the Devil and the Author totalize the world through evil. Our young convert smells the sulphur:

it is against Satan that he must play the game. Yet he would lose everything with no reward. Therefore, he must address himself to God: to a demonic God who would not be a bad Devil. Is there such confusion in this tormented soul?

Let us acknowledge, to begin with, that Flaubert has a penchant for black masses and has even taken himself for Satan on occasion. The legend seized him belatedly, making him a benevolent boor, but his contemporaries were not all fooled by it. Everywhere he announced his misanthropy; Jules himself, after several suspect enthusiasms, proudly confesses his hatred of men. Is this a reason not to invoke God? The churches are full of worshipers ardently imploring Him to chastise their fellow men. If wishing for Good were all that was needed to enter a church, churches would be empty. You retort that at least by all this black magic, by these antemortem and postmortem sanctions demanded out of goodness of heart, it is the Good that one claims to serve, and the believer, thank God, has a good conscience. Thus logic is saved if not morality: of the just God one asks only just interventions, which reward the pure and punish the wicked. Whereas Gustave, it must be confessed, demands that the Creator commit genocide. And later? If he judges the whole human race corrupt—without even excepting himself—between the desire that is savage but conscious of its own futility and the homicidal prayers of pious souls, there is merely a difference of degree. God serves Evil as well as Good, since man created Him. He even has the properly satanic job of making Evil seem like Good and Good like Evil, if only it is asked of Him.

This is not the issue, however. At the moment in the pitch-black night of Pont-l'Évêque when Flaubert resolved to endure the worst, he felt distantly, deep within him, the obscure need for the worst not always to be certain. In Gustave's mad stubbornness as he runs toward his doom, there is the somber conviction that the Devil gives nothing away, that his atrocious and definitive debasement will not even give him the chance to write. Consequently, gripped by the flashing terror that the truth of this world really is atrocious (he *believed* it until this point, that is, he played at believing it), he revives his dead God and puts himself entirely in His hands. There is no time for this resigned intention to be made explicit: in that "fatal moment," Gustave is concerned not with inventing new structures for himself but with recovering those of his childhood—which have always persisted beneath the black feudalism. Gustave calls the Father to his aid.

We have discovered, on the tactical level, that the original attack involved an intention of love: the unloved boy tried to find paternal tenderness in it once again. We understand now that on another level this regression had a strategic meaning, more obscure but fundamental: it was a matter of falling back again forever into the golden age, that beneficent time when the world was good, when the all-powerful Father and the gracious God sustained each other and indeed were one. In that golden age, paternal feudalism was the symbol of religious feudalism, and vice versa; for the little vassal it was the moment of innocence, of accord with the self. Beyond his present conflicts, beyond his resentment of the dark Lord, what the convert of Pont-l'Évêque attempts to recover is this identification of the Father with God, which guaranteed his personal identity. Then, pain was *merit*: one suffered *in order to be consoled*; wasn't this the underlying meaning of Flaubertian dolorism? Already passive, little Gustave had merely to display his wounds: they would certainly confer *no right* upon him since the generous love that enveloped him gave *more* than anything one could expect of it. But the merit was a humble appeal, and the child put trust in his Lord: he would be heard. All he had to do was to *abandon himself* to him, to follow the inclinations of his constitutional passivity, certain of being fulfilled. The future was already a destiny since it came to him through another, but it was a happy destiny. And here is Flaubert in January '44, at once one of the damned, sinking toward his doom, and a passive agent *abandoning himself* (simply because he will attain the worst only by *letting himself go*). But the meaning of the abandon—not only in the case we are describing but in general and as it appears to eidetic intuition—is *never* despair, that bristling, horrified, abstract tetanus, neither is it the calculated hope of the practical agent, but rather a hope without qualities, an act of faith in the future.

Something is going to happen; the Other, in whatever way, will take charge of this life that one refuses to assume. Such is the meaning of the "Loser wins" of Pont-l'Évêque: "Father, I am sick, take me in your arms and comfort me!" As if this fierce, total shipwreck had the effect and purpose of causing hope to be reborn, as if this desolate proof that Evil triumphs, whatever you do, could not be lived as a Passion without prompting the rebirth of a childish belief in the Good.

The real "Loser wins" appears as the inevitable counterpart of the determination to lose. Just when Gustave, drunk with resentment and unhappiness, topples over in protest against the black Father, against Satan—"Here is what you have made me"—he transforms this disaster into a human sacrifice of which he becomes both author and victim in order to attract to himself the divine benediction; or, if you will, it is homage that restores *good* feudalism. But obviously the awaited Gift cannot be *just anything*. God the Father is solicited by a pious boy of twenty-two, who has lived, whom a painful childhood has formed, who formed himself from it; when he asks that his sufferings be rewarded, he has long decided on the only fitting compensation—genius—and has long conceived of Art as a black mass. If God exists, if He is the All-Good, He *will give* what is asked of Him: His infinite and gratuitous generosity, the magnificence of the awaited gift that involves nothing less than the provisional suspension of natural laws, everything conspires to hide from Gustave the fact that he intends to make the Lord play the role of the Evil One and that he solicits from Him the disqualification of His Creation to the advantage of its diabolical image. Actually, he hopes for a boon from the Other. A boon for himself alone, a mark of love that comes to reward his merit: the contents of the boon, perfectly defined, are not put in question. Only one thing is certain: if Gustave's wishes are fulfilled, it can be only by a good Lord. As for the ordeals, the sadistic absenteeism of this high personage, that can hardly surprise him: indeed, his relation to the symbolic Father has been lived too long in ambivalence; behind the "eternal silence of the divinity" he will *assume-without telling himself so*, of course—the infinite love of which he is perhaps the object, just as after the fall, around the age of seven, he tried for some time to imagine that Achille-Cléophas's irritated indifference was only a crust that hid an infinite tenderness for his younger son.

Thus Gustave finds himself engaged by his entire history in a contradictory process which consists of earning through his painful agnosticism the Almighty's gift of the keys to Nonbeing, the Good Lord's bestowal upon him of the right to Evil, the Father of Man's authorization to demoralize the human race. Has he understood this? The end of *L'Education* would seem in this case to be an attempt—hardly conscious but systematic—to resolve the contradiction: if "Loser wins" is a strict succession of events, God is eliminated by Himself, His mediation is useless, and the reversal occurs automatically. In other words, we do not leave hell, since failure issues in nonbeing, or, if you like, since the impossibility of being represents the deepest essence of Beauty. Beauty, indeed, is not a plenitude but its contrary: it appears to the public as frustration; better still, even made manifest through a work, it *finds no public*. Jules doesn't even need to refuse publication—out of purity, out of fidelity to nonbeing; *the fact is* that no one ever offers to publish his works: were he to show them, they would be too beautiful to give pleasure. In *L'Education*, Art is not a reward for failure, it is failure itself totalized in depth with all its consequences: Jules, one of the living dead, takes death's point of view on life, all the while knowing, since he persists in living—at a minimum, it is true—that this point of view itself is an Illusion. In a sense, failure has *given* nothing at all except those famous coins that turn into dead leaves if you try to use them. But it is precisely the afterglow of the *idea* of the coin in the dead leaves that manifests the absolute contestation (derealization of metal by its metamorphosis, derealization of leaves by their past essence, surpassed, unrealizable, yet sustained by the reminiscence of that unforgettable entity, gold) and defines itself as a sorcery worked by Beauty. Jules owes nothing. To anyone.

Gustave Has Become the Author of *Madame Bovary*

At this time we can offer merely provisional conclusions concerning the strategy of this neurosis. It seems clear, in any case, that the rationalized "Loser wins," born of a rather profound intuition of the meaning of the fall at Pont-l'Évêque, was developed to the extreme by Gustave in a moment of alacrity that I place between June 1844, when the illness subsides, and January 1845, when the first *Education* is being completed. Consequently, as I believe I have shown, he rarely alludes to it, and it is the underlying and original "Loser wins" that explains most of his procedures as an artist. Julien is his man—much more than Jules, about whom we shall speak no further. Let us not imagine, however, that this rationalization was useless: as we have seen, it allowed him for the first time to understand *his* art. Moreover, it is not unthinkable that it remained inside him on a certain level, and that he did not speak of it for fear of the Devil.

At this point we lack two dimensions for understanding Flaubert's illness completely, and we shall now examine them in turn. First, the neurosis is historical and social: it constitutes an objective, dated fact in which the characteristics of a certain society—bourgeois France under Louis-Philippe—are brought together and totalized. In the next volume we shall try to compare it as such with other neuroses to see whether it might not belong to a family of ailments that appeared for the first time in that period. This study will allow us to approach the *artistic movement* around 1850. Second, Gustave's malady expresses in its plenitude what must indeed be called his freedom: what this means we shall understand only at the conclusion of this work, after we have reread *Madame Bovary*.

CHAPTER FOURTEEN

The (Second) Problem

{Editor's Note: Let us recall that this vast work began with a chapter titled "Problem," and now it nears its conclusion with a similarly titled chapter. The first Problem clarified the task that lay ahead—namely, of understanding how this "idiot of the family," Gustave, could mature to write *Madame Bovary*, which for Sartre is a thoroughly nihilistic work. The Problem now to be considered is why this nihilistic work succeeded. That is, why was it not dismissed as peculiar to its author but rather became the symbol of "realism" for its own time and for our time as well? Thus, the task in the roughly six hundred pages that follow chapter 20 in the original work and conclude the published part of Sartre's study is that of a new progressive movement, which aims to reveal how both the literary and the social milieus forged an "Objective Spirit"—a web of literary and social norms which was itself neurotic, and which meshed with Gustave Flaubert's private neurosis (more on this in my comments in the next chapter). Moreover, we begin now to understand Gustave's uniqueness, recalling Sartre's distinction between the singular universal and the universal singular: as we develop our lives, what is universal in us arises more and more from what is unique to us—but this process is different for each person as it reveals our freedom. For Gustave, it is a constant returning, and to his unloved childhood.}

Thus far we have tried to understand Flaubert's neurosis from within, to reconstruct its protohistorical genesis, its history, and to discover the *subjective* teleological intentions it constitutes and by which it is structured in turn. When I call these structuring intentions *subjective*, I mean of course to select and designate only those arising from his particular—originally familial—situation which have meaning with respect to his particular case and, when applied to an "unspeakable" but disturbing anomaly, integrate it with what he himself calls a "particular system made for one man alone." We have seen his neurosis develop, in short, on the well-defined terrain of passive activity, which also conditioned it. And we have distinguished two discrete elements in it, which can be separated only through discourse, namely, the primal disturbance and stress, a self-defensive reaction attempting to enclose the disturbance and to dissolve it, or at least to neutralize it, and which through this very attempt (through the general mobilization of lived experience it requires and its dialectical relations to that throbbing discomfort it encloses, hardly digests, then suffers as its motivating, and unforeseeable, determination) finally produces the greatest possible disruptions in the area of habitus and conduct. We thus perceived Flaubert's neurosis, intentional and suffered, as an adaptation to illness, bringing in its wake more disturbances than the illness itself.

Yet though we have enumerated these disturbances according to Gustave's own testimony, we have not tried to *evaluate* them. In other words, we have indeed seen that, far from suppressing the anomaly, they reinforced it, and even in a way *constituted* it, by making Gustave a man profoundly different from other men. But lacking a system of values, we have been unable until now to decide objectively whether the neurosis harmed Flaubert—and to what degree—or whether, to the contrary, it was useful to him.

Certainly there is no lack of objective structures, and we have used this as our starting point. There is the institutional whole, a product and expression of certain infrastructures; there is historical contingency, which, conditioned by that whole, goes beyond it even while preserving it by reviving its internal contradictions; there is the Flaubert family, a metastable result of certain structures and history, whose disequilibrium—common at this period—bears witness at once to the survivals of the past and the difficult advent of a new order. Finally there is the father, both rural and urban, both feudal and bourgeois, a man of science, therefore agnostic at this period when faith, slain by Jacobinism, attempts a rebirth without great success and manifests itself in the new generation as a dead loss, a diminution of being with nothing to counterbalance it. But these abstract and general determinations are already highly particularized in the familial intersubjectivity of the Flauberts: that famous father, nervous to the point of tears, that "done me wrong," a good-natured or fearsome tyrant; that mother, burdened forever by the death of her mother, outdoing herself in wifely servility, adoring her husband as a spouse and even more as a substitute father;

the gloomy atmosphere of the Hôtel-Dieu—all this contributes to enriching institutional determinations and to surpassing them toward the concrete history of an irreducible microorganism that cannot escape historical contingency but suffers it and totalizes it in its own way.

And, above all, we have had to imagine that concrete whole—the rise of the bourgeoisie refracted in one particular daily life—as it was lived in ignorance and panic *by a child*, by a constituted product of this social cell, a son of man, predestined even before conception, who surpassed these conditionings blindly, in the dark, toward his own ends, and consequently ran up against alien objectives that an *other* will had imposed on him and that he internalized despite himself as if they were *also* his. Ignorance and passive constitution, the devoted coldness of the mother, and that second weaning, the sudden disaffection of the father—or what was felt as such—then, the jealousy and exasperation of a kid caught between given incapacities and the familial ambition he had already internalized: that nest of vipers could not be untangled; it had to be *lived*, to be obscurely constituted as a *subjective* determination. And Gustave's subjectivity manifests itself precisely in this, that the only tools at his disposal for understanding himself and those around him are symbols (the curse of Adam, the paternal curse), myths (fatality, the ultra-Manichaeanism that consecrates the victory of evil over good), false constructions (Achille conceived as usurper, Achille-Cléophas sometimes identified with the Devil), and fantasies of resentment (connected to that cruelty he calls "meanness" in his youth and which Sainte-Beuve will call sadism in his critique of *Salammbô*, but which, as we have seen, is rather a *variety* of sadomasochism connected to the problem of fiction and incarnation).

Thus, the attempt to demonstrate the objective conditions of neurosis in the institutions and historical existence of the Flaubert group has been futile, and we are forced to state that well before the crisis of 1844, indeed from early childhood and throughout that adolescence I will call preneurotic—for in it we see future disturbances emerging and gradually taking shape—Gustave does not react to the *objective* aggressions explained by his real situation but to the coded interpretations he gives them, which originate in the prefabricated schemes of his subjectivity. Any attention Achille-Cléophas might pay to Achille will appear very early on as a frustration diabolically premeditated by the symbolic father, that dark Lord, and Gustave's response will be the *literary* hatred that makes him write *Un Parfum à Sentir* or *La Peste à Florence*. At the *collège*, his comrades' innocent gossip or inopportune smiles strike him as the murderous cruelty of the multitude scandalized by his anomaly.

Against this thorough but dreamed ostracism—he actually seems to have enjoyed real popularity and even a certain prestige—he defends himself with passive ecstasy.

In other words, this preneurotic and perfectly subjective behavior (which might, strictly speaking, be called neurotic, and is subjective since it seeks in stupor a purely imaginary compensation understood as such) is a defensive reaction to an erroneous, hyperbolic interpretation of the real situation, whose strictly symbolic aspect is dictated by preconstituted schemata. Thus not only is the induced behavior a modification of subjectivity, but the inductive determination, though it appears to be a simple perception of the objective event, is a subjective evaluation of that event. We might say that everyone shares this condition, and it is true: to perceive is *to situate oneself*; so in any case there is a dialectic of internalization and externalization. The important point here, however, is proportion: while a part of the object is revealed as it is, by revealing to us what we are (that is, our relation to it and our anchorage), we can hope, at the end of an extended quest, to achieve that reciprocity of position (the object defining us to the same degree that we define the object) which is the truth of the human condition. In Gustave's case, subjectivity gnaws away at the objective and leaves it only enough exteriority for it to transmit its inductive power to the phantasms that digested it. His effort is entirely to desituate himself.[1]

We have therefore followed his preneurotic life until the explosion of his neurosis and have restrained ourselves from objectively evaluating his behavior; we have preferred to *understand* him, to study his behavior with regard to its ends, and to conceive of that behavior as a response to *experienced* situations rather than declare it *aberrant* in comparison to "real" stimuli or to the behavior of others. Indeed, in principle it is impossible to determine what is *reality* without invoking a system of values. Who is more adapted to the real: Gustave, who uses every means possible to try to interrupt his legal studies because he knows deep down that they will lead him to take up a profession, thus to become that abhorrent "bourgeois"? Or Ernest, who was also a romantic and thoroughly despised "philistine" but never nurtured the intention to escape his class; who climbed skillfully, flexibly, each rung of his career ladder, beginning as prosecutor in Corsica and ending as a parliamentary representative; whose primary concern, when asked for the letters of his deceased friend for publication, was to expurgate them? For a psychiatrist, for a bourgeois analyst—and they are all bourgeois—Ernest is the very type of the adult: social, sociable, adapted to his task and even to the evolution of French society. Those practitioners are too well trained to deny Gustave his exceptional personality, but for them he remains a man to be cured. Maybe so, but *of what*? None of them, of course, would dream of preventing him from writing. They might look for slight behavior modifications, that's all. But to what end? So he could go to Paris more often? Live there? Spend all his nights in the Muse's bed? Write different books? Get elected someday to the Academy, like his friend Maxime, the photographer? Would they try to make him acknowledge that he is bourgeois whatever he does, and that his struggle against his class, lost in advance, is simply wasted effort, a futile waste of his talents? He does tear himself apart. And Josephin Soulary is certainly more adult, stronger, more reconciled, when he admits, with an amused smile: "What do you expect? I am bourgeois." I am reminded of the advice given by a psychotherapist to one of my friends who liked young boys: "My dear man, you must choose: become a passive homosexual or try heterosexuality." Should Flaubert be told, "My dear man, you must choose: *be* consciously the bourgeois you have under your skin, become the great poet Soulary, or go over to the people, work in a factory and despise your class of origin by becoming one of the exploited?" This is a contemporary solution and was not possible earlier, as we know.

In other words, it is totally impossible to relive Gustave's neurosis *sympathetically*, to grasp its origins and intentions, to affirm *with him* that it allows him to live, therefore to be faithful to his ultimate ends—and at the same time to evaluate it from the outside in the name of a doubtful concept of normality. There is indeed neurosis, however, as Flaubert himself admits. Ten years of "epileptiform" attacks, hallucinations, anguish, extreme nervousness, and near sequestration. This is what he calls "my nervous illness." We have seen its meaning: that sacrificial choice to be a man-failure, and beneath it the negative theology of "Loser Wins," which reestablishes hope in the depths of this desperate soul. There is no doubt that in response to an emergency situation (an emergency for him, as he had been made, as he was making himself) this illness saved him from the worst. But *at what price*? For the disturbances are incontestable. And invasive. Although he always understood, in some obscure way, "just how far he could go."

But ask yourself: this man wanted only to write. If he is writing, what does it matter to him, basically, if he is sometimes compelled to have convulsions on his couch? We cannot judge his forced seclusion as would a man of the world, a politician, or a soldier. If there are *damages* and we must evaluate them, we have only one scale of measurement available, the one he himself accepts. The illness removes him from the law and assures him the freedom to write—quite simply, the freedom of leisure. He says so, and that is not in doubt. But *without the illness*, more torn perhaps, more unhappy but more adapted, wouldn't he have *written better*? While claiming to serve his supreme end, art, didn't the neurosis subtly degrade him? Didn't it make him a second-rate artist when without it he could have aspired to be first-rate?

This evaluation, which seems to use criteria acceptable to Flaubert himself and reestablishes us, or means to reestablish us, on the terrain of objectivity—on the terrain of the work as an assessable object—is what Maxime attempted after his friend's death. According to him, Gustave was a writer of very great talent. Without his illness *there* is *no doubt* he would have been a genius. Despite the quarrels that divided them after 1850 and until Flaubert's death, this affirmation is of interest because Du Camp knew him before his crisis at Pont-l'Évêque and seems to have sincerely admired him at that time. *Novembre* had touched him; he found himself in it, strangely enough. And of these two friends, the future member of the Academy is the one who experienced the other's superiority. He sensed a withheld strength, an explosive power in Gustave that would soon become manifest. After the first attack, Maxime went frequently to Rouen and thought he could see a certain *deficit*. Gustave was in a panic, he feared he was going mad, was dying. In the midst of his cozy life, the slightest vexation plunged him into a frenzy. This was the least of it; he lost all interest in external events, no longer even read newspapers, lived in a dream from which he could rouse himself only with difficulty, and, above all, he *didn't change anymore*, like a clock forever marking the time of the accident that destroyed its mechanism: the same readings, often grossly obscene, the same behavior, the same witticisms.

It must first be observed that Maxime's judgment is secretly dictated by the name he gives Flaubert's illness. He calls it epilepsy, a somatic ailment which nonetheless has formidable effects on one's mental life. In other words, the amateur physician's diagnosis already involves the certainty of a psychic *deficit*. In those days there was no conception of the existence of neuroses. Moreover, the system of evaluation proposed by Du Camp is hardly used today: the contrast between genius and talent has a historical background (to which we shall return) that implicates Providence; it was abused during the Romantic period, and the generation of 1830–40, to its misfortune, inherited it. We do not reject the distinction out of hand because we want to form our own estimation in accord with Gustave, who, like all his contemporaries, made ample use of it.

Still, this type of estimation presupposes that Flaubert's works should be judged by Maxime's aesthetic criteria, which are no longer acceptable. Du Camp, of course, has the right to apply them, provided he knows that in passing judgment he is judging himself, as we all do. But in

1970 it is impossible to make those aesthetic criteria our own. Gustave's work, he tells us, could have been better than it is. It reaches a certain level and never goes beyond it. The fruit did not fulfill the promise of the flower. This judgment is revocable, however. It was, and is, revoked daily: first—even before it was formulated—in 1857, by the thundering success of *Madame Bovary*;[2] later by the generations of [Émile] Zola, of [Alphonse] Daudet, and of [Guy de] Maupassant. In other times, Flaubert was out of fashion: [Paul] Valéry didn't like him; some critics tried to demonstrate that he wrote badly; literature was following other paths and defined style differently; but *Madame Bovary* was not condemned for the reasons Maxime proposed. And that period ended in its turn. Gustave is now back in favor, and the new novelists see him as their precursor; they admire him for his justifiable concern in the mid-nineteenth century with the problem they consider essential, that of language, which puts in question the very being of literature. Again a revocable judgment that will one day be revoked and whose revocation will in turn be annulled. In short, like all great bodies of work, Flaubert's has a history that began in the author's lifetime and has not approached completion. Every negation of a negation enriches it and leads it toward its *potential evolved truth*, an ideal totalization that can be imagined only at the end of history, if words still have any meaning. And every negation is merely Flaubert's *situation* by a literature that redefines its objectives and the means of reaching them.

As for Maxime, he is out of the game, swallowed up along with his ideas. He is still, however, of some interest: he *alone* posed the question of damages. And on what does he base his daring assertion that Gustave, without his "epilepsy," might have written better? On a critical appraisal of the novels? No, on the man's behavior.[3] The text is clear: Flaubert is living in a state of permanent distraction, the present does not interest him, does not touch him. As a result, he remains immutable. Conclusion: *he has nothing to say* simply because *he refuses to draw his inspiration from lived experience*.

This negative judgment issues from a positive aesthetic. When Flaubert, sullen and peevish, was dozing on his horse or camel, Maxime, lively, watchful, was scrutinizing the countryside, slipping out of the saddle and photographing the Nile or the Pyramids; to him we owe the first photographic reporting on the Middle East—his claim to immortality. This achievement presupposes an admirable dual adaptation to reality: not only can he organize himself to realize his dreams—the dreams of his generation—but he manages to fix them, to reproduce them, and to offer them to those who have remained in France, by skillfully using an instrument that has just made its appearance, the newest product of technology. An aesthete, he has understood the possibilities of using a modern piece of equipment to capture *as an artist* the most ancient monuments. Thus he claims to be the permanent contemporary of his time, and nothing is lost on him: he internalizes immediate reality as lived experience and reexternalizes it as a work of art. Inspiration comes to him in the course of things; he bathes in it and lets it penetrate him.

A profoundly bourgeois conception, as we shall soon see. The artist, according to Maxime, is not concerned with depicting man in the world, with rendering in each of his books the totalizing relation of the macrocosm to the microcosm; in each of his works he seeks to *detail* a *particular* novelty. By the same token, he affirms his faith in progress, not the progress of art as form but the progress of its content, which will be enriched by all political or technical innovation. The bourgeois cry out for such an art, which would be both anecdotal and present in the social and scientific evolution; they want a high-toned literature to make an inventory of *their* world and reflect back to them the constant improvements that will nourish in every reader the great *necessary* myth of creative evolution. But to the extent that this conception remains without principles for Maxime, it establishes the foundations, several years in advance, of what will later be called the art of journalism.

Writing without a Public

But if in order to write you have to be on the lookout, to be tuned into both history and its footnotes, to live with your times, to be informed, Maxime had of necessity to condemn Flaubert and to declare that his illness had cut him off from the world, had made him incapable of *observing* and *feeling*. This is the very type of false condemnation, or, if you will, falsely objective condemnation, because it clings resolutely to the exterior of its object—by rejecting a priori situational reciprocity. Maxime's notion of genius is supreme attention to the real, contemporaneity itself as it is lived; this means the work will be inspired by new needs that industry—strange as it may seem—hatches in man solely for the purpose of satisfying those needs. According to these observations, genius would be the normal thing. This conception, which is well suited to the bourgeoisie of the Second Empire, is—taken at face value—merely an incomplete idea and hence false. Assuming that the writer gives an account of his own period as he experiences it through his own facticity, how can he adopt his anchorage as a point of view without probing more deeply and redefining it in terms of the class struggle? How can he vaunt the bourgeois century without showing the progressive constitution of a proletariat that is its truth? And a writer of 1860, of course, will not be expected to discover that truth by some blinding intuition and then make us see it, then use it to denounce us. No, but simply not to be inferior to his public, to M{onsieur Émile} de Girardin {French journalist, publisher, and politician}, whose prophetic reaction we saw at the time of the revolt of the *canuts* {that is, of the Lyonnais silk workers}, to the notables of 1848, who after the June massacres clearly understood the dangers of universal suffrage and, having abolished it, judged it safer to put themselves in the hands of a "strong man." The ruling class has no desire to share this farsightedness, or at least this anxiety, with its writers. The Nile and photography—that is the fantasied alliance, the past revived by ultramodernism. But the author is urged to stop there, not to reveal the other dimension, labor, not to refer with his camera, an egg laid effortlessly by modernity, to the factory, to machines, to the worker—even to denounce his "barbarity," as a bourgeois conscious of himself as such would take it upon himself to do.

Even after 1871 and the massacres organized by {Marie Joseph Louis Adolphe} Thiers {French statesman and historian, second president of France} with the plenary approbation of the ruling and middle classes, the bourgeoisie was aware of its fundamental hatred of those spoilsports, the exploited, but its writers were not allowed to mention it. That would be to acknowledge that classes exist, and that relations of production arouse in the individual, as a member of his class, what might be called an affective a priori. So Maxime will gloss silently over real history, peopling his books with flat figures animated by flat sentiments—by emotions that seem uniquely born of human nature, meaning of course bourgeois "nature" (an abstraction created by its constitutive relations with the working classes) and its progressive transformation by modernity. Yet those relations are never revealed for what they are: the singular determinations of a fundamental and hidden affectivity, which is our real way of living our anchorage *among men*, in a class, in a particular milieu, in a social "stratum" defined at the core of this class by antagonisms aroused by the division of labor and its resulting conflicts. Maxime's "modernism" will serve the mystifications organized by his masters, since he makes modernity a state of the soul sustained by the benefits of a heartless industrialization. And when he judges Flaubert in the name of that pliant, loquacious, and untruthful art which, beneath its perpetual adaptation to *gadgets*, hides a profound and deliberate maladaptation to the social world and its contradictions, an inert lacuna, a rigid nonwill hidden by the darkness of the depths, it is the bourgeois public that judges Gustave through Maxime and reproaches him, finally, for having failed to write a literature affirming the values of his class. Apart from the fact that it is difficult to condemn a writer for never having undertaken what he refused to undertake even in his first works, Maxime's bourgeois monarchic conceptions (which will find their public under Napoleon III) represent, crudely speaking, the doctrines of hack writers who have vanished without a trace.

Perhaps he thought these doctrines were in conflict with Romanticism; but he did not perceive that Romanticism, by means of a rigorous dialectic, had already been challenged, surpassed, and preserved by a new determination of the Objective Spirit first *revealed*—precisely—*by* Flaubert (and at the same time by his contemporary, Baudelaire, as well as—although less clearly, we shall see—by Leconte de Lisle, their elder by three years, and of course by the Goncourts), that it was enriched and developed during the second half of the century until it found its theorist and hero in Mallarmé, then died of senility after the Symbolist decadence. Maxime would be unwitting witness to this fecund *deviation* of literature; he would not see the clear evidence that all the *good* works between 1850 and 1880 were born—directly or indirectly—from this new current.

Always seeking the master stroke that would make him rich, trying to write and sometimes writing a best seller, enjoying, or imagining that he enjoys, a large audience—in proportion to his compromises—he aspires to communicate with his reader and succeeds easily; yet this facile victory conceals the most important *literary fact* of that half century: the divorce—unique in history—of the writer from the public. This event will be experienced *as a drama* by all the "artists" of the period, and their works, behind a facade of deceptive serenity, bear witness to it.

In order to assess the *damages* of the neurosis, it is therefore necessary, though not sufficient, to confine our research to the domain of literary production. We must, moreover, refrain from imagining this production in terms of norms that claim to be transhistorical and are actually just the product of another moment in history or, at the same moment, of another social stratum having other interests and other internal relations with the bourgeois class. The only possible principle is the one that Flaubert continued so lucidly to recall throughout his long correspondence: critics must judge the work of art by the artist's intentions, that is, in terms of his initial project, which itself depends on a structured set of aesthetic norms. Gustave obviously does not require his judges to have a subjective sympathy for the phantasms of his subjectivity; he is demanding an objective criticism, rigorous in its *comprehension*, that would grasp in the finished work the principles of the enterprise implicitly inscribed in it, and appraise what the artist did in terms of what he intended to do.

For—as we shall see more clearly as we go along—all literature, as a historical determination bound to contingency and to tradition, defines its own subject; that is, it demarcates and isolates a certain sector for cultivation by the structures it generates, and in this connection it discovers a new use of language, its instrument and raw material. Or, if you will, it understands *linguistic being* in a new light; starting with an original goal, it assigns it real *possibilities* never before envisaged.

Considering Flaubert from this point of view, we shall suggest that what Maxime would call his *deficit* is merely the organization of a neurotic instrumentality intended to give him the means to "make art" according to the principles he has established. Certainly not by deliberate choice, but because he *found* them within himself *already adopted*. The *rejection of immediate reality* is not, as Maxime insinuates, a lesser presence in the world due to a psychoneurotic sclerosis of his adaptation to the real. It is the firm determination never to be inspired by the event; in other words, it is the intention to purify inspiration. Inspiration born in the course of events sometimes seems dazzling but in fact remains variable and hazardous, obscured by passions; it comes from chance, and chance kills it. Sullied by the materiality of life, the work issuing from such inspiration is itself hazardous and bears the traces of original filth. This does not mean that the artist cannot *utilize* immediate reality. He can recount the sad story of the Delmarre couple or the life of a group of young men between 1846 and 1860. But he keeps his distance from the events he retraces; he is not inspired by them because his subject lies elsewhere; he handles them from afar, modifies them at will, and assigns them the job of incarnating the nonimmediate in the contemporary world. The incarnation is imperfect because the real subject has nothing in common with the plot; yet this imperfection must persist and become meaningful allusively, referring to a silent totality all the more present as it continually calls attention to itself, given the impossibility of *rendering* it, as the whole which, canceled by the singular determination, resides in each of its parts.

When writing *Madame Bovary*, Flaubert shares with Louise his deep desire as an artist: *to appear* to treat one subject but in fact to be treating another, quite different in quality and scope, or not to treat it at all, by which he does not mean writing to say nothing, but writing to say, Nothing. *This is the role of the immediate in Madame Bovary: to symbolize, strictly speaking, to allude to the macrocosm or the void that is its equivalent, and above all to distract attention, to fool the reader, and while the reader is absorbed in reading a contemporary story, to inject him with an ancient, eternal poison through style* {editor's italics}. For Gustave the subject of literature is given a priori. He would say later to George Sand:

one does not write what one wants. And it is true; Maxime does write what he wants, or almost, but this is not writing. The content of the work cannot be provided by the course of things, a succession of opaque and trivial singularities, nor can it be provided by caprice. The only *possible* content, for Flaubert, is the judgment the adolescent made of the world at the end of childhood, which was always the same despite the various ways he expressed it: “The earth is the realm of Satan”; “At a quite early age I had a complete presentiment of life”; “I believe in the curse of Adam.” In short, the worst is always certain, I believe in Nothing. The Delmarre woman never interested him for herself. But he charged her and all her petty world with developing before our eyes that obscure a priori, human life as he perceived it at the end of his childhood.

In reality, Flaubert knows the grayness of the quotidian; this world is *not enough* to be truly assimilated to hell. But we have seen why the task of the artist is to *represent* it by a totalizing tightening of its slackened bonds, by imperceptible additions, by discreet eliminations, as if it were that perfection. The content of the work will thus be its form: the world must be reproduced as if it were the work of a freedom whose goal is to realize radical evil; this presupposes that everything, of itself and beneath the level of action joined to all other things, must lead to the worst. And this enterprise requires such rigor in the writing, such a multiplicity of connections between the elements of the narrative, such adroitness at offering glimpses of the savage and menacing All through every part, and then at suppressing each one so the totality can manifest itself stripped bare and reveal in the final instant that it is quite simply nothingness. Such effort, care, and calculation are required that radical evil is merely an ethical designation of that other absolute norm, beauty. And as evil cannot identify with being as being, which is simple positivity, or with nonbeing, which taken as such is nonexistence pure and indescribable, it must reside in the dialectical movement between the two: the nonbeing of being expressed by the being of nonbeing. *The nonbeing of being* is the prophesied result of totalization when still in progress, the meaning of the narrated story while there are still characters to live it and while it is still sensed through their tumultuous passions. Totalized, being identifies with the void, and evil is not that ultimate, colorless, odorless, tasteless void but allows itself to be glimpsed at every step of the totalizing narrative; this happens when, through the reciprocal determination of the parts by the All grasped as the rule of unification by the annihilating future (fate), and of the All by the parts (the part, by managing a painful disappearance *as part* so that the All should be manifest in its radical unity, becomes the symbol of the All taken as permanent disappearance), the violent, massive and variegated multiplicity of the present denounces itself, in the heart of its permanent affirmation, as having no substance other than an eternal and featureless void. Evil is that gnawing contradiction at the heart of being, that discovery in every being, when it invests all its forces in persevering, that it is merely an illusory modulation of nothingness and, in sum, the futile contention of that truth sensed in the rage and turbulence of passions.

The Magic of Fiction

{Editor's Note: In *Being and Nothingness*, Sartre considers nothingness not as a void but as that which distinguishes one being from another—a tree from a bird, for example. Nothingness resides in all being, allowing change, and, in humans, it is that which gives us our freedom. I examined this idea at some length in my *Commentary* on this work (cited earlier in Editor's Introduction). Fiction uses this distinction by allowing characters to exist in a novel through words which both are and are not their sounds and marks. This is a complex issue that Sartre here merely touches upon but has never fully developed. I made an attempt in a few articles (e.g., "Crafting Marks into Meanings and Things").[4]}

The being of nonbeing is the raw material itself of the work as fiction; it is *appearance*, which is diabolical because the being of nothing, always borrowed, relative to being, suddenly shows us the disturbing, vampirizing power of what is not. In this sense—as I have demonstrated elsewhere—absolute evil is none other than the imagination. But in the Book as Gustave conceives it, appearance reveals its borrowed being and its nonexistence at the moment when being, in the course of the narration, is itself revealed as appearance. Hence being, maintained in the fictional setting, can no longer challenge appearance the way truth challenges error. Quite to the contrary, the two strata of appearance reinforce and challenge each other, and the work remains in suspense like a nightmare that would at the same time be true. The extraordinary purpose of art, in Gustave's view, is *to manifest* the ineluctable slippage of being toward Nothingness through the imaginary totalization of the work; *at the same time* its purpose is to preserve indefinitely, by that regulated illusion which is the work, a sense of endlessness in this slippage, fixing it through the restraining power of words whose permanence assures us *in the imaginary* that it will never reach its end and will always remain ineluctable, irreversible but *unachieved*.

Thus the nonbeing of being—which is realized, according to Flaubert, only at the end of an exhaustive totalization symbolized by the anecdote—is signified by the being of nonbeing, which confers upon it in the work a perfect but imaginary *atemporality*. Temporalization (Gustave's worm in the apple) is exhibited in the work that denounces it, like destiny or a fatal slippage toward the worst: it is a fundamental structure of the *Subject*. But at the same time the work enfolds it in its calm eternity. So that the temporal, maintained, sustained at every moment of the Book by a continuous creation, manifests itself during reading as a byproduct of atemporality. The work is born of an interference in which two movements annul each other: being slips into nonbeing, and this very nonbeing saves it by vampirizing it. Flaubert's sadism is thus unleashed. This is not just a transparent display of the nothing at the basis of being; Gustave adds insult to injury by subjecting being to nothing: he compels it to take the little substance and permanence he concedes it from the imaginary.

The sole problem, the sole concern of the artist as Flaubert conceives of him, is therefore art, by which I mean the set of procedures that allow putrefying being to be preserved in the alcohol of nonbeing. The *idea*—the totalizing conception of the work and hence the unique subject of literature—has always intoxicated Flaubert. For this reason, no particular circumstance is at the source of his writings. Breughel's *Saint Antoine*, the *Saint Julien* of Rouen Cathedral, are *already* works of art, and of the kind he would wish: they are totalizing. No doubt he *encounters* them, they impress him; but this is because he *recognizes* them. They provide him with what the formalists call the form of content, that bit of unformed matter without which the idea would vanish. Standing before that picture, before the stained glass window, his fervor is engaged because the object grasped—itself imaginary—spontaneously offers him the thing that gives meaning to *any* great work (in his eyes): a circularity of being and nothingness, in which nothingness must triumph over being although that is the source of its false substance. A circularity that is *unthinkable, unspeakable* (at least directly) and essentially *irrational* (merely one of its charms for Gustave), and that can be expressed only in the work—a center of unrealization which is already in itself a hybrid mixture of being and nothingness. In other words, the meaning of the work of art is to give—indirectly and in the imaginary—the only form of existence possible to that inchoate idea which, Gustave tells us in *Mémoires d'un fou*, is confused with his life.

In short, the form of content will be quickly found. What is *essential* are the techniques of creation, its procedures and directed inventions, all the manipulations that aim—blindly—at *making visible* what cannot be thought and in this way introduce into other minds an inchoate thought, the meaning of the work, a lingering phantom they cannot confront, a perpetual and disturbing incitement to conceive of something inconceivable that escapes them the moment they think they've grasped it. But these aesthetic means are themselves almost impossible to find. Indeed, as their purpose is to render the irrational, they are by nature inaccessible to reason; and the idea cannot help to define them, for without them it would have no existence, remaining latent or vague to Flaubert *unless* he has discovered a way to embody it. Hence the young author's alternating enthusiasm and discouragement, then his bitterness, finally his despair; for the idea—immutable in itself—is nothing (being, stripped down, the unthinkable idea of the nothingness of being). When Flaubert is carried away with excitement, it's because he thinks he has found the lens to refract it; when he abandons his project in disgust, it's because the idea proves elusive. The techniques weren't good enough: for lack of appropriate treatment, the anecdote has shriveled and is reduced to its particularity.

CHAPTER FIFTEEN

(The Problem Concluded)

THE OBJECTIVE SPIRIT

{Editor's Note: Sartre continues by reinterpreting the Hegelian notion of the Objective Spirit. He writes, "In fact, the Objective Spirit—in a defined society and in a given era—is nothing more than culture as practico-inert" (Cosman 5:35). The term "practico-inert" comes from Sartre's *Critique of Dialectical Reason*, and it points to the "weight" of the social structures of a time—namely, the forms of art and architecture, the codification of laws that tend to regulate our behavior and which also reflect our beliefs, as complex and as contradictory as these may be. We develop our freedom within this web, sustaining it or challenging it. Sartre continues, "The Objective Spirit, while never on the side of pure lived experience and free thought, exists as an act only through the activity of individuals" (Cosman 5:41). To give an example, if I as a white person am looking to rent an apartment and I find one that I like very much but which is in an all-white neighborhood that clearly discriminates against nonwhite persons, I am not responsible for that condition, and yet my act of renting or not renting either deepens the prejudice or works against it. Sartre's point about Gustave Flaubert is that he freely accepts and deepens his unjust social conditions, even to the extent of approving of the murders of the weak and unfortunate people of his times. And, it is within this acceptance of the injustice of his age that these final three chapters aim at revealing how the neurotic age of the Second Empire required its greatest writers, its so-called Knights of Nothingness, to represent a beauty that was supposedly beyond the human realm but actually below it. That is, a beauty seemingly "for its own sake"; in reality, a beauty empty of all meaning and devoid of any possible relation to truth. The individual Gustave Flaubert both personified and gave life to the Objective Spirit of Second Empire.}

In short, Maxime has understood nothing. For Gustave, the work's meaning and content are given in advance. So what's the good of living? Life is disruptive; its tepid passions and petty cares could distract the artist from his true task, which is to perpetuate the wreckage of the world through *style*. And, indeed, why *change*? What is there to change since his task is fixed? The refusal to seek inspiration in the event, which is clearly formulated in the first *Education* ("it merely refers to itself") must be accompanied by the refinement of a defensive lens against any alterations. Art requires a *guaranteed immutability*. First of all, living distracts us; the main thing is, we must think only of the means to construct the irrational object that will indirectly suggest the unthinkable idea; in fact, we must think only of style. From this point of view, convinced that he is aiming too high for his feeble powers and that, lacking taste, he might destroy himself if impotence doesn't silence him first, Flaubert thinks he hasn't a minute to lose. Writing to Louise one day, he expresses his amazement: how could Leconte de Lisle, an artist, fritter away two years in tempestuous and disappointing love affairs while he forgot his art? Gustave's stupor will provoke laughter; it is typical of him, however. Why love when the artist's only concern is to write, and style, an absolute point of view, is constantly slipping away? "Think of style," he says to the Muse, "think of it always." He could be a believer speaking of his God. That is what it is, and even worse: for that uninterrupted meditation on language is pursued in anguish, in disgust; this Christian believes he is damned. His only chance for salvation is time. A time that is uniform and empty of all content, that smacks of boredom, whose every moment is like the last, a time that he can put to good use for inventing the form adequate to his unique subject, which was fixed since adolescence and yet never treated.

On this level, perspectives are reversed. Like Maxime, we wonder whether Gustave's neurosis did not hamper him in his work as a writer. Shouldn't the question be, rather, whether it was *useful* to him? I don't mean that kind of immediate appeasement procured subjectively by certain neurotic *stresses* to the detriment of psychic integrity. I am wondering about the *objective* results of his "nervous illness": doesn't it furnish him with the *means* to write *Madame Bovary*? I have said that art, according to Flaubert, requires a *consolidated immutability*. It is not enough to reject the accidental and think only of the very essence of beauty, of the means of capturing its light; you must be *protected from changes*. This is something no choice, no decision, even in the form of a vow, can provide. I cannot commit myself in relation to myself; and the vow not to change, even as it is made, invokes the possibility of being broken, which becomes *my* permanent possibility and perhaps my vertigo, my temptation. And then, even when I for my part would be faithful to the pledge, who can guarantee that a change in my moods or taste will not be the result of external forces? Immediate reality seeps in everywhere: How shall I defend myself against it? Making vows is all very well—no sooner said than done; they take you off, tonsure you, and shut you up in a monastery. But that commitment has meaning only in a religious society: it is integrated by a constituted body, by an *Order*, and this order is entrusted with recalling the commitment, with imposing it in case of failure; in short, the order takes responsibility for that commitment, and the new recruit must internalize it as an *other will*, or the *will of the Collective*, sustained by the constraint of the serial, by the constraint of the sworn group, if need be by bodily constraint. The newcomer is protected against the outside by high walls, against himself by the simple fact that it is much more difficult to leave the Order than to enter it. In these communities, mystic flights are often merely rebellion turned inside out by the consciousness of its impossibility.

For Flaubert, an agnostic who wants to devote himself in solitude to a profane occupation, the only conceivable equivalent to constraint is neurosis as a suffered option. The public solemnity of vows—which helps to make them irreversible—is here replaced by the publicity of scandal: the declared unworthiness of the Flaubert son protects him from temptation, compels his sequestration. The illness itself, six months of bed rest, the irregular, always imminent return of the attacks, defends him against himself and confines him to his room; the will of the family is substituted for his own: Doctor Flaubert personally forbids his return to Paris. Finally—as he so often repeated!—this profound upheaval has killed him; his heart is dead: even if he wanted to, he would be incapable of falling into the amorous senility that doomed Leconte de Lisle. "I am not made for pleasure." Opportunities can proliferate, but for this phantom, void of his affective substance, they will never again be tempting. Public commitment, *other* will, prohibitions, bodily constraint, high defensive walls—all replaced by his neurosis. And, like a monastic order, it is easier to enter than to leave. Beginning in January 1844, Flaubert is nothing more than a mediation between the idea that ravages his life and the style that must indirectly render it.

The question of "damages," however, has so far been answered only in part. It has, if you will, shifted its ground. It seems evident that Flaubert's conception of art requires the immutability of the artist. But isn't this conception of art itself neurotic? Let us not forget that the desire for immutability seems to have long preceded his aesthetic ideas. When he stoutly declared to Ernest that he was and would remain the same, he was fifteen years old and still relied upon his spontaneity as a "poet."

At that period—and during the following years—the young man was engaged in a struggle against his fate. And the primary goal of this clearly affirmed "immutability" was not to serve his artistic vocation but to give him symbolically, and preserve for him, the inert present of inanimate matter *against time*, which would perforce change him into a prosecutor or a notary. Couldn't it be said, then, that immutability—the refusal to live the life others wanted to impose on him—was a singular and primitive neurotic goal; that he desired it, or believed he was afflicted by it, to escape the paternal curse and because it satisfied his obsessive desire to be a mortuary figure, a dead man, a being beyond life; that before a suffered *exis* it was a role, and far from being required by art as a condition of its possibility, it was, on the contrary, immutability as a neurotic attitude that imposed on Gustave a conception of art to justify it? Indeed, for that which is immutable, a totalizing art that rejects life becomes the *only possible*; and so immobilism, dissembling its identity as primary cause, poses as the indispensable means of attaining beauty.

Shouldn't we consider, indeed, that in *L'Education sentimentale* and in his correspondence Gustave presents as aesthetic *norms* certain *factual* determinations encountered in psychoneuroses as definite symptoms, some of which even seem to belong to the psychotic universe? His refusal to change is accompanied by a refuse to live, to adapt himself. Isn't that impassive witness, the artist, the final incarnation of the Old Man—a role so favored by Gustave—or of that other role, the dead man? And haven't his morbid passivity and pithiatism made him choose the Imaginary as a permanent milieu *against the Real*, even before he decided on his vocation? In this case the *subject* of art—the oneiric world and the directed dream of a continuous annihilation of being—merely provided the expression of a neurotic option prompted by resentment and an unrealizable desire for compensation. Isn't there an obscure, *unthinkable* nucleus in this breachless circularity of being and appearance? We might say he *rationalizes* in the form of aesthetic, hence in some way universal, imperatives that "system made for one man," whose profound finality—to mask his anomaly and escape the paternal curse—is strictly *singular*.

In a way, this interpretation is irrefutable. Neurosis is the subjective—at least as it is lived by the neurotic. And while *maladaptation*—which is essentially psychotic—does not characterize neurotic disturbances and isn't a symptom *required* for their clinical definition, neurosis always implies a certain refusal, a break with the real. This is what happens in the case of hysterical disturbances, which alone concern us here. When {the French neurologist Jean Martin} Charcot was teaching at Salpêtrière, hysteria was seen by his students as a *refusal* that was somatized through spasms. But we know today that this brutal and manifest refusal represented the only response that uneducated, often illiterate subjects could offer to questions raised in the course of things. By studying this same neurosis in the most cultivated circles of Vienna, Freud proved indirectly that the spasms were merely extreme and *meager* reactions to the permanent aggression of objectivity. In the most intelligent patients, these symptoms did not appear—and today it seems that with the general rise in the level of culture, they have nearly vanished. Hysteria becomes characterized, to the contrary, by flexibility and docility, by an incontrovertible comprehension of the real and by an *apparent* adaptation to objective situations. But this adaptation is deceptive: the patient deciphers questions posed by his surroundings and events at hand in terms of a fundamental intention of *rupture*. If the intention is given at the outset, it proposes the rupture as long-term objective: the patient will espouse the real to the point where he can detach himself from it by a role that at once embraces and neutralizes it. He investigates the traps that history and the environment might conceal only so as not to be discovered when he focuses on believing in the role he is playing. Of course, the game and the investigation—when the neurosis is in place—happen simultaneously: the role as it is now interpreted is merely an adaptation already passed, surpassed—however valid it still might be in its general features—and the investigation is prospective; the patient sniffs out ambushes, and in this search he is already outlining his future response, the character he will try to interpret. In Flaubert's case we might say that, although unfamiliar with either of these illnesses, he orients his *neurotic* pithiatism toward the imitation of the kind of *psychotic* refusal of reality associated with schizophrenics.

The trouble is that *Madame Bovary*, incontestably the work of a neurotic, is in no way *in itself* a *neurotic work*. Writings certainly exist that in themselves bear witness to disturbances in the mind of their creator; these are often deeply interesting documents, of brilliant and terrible beauty, but revealing to the reader—even if he understands nothing of psychiatry—the disturbing universe of mental pathology. I am referring to that vast collection of what we might call "morbid literature," journals, narratives, memoirs, tales and stories, very few of them published and remaining for the most part in the archives of psychiatrists or psychiatric hospitals. Haunted by phantasms, loaded with symbols, torn by obsessions that generate the work and yet rip its texture, sometimes simplified by a pathological geometry or hyperlogic to the point of extreme poverty or to a strange elegance that throws us into discomfort, sometimes obscured by the richness of an autistically structured thought that can render them unintelligible to everyone and primarily to their author, these productions are in themselves symptoms.

Their ambiguity will seem clear if we compare them to patients' drawings, which are better known to the general public. Such drawings do have clinical value for the psychiatrist; they reveal to him the morbid schemes and hidden intentions that structure a patient's psychic life. During treatment they can in turn confirm the diagnosis and the cure by the progressive disappearance of a symbol and hence of the obsession or inhibition expressed by it. But these drawings are often exhibited as though they were the canvases of a "normal" painter. Then, although visitors instantly *perceive—in* a state of estrangement[1]—the *other thought* present in the style of drawing and self-proclaimed in all its otherness, they cannot help being sensitive to the *aesthetic* character of the productions. This is not surprising, for in most cases the drawing bears witness to a rupture with the real and to the choice of the Imaginary, even as the artist's pencil allows the neurosis or psychosis to act as a totalizing idea in Flaubert's sense. So it is with pathological writings, although the difficulty inherent in using linguistic signs rarely permits them to be entirely beautiful. The evolution of the Objective Spirit is such that in our day the best of these productions are integrated into literature, which is defined for us as a hermeneutics of silence rather than a rigorous construction according to rules. It does not much matter that the literary is incomplete or incoherent if its allusive value is incontestable.

But while the essential quality of Flaubert's works is undoubtedly *allusion*, his works do not fall into this category. They are finished products, wrought, polished, up to the standards of his time—*first-rate*. In other words, what they first reveal is rationality as the rule of literary praxis. No doubt the essential goal of this achievement is to "render thought indirectly through form." Be that as it may, it is there in its density, its irreducibility, making *Madame Bovary* what its author wanted: a *natural being*, like a tree or a landscape, which new generations accept as they would *things* of the urban or rural world, and institutions. And this can never be said of "morbid works"—even the most beautiful—for even as they fascinate us they unravel before our eyes. Their essence is that inconsistency which does not allow them to stand alone; incomplete, confused, ambiguous, their "vibrating disappearance" is effected in the very process of reading as an attempt at recomposition, and leaves us face-to-face with pure horror. Such horror is the *meaning* of Flaubert's novels, but their density prevents them from dissolving. Thus the literary object *is composed* through us, during the reading, and is posed for itself in its unity. As a result, the horror is never present, it haunts the book without becoming visible; always intended, it escapes. For that very reason, *Madame Bovary* as a work does not fall into the categories of the pathological; by itself it refers neither to the subject who wrote it nor to his obsessions. Pathological writing is continually transparent to subjectivity: hence it offers us the horror of living but doesn't convince us directly. Flaubert's work is classical because it convinces us of that horror without bringing us up against it. And we can be sure that this is how it seemed to the public of 1857, who would never have accepted it otherwise.

If neurosis defines itself as the more or less radical choice of subjectivity—and this is indeed its function for Gustave—it offers no means of escape from that subjectivity; and the work issuing from it must be morbid, must mark the singularity of its author without becoming the *singular universal* that self-evidently wins our adherence, for singularity touches us by designating us through its aesthetic universality to precisely the degree that universality masks subjective idiosyncrasy. Indeed, neurotic writing is masturbatory: its only end is neurosis itself, and the intention to communicate is absent or reduced to its simplest expression.[2] And while Flaubert's relation to the public may be poor a priori, while he may write *in the absolute* rather than for readers, his works are unreal determinations of objectivity. He wants to produce centers of unrealization that escape him, little metaphysical events that close up and turn against him—and not to assemble words that would reflect his neurosis to him alone.

In other words, it is quite true that Gustave's intentions are neurotic, and that they are aimed primarily at his idiosyncratic subjectivity. But it is also true that he has produced an objective work that presents itself to the reader as a singular universal. It seems we have come to an impasse: Is it conceivable that the return to the subjective could in practice result in the production of an object in the social world? And it hardly matters, in this case, that the object is imaginary since it is, as such, a *real* determination of the society. Are we to claim that in this case, quite by chance, neurosis is counterbalanced by talent? That means nothing. First of all, talent is indefinable: that "gift" is revealed only in the work; it is the very success of the work projected a posteriori onto the subjectivity of the author. Then, too, it is a metaphysical virtue, in Comte's sense of the term, the abstract explanation of a shift from the subjective to the objective by a power analogous to the soporific virtue of opium. Even this absurdity would be less manifest if the imagined author, a mixture of the objective and the subjective, attempted to emerge into objectivity by expressing himself.

But if he is neurotic, if he writes to satisfy his neurosis, it is subjectivity he is aiming at—and the incommunicable; then talent becomes providential grace, or, better yet, the *miracle* by which God would transform this systematic subjectivization into objectivity, and would transform the refusal to communicate into communication. For at the extreme we would have to conceive of a schizophrenic turned toward absolute autism and, *thanks to talent*, offering to share with the reader the pure asocial nature of his autistic thought. This is inconceivable since in this case writing is merely a means used by the illness, an effort to steal language from others and use it to take refuge in an inexpressible self. Talent—like *exis*—would, if it existed, contain a communicative intention that would be denied and shattered by the systematic rejection of all communication and the quest for that absolute point at which lived experience, heavily charged with social desires, would realize them by ridding itself of all intersubjective conditioning, primarily by rejecting the distinction between the possible and the real, as we do in dreams.

It may be asserted that we write to free ourselves of our neurosis, and that talent, in this case, is the good fortune that allows such a deliverance by projecting it into the world, inscribing it there. But this solution is merely word games, and a vicious circle at that: we would write to detach ourselves from the subjective, but how can we do this if we haven't already taken our distance? And what would be the significance of the neurosis–talent dichotomy, reminiscent as it is of the abstract opposition between reason and the passions introduced by classical philosophers? Talent, if it existed, would be spoiled from the first by neurotic infiltrations, and so would be ever more resistant to itself the more it was dazzled by the "unspeakable" illuminations of neurosis. Why should one go through hell, then, to express what is in theory inexpressible, not as an inert determination escaping verbal expression by its very nature, but as a fundamental refusal to be made rational, fixed, and displayed through a systematic effort of expression? And what *would* that talent *express*? For literature flushes out words hidden in things and feelings; but if there are no words, or if they are stolen and used against speech as obscure talismans, what can this literary probing lead to? We can name only that which demands a name; in a word, if neurosis issues in a *work*, then talent, a view of the mind, has nothing to do with it, and we must seek its explanation in the neurotic process as a whole.

Madame Bovary as an Escape from the Father

And even that would not suffice. We can easily demonstrate—and we have done so—that for Flaubert, fame and literature were, at first, merely neurotic phantasms closely linked to that other phantasm, the paternal curse, and that in order to write and to be reborn (a secondary and phantasmatic desire), and equally to escape the arid wisdom of his father, he chose to go deeper into subjectivization and *realize*, through a memorable crisis, the principal themes of his preneurosis—old age, the infantilism of regression, the rejection of change, a break with the real, and living death—as a set of suffered prohibitions that condemned him to sequestration and to dreaming. We know too that at that time he was rationalizing and universalizing his neurotic qualities by using them to build a system of aesthetic norms, which amounted to defining *his task*. Defining it but not accomplishing it until 1848 it remained more a dream than an enterprise. Hence two related questions: How does he shift to execution—that is, how does he objectify the subjective, which is a way of turning his back on subjectivization? And since he always remained faithful to his values, that is, to the transposition of his neurotic phantasms into canons of art and style, how could the work that was the issue of this fidelity become integrated with the Objective Spirit? In other words, how could one man's madness become a collective madness and even the *aesthetic justification* of his times? For in our investigation to this point we have not yet succeeded in generating the *writer* Flaubert from Gustave the family idiot, who dreamed of writing but also imagined he was a musician without understanding anything of music. Which means, of course, that his writing—at least until and excluding the first *Education*—remained incantatory and masturbatory, whatever its quality. But this also reveals new difficulties. To be a writer is not only to write words in a notebook, it is to be published and then read. To be a *famous* writer, as he became from one day to the next, is to create scandal but also to arouse admiration and enthusiasm. These apparently opposite reactions have the same meaning: the resistances of certain social strata (today we can define them by class, socioprofessional milieu, residential area, age, sex, etc.) are accompanied by a new awareness in others, and the intensity of the awareness to resistance bears witness to the aptness of the work, its topicality. It was unexpected, of course: the most enlightened public merely expects the reprise of the same works under other signatures. But when it appears, it wounds to the quick or reveals the need it has fulfilled. And when the fulfillment far surpasses the scandal—as was the case with *Madame Bovary*—*there* is *at once*, of course, *misunderstanding* (we shall see Gustave in the next volume labeled a realist and shouting his rage) and, beneath these errors of interpretation, readers and author discovering their *synchronism*. {Editor's Note: The "next volume" Sartre refers to was never published.}

But if the public demands to recognize itself in the work, the writer would have to live the most typical or, as the Americans say, the most "popular" common experience. With more or less distance, to be sure, and *in his own way*. This would be his only chance to produce what *in any case* a work must be: a singular universal. The singularization of the universal (the idiosyncratic internalization of the external in and through the author's experience) produces in the reader the universalization of the singular. This means he understands that particular experience through the obscure abstract generalizations that refer him to his own particularity. But how is it conceivable that a neurotic work, produced by a patient as a means of subjectivization, could disclose to the reader anything other than a singularity that is posed for itself *against the universal*, and consequently presents itself during reading as the absolute Other, crying out to the public: "*You are not me* because *I don't want to be you*"? Perhaps, despite everything, we feel distantly touched in that slime resting on the bottom of every pond. But the explicit refusal to communicate, which characterizes the neurotic (or psychotic) work, serves as a pretext to each of us to refuse in turn to be *affected* by alien phantasms. The work seems to be closed in on itself, meant only for itself, limited despite certain beauties to the complacent exposition of a case. The interest we bring to it, then, limited as it is, can only be objective and documentary: "There are people like this." Yet it will quickly fade—a clinical study will be more compelling; it describes symptoms, isolates the illness, classifies it in one of the great psychoneurotic categories, and in some cases attempts at least a conjectural etiology. In short, it is informative. A morbid work, *experienced* neurosis, is not informative; it is merely upsetting. Assuming that, under exceptional circumstances, it holds one's attention for a moment, can we imagine it has anything to teach us? It would have to create a certain need in the public that it alone can fill, *and at the same time* specialized readers—writers and "artistic people"—would have to see it as a revelation of the true meaning of their enterprise and appropriate it to surpass it toward their own ends.

Two impossibilities: the neurosis, by posing its singularity in the work, deprives itself of the means to transform itself into the required Objective Spirit; boxed into the present, it cannot in principle initiate a future cycle. Yet today's reader may find it to his liking: historical circumstances—too numerous to indicate here—have caused us, as I have said, to prefer the infinite to the finite and consequently the incomplete to the complete, the monster to the pure product of art. But it is unimaginable that our great-grandfathers in 1857 could have recognized themselves in a morbid book, or that a neurotic, offering himself as such in his writings, could have enlisted followers and changed the form, the content, the meaning of literature.

"Neurosis of the Objective Spirit"

We return to our point of departure. In 1844 Gustave is locked into his neurosis; his intention to write is the neurotic consequence of the Flaubert family's disequilibrium, being structurally half-bourgeois, half-rural, with the relation to the father predominant. Achille-Cléophas's death clearly diminishes the adverse pressure on his son. But he is far from being cured: he loiters and daydreams, literature as a neurotic demand is manifest to him as a prohibition, and condemns him to impotence. We could not, moreover, reconcile the decreasing frequency of the attacks or even their later disappearance with a perfect cure: Gustave is a hysteric and will be one all his life. His life is organized around his neurosis to such an extent that it sometimes seems to him, in his hours of discouragement, that far from sacrificing his life to art, art serves him as an excuse not to live. The principles and norms of his aesthetic, moreover, seemed a short while ago merely a transposition of the chief intentions of his hysteria. It is the particular system "made for one man," and therefore incommunicable; it is the sequestration Flaubert attributes in his last years "to the fear of living"; it is the absolute pessimism and frantic misanthropy whose origin is not knowledge of the world or men but a certain "presentiment," the basic condition of neurosis, which is itself the product of a preneurotic *universalization* of the original (hence familial) situation. Unable to denounce or change it, the child masks it to himself (and masks his anomaly) by seizing upon radical evil as the ruling principle of human relations. This self-defensive reaction to the ostracism he believes he suffers is finally just the abstract thought of the negative: Is it possible to derive from it a system of norms, a synthetic and concrete idea of artistic labor, a form as imperative, a content as requisite? No, *that cannot really happen*; morbid universalization is here falsely objective and can generate neither rule nor content; at most it can delude itself by generating symbolic and sadomasochistic narratives in which everything is arranged to show vice rewarded and virtue punished. Moreover, Flaubert's radical misanthropy—often translated by that dream of dying unknown, *his very name* forgotten—may not prevent him at other moments from desiring glory (he imagines it as a way of debasing the human race); but I contend that it creates in him, from adolescence on, a pathology of communication which deteriorates until his project of writing.

Hence this paradox: Gustave's neurosis could produce, *strictly speaking*, only neurotic works that would have repelled the public of 1850. Yet *because of it*, between the ages of thirty and forty he wrote a book that is dense and full, with an aesthetic rigor (not classical, however, since the "form of its content" is a draining away and it owes its beauty to the union of these opposites, the "marble" stability of the sentence subservient to the sliding toward death, or, if you will, the immutable charged with representing both immobility and movement) that imposes itself on the public and, for the writers of his time, initiates a future cycle, though the norms of the new art are still unclear (for until his preface to *Dernières chansons*, which is not even very good, Gustave never wrote about those norms publicly) and, *just because of that*, as if a concrete task were to be invented and achieved. This book, a concrete reality posed to the public as an enigma—because its mode of production remains unknown—becomes, as do all great works, institutional. Gustave, of course, is not the one who institutes it (as the normative determination of a certain sector of the social imagination); whoever its author, this operation does not belong to him; by a profound affinity with his time, he merely provides the means of the consecration. And his integration into that totality called the *Objective Spirit* of his society provokes a totalizing transformation of that organism, which must be altered from top to bottom to assimilate him.[3]

This paradox can be explained only if we assume that a work by itself transcends the stage of neurotic complacence and contains the structures of objectivity. But, being the issue of that *subjectivization* characteristic of neurosis, it can in fact generate in itself only the elements of *false objectivity* (for example, pathological universalization). Its author, then, is incapable of accomplishing this transcendence and objectifying himself in it as a singular universal, furnishing the public with a critical mirror held up to contemporary society. The public itself, in this particular case, is the agent that transforms this false witness into a true witness of his time. And since the work's objectivity remains false *in principle* (there is nothing to prevent panoramic consciousness, immobilism, and radical misanthropy from being mistakenly adopted with the resulting familiar contradictions), its truth—its power to express the times—can come to it, through an external qualification which it internalizes, only from the times themselves.

In other words, its false objectivity will become true in its very falsity if the various social strata that constitute its public see its past and present circumstances *with false objectivity*. But this is not all. There is no society based on the division of labor and on exploitation that does not have an objective but false idea of itself, in particular when that idea is produced by the ruling classes as their self-justification and as the edifying mystification that the exploited classes must be made to swallow. We call this unreal but quite rigorously constructed totality *ideology*. Can we say that all ideology is a collective neurosis? To do so would be to abuse a rigorous concept. This abuse, moreover, would serve no purpose; in other times, with other ideologies, morbid works have gone unnoticed, unremarked, slipping into nothingness before awakening the slightest resonance. And such public indifference results when the norms of art imply the rationality of the work. In the age of Voltaire and the Encyclopedists, the idea of beauty imposed by a combative bourgeoisie whose most potent weapon was critical reason suggests a rigorous construction, rules based on rationality rather than custom, communication between author and reader, the final objective of the universalizing enterprise, which is the aesthetic agreement (a universal determination of sensibility pathos-demand) of all readers. By the same token, art was defined by health, normality, the equilibrium of the artist, and even without making this negative consequence explicit, it was agreed that a madman cannot be an artist since madness *makes no concessions*. At that time, as in many other times, a morbid work hadn't the slightest chance of being read; furthermore—whatever it might be—it would bear witness neither to the miserly and conscientious bourgeois busy making their pile, trying to find the laws of mercantile capitalism by conceiving of them as rules of the economy *in general* and on the model of natural laws, encouraging scientific research with a view to its future practical utility, and combating customary privilege by substituting analytic positivism for history; nor to the aristocrats, whether traditionalist or enlightened, skeptical and sometimes even cynical, who would initiate the Revolution even before the third estate. They read Nerciat, they enjoyed Faublas because that superficial eroticism is a *rational* diversion; but de Sade's black, profound eroticism found no public because the books it produced, despite the undeniable beauty of their extravagance and the radicalism of the questions they raised, manifestly fell into the category of neurotic works.

This society, however, is fueled by false ideas: the idea of nature, of human nature, of natural law, is false; the fundamental conception of a bourgeoisie conceiving of itself as a universal class is false. The public of 1850 must have not only an erroneous notion of the structures of its society and its origins; in the cultivated strata of the society those errors must be of a *neurotic* sort and manifest in themselves underlying affinities with Flaubert's neurosis. Only in this way will Flaubert's neurosis, even in its systematic subjectivization, bear witness to those errors. Going one step further we can say that Gustave's malady will allow him to be objectified in representative works only if it appears as a particularization of what must surely be called a *neurosis of the Objective Spirit*. Not only does Flaubert's deviation become the measure and expression of a certain loss of direction of the community on the sociocultural level, but in the objective neurosis in which he participates the young patient finds general aims that surpass his own and give them universality; even his abstractions will a priori find their flesh and blood, their concrete substance, in the multiple determinations of the multitude. The tools of his creation, the techniques and especially that "taste" he has coveted, everything that seemed to escape him in the preneurotic state he will have the good fortune to fix *in objectivity* not only as products of a culture going off the deep end but also as the still unnoticed or unexplicit means of objectively structuring his works.

In other words, if his neurosis is the result of an objective illness, the work resulting from it doubly escapes neurotic subjectivization. As testimony, its truth expresses the false collective testimony; as irreducible novelty, it derives from the objective realm—especially from the works of contemporaries—methods that will endow it, at the very least, with that rigorous and nonneurotic necessity, aesthetic unity, and will consequently transform it into a singular imperative.

At this stage of our investigation we are compelled to reverse the terms and ask ourselves if art does not affirm one of its historic moments—that very moment fitting to the second half of the nineteenth century—through the neuroses of Flaubert and the great authors of his generation. In this case, instead of conceiving of Flaubert's art and its normative principles as the result of his neurosis—which brings us back to a pure subjectivization contradicted by his work—shouldn't we conceive of Gustave's neurosis as a product of art-to-be-made, its pathological aspect originating in the impasses of art-already-made and its objective requirement? Its meaning being that for art to be possible, these impasses must be surmounted—a requirement which, by the very nature of those impasses, will never be satisfied except by neurotic inventions? In Flaubert, art would become neurosis to survive its contradictions by an illusory surpassing and *hold on* until the general movement of the society has surpassed but not resolved them. In this case we would have to seek, at the core of subjectivization, elements of objectivity that, far from arising from the neurosis, would take possession of it, penetrate it, direct it in the name of a transcendent finality—a finality that is external, even in the very core of neurotic immanence—but without any *personal* agent.

In contrast to the Father's curse—which is a factor of subjectivization since the subject grasps it at the heart of lived experience as an *other* will and relates it to a well-defined person—a teleological and normative system would be organized in and through Flaubert's mental troubles without, however, leaving the realm of the anonymous and without being defined other than as the surpassing required by the objective contradictions of literature. In mentioning this rigorous structuring—and the transcendent imperative: if you want to write *today*, you must go crazy—in conjunction with the curse of Achille-Cléophas, an idiosyncratic and purely familial fact, whose consequence is a particular and purely subjective neurosis (which can, strictly speaking, be conceived of as a mode of Flaubert's intersubjectivity), I wanted to indicate the complexity of the problem. Indeed, if we must accept the hypothesis that Gustave's subjective neurosis is the internalization, and then the reexternalization, of *art-to-be-made* as a contradictory set of impersonal imperatives, we would be equally compelled to take account of familial structures and the will of the symbolic Father, which are the determining factors of Gustave's neurosis in its *other* guise as an irreducible singularity. What relation can be established between these two types of conditionings? And how can the same illness *at the same time* be valid as a solution to social antinomies and as an individual issue? We have witnessed the genesis of the Flaubertian aesthetic, and we have seen in its principles—immutability, panoramic consciousness, impersonalism, an identification of beauty and evil—the rationalization and universalization of a self-defensive system that at other moments acknowledges it is "made for one man."

If we must now admit that when he chose—during the preneurotic period—to reward his exile with literary glory, he released an objective process that directs the internal evolution of his malaise and ineluctably transforms that malaise into neurosis because art, to remain vital and survive this thankless period, needs neurotic ministers, we are faced with two contradictory interpretations of the attacks ravaging Gustave's existence. The first supports Maxime: immutability, the rejection of immediate reality, and the principle of panoramic consciousness (speaking only of those fundamental determinations originating exclusively in the structures of the Flaubert family for the sole purpose of elaborating a defensive strategy—when all is already lost) offer themselves as false aesthetic norms; art, defined and conceived exclusively for Gustave's individual salvation, loses all its substance, which is a considerable impoverishment. In the second hypothesis, art, as a function of its very impossibility, transforms Gustave into that chosen vehicle by which literature, already half shipwrecked, will be saved and brought into port. The neurosis is thus *positive*, appearing to be the only means conceivable in 1850 by which something like art might be possible, despite its new impossibility and especially *because* of that impossibility. Flaubert would then be a martyr, his difficulties requisite and his life *exemplary*. The erroneous principles at the origin of his aesthetic system by no means represent—as Maxime would have it—abstract, empty rules, a sort of artistic Eleaticism, but should be imagined—starting from its *results*, from *Madame Bovary*, for example—as the substructure necessary to a new and concrete conception of literary art and its object. Flaubert's Catharism would then appear as the monastic rule that imposes itself for half a century on respectable writers. Can these contradictory interpretations be entertained at once? We cannot say as yet. Whether one *can* accept them together or not, however, they *must* certainly be taken at the same time; for without the first, how do we explain the attacks, the sequestration, the stupor, the conduct of failure? And without the second, how do we explain *Madame Bovary*?

To conceive of the strange reciprocity uniting the singular and the collective in Gustave, we must first define what we call the Objective Spirit and its neurotic determination. In what follows we shall see the exigencies and contradictions of literature during this period, the questions it raised for the post-Romantics, and the reason why the only responses possible, not only for Flaubert but for his contemporaries, were psychopathic. We shall then endeavor to return to Gustave and determine *to what extent* and *how* the insoluble problems of art are at the heart of his troubles: how these can be—despite apparent contradictions—a neurotic response both to a subjective malaise and to the objective malaise of literature. Only by this method shall we perhaps manage to discover whether Flaubert's illness produced a mental deficit of some kind or whether, to the contrary, it was the means for him to accede to *literature-to-be-done*, more precisely, *to do it*.

CHAPTER SIXTEEN

Neurosis

PERSONAL AND OBJECTIVE

Let us avoid any misunderstanding. At the beginning of the twentieth century, the long literary dream that began with Gustave at age twenty was completed with the last of the Symbolists. At that moment many young writers who wanted to preserve the heritage of the preceding generation and go beyond it toward a new classicism, influenced by the strange attitude of their fathers and older brothers, decided that neurosis was the necessary condition for genius, as Gide wrote of Dostoyevsky. But this post-Symbolist generation was judging conditions necessary to the work of art according to those art demanded of their immediate predecessors. In this sense they were attesting to the fact that between 1850 and the end of the century you had to be mad to write. Quite true: their ideas only confirm my own. Only I cannot accept their *generalizing*, as if the meaning and function of literature—for the individual and society—were not constantly changing in the course of history; as if, depending on the period, art did not recruit its artists according to different criteria. It is true that from 1830 on, for reasons I shall enumerate, some of which are still valid today if less virulent, neurosis was the royal road to the masterpiece. But this doesn't seem to me to have been the case in the eighteenth century, and even less so in the seventeenth. In those times the author was chiefly required to be a "respectable man," integrated into the society as long as he strictly observed certain rules.

The point is that in integrated societies the psychoneurotic element, if it exists, is never regarded as the artist's aim, and even less as the reason for his art. I have said elsewhere that genius is a way out, the only one left when all is lost. I say so again, specifying that this way out is not neurotic and usually even allows one to spare oneself a neurosis.

In a word, when literature does not appeal to psychopathology, neurotic accidents do not take place, or, if they are produced in an author, this fact—of prime importance for understanding the individual—is annulled in the Objective Spirit because it is a matter of chance, a nonmeaning in relation to the meaning of that cultural moment. And although the substitution of one form for another is made *by men* and motivated by discomfort (there is a contradiction between the earlier form and content that asks to be treated in the present), there is no reason why this discomfort, which is of a specifically cultural order, should be experienced *neurotically*, *unless* the particular structures of the historical moment require it.

And this is precisely what happens around 1850, a moment in which the condition for creating art is to be neurotic.[1] Not in just any way but in a specific way, which we shall attempt to define; the objective movement that transforms culture on the basis of deeper transformations—but also as a function of traditions and laws proper to the cultural sector—produces such strict and contradictory norms that the contemporary moment of art cannot be realized as a determination of the Objective Spirit except in the form of *art-neurosis*. This does not mean that the works will be neurotic but that literary doctrines and the "poetic arts" will be, and that artists will have to act, or actually be, neurotic. And because of the dual nature of the literary act, reading, while it is taking place, becomes the public's brief, induced neurosis.

The Objective Spirit of an Age

{Editor's Note: Sartre has elaborated many of the notions relative to his use of the objective spirit of an age in his *Critique of Dialectical Reason*. He examines the way our best intentions frequently run up against the requirements of nature that we may not be aware of, what he terms, the "practico-inert." He writes, "History has two principles. One is human activity, simultaneously all and nothing, without which the inertia of things would evaporate like a volatile spirit. The other is inert matter, within the agents themselves and outside them which supports and deviates the whole practical edifice at the same time as having stimulated its construction (inasmuch as it was already a synthetic and passive deviation of previous praxis)" (2:135–36). Earlier in the first volume, he had given the example of Chinese peasants who, in order to make their land arable, deforested it and were thereby themselves the cause of floods (1:161).}

This cannot be understood without several general clarifications regarding the Objective Spirit. We may well wonder if it isn't dangerous to preserve this suspect notion still bearing traces of its origins in Hegelian idealism. But there is some use in reviving it and indicating the instrumental function it can perform in the perspective of historical materialism. In fact, the Objective Spirit—in a defined society, in a given era—is nothing more than culture as practico-inert. Let us understand, first of all, that at the origin of culture is work, *lived, actual* work insofar as it surpasses and retains nature in itself by definition. Nature is the given environment during a specific period, and work reveals this environment as simultaneously that which presently exists *and* the field of possibles that can be made use of to give that environment a new being consonant with the goal fixed by the worker, in short, with a certain condition, called the environment, that does not yet exist. Thus work is by itself antiphysis; its definition is to be antinature nature, which is precisely the essence of every cultural phenomenon. It seeks knowledge in order to transform, which implies, elementary as the work night be, that for the worker it bears witness to a type of exploitation, to a regime and the class struggle, ultimately to an ideology.

And for the worker himself immersed in this exploitation, work itself redounds upon him as an enemy force; being praxis, hence an illuminating surpassing of being toward an end (a surpassing of raw material toward the production of a change within the practical field), work is the internalization of the external and the reexternalization of the internal. As such, it is lived experience and consequently reveals both itself—as imposed, for example, and remaining external even while internalized—and, through it, the fundamental human relations proper to this mode of production (the kind of reciprocity established on the level of its concrete labor, the kind of nonreciprocity generated by the division of labor and possibly by the resulting exploitation). Moreover, this work is accomplished by means of an instrument—that would alone suffice to define society and man's relation to nature, at once antiphysis (which appears on the level of carved stone) and nature appearing beyond antiphysis (on the level of carved stone) and nature appearing beyond antiphysis and in it (even at the level of automation) as its internal and external limit, continually displaced. By the use he makes *of* it, the instrument therefore becomes the worker's *organ of perception*: it reveals the world and man in the world.

Thus the most elementary praxis, insofar as it is actual and lived from the inside, already contains as an immediate condition of its later development and as a real moment of that development, *in the living state*, an intuitive, implicit and *nonverbal* knowledge, a certain direct and totalizing yet wordless understanding of contemporary man among men and in the world, hence an immediate grasp of the inhumanity of man and his subhumanity, the first seed of a *political* attitude of refusal. On this level all thought is given, but it is not posed for itself, and so in its extreme compression it escapes verbal elaboration. I have said enough about it, however, to make it clear that superstructures are not the site of this revealing but merely the upper levels of elaboration in which this practico-theoretical knowledge is isolated, posed for itself, and systematically made explicit, hence becoming theoretico-practical.

Here we must take reflection as a starting point, for reflection shapes lived experience according to its own ends, though that experience is originally unreflected and becomes reflected according to certain rules that themselves issue from certain reflexive needs. In other words, in the totality of praxis reflection isolates the moment of theory, which has never existed alone but only as a practical mediation determined by the end itself. Recourse to language thus becomes necessary. And language, on the one hand, isolates and transforms into a finished product the knowledge that existed implicitly in the worker's act. It provides names and hardens in the form of defined structures all the elements that have interpenetrated in the cultural revealing of work (mode of production, relations of production, institutional whole, mores, law, etc.). Named and thus perpetuated, these fragments of the real becoming fragments of knowledge are thereby falsified. Through this quality of false knowledge they come close to being a nonknowledge, which also exists on the elementary level of the living actualization of praxis—that set of opinions arising from pathos that are proffered, at this higher degree of elaboration, as learning from experience.

In fact, these extrapolations are inseparable from lived experience, and they form, if you will, class subjectivity. After processing they will become the clearest of what we call ideologies. Thus, alongside false knowledge, whose origin is a practical and nonverbalized knowledge, ideologies that impose themselves on the worker—ideologies of his class, of the middle or ruling classes—are introduced or reintroduced into him in the form of recipes explicitly presented as a verbal exposé or a related set of determinations of discourse that would illuminate his condition and offer him the means to tolerate it. This involves chiefly, of course, a conception of the world and of men formed by the ruling class in taking possession of its environment through the systematic exercise of power, and inculcated—by familiar means—in the working classes as though it were a universal ideology, or a body of knowledge. In the worker, of course, these ideologies come into permanent conflict with *his own* ideology—which issues communally, like a myth, from his hopes, his despairs, the refusal to accept his condition as an inevitable destiny—and they have the upper hand as long as working-class ideology is not *verbalized*. Were it to be so, moreover, it might encourage a sudden awareness but might just as easily retard it: class consciousness appears only at the end of a theoretico-practical effort that aims at dissolving ideology into knowledge as much as possible.

I will merely cite as an example the slow emancipation of the worker in the nineteenth century. Between 1830 and 1840, his ideas were so effectively confused that *L'Atelier*, the first proletarian newspaper, insisted on Catholicism, or at least theism, in face of the Jacobin bourgeoisie who had deprived the worker of the consolation of God. He set his knowledge in the practical realm against alien ideologies—as did the *canuts* in Lyon; when wages were lowered, he rebelled. But as soon as the revolt was either victorious or suppressed, he could think explicitly about this knowledge only through alien ideologies, words and phrases that did not apply to it—quite to the contrary and that distorted it while claiming to articulate it.

The Objective Spirit, Ideologies, and the Written Word

Thus, elaborated ideologies are quite distinct from that intuitive and immediate constellation I have just described, which involves an implicit ideology spun around a kernel of knowledge, accompanied by myths and a system of values tacitly applied by agents who have never articulated its basis. Not only are these elaborated ideologies distinct from it but they are in conflict with it by providing immediate and nonverbalized thought with translations that conceal it from itself. Yet it will be observed that the force of these inadequate systems comes from their inertia. Primitive and immediate thought is none other than the practical behavior of the worker insofar as it discloses in order to effect change and is necessarily accompanied by a nonpositional consciousness of itself; this presupposes a constant "syntony" of that tacit body and the real, whence its perpetual flexibility. It must exist as an act and as part of an act, or it does not exist at all. In other words, it issues from work and vanishes with it. On the other hand, *verbalized* value systems and ideologies remain in the mind, or at the very least in the memory, because language is matter and because their elaboration has given them material inertia.

Written words are stones. Learning them, internalizing their combinations, we introduce into ourselves a mineralized thought that will subsist in us by virtue of its very minerality, until such time as some kind of material labor, acting on it from outside, might come to relieve us of it. I call these irreducible passivities *as a whole* the Objective Spirit. And this definition has no negative intent, no voluntary deprecation. In a society of exploitation, of course, these structured wholes are harmful to the exploited classes to the extent that they are introduced into everyone from the outside and recast in the memory as ramparts against any sudden awareness. But taken in themselves they simply manifest this necessity: matter is the mediating element between men to the same degree that through their praxis they become mediators between different states of matter.

The Objective Spirit is culture itself but only in accordance with its becoming the *practico-inert*. That is valid for all its aspects, as much for the mode of production, defined by that particular wrought matter which is the instrument, as for relations between men as they are established as *institutions* and become lived institutionally. And the relational mode of wrought matter to the agent is, as I have proved elsewhere, imperative. Every object produced presents to me its directions for use as an order ("Shake contents before using," "Slow, school zone," etc.). We understand that even if, as frequently happens, the sponsor of the object in question finds his interest in the imperative form—which guarantees the proper usage of the thing—he is not the source of that form. Strictly speaking, he can present his advice only in the form of a hypothetical imperative, such as: "If you want to use this object, you must . . . ," and so forth.

For the real relation between men is actually reciprocity, which excludes orders. But whatever the object produced—even a machine—the utilization that Society or any such group recommends by way of it necessarily passes *through* and consequently undergoes the transformation imposed on it by the practico-inert. Its directions for use become an inert discourse participating in the inertia of matter. As such it imposes itself on the agent as *not to be* modified by any subjective intention—not because it represents the universal in the face of the particular, but because the practical seal imposed on the raw material participates in its materiality and is introduced into everyone as an inert thought that belongs to no one but must be preserved, whose practical consequences must be derived and applied on pain of seeing the practical thing burst out. In the internal structure of this thought, in any case, we encounter material inertia (for example, in a particular and mechanical relation between premises and consequences). In sum, it represents at once the beyond of matter here present and a kind of materialization of that beyond. And if there have always been men to give orders, they should rather be considered transmitters. Besides, the "master" who commands, and usurps the inorganic minerality of the commandments given by the object, clearly plays an inorganic role in relation to the slave, and his orders obviously issue from a stone mouth, his own. Indeed, he commands as a function of his mineral being, of his interest, which is something imperative, and he augments its status as thing by depositing it into that other thing, discourse.

In our view, the Objective Spirit represents culture as practico-inert, as the totality to this day (in any day) of the imperatives imposed on man by any given society. But for our purpose, which is to study art-neurosis as a historically specific determination of the Objective Spirit, it is preferable to imagine only a sector of that spirit: the elaborated unity of ideologies, cosmogonies, ethicoaesthetic and confessional systems as they manifest themselves as the structuring of a discourse. We have no reason to consider them in themselves, as ideas that are institutionalized, but should consider them rather as they pose to language the question of their adequate expression, and thereby define literature in the abstract as a work of material production. We are at the top of a hierarchy, and thoughts seem almost dead. But they are merely exhausted along the way: they are neither reflections nor byproducts of an infrastructural, unthinking reality but must simply be seen as the last avatars of total ideas, mute and practical, that are merely one at the outset with the act of work, of appropriation and exploitation, or a hundred other acts. This explosive combination of values, verities, ideologies, myths, and mystifications, contradicting each other insofar as they emanate from classes and—within classes—from different social strata, nonetheless poses itself as a multiple and contradictory comprehension of our species as the product of its history, of present circumstances, and of the future that it is preparing for itself "on the basis of prior circumstances." Enclosed in writing, it has become canned thought. But written language, by lending its material and institutional reality to those "expressible" thoughts, has bent them to its laws. Intellection—and likewise comprehension—is surely a synthetic surpassing of signifying materiality toward signification. Nonetheless, that surpassed matter is preserved in the act that transcends it, and it both limits and determines that act in spite of itself. Materialized in writing, culture—at this level—burdens thought with its own weight and does not derive its permanencies from a firm and sustained but still lively intention; quite to the contrary, they are the passive aspect of the idea.

I am speaking, of course, of the written thing, and I am well aware that no judgment on it is ever definitive. Posterity will return to it and situate itself by situating it in new circumstances. Still, certain internal articulations, certain structures—manifest or implicit—are unvarying. Consequently, living thought as a surpassing is at once aroused, advanced, and retarded by that opacity to be surpassed which is precisely the idea as written, "thingafied." Indeed, this written idea has set its seal upon matter, but matter has in turn invaded the idea-seal, infected it with its heteronomy, better known as the principle of exteriority. It has broken the interiority of the original thought—a translucid presence of the all in the parts and the parts in the all—and substituted the *letter* in its place by penetrating even its minutest aspect with an external scattering. The idea becomes a thing: once imprinted, its tendency to persevere in its being is precisely that of the thing. When the library is deserted, thought dies; the thing alone remains, made of paper and ink.

Writing operates on a dual principle: one person writes, the other reads. Without the reader, nothing is left, not even signs—for their only function is to guide the project of transcendence. We might almost speak of an abstract virtuality, which does not come from the book itself but determines it from the outside insofar as it becomes the object of various intentions: of the librarian who arranges a catalogue, or of future readers who promise themselves that "one day" they will read or reread the work. These considerations lead us to several conclusions.

The Objective Spirit: Three Clarifications

1. *The Objective Spirit*, while *never* on the side of pure lived experience and free thought, exists *as an act* only through the activity of men and, more precisely, through the activity of *individuals*. As far as we are concerned, it is clear that without readers it simply would not exist. On the other hand, in the intimacy of a room, in classrooms or libraries, millions of people read millions of books, each of which contains references to other works not consulted at that moment. A detotalized totalization is thereby effected; each reader totalizes his reading *in his own way*, which is at once similar to and radically distinct from the totalization that another reader, in another town, another neighborhood, tries to realize *with the same book*. From this point of view, the multiplicity of individual totalizations (they are not all related to the same book but to different sectors of written knowledge, many implicitly referring to each other) seems irreducible. It would take too long to explain here how, despite the apparent atomization, this set of circumstances continually effects an exhaustive totalization without a totalizer.

My point is, rather, that following generations will make today's lived present into a totality that is past, surpassed, still virulent in certain ways, and readers, individually or as a group, vaguely sense this. So they feel they must work their particular synthesis of one detail of a sector of knowledge in the stable and inherently dated milieu of accomplished totality. And this totality—as it appears to them, an invisible unity of the diverse, a transcendence that destroys their present immanence, a future that eradicates experience in men's hearts as it is being lived in the name of experience to be lived by future readers—represents for each of them the totalitarian objectivization of each one's particular efforts of acculturation. In this future objectivization, whose meaning is still unknown and which, as such, is aspired to only through empty intentions, they find their ineffable objective unity: it makes them, for themselves, representatives of *the times*. But as their praxis at this moment is reading—an effort, indeed, of acculturation—these living times that have already been fixed and described appear to them in their cultural aspect (the limits of knowledge, unresolved problems, areas of ignorance, established convictions to be revoked by the future). Seen from another angle, this is precisely the Objective Spirit of the age, an imperative constellation, unlimited but finite, whose thought cannot yet emerge.

2. However, although a gaze is needed to restore it by making it readable today, the Objective Spirit is characterized on this level by its position *outside*, not the present product of an effort of thought but first and foremost *in books*, in the writings of *others*. In this sense its materiality expresses at once its alterity (in relation to the reader) and its pastness (it bears a date, *it may already be dated*; recent works may be better informed, it may be challenged six months from now by works as yet unpublished). In any event, reading is an attempt to transform a thing into an idea. The eye must recover the ideative act of the other through its vestiges, gather up the scattering of signs, and discursively recompose according to learned codes what may formerly have been the object of flashes of intuition. Our concern, for the moment, is with the double character of the Objective Spirit, which can be a surpassing toward the idea *in us* only if it is *outside*, as worked matter. The guarantee of its permanence is its status as thing: it does not exist, it is, and the only dangers threatening it come from outside, from great natural forces and social disorders. And when I transform the thing into an idea by reading, the metamorphosis is never complete; it is an idea-thing penetrating me because the reality of that hybrid being which I alone can revive is necessarily outside me as thought frozen in matter, and because that thought, even as I make it mine, remains definitively *other*, thought surpassed by another who orders me to revive it.

Furthermore, the idea I appropriate is also, I know, appropriated by other readers at the same time; these are people I don't know, who are not like me, and who surpass the same material toward similar but perceptibly different significations. Thus every lexeme remains *within me* external to me to the extent that I perceive it as enriched by a thousand interpretations that escape me; the book, a finite mode of the Objective Spirit, appears both internal and external in relation to the reader. Reading is an internalization according to definite procedures, but the sentence is never entirely soluble. Its indestructible materiality derives at once from the frozen rigidity of the *vestige* and from its multiple relation—for every reader—to others. In other words, its *virtual* extension to a whole public and its current connections with *series* or readers or *groups*, or the two together. In this sense, writing gives us a glimpse of society as one of the elements of its essential duality. Or, if you will, the exteriority of writing makes it appear to every reader as a *social object*. This, indeed, is *what it is*. If apprehended in its relations to the seriality of readings, it seems to be a *collective*, a real index of social detotalization. Through it we measure the *separation* of individuals in an envisaged society; its mystery represents the false union of readers, each of whom is unaware of the other's thoughts.

In our societies this may be the result of the creation of mass culture; in this case, as the words penetrate the person reading, that person internalizes *his own solitude* in the face of an impenetrable block of exigent sociality, without considering that this sociality is nothing but the detotalization of a collectivity as lived socially by each of its members. In short, the social opacity of the book and its institutional character refer quite simply to an indefinite number of other solitudes. In this way, the book as *collective* is, in a sense, a *sacred* object; its "numinous" character is manifest most clearly when we imagine it in its occasional relations with uniformed people who read very little. When they approach a work recommended by others whom they trust—they treat the text as if it were composed of *carmina sacra* {sacred music}, according it the same *respect*. In effect, they are dimly if inarticulately aware that by absorbing those little pointed black splinters we call words, they are about to swallow society whole. But they also know that it will remain *outside* as the collective character of the book, even as they are trying to install in themselves the content of the work as *knowledge*. Thus, through its exteriority the duality becomes a trinity: the relation reader–author refers to the usually serial relation among readers. The profundity of an *idea* I have *read*, as I have retained and understood it, *is others*: those significations that I have not grasped but that I know to have been awakened by the gaze of others as *underlying structures* of the legible object.

Profundity is therefore an abstraction that haunts me, especially if I know and lament the gaps in my education, and it is an intention that misses its mark insofar as it *escapes me* in certain respects. It is a way of isolating myself with respect to society *grasped through its culture*; moreover, this abstract but present profundity defining the work in its objectivity comes to me as an imperative: I *must* understand what the author wanted to say as best I can, and in its totality, to the extent that others have exalted the meaning of the work and made those ideas-things incandescent. Obviously I will not complete this task—I know that well enough, and how far I get depends on my education, my greater or lesser degree of familiarity with abstractions, the time I have at my disposal, etc. But the imperative is to push as far as I can, to become integrated with new social strata; when I can go no further, the mysterious residue represents the unfathomable, indefinite social realm, or, more precisely, seriality.

If the work refers to a group—and it must be a sworn group—the imperatives are much more rigorous. For a young communist, the *Manifesto* of 1848 is at once the work of Marx, an objective description of reality, and the theory-practice that creates the unity of the Party to which he has just given his allegiance. The individual aspect of the work, its relation to the dead author, tends to be effaced (as does the relation of Carnot's principle, or some other discovery in the natural sciences, to the living man who invented it). On the other hand, the second characteristic is sustained and exalted by the third: the *processes* articulated by Marx and Engels, the events presented and illuminated by the class struggle, are not purely and simply facts for this neophyte. They are *also* facts and perhaps *primarily* facts, as we have just seen, insofar as knowledge absorbs such thinkers and eliminates them, but they are also what he *must* understand to realize a total integration with the group; and furthermore they are practical considerations which *must* illuminate his understanding of the current politics of his Party and his individual tasks.

The book is structured as a collective to the extent that any group is necessarily penetrated by seriality (it may be that students or young workers meet regularly to read the book and discuss it). Only *this evening* the young man has gone to his room and reads without friends or witnesses. But while this ambiguous structure reminds the isolated reader *in this fashion* of his present solitude, it defines it not as a real and permanent state but as both a product of bourgeois society (therefore as a yoke to be thrown off) and a danger: all alone, I have no one to stop me from making a mistake. I must try to read as if I were *everyone together*. It is my vow—my commitment to the Party—that determines my reading; the book restores the group as the normative determination of my activities.

All these remarks, of course, derive from the fact that the work, something inert, continues to *be-there* passively, the way an object in motion continues to move indefinitely if nothing comes along to stop it. And the work presents itself to everyone in the name of that inertia as having existed before the current act of reading, existing elsewhere, in other libraries, and living on after the present reading. The book, whatever it is, and whether it conveys fact or fiction, virtually gives us the assertoric itself in the imperative form. Indeed, I distinguish two imperatives: the first—crude, obscure and solitary—is linked to seriality. We *must* read the Goncourts because everyone reads them and we should be able to discuss them; so we also *must* understand and judge them. The second imperative, which refers to the platoon and its unity, is the imperative of freedom—at least in principle. But in both we see that comprehension is not defined in each reader by the free play of his possibilities and the quiet recognition of their limits; rather it is required, and when at the end of his resources the reader halts midway, he feels guilty and regards his limits not as factual givens (linked to the empirical conditions of his intellectual development) but as a moral fault and a premeditated failure (in the past he *could* have learned more, even today he *should have been able* to concentrate more, to ask more of his intelligence and of course none of this is true).

In other words, when human intentions are addressed to us through worked matter, materiality renders them *other*; inert but indelible, they designate us as *other* than ourselves and our fellow citizens. Human reciprocity is broken by the mediation of the thing, and the frozen intention that summoned us *as others* can have only the structure of obligation. Thus the Objective Spirit—which is culture as practico-inert—can address itself to us, even in literature, only as an *imperative*. This is its very constitution, and it cannot be changed, even if we accomplish the task of intellection or comprehension prescribed to us, because of the indestructible residue of materiality that remains in us after reading, and which we apprehend as a failure or an unjustifiable halt in our mental operations. The Objective Spirit reveals our finitude and compels us to regard it as a fault.

These remarks, of course, are not meant to restore reading—or the transformation of the thing-idea into an idea-thing—into its plenitude. The syntheses of recomposition are in fact accomplished according to objective rules (the structures of language, the author's explicit and implicit intentions, the judgments on the author made by other authors we have already read, etc.) *and*, simultaneously, according to the idiosyncratic habitus of a singular internalization (oneirism, resonances, bad faith, ideological interests, etc.). As a result, the work, apprehended by a developed—at least partially closed individuality, is never entirely taken for what it is; it is read in the light of the historical moment and of the cultural means at the reader's disposal (which indeed rank him in one social stratum or another); and at the same time the act of reading serves as a pretext for each reader to relive his own history and perhaps the primal scene. Be that as it may, under this subjective camouflage the skeleton of imperatives remains, directing the readerly thoughts as much as and more than they seem guided by the reader's oneiric (and purely factual) compliance.

3. This would be of little importance if, in the sector concerning us, the Objective Spirit as it is fundamentally materialized did not manifest itself to readers as the disparate contiguity of works belonging to all social categories and all periods. As soon as this atemporal juxtaposition is internalized and realized in me, it becomes explosive. I may have chosen *these* books and tried to digest them to satisfy my singular needs; as a systematic resurrection, reading constitutes me as the objective mediation between the cultural past and present, and between different conceptions to which contemporary works appeal. By awakening *meanings* through a totalizing movement whose source is my personal unity, I provoke collisions of ideas and feelings, and by lending them my time and my life I exalt and exacerbate innumerable contradictions. Now, given our earlier descriptions, we already know that these contradictions are written in stone: they are rooted in the inertia of thesis and antithesis. They coexist outside me in the pure, nonsignifying being-there of the thing; internalized, they are revealed through my subjectivity, but still retain the rigidity that characterizes them on the outside. We are not, in effect, dealing with a flexible and fluctuating confrontation with an idea, which in a practical totalization would set the all against the part and the parts against each other. There is no whole; only disjunctures, contradictory theses, whose authors were often unaware they contradicted each other since they were unacquainted. Thus the oppositions are at once rigid and without real consistency, not having been generated by a rigorous totalization. The operation proposed to the reader here is the reverse: he must totalize and surpass toward a synthesis starting from those given contradictions revealed in contingency.

I say he *must* totalize because, as we have seen, every idea of the Objective Spirit imposes itself as a demand as soon as it is invoked.

Furthermore, when two ideas—demands are manifest at the same time in a reading, these contrary imperatives imply a third imperative: to reconcile or transcend toward a synthesis, to integrate these notions gleaned somewhat at a random into the organic unity of a totalization that produces and surpasses them, and will itself be an imperative. Thus the Objective Spirit, an external-internal reality whose source—as far as we are now concerned—is the dual aspect of writing, is characterized both as a sum of inert demands and as a supreme, ubiquitous imperative that summons the reader to dissolve contradictions in the unity of an ongoing totalization.

I say "ongoing" because the Objective Spirit renews itself: every day it is enriched by new books, new demands. And these new writings can very well become integrated into one or another personal totalization effected by readers. But they can also set themselves against any such a totalization. In this case, everyone must get back to work again and break the determinations (the negations, the limits) of his totalization with respect to the new work and its silent demand, so it can be included. And as the number of books published each day far surpasses the individual possibility of totalizing written culture, the perpetual addition of new material has the effect of preventing the totalization from closing in on itself and being transformed into a tranquil totality.

This is what we will call the life of the Objective Spirit, a material detotalization internalized as a demand to be totalized which contradicts that dream of stone, totality in inertia, by the constant and nullifying appearance of new productions. The Objective Spirit of an age (I am, of course, defining it only in the realm of writing) is at once the sum of works published during a specific period and the multiplicity of totalizations effected by contemporary readers. As we know, thoughts are living things. They are born of original thought, which is merely practical behavior as it reveals the environment from the totalizing perspective of its reorganization. When thoughts are in libraries, they are petrified by writing and therefore dead. The reader recomposes them, yet he does not reach the profound and naked life of the root-thought; the *lived* reality he confers by internalizing them cannot be a return to thought before writing: it assumes the written word and can merely animate the graphemes by binding them together in an interior synthesis. In this sense he is still distancing himself from primal spontaneity; his own personal, practical field is not defined by needs and physical dangers but is composed of books and words, and his work is the perpetual stirring up and reorganization of this field on command. Yet his practical thoughts are indeed spontaneous in that they represent his conscious behavior (reflexive or unreflected) as a reader.

Hence, whatever the content of the Objective Spirit as canned thoughts, we can say that every cultivated reader formally intuits it—totalizing it in the abstract—insofar as that intuition simply illuminates the multiple aspects of reading. Awakened significations do not demand only to be understood or even totalized: these engraved signs refer to the universe, to our being-in-the-world, and primarily to our conduct. We are led back to the real environment, full of surprising traps, that we left behind upon entering the library. Knowledge and ideas are—more or less directly—practical; so it is through our personal praxis that we must try to accomplish this veritable totalization demanded by books (through techniques, ethics, religions, etc.). Action, being the totalizing of doctrines, thus transforms us; we become representatives of a past or future group that we intuit behind the imposed practico-inert idea, or a group we will form by winning it over to our practical totalization. For the Objective Spirit tells us, contradictorily but imperatively, who we are: in other words, what we have to do.

We are chiefly concerned, however, with a category of specialized readers who read in order to write. In them, literature plays the role of recruiting officer. No doubt their choice to become writers represents a subjective way out of their difficulties and problems. We have seen this in Flaubert's case. But just as you can become a shoemaker for accidental reasons and through particular events, and those reasons and events do not alter the objective need to know how to repair shoes according to current techniques and use an awl *properly*, so every reader who reads in order to write will discover literature as it is in his time even before deciding to be an apprentice author. In short, none of them, in any age, invented or reinvented literature. We might say that it is reinvented in them as an obligation to write from the starting point of literature already written. In every historical society in which an individual decides to be a writer—whatever the outcome—literature is given to him primarily as a totality he chooses to enter. This totality, of course, is not given to him in all its details, by which I mean in all works of literature; quite the contrary, the individual's approach to the All is variable. We have Flaubert's totality, Proust's—which might be called "highly literate"—as well as that of the young shepherd whose writings were published by *Les Temps modernes*, who had read only almanacs, newspapers, and a few books by Victor Hugo. Yet none of them *invented* literature for his own ends. It existed, and each of those would-be writers, according to certain features of what I call literature-already-written, deemed it advisable to enter an apprenticeship and become a representative of literature-to-be-written. So literature seems to be a practical activity and manifests itself by the existing results of that activity, literary works, which the aspiring writer reads differently than a simple reader, in order to discover through inspection of the finished product the rules that aided its production and which he wants to know for his own use.

CHAPTER SEVENTEEN

Objective Neurosis and *Madame Bovary*

{Editor's Note: As we conclude our study, let us recall that Sartre's intention in the last volume of his huge work, reflected in this final chapter of the present abridged edition, is to show why *Madame Bovary*, a work advocating nihilism—the doctrine that the worst is always true in human affairs and that efforts to put meaning and value into our lives are hopeless—was accepted by the French people of Gustave's time, and, with appropriate changes, by people of our own time, as a "realist" novel. The reason is that it masks the unjust ways the rich and the well-to-do middle classes sacrifice the lives and work of the poor and the workers, even to the extent of condoning their deaths as necessary but unfortunate happenings for which they are not responsible. On the other hand, this had to be done in such a way that it seems to be merely the ordinary ways everyday people live their lives, a perfectly written work, one that seems to be so true that it appears to be a thing of nature, beyond human criticism. It is Sartre's claim that Gustave Flaubert's entire life prepared him to write such a work since he *freely* chose to remain close to a family that regarded him as a failure and indeed the "idiot" of the family, whose writings could only be the scribbling of a son who could not live up to the standards of his eminent family.

Moreover, throughout the last hundreds of pages, it is Sartre's intention to show that Gustave's "fall," his collapse before his brother doctor Achille, was an "oracular" anticipation of the false realism that was characteristic of the bourgeoisie. In the abstract, this would be a stupid view to hold; but, for Sartre, it was true (and is true) because of the neurosis of the Objective Spirit that rules our times.

Finally, Sartre has been engaged in a long discussion of Charles

Marie René Leconte de Lisle, who formally might have taken Gustave's place, except that his hatred of man is, for Sartre, only abstract.}

For literature to posit itself as an absolute, not in theory but in the imaginary object it produces, we must be able to discover in the work a singular quality attesting to the indissoluble unity of an objective neurosis in the author—the internalization of contradictory imperatives and the surpassing of all these contradictions by art failure—and of a clearly delineated subjective neurosis, with roots reaching down to his early childhood.

If the creator is lucky, each of these determinations will reflect the other in a constant reciprocity, and it will be unclear whether the first simply facilitated the internalization of the second or whether, on the contrary, the second produced the first, in the course of its evolution, as an invented and universal consequence of its individual contradictions by projecting itself into the objectivity of a work to escape stewing in its subjectivity. Or whether, as a consequence of the original situation, art neurosis was able to *become incarnate* in a particular subject and, far from remaining a set of formulas and pseudophilosophical aphorisms, to live through him as an endured delirium and as an accepted Passion. If anyone is to have a chance of moving this sullen society, its bitterness and anguish masked by its superficial fires, he must clearly be a member of the professional elite or must be wealthy and, as such, conscious of belonging to the most favored classes—those called, at the time, the bourgeoisie. This class consciousness must be the source of his malaise. Let him regard himself with the scornful eyes of the nobility: he will be all the more acceptable since at this time a depiction of the bourgeois as seen from below by the brothers of the massacred must be avoided at all costs. {In an earlier footnote Sartre had written, "There had been many massacres since 1794. Each time, however, the bourgeoisie was able to deceive itself and preserve its facade as the universal class. . . . In June '48 the veils were torn away: the bourgeoisie fulfilled its class reality by means of a crime. It lost its universality and defined itself by its power relations with the other classes in a divided society." And, thus the educated reader must see these massacres as necessary and as having nothing to do with themselves.}

Thus hatred is more tolerable; for the reader, it is reversed—the author makes him experience that internalization of the sentiment the "lower classes" harbor for the murderers of June '48 as the internalization of a privileged disgust for the commoner's condition. With one proviso: that self-hatred appear as the burning core of misanthropy; the aristocratic gaze will not be the gaze the writer—in the manner of Vigny and, comically, of Leconte de Lisle—levels on his public, but *first and foremost*, to the contrary, the gaze he feels leveled from above on his own life, the vivid light from that dead star, the nobility. It is not anyone's gaze, yet it must be *endured*; that is the reflexive consciousness of the true nihilist—or, if you will, his reflexive phantom; in fact, reflection does not *exist* in this realm. Rather, whatever the reflexive scissiparity, the last reflexive consciousness does not grasp itself as the consciousness *of* consciousness but as a superior degree of the reflected; in other words, it refers by a transascendant intention to the reflection *of another*, and is thereby constituted *in its being* as pseudoreflected, meaning that this other being constitutes it in that this other is *elsewhere*. Moreover, this consciousness, from the depths of its baseness, thereby reveals itself to the *scorn* of that dead eye as *exis*. And the pseudoreflected feels constituted as an object by that gaze—which is identified increasingly with an illumination—without ever being able to enjoy that fundamental character of its objective essence: a contemptible-being-held-in-contempt.

In short, he must first be discontent with himself, and he must not be able to *live* this discontent even while presenting it as constitutive of lived experience; in one respect this discontent must be nothing more than what haunts him, and in another merely his first *concern*; haunted by his insubstantiality, as contemptible-being-held-in-contempt, he must turn constantly toward reflexive scissiparity in order to coincide with the *absent* reflection of contempt. Nor must he ever succeed—obviously—and from this fundamental concern, from this never abandoned, never entirely successful effort to *realize* himself as the horror he inspires in the *other*, he must derive some metaphysical merit, owing entirely to his dissatisfaction with himself and to the profound failure that is his identifying mark—not primarily or even chiefly an incapacity to cast off his baseness but an incapacity merely to *see* it (or to *see* it *seen*). Given this self-hatred conceived as the mystical relation of the feudal to the bourgeois, which—insofar as it *does not have* its roots in an inexpiable and irreversible crime—is never altogether felt as real and remains in suspense, proffering itself as always future, always capable of pouncing on its man and leaving him struck by a blinding intuition (an intuition that is forever impossible, of course, but which, from the depths of the future where it claims to be hiding, seems to be the ever *realizable* meaning of lived experience); given this internalized and reversed hatred, the author has the perfect right to hate others. The public will believe this is only an incitement to each reader to win salvation by hating himself, but in fact this is not true. Here, all is alienation:

its source is a hatred clearly proclaimed by the other (or believed to be so); this alienating primacy of the symbolic father, the aristocrat or any *other*, is not truly experienced—except as a Destiny—and so provokes a neurotic hatred of the other (not necessarily, of course, hatred against someone we believe we are hated by), the intentional and dialectically rigorous displacement, masked by syncretism, of one unrealizable objective by another, which the reader is only too inclined to *realize*.

In this sense the *misanthropy* of the neurotic author of 1850 is a realistic impulse aimed at real objects, although it is dialectically conditioned by an unreal and unrealizing—if true—hatred of oneself. *Hatred of* others—whatever its origin—remains at the center; and obviously in that society devoured by hatred one wants to satisfy hatred still more than contempt. But that hypocritical and puritanical public can give itself such license—and thereby welcome a writer-witness, looking at the world in complicity with him—only if the work that invites him to do so presents itself initially as the product of a centripetal hatred whereby the author claims to discover *first the hateful universal*, namely our universality, human nature, in the contempt he inspires in himself or does his utmost to inspire.

Thus we find the tendency, which is detectable everywhere at the time, to dissolve vulgarly historical crimes in the anguished metaphysical and nontemporal self-condemnation of the species in the heart of the man who committed them. They disappear, they are merely symbols, merely the necessary temporalization of intelligible character; the worst is necessarily and always certain, for it is merely the expression—in circumstances otherwise random and negligible—of radical evil as it is posited, sensed, sought, and never attained. And this evil is none other than the return in force of universality, the bourgeoisie posing once again as the universal class but this time *negatively*, by attributing to human nature the contradictions, conflicts, alienation, and hatred that are the products of bourgeois society in France in the mid-nineteenth century. This means, of course, that the chosen writer must *keep silent about the events of '48*; that is indeed Leconte de Lisle's strategy, and, as we have seen, he admits it freely. But this isn't sufficient; or, rather, it is too much and not enough: too much because it might be seen, *it* is *seen* as a *historic* silence based on a specific contempt (and on an equally specific fear); not enough because misanthropy must not remain abstract and rail against man without giving its reasons. It would be unconvincing; the only way to make it attractive is to give it content, which is to say that the optimal attraction at this time will be produced by the reading of a work that in its subject matter, and even in its form, engenders the man of misanthropy, a work that *makes visible* the curse of Adam and its eternal consequences. But it must do this through the ordinary anecdote, in the banality of *apolitical* life, so that abjection, discovered in simple, "habitual" lived experience, justifies in advance political crimes and depoliticization without *ever* recalling them. This last condition implies that the *atemporality* of the presentation is based, in fact, on a temporal discrepancy: if the author's manifest misanthropy is to be welcomed as "genuine" and presented as an actually felt sense of shame, and not as something coldly manipulated for promotional purposes (or as a denunciation of the bourgeois, tied to the events of '48), it cannot present itself—unlike the misanthropy flaunted by de Lisle—as the simple result, eternal and calm, of a stoical or "brahman" panoramic consciousness. In other words, it must be *generated at the time* not as a blind passion forged by accidental causes but as a *conversion*, as the discovery of the truth in the light of an individual event that is specific and yet archetypal; this event can only be failure.

Abstract Hatred

But it had to be felt by the author in his very marrow; Leconte de Lisle's failure was doubly defective in not being truly lived as such and in being related to the taboo date. The only way an experienced failure might have escaped the reader's suspicion, then, was to have taken place *prior* to the catastrophe of '48—not by much, however, three or four years would suffice, otherwise that particular defeat might have been explained by the previous regime (the stupidity of the Restoration, the violence of the Empire, the revolutionary Terror, the privileges of the Old Regime). And it had to leave visible traces: the meaning of that shipwreck would then be that man is impossible, a life had to be broken under the July monarchy, and only that living deadman, the artist, could survive this singular experience of our universal impossibility. A small, obscure disaster, inexplicable, irreparable, this shipwreck had to be lived as an irreversible degradation, the frigate had to sink into the lower depths of subhumanity. Through his martyrdom and through it alone, lived through *for nothing* and without compensation on condition that it reveal to him the indissoluble bond between misfortune and evil, between our total impotence and our original culpability, the victim can be *convincing*; dead and already cold, the public's welcome can raise him to the rank of *fascinating writer*. For this original failure—precisely because it is prior to the collective failure of 1848 and implicates only humanity—can be recomposed by reading and thus established for *this* public *as an oracle*, and—through a disaster that will become manifest in and through the work as a singular universal—as the symbolization of the advent of the Second Republic, of its impotence and its crimes, of its collapse and its death, crushed under the boot.

For although that memorable historical moment distantly follows the individual misadventure of the author, it is nonetheless a singular universal as well. Through tens of thousands of individuals, something was begun in pain and blood, then broke apart, that bore general *significations* even at the outset, but its *meaning*—even in the midst of generality—is a singular temporalization, a lived and plural determination of the intersubjectivity that marks the era at least as much as the era marks it, and that "will never be seen twice."

With this in mind, we shall more firmly grasp the prophetic character of personal failure—insofar as it is the meaning of the work and its possibility—for that failure, while utterly condemning *man*, relieves the *men* of '48, even the murderers, of all particular responsibility. Yes, unremittingly guilty. But guilty *by nature*, guilty of *being born*, pledged on principle wherever they come from, whatever they've done, whatever side they've taken, to a destiny of impotence, endured misfortune, and *ontological* culpability. Finding himself in the *anecdotal* wretchedness and abjection of a singular life, especially if an always possible universalization is never accomplished, if no conclusion is drawn from it, and mutely deciphering it as a free rendering of the abortive revolution, the reader will not necessarily be touched by a new innocence but rather he *will derealize* his culpability. He will strip it of its historicity; the fault is no longer specific, it is not engendered by certain immediately irreversible decisions that one might not have made; it is the human tragedy. Certainly one can distinguish between the moments of the act: there is a *before*—the crime is not yet committed—and an *after*—it is committed for all time. But this *before* and this *after* are fictive since in *any event* the act of deciding produces a crime (at once because our acts resemble us and because they don't resemble us, because—resembling—they betray our egotism and our foolishness, and because, derailed by the force of circumstance, falsified, misunderstood, their violence and their harmfulness become exacerbated: and more generally because human activity is an illusion, an appearance taken on by great cosmic and inhuman forces). This culpability does not seem to be a historicization but the a priori irreversibility of a process of inevitable decline; time and history are at once preserved and adeptly reduced to impotence. There is a duration, a flash of lightning that illuminates a fall—and there is no duration since the fall, which defines human action and enters into the definition of man, begun anew with every man, with every group of men; predictable and repeated, it takes place in the cyclical time of eternity.

Failure will therefore be oracular if the readers of the Second Empire read into it their own political and social history and see it dissolved in an eternity forever begun anew. And since it is easier to succeed than to fail on command, as the voluntarism of defeat would have the immediate result (as we have seen) of changing it into a victory that dare not speak its name, the ascribed failure—as a universal singularity, as the *always possible* universalization of the singular—must be assured, shall we say fatal, *from the outset*, must become for the reader, after ten pages, the object of a certainty and an expectation corresponding to certainties lived by the author himself in the course of the process of degradation he is retracing. This forecast, imposed before 1846, before the decisions of the individual had been implemented even to the slightest degree, like the anticipation of his death and resurrection, had to have for that individual the mysterious clarity and irrationality of a sibylline message; he would be able to ground it neither on his familiarity with the human condition (if he had experience of our impotence, of the lie that makes our illusory acts qualify us without belonging to us, why would he decide to act? Experience comes *after* the fall, that totalizing abolition) nor on a show of will which, while giving him no certainty (indeed, the worst is not always certain), would replace the anguished feeling of a fatal seduction with a cold, abstract determination.

Indeed, it is *precisely* that anxious apprehension of a *suffered* seduction—without any justification—that must be *prophecy itself* as an indefinable quality of lived experience. Not only the prophecy that the future reader will find in the as yet unwritten work, but the prophecy that, passed over in silence, makes the *end* of an enterprise—as the radical condemnation by being of all praxis—the fatal meaning, *tasted* rather than understood, of its beginning. In this disturbing prescience, *denial* and *lack of awareness* are clearly marked by anguish: the destiny about to be imposed, whatever it might be, is abhorrent to the individual at any price. The shipwreck is certain but indeterminate, otherwise anguish would become horror and denial would become specific, defensive forces would be organized. The unqualified purity of the anguish reveals, here, that failure is grasped from within and in anticipation as though already *suffered*. But certainty of the worst, the flavor of lived experience, implies in a way that the victim is in on the secret being hatched against him; in other words, he *organizes* what he *will suffer*, not on the level of the more or less deliberate decision but on that of implicit intentions—by a refusal to know himself—which teleologically structure and orient the temporalization of lived experience.

Prophetic anguish therefore finds its basis in these pithiatic depths where, for certain individuals, inventing oneself and enduring oneself are indiscernible. Furthermore, anguish is itself the bias of failure; to foresee it is to be affected by it first, not in the *active* form of wanting but in the passive and hysterical form of *belief*. In other words, the requisite failure, if it is to fascinate readers as their own historical failure and the eternal failure of man connected by the singular mediation of an anecdotal defeat that took place several years before, will result only from a *conduct of failure*, the apparition in some haunted young soul of a subjective neurosis whose origin is to be sought in the singular and specific givens of his early history. The objectives, in this case, are set by the Other; the young man affirms them as *his* because he cannot reject them, but they continue to seem alien to him, as evidenced by his defensive belief that he cannot attain them. Yet as he considers nonsuccess to be synonymous with subhumanity—because the primacy of the Other confers on him the right to define humanism to his liking, so that the human race, in the eyes of its victim, continues to appear as *his other-essence*—the neurosis in this instance consists of the humiliating expectation of a fall that will deliver him at once from the mandate imposed on him despite himself, and from his destiny as man.

The failure of 1848 will find its justification only in the narrative of prior facts inspired by the pathological metamorphosis of an ordinary man into a man-failure. Art-neurosis does not demand that the artist be *truly* neurotic; in principle, it is of little consequence whether he *is playing the role* of a mental patient or really affected by psychic difficulties; in one way or the other, the themes required by absolute-literature—noncommunication, the solitude of the artist, derealization, failure, panoramic consciousness, and nihilism—will become manifest and determine the meaning of the work. If, however, the best candidates for glory turn out to be two authentic neurotics, Baudelaire and Flaubert (both born in 1821); *if Madame Bovary seems to the readers of 1857 to be the book of their times and, even more, their book; if they unwittingly find in Emma's destiny the image of the fatalities that gave birth, and dealt a dirty death, to the Second Republic—if all this is true, it is because beyond the practico-inert imperatives of the objective spirit, the public can admit only a work of fascination* {editor's emphasis}. As I have said, this is an era in which reading is either listless or neurotic; and in the second case it involves an oneiric satisfaction whose meaning is highly ambiguous. Each person assuages his hatred of all others and justifies his misanthropy—in the margins of a falsely humanistic ideology—while *unrealizing* his personal culpability and even finding an obscure merit in his sufferings, his abjection. And in order to be temporalized, this reading-neurosis requires that the general themes of absolute-art are presented through a true and unique experience that enriches them, veils them, deflects them, and above all, far from drawing all too obvious conclusions from them, *makes them palpable* as the very flavor of lived experience. This means that the public *wants to conclude nothing*, that it is afraid of changing concrete givens into ideas too quickly and of being obliged, after closing the book, to declare its own misanthropy. It means that misanthropy must inhere in the connective tissue of the book, as an *other* thought, a thought *of the other*, of the author, always on the verge of being formulated, always elusive; the public must be able to recompose in secret, reading *another's* failure as *an other* failure and, reassured by this alibi, as its own failure. In a word, it must be appeased and protected against itself by the substance and authenticity of an experience that *cannot be* its own, and that is lived out before its eyes by a spellbound consciousness, a consciousness the reader reconstitutes in the process of reading as his product, and at the same time as an alien reality.

This reader is not a man-failure: his defeat is historic and real, therefore it is not proof that the shipwreck is characteristic of man; quite the contrary, it *characterizes* this midpoint of the nineteenth century and defines the bourgeois and the professional elite. Others in other times could have vanquished their adversaries; in France, after June '48, there is no one but the vanquished—and so they remain defined indefinitely in the history books. To tear themselves away from the historicity that condemns them, they will recognize themselves in their writers only if they find in each one the survivor of a nontemporal, absolute shipwreck, in short a *man-failure* having lived his fall into subhumanity as the singular realization of the original sin, of the archetypal disaster, repeated daily, that gave our father Adam his true nature.

Deep Hatred Must Seem Ordinary

The public of 1850, overwhelmed by real crimes, will heartily welcome the writer whose semisincerity will allow him more effectively to lie to himself, the writer who *really* believes in the "curse of Adam." But since this curse cannot be considered a truth, since the prophetic evidence of bankruptcy cannot, except in neurosis, accompany the establishment of an enterprise it so essentially contradicts, the reader in this era will recruit his misanthropic authors from among those who are authentically neurotic. A subjective neurosis of failure expressing itself in works conceived according to the objective imperatives of art-neurosis and communicating to them the opaque and convincing richness of lived experience—that is what will best support the lies of this society disgusted with itself, unable to recover its equilibrium. This society is not awaiting anything, of course; but *after Madame Bovary* it discovers in itself the need Flaubert awakened, and which for some years would be its properly literary demand.

It is clear, then, that in the 1850s the votes of a public inadequately recovered from its collapse will go to authors whose subjective neurosis consists *precisely* of an intention to fail, and who, apprehending it as *other*, see it as the manifestation of the *impossibility of being man*. In their works, *lived experience* prophesies *after the fact* and universalizes the disaster of '48. In this sense we can say that Gustave offered *this era* the image of the exemplary artist. Conceived this way, however, Gustave's relation to his times seems contingent; we have gone from the necessary and sufficient conditions for his welcome by the public to the proposition that he was, in effect, fulfilling them. But comparisons, especially this entirely empirical one, do not an *argument* make. The striking fact is that the public of the Second Empire *rejects* Leconte de Lisle, its worthy interlocutor, the man who, *like his readers and at the same time*, was determined by the *watershed* of '48—and that this same public, by contrast, adopts as *its* author a young man indifferent to all politics, *whose own watershed* was accomplished, for idiosyncratic reasons, in January 1844. That readers recognized Flaubert as *the exemplary artist* can surely be explained by the structures of the new society, by its historic pessimism, its culpability, its misanthropy. But this selective attitude applies exclusively to the public, which is so constructed that it can recognize itself only in *Madame Bovary*; there is no indication that Gustave's failure—produced and suffered at Pont-l'Évêque—was socially prophetic. Especially since that same public asks him *at once* to be the oracle of the metamorphosis and to derealize its sin by a universalizing lie.

This last quality implies that thirteen years after the fateful night, Flaubert is chosen not for his *truth* but as the instrument of a self-deceiving lie; Gustave therefore seems to have been chosen *by a misunderstanding*, and in a way it is not his *truth* that reading obscurely deciphers but, quite the opposite, his insincerity. So it is hardly possible that Gustave's Fall of '44 can *authentically* reflect the general collapse in 1848 to the readers of '57. All neuroses are insincere; Gustave's seems to be a happy accident that is immediately *exploited* by the disingenuous of 1857; in this case there would be merely a fortuitous connection between the author and the public: the double insincerity and the diachronic time lag could not establish the organic bond of interiority that is regarded as indispensable when we say that a writer *expresses his times*. But it must be acknowledged that this rather awkward notion was simplified to an extreme by criticism—notably by the "scientific" studies of Marxism. We shall be able to grasp the truth and necessity of the reciprocity of *expression* that makes the work an illumination of the general praxis in a given society and makes that society a guarantee, a realization of the work as imaginary prophecy, only if, *on the one hand*, we assume that the book takes account of an entire collectivity, with its lacerations and its struggles, but from a partial perspective that confuses everything and belongs, *in general* (exceptions abound), to the writer himself and to his class of origin, and, *on the other hand*, we assume that what we call an era is the meeting place of numerous generations that distinguish themselves from one another by different pasts and futures, while uniting in a contradictory synthesis because they *share the same present*—a present imposed on them by the force of circumstance even if they interpret it differently. Moreover, it is to this concrete and plural unity that the author must bear witness, though he can do so only *from the perspective of his generation*, that is, on the basis of a past and a future that are unknown to his younger readers. Class bias and diachronic discrepancy—which are, of course, not unrelated dialectically—have the effect of muddying the message and at the same time giving it a *plural* meaning. Engaged in an inflexible present, which he interprets through his projects (the double ecstasy "past-future," which defines him), but thoroughly penetrated by anachronistic *meanings* born of futures and pasts that are not his own, the author can be the contemporary of his contemporaries only if he is both behind and ahead of them. Quite often, moreover, not to say always, what is ahead is determined by what is behind. And that is indeed the case with Flaubert.

Thus, the young bourgeois generation (*the one that was born around 1820* and lived through the entire "July monarchy") *perceives* the bourgeoisie, its own class, *almost* undisguised: the environment—their parents—is revealed as ignoble, the expression of utilitarianism. The denial is *total*. Yet it must be understood that this generation cannot bear *utilitarianism*, that is a fact. These young men, however, cannot *see* the bourgeoisie unless they adopt the (realistic) point of view of the disadvantaged classes; and while a few of them will love the people from afar, the majority merely have contempt for them. They are passably reactionary bourgeois, which for them corresponds, even before they formulate it, to opting for an order maintained by a hierarchical power.

This feeling is deeper and more precocious in Flaubert than in many of the others. The son of a practitioner, he is denied by his family and his studies the possibility of being a scientist or a technician of practical knowledge. And the crisis of the bourgeoisie is manifest for him as an exclusion of utilitarianism and reality. He is therefore compelled to choose the *unreal* and panoramic thought—which claims to see the bourgeoisie from above, as it *is*. But this choice—a forced hand—is accompanied in him from the first, as we have seen, by guilt: he will be a conjurer of shadows, he says bitterly. Furthermore, choosing not to be useful is choosing to *do* nothing; later, he will make a small change and say he is doing *nothing*. Disgusted by utilitarianism, he chooses not only to be useless but to be harmful. All this hides a deep wound: not only is he disinclined to leave his class, but, since that class is the source of all evil, he would also hope it would compensate for its evil through the acknowledgment and selection of an elite to which he would belong. He enters into literature on this basis, that is, solicited from this point of view, literature-already-written (eighteenth century, Romanticism) is about to reveal its contradictory (practico-inert) imperatives to him. He wants to become a writer *so as not to take up a profession*. That is the possible choice for a small soul already penetrated by classical culture but still rather vague. The rest comes from things, inert objective demands that reveal themselves in considerable tension when seized from this angle. Certainly for another bourgeois, more reconciled to his class, for Maxime, for {the playwright Émile} Augier, such demands are scarcely, if at all, apparent: those men want a bourgeois art against their class, which does not consider it necessary to have an art of its own and *for* itself.

But from the moment that the Father, physician and lord, categorically condemns art in the name of science, the young apprentice wants art to be the reverse condemnation, the condemnation of the bourgeoisie—of the real—in the name of an imaginary feudal order, the aristocracy of the Good Lord. As a result, art-to-be-made reveals its triple objective demand: the failure of the man, the failure of the artist, the failure of the work. Which necessarily implies an objective neurosis. Flaubert and Baudelaire are the first to have understood this, precisely because their early history disposed them to become neurotic; the purpose of Flaubert's subjective neurosis is the same as that of the objective neurosis (demanded by the requirements of the objective spirit). We can even say that the imperatives of the objective neurosis universalize and objectify what remained singular and subjective in him: the failure of the man (of his bourgeois self) involves the denial of the real and naked bourgeoisie, and the creation of an imaginary *consolidated* man. He alone can conceive of art for art's sake and realize a work as its own end. This means that art is a treatment imposed on the totality of the imaginary by a man who has himself become imaginary: art and the artist are homogeneous. It goes without saying, however, that Gustave, subjected to the will of his father (who conducts himself in a typically bourgeois fashion by choosing his son's profession), can imagine changing his being only by changing his subjugation. Impossible and even harmful art (demoralization) becomes his daily task.

Objectively, then, art for art's sake seems to be a black feudal order whose principle, beauty, is hidden, but whose artists are, in the imaginary, the Knights of Nothingness. Flaubert's relation to the (bourgeois) real is *imaginary destruction*. We thereby understand that art for art's sake, an unreal feudalism, is in truth the "cover" that writers and artists draw in advance over the bourgeoisie, which is dangerously exposed. An imaginary cover, to be sure, but one that appeals to another cover, also imaginary, that nonetheless *consolidates* it by *distinguishing* the Knights of Nothingness in the name of another knighthood, the chivalry of death (the military). Pushed by his family outside the bourgeois world and into anomaly, Flaubert's deepest, most intense desire (without admitting it to himself) was always to be reintegrated into the elite of his class (inhabited, naturally, by his father and brother) as a mandarin, but he disguised this unrealizable desire with his (equally unrealizable) wish to *change class*.

So we must see that Gustave's profound intention in 1844 is not to *liberate* himself from his father but, quite the contrary, to become reintegrated with his family and live in it under the authority of the black Lord. The complexity and ambiguity of this *subjective* decision rests in the fact that Achille-Cléophas, who was a country gentleman and a bourgeois, a prince of science, appeared simultaneously to be a member of the bourgeois elite and a *modern* aristocrat. Flaubert therefore conceives hierarchy in civil society as an ideal, families being dominated by the paterfamilias, which necessarily implies, in his case, that to guarantee this dream, political society must be a black dictatorship creating an imaginary nobility all of a piece (as the result of a voluntarist selection). Gustave demands a cover because he wants to veil real *property* and self-interest, the basis of utilitarianism (which is this same property insofar as it objectively develops its requirements), with an impossible object, the beautiful, something one does not possess and that must be realized only occasionally as a presentiment, in the work of art. In short, at Pont-l'Évêque, by the realization of the objective neurosis through a subjective attack, Gustave demands an objective cover for his being-as-property-owner four years before the bourgeoisie sought one. He would continue to *possess* but by means of an alienation that made him forget it; he would be the bourgeois-gentleman, like the Goncourts or

Baudelaire, because after 1840 the requirements of autonomous art compelled them to desire the reestablishment of patronage. It was the princes and dukes of the Empire who ought to have taken the place of that false nobility which achieved the appearance of changing class. We know, however, that under the authoritarian Empire, the ideology of this borrowed aristocracy was rosy and benevolent. There was misunderstanding, and certain trials took place as a result. But from 1861 onward, the Empire was liberalized, and it more or less understood its cultural mission. To a degree, political society and the writers become better suited to meet each other's needs. But the liberal Empire was the bourgeoisie triumphant: in it, writers found their class and their public. Until 1870 they would be sullenly attached to the Empire that hid reality from them.

It is clear, then, that in 1844 Gustave was struck down by an attack whose motives were subjective, and whose objective meaning—coming from the conflict of two bourgeois generations and the requirements of the objective spirit grasped from this perspective—was a prophetic summoning of the society of the Second Empire, the only society, strictly speaking, in which Jules the Hermit could live. This society, which the bourgeois would choose on the occasion of real events originating in the class struggle, was an imaginary society, the waking dream of the bourgeoisie of the 1850s, with the advantages and inconveniences attendant upon such a social accident. For the proponents of art for art's sake, there was indeed a kind of diachronic progress. Gustave, in particular, had already constituted himself a subject of the Second Empire in 1844. This is why he missed the rendezvous in '48. It's as if *his* February revolution had taken place in January of '44.

All the artists were attempting to do this around the same time, with more or less success, whether dandyism was taken as a substitute for the defunct nobility, as it was for Baudelaire; whether they really believed in their nobility, as the Goncourts did; or whether an affectation of republican zeal dissimulated pseudoaristocratic memories, as was the case for Bouilhet and Leconte de Lisle. That was art under the Empire. All these men, haunted by the idea of "nervous illness," read each other's work and confirmed each other. By their communion and solidarity they consolidated the unreal in themselves, that is, aesthetic perception. It remains to be shown how the bourgeoisie of the Second Empire would support them because it preferred an apolitical art for art's sake to any manifestation of *engaged* art.

Art for art's sake, however, is not a school. Each of the writers considered here is doing something unique. Flaubert, in particular, is absolutely not a poet. If he wrote some verse in Alfred's time, none has survived. He also declares that he is *not* a novelist, yet he wrote only novels and *La Tentation*. "I am a writer," he says. What does he mean by that? How shall we explain that the common idea of pure art prompted him to produce *those* particular works? We shall try to answer these questions by rereading *Madame Bovary*.

Editor's Conclusion

As I noted in my Editor's Introduction, Jean-Paul Sartre gave Hazel E. Barnes his notes on Gustave Flaubert's *Madame Bovary* and she completed her book *Sartre & Flaubert* (1981). Barnes observes that these notes do not contradict Sartre's view in his published work. Relying on what we have already noted and using Barnes, it seems appropriate to end this abridged study with a short summary of Sartre's view of *Madame Bovary*, its nihilistic realism, and its enduring success both in Gustave's time and in our own.

I will not attempt to gloss the actual text of *Madame Bovary* to see whether I can understand how the story points to nihilism. In truth, when I first read the book, I did not see anything particularly remarkable in it. It did not affect me as did, for example, Herman Melville's *Moby-Dick*. One's first mature reading is what counts, and I think that we must grant that Sartre's first reading revealed the book to him as preaching a false, nihilistic realism. It will prove nothing to go back and read the book with Sartre's interpretation in mind; this sort of thing can always be done. My aim, rather, is to acquire a firmer and clearer grasp on the exact meaning of Sartre's interpretation, regardless of its truth, which I must leave to others to decide.

The preceding discussion has presented us with enough references to allow us to glimpse the direction in which Sartre was heading. I here merely wish to put a particular focus on what has already been mentioned. Let us begin with a few obvious remarks. All of Sartre's works aim at bringing to light our responsibility for making our world and our humanity. This commitment to "making the human" separates Sartre from Flaubert, and it was the initial reason for Sartre's antipathy toward him, following the need to acquire empathy if he was going to understand Flaubert. Indeed, we are again concerned with the purpose of writing. For Sartre, a committed writer invites the reader to become engaged in changing the world toward a more human condition, without, however, preaching this message. This is opposed to Flaubert's notion of art for art's sake. On the other hand, Sartre's concern is with Gustave Flaubert, and here we have to note again that Gustave's appeal to pure art is not born from meditating on art; rather, as we have seen, it arises as a disguised hatred of his family:

> Gustave, as we have seen, wants to escape his familial alienations and screams this out by subjecting himself to art, that is, by presenting it as a nonhuman end, as an inhuman and ultimately antihuman imperative; he cannot conceive of humanity establishing its task as the dissolution of the Other in the bosom of the Same. Ruled and cursed by the Other, Gustave can admit man only insofar as his essence is outside him, in a cruel Other who scorns and devours him. (Cosman 5:425)

As we turn to *Madame Bovary*, Sartre sees all this hatred of humanity simultaneously embodied and hidden in the work on at least three levels, of which Gustave is aware of only two. First, there is the conscious crafting that disguises the deep and general misanthropy in a concrete tragedy of a socially condemned love that cannot be realized in this world. Reading this narrative, we say to ourselves, "If only this or that circumstance had been different—if only Emma or Léon had been honest, or Charles a little more astute in the ways of women's love and if only the social climate more open—Madame Bovary might have had lovers and a devoted husband and would have been moderately happy." Indeed, it is tempting to offer a standard exegesis based on Sartre's understanding of the relation of the novel to Flaubert. After all, we meet again the theme of the doctor. But, according to Sartre, Flaubert is aware that he has fashioned a false realistic novel, and, indeed, that was his purpose in writing it.

The second level of Flaubert's awareness concerns the real message of the book, which we can put simply as: "Why are you concerned with the little misdeeds of Madame Bovary when the best of life is doomed in advance to utter meaninglessness? Don't you know that the bourgeoisie surrounds itself with petty evils, which it then recognizes and rejects—while all the while a deepest of all evils, art for art's sake, has already judged and condemned the entire bourgeoisie class for its 'apelike' existence."

I think it is clear that Sartre believes Gustave is aware of these two levels of reading *Madame Bovary*. The third level—written by him but not known explicitly—is that this message of misanthropy is itself a disguised hatred of his father. In Sartre's study of Jean Genet, we read the simple story of a king who makes a picture of his beloved to bring with him to war. When he returns, the king prefers to contemplate the picture that had captured his beloved beauty rather than the beloved herself. "Right-thinking people will say that the king is mad." Sartre replies, "No, he was not mad; he had become evil."[1] Let us alter the story. A king, fully aware that the beauty of his beloved will fade, has it captured in a picture, which he then takes to war. He returns from war, preferring to contemplate the picture rather than the person of his beloved. In my version, the king was always evil; from the start, he hated the temporality of the human condition, fixing his attention on the portrait the moment it was completed. I suggest that Sartre interpreted *Madame Bovary* in this way—evil is already present in the first line of text and runs throughout the narrative. Even if my remark is true, it is very general. Let us begin anew.

For the sake of argument, I am willing to grant that Sartre could properly gloss the text, revealing all three levels of discourse: surface narrative, general misanthropy, and hatred of family. I do not know exactly how Sartre would go about it; I prefer to merely make a few observations that interest me. Let us then grant that the realm of evil in *Madame Bovary* is in the way the words meld and hold together, revealing, as it were, their underside. Still, these words are "being"; that is, they are marks on a page delivering their message to the reader. But, as in every work of fiction, these marks point to appearance. Thus, returning to the terms of *Being and Nothingness*, while adapting them to a new context, Sartre writes, "The being of nonbeing is the raw material itself of the work as fiction" (Cosman 5:15). The written words are themselves the fictional narrative, in the sense that when reading these words, we dematerialize them into meanings that deliver to us the narrative. Simply, the physical marks of the sentence I am writing become when we read the meaning of the sentence. If the sentence concerns characters in a story, the physical marks are dematerialized into the story itself, otherwise we could never become engrossed in our reading. While this brief explanation is not meant to unveil the mystery of reading fiction, it can be said to point to the normal process of what happens in writing and reading fiction.

But now the door is open to a different use of the way the written words allow the appearance of characters and events to be delivered to us on the pages of a book. The appearances, which play within and on the pages of our book and which we give ourselves to for a temporary respite from the cares of the real world, can be forged so that their aim is to make the real world a respite from action, not a temporary relief but a deep giving of ourselves to the imaginary. We thus carry this imaginary ideal with us throughout the day. Our real actions tend to fade into the imaginary world of fiction. Indeed, the meanings of our actions appear to take their substance and unity from the imaginary perfection of the written work, a perfection hidden by the sturdiness of the letters and spaces on the printed page.

Still, even granting all of the above, I think this would be only a small part of the task to be accomplished in the projected volume on *Madame Bovary*. In the concluding paragraph of the actual work, Sartre hints that a proper reading of the text will reveal that the spirit of art for art's sake prompted Flaubert to write the specific works which he in fact did write. Now either this is a repetition of what Sartre has already said or he is pointing to something new. We already know in great detail how Flaubert's neurosis meshed with the inhuman notion of pure art to cloak both his general misanthropy and that of his father. What, then, is his further question? I suspect that Sartre's aim is to show how the objective spirit of the times demanded the kind of neurosis that was characteristic of Flaubert and which he embodied in his works, specifically *Madame Bovary*. What can this possibly mean? Of itself, the objective spirit of a time must be activated by real people, for it gives only the conditions for actions. Existing individuals may act against the spirit of the time, regardless of the success of their actions; or, they may incorporate this spirit, moving it deeper into itself. This seems to be Sartre's view of Gustave Flaubert. With this in mind, can we reveal an aspect of the objective spirit of Flaubert's time to be such that it, the objective spirit, also masked its misanthropy by a hatred of the father? Which father? The male bourgeois, guardian of those lesser beings, women; the white male property owner, whose intelligence and hard work justified slavery and colonizing for profit; the father, the man of rights, who begrudgingly bequeathed some of these rights to his lesser subjects—could this pervading aspect of the objective spirit of the times be said to demand a work that screamed the hatred of the paterfamilias?

Moreover, it would still be necessary to distinguish progressive from regressive aspects of our reflection. The initial progressive movement would require a deeper look at the phenomenon of the acceptance of a work that proclaimed the hatred of humanity as a "realist" work as well as a new look at Flaubert's status in our contemporary literature. The regressive stage would, I believe, have at least two levels; the first has already been noted; namely, the way the objective spirit of the liberal part of the Second Empire demanded neurotic works, which others approximated but that only Flaubert provided because his neurosis arose from his sustaining hatred of his father. The second regressive stage would have to bring us to the present and explain more fully why Flaubert is still regarded as the father of realism. Sartre does some of this explaining in the work we have examined.

Each regressive stage would then have to be followed by a synthetic-progressive movement, which would reveal the moments of freedom that sustained the dialectical tension between hatred and need. That is, we would have to take a closer look at how and why the Knights of Nothingness sustained the milieu of the primacy of the imaginary, allowing Flaubert to enter within and, at least, for a time, be its king. All of this has already, to a great extent, been accomplished. This new reflection would begin and end from a detailed reading of *Madame Bovary*. That is to say, the dialectical tension between the singularity of Flaubert and universality of the times would concern not only the man and his times but also the specificity of this particular work, *Madame Bovary*. It would almost seem as if the objective spirit had indeed written *Madame Bovary*, with Flaubert as the mediator.

Thus, that strange claim of art for art's sake would now appear to be more than an abstract error, born of the impossible dream of a pure art that can exist apart from humanity. On the contrary, the bad-faith ideal, art for art's sake, would now be manifest as a concrete historical event, the Second Empire, in which the man Gustave Flaubert and the work *Madame Bovary* mesh so perfectly that the each demands the other.

Acknowledgments

Kyle Wagner accepted my suggestion about doing an abridgment of Sartre's massive *The Family Idiot* and carried the project through to completion. Of course, I owe a special word of thanks to the translator of Sartre's text, Carol Cosman. Moreover, I extend my thanks to Sartre's Trust, for allowing the abridgment, and to the readers who approved of the project. James L. Marsh and several others helped me in the beginning stages of this project. The complete editorial staff at the University of Chicago Press has given their usual efficient help. Dylan Joseph Montanari contributed valuable editorial assistance, Lindsy Rice was the production editor, and the press's copyeditor Lori Meek Schuldt carefully edited the manuscript. Nathan Petrie was the promotions manager, and Kristin Rawlings guided me through the questionnaires. Finally, Spencer Fuller of Faceout Studio designed the cover. Marisa Pagin Catalano carefully guided me through the entire manuscript as well as the index.

Notes

EDITOR'S INTRODUCTION

1. Jean-Paul Sartre, *The Family Idiot: Gustave Flaubert, 1821–1857*, trans. Carol Cosman, 5 vols. (Chicago: University of Chicago Press, 1981–93). Parenthetical text citations are identified by translator's name and refer to volume and page number of this edition.
2. Jean-Paul Sartre, *Being and Nothingness: An Essay on Phenomenological Ontology*, trans. and with an introduction by Hazel Barnes (New York: Philosophical Library, 1956), pt. 4, ch. 2, sec. 1, "Existential Psychoanalysis." See Joseph S. Catalano, *A Commentary on Jean-Paul Sartre's "Being and Nothingness"* (Chicago: University of Chicago Press, 1980), 214–18.
3. Jean-Paul Sartre, *The Search for a Method*, trans. and with an introduction by Hazel E. Barnes (New York: Alfred Knopf, 1963), 145.
4. Jean-Paul Sartre, *Saint Genet: Actor and Martyr*, trans. Bernard Frechtman (New York: George Braziller, 1963), 584.
5. Sartre, *Saint Genet*, 34.
6. Jean-Paul Sartre, *The Transcendence of the Ego*, trans. Forest Williams and Robert Kirkpatrick (New York: Noonday Press, 1957), 104.
7. Sartre, *Being and Nothingness*, 463.
8. Sartre, *Being and Nothingness*, 464.
9. Sartre, *Search for a Method*.
10. Jean-Paul Sartre, *The Critique of Dialectical Reason*, 2 vols. 1, ed. Jonathan Rée, trans. Alan Sheridan-Smith (London: NLB; Atlantic Highlands, NJ: Humanities Press, 1976), 1:96. See also Joseph S. Catalano, *Commentary on Jean-Paul Sartre's "Critique of Dialectical Reason, Volume 1: Theory of Practical Ensembles"* (Chicago: University of Chicago Press, 1986).
11. I do not have a deep knowledge of French literature. I am not about to attempt to gloss the actual text of *Madame Bovary* to see whether I can understand how the obvious story points to nihilism. In truth, when I first read the book, I did not see anything particularly remarkable in it. It did not affect me as did Herman Melville's *Moby-Dick*. My aim, rather, is to acquire a firmer and clearer grasp on the exact meaning of Sartre's interpretation. For a better grasp of Gustave's

works, I recommend Hazel Barnes, *Sartre & Flaubert* (Chicago: University of Chicago Press, 1982). On the other hand, I did make an attempt to take a deeper look at *Madame Bovary* and other aspects of *The Family Idiot* in Joseph S. Catalano, *Reading Sartre* (Cambridge: Cambridge University Press, 2010), 3–80, 82–205.

12. Sartre, *Saint Genet*, 557.

CHAPTER ONE

1. A letter to Mlle Leroyer de Chantepie, Croisset, 6 October 1864.
2. {Editor's Note: All quotations from Caroline Commanville seem to come from Gustave Flaubert, *Correspondance*, 9 vols. (Paris: Conard, 1926–33); and supplement, 4 vols. (1954). Sartre does not indicate an exact page reference, and he seems to consider the edition uncritical to the extent that it is not clear where one correspondence ends and another begins.}
3. {Quoted in Flaubert, *Correspondance*, 1:355, as cited by Barnes, *Sartre & Flaubert*, 421.}
4. This is Lacan's translation of the Freudian term *Unheimlichkeit*. [Translator's Note: The usual English translation is "the uncanny."]

CHAPTER TWO

1. It is not *only that—it* is first to work. But work as objectification is also a signifier.
2. Any of Gustave's tales written at this period would reveal, upon inspection, the same theme. Marguerite, Garcia, the *bibliomane*, and Mazza are as much incarnations of Gustave as Djalioh. I have chosen *Quidquid volueris* because here the author's effort to describe his childhood aberration is more explicit. We shall later explore the strange "object relations" that can be glimpsed through these fantasms. It is to the point, nevertheless, to stress that the monkey and the slave represent not only Flaubert's parents. This is the period when Gustave, who was in love with Mme Schlesinger, delighted in sadomasochistic fantasies of Schlesinger's sexual relations with his wife. Gustave imagines the woman he loves in grotesque and obscene postures; she is the debased slave of her supposed husband. He too, then, is surely symbolized by the orangutan. Achille-Cléophas, by contrast, is—as we shall see—doubled: he is at once Monsieur Paul, who presides at the monstrous breeding out of a love of science, and the simian beast who impregnates a woman.
3. Comparing this passage with Caroline Commanville's text—"in the face of their laughter he remained a dreamer, glimpsing a mystery"—we can see that it involves an actual memory.
4. These passions, violent as they are, do not involve the harsh fury of human passions. Such passions, Gustave notes, contain no jealousy or even possessiveness; they address themselves to the whole of creation.

CHAPTER FOUR

1. An insignificant man is as fully signified and signifier as his neighbor, even if his neighbor is the "original" product of an extravagant childhood. All the

significations of the human world determine his insignificance, be it by deprivation. He is compelled by his psychosomatic reality to signify *insignificance* through his projects; inversely, others and the world make of him a *signified insignificant*.

2. Flaubert, we shall see, is one of these few. That is the greatness of his work.
3. Without going into details—we shall come to these as we proceed—it goes without saying that Gustave, even before being conceived, could only be a *younger* child.
4. Let us understand that it can be perpetuated as it is, reappear intermittently, and consequently be integrated into a cycle of repetition, or be abolished in the more or less long term. In any event, however, the only change that can affect it is sclerosis or stereotyping.
5. Cf. Gustave Flaubert, *Souvenirs: notes et pensées intimes*, Avant-propos de Lucie Chevalley Sabatier. Paris: Buchet/Chastel, 1965, 107.
6. Their meaning and their function have continued to vary, for each revolution forms them into a richer aggregate, more differentiated and better integrated. It is in terms of the retotalization at a given juncture, at whatever level it is operative, that the constituting determinations are themselves determined as being or not being assimilable; and in the latter case that they are seen as having a role to play—real or imaginary according to whether the integration is actual or dreamed.

CHAPTER FIVE

1. In another sense, however, unrealization must be taken for total in each case. But this is not crucial here.
2. Of course, the general concern with *rendering* Hamlet ends by becoming an obsession in that every detail of real life is seized upon as an incentive for derealization.
3. I do not claim that the unrealization is continuous. It takes very little for it to give way to cynicism (crazy laughter onstage, an aside to one's partner in front of the audience, etc.); but no more is needed to pass from cynicism to exaltation and its unrealizing exploitation. It all happens in the framework of a general project of unrealization in which recurrences of the real simply happen as a matter of course.
4. What supports him in his effort and is perhaps effortlessly unrealized is his "staging"—a collection of positions, movements, and attitudes indicated by the other or the director. We often hear an actor, in the course of rehearsals, say that he *does not feel* the stage direction that is provided: "Play that sitting down? Say that while moving toward the back? No, my friend, I *don't feel it*." The *feeling*—the attitude accompanying the speech—represents here a mediation between real sensations (kinesthesia, coenesthesia, postures) and their exploitation by the imaginary: if he stands up to speak, the sudden action of springing out of the armchair will dispose him to feel the indignation that has made the fictive character jump to his feet.
5. We shall soon see that this is not true of Gustave.
6. If I did not advance, the Germans would shoot; if I did, I would find myself under French fire. I made a choice, however: the danger was worse on the German side—they wouldn't miss me. But this choice, imposed by the circumstances,

was so little *mine* that it seemed like an integral part of a role I had to play.

7. Maurice Merleau-Ponty, *Signes*, Gallimard, 1960.
8. See the story told by the second narrator in *Novembre*.
9. They don't need much time to judge an audience. Depending on the case, they act in a restrained fashion, give themselves liberties, force certain effects, etc. But for each interpretation of the role to be successful, they must not be in on the secret of what they are doing. The warning of "a tough audience" or "an inexperienced public" or "a cold crowd, look out!" remains inside them as a guiding and almost always nonverbal indication.
10. This is precisely what Hegel calls *pathos*. It will be understood that we have used the word *in this sense* in the preceding pages.

CHAPTER SIX

1. For this reason, photographs of ourselves or a film in which we appear are more revealing than a mirror. The attitude I took in front of the camera, the gestures I made, are mine, I recognize them, but I can observe them to the extent that at the moment I am *looking* I am no longer doing these very things. My image, liberated from myself, tends to become *the image of another*, and I tend to judge it through the eyes of others.
2. As we might expect, a third theme appears *in reaction*: the mirror *frees us from others*, it is our relation to our self. Our only victories, he says to Louise to console her for a failure, are those we have in front of our mirror. And to Louis Bouilhet, who was "in a depression," he wrote: "Come now, little man! Chin up! Bawl all alone in your room. Give yourself a good talking-to in the mirror" (4 September 1850, *Correspondance* 2:237). But the situations in relation to which this theme is evoked (defeats throughout the century) sufficiently demonstrate that it is prompted by wounded pride and is therefore subsequent to the other two. Of course the mirror, here, has only a metaphoric role; Flaubert says to the Muse and to Bouilhet: it is enough that we are content with ourselves; we are our own judges. But the choice of the metaphor speaks volumes: for the image of the *For-itself*, Gustave chose the object that manifests his *being-for-others*. This is not tearing himself away from the hands of others but putting himself in the hands of the imaginary "happy few" who will recognize his merit.
3. June 1845, *Correspondance* 1:182. (Flaubert, Gustave, the complete edition is as follows: *Correspondance*. Paris: Conard, 1926–33, 9 vols; and supplement, 1954, 4 vols.)
4. We shall see later that the audiovisual aspect of language is the source of his taste for puns.
5. Though of course they belong to the same category.
6. The basic choice of artists is polyvalent in childhood because it is above all a choice of the *ludic* and of derealization through the imaginary. External circumstances, internalized, make that choice specific and orient it but it always remains *plural*.
7. To Ernest, 15 April 1838: "Yesterday I finished a mystery that takes three hours to read. Only the subject is worthwhile." 13 September of the same year: "The famous mystery I did in the spring takes only three hours' reading, continues with an unbelievable rigamarole [*galimatias*] or, as Voltaire would have said, pompous nonsense [*galiflaubert*]." We note the importance of oral reading: Gustave

has *timed* his text. He adds: "(for your next visit) . . . I have enough to bore you with my productions for a long time, more noisy than agreeable." Unbelievable rigamarole, a reading more noisy than agreeable—these words shouldn't fool us; we are accustomed to Gustave's insincerity, his false modesty. After all, he was not so disgusted with *Smarh* at the time since he envisaged reading it to his friend. Yet these words, this time particularly violent, nonetheless betray his *fear*: of having failed in his work. No doubt he was counting on Ernest's admiration to convince him that he had succeeded. As we see, Gustave's great disgust with writing is proclaimed in the month of July, sandwiched between two other letters that shed light on it.

8. A comparison between the artist's work and masturbation is often found in his written remarks: "Let us masturbate the old art to its deepest joints." "The erection has finally come, Monsieur, by dint of beating and manumauling myself," etc. Cf. Roger Kempf: "Le Double pupitre" in *Cahiers du Chenevis*, October 1969.
9. I am not saying that solitude is imposed *by definition* on the writer; *social* forms of literary creation exist—collaboration is one such form. There are others: the cultural revolution can lead to the collective production of a written work (as well as to the challenge of art in the name of practical creation). I am describing the situation most common in the nineteenth century, symbolized by the fact that many writers, in order to find extreme isolation (like Balzac or George Sand), worked *at night*, when sleep abolished the society around them (Stendhal, by rising at dawn, demonstrated that he still belonged to the classical centuries and that he brought the literary attitude of the eighteenth century into the era of "romanticist" solitude).

CHAPTER SEVEN

1. "If I take the risk of showing [these pages] to a small number of friends, it will be a sign of confidence" (*Un Parfum à sentir: Deux mots*). "Perhaps you will laugh afterward . . . looking back on a poor child who loved you more than anything else and whose soul was already tormented with such foolishness" (*Agonies*: dedication to Alfred). "And then Christ wept . . . and Satan, laughing more horribly than one of the dead" (ibid., conclusion). Etc., etc.
2. End of *Un Parfum à sentir*.
3. *Correspondance*, 2:268.
4. *Sic*.
5. *Correspondance* 4:141, 3 January 1857.
6. *Correspondance* 4:143.
7. Ibid., [vol. 4,] pp. 158–59.
8. The suicide of bankrupts is a frequent theme in the literature of the nineteenth century. Not without reason.
9. Can he prevent a newcomer entering the school during the year, someone better taught and more competent, from stealing his ranking and with that his grade (the tendency of teachers being, in general, only rarely to exceed a certain *maximum* quota which they have fixed in advance, so if the new boy holding first place is graded 15/20, the former first has a good chance of falling to 14)? Or a schoolmate, until now more mediocre, from suddenly waking up, catching up with him, and overtaking him? Or a new teacher from disconcerting him with his teaching methods? Etc.

10. It will be noted that Charles Bovary is rather poor and enters the *collège* because his mother has ambition. And he will feel displaced there.
11. The baccalaureate at first seemed to be a simple rite of passage allowing the sons of the bourgeoisie to accede to the direct exercise of the powers of their class. But from the beginning of the twentieth century it has tended increasingly to take on the character of a competition, which allows the unmasking of its selective nature.

CHAPTER EIGHT

1. Cf. 26 August 1834. To Ernest [Chevalier], *Correspondance* 1: 13. Here Flaubert tells the story of a drowning and the comments it inspires.
2. An exception, however, is the letter of 31 March 1832: "One student at Pere Langlois's nearly . . . fell into the privy. . . . If he had not pulled himself out, he would have fallen into Pere Langlois's excrement." Here we find once more the scatological vein of the "Explication de la fameuse constipation."
3. *Correspondance* 1: 16–17, 2 July 1835.
4. Edition de Monaco, 3:247. Goncourt, Edmond and Jules de. *Journal: Mémoires de la vie littéraire*. Monaco: Fasquelle and Flammarion, 1956.
5. As the dedications of *Agonies* and the *Mémoires* prove.
6. *Souvenirs*, 96. as above?
7. *Souvenirs*, 90 and 109.
8. We should note that Flaubert's thought, as often happens to him at this time, immediately goes astray. Indeed, he adds: "How could I tell you everything I've felt, everything I've thought, all the things I enjoyed that evening? . . . Could I ever tell you all the melodies of its voice," etc. There are two themes here: the first is the "mysteries of the soul unknown to itself," the second, quite different, is the inadequacy of words when it is matter of rendering sensation or feeling, even when they are the object of a clear reflexive consciousness.
9. Or unless it is offered, as in the German Romantics and in *Louis Lambert*, as a sign of our double nature. Indeed, Balzac writes: "How is it that men have reflected so little until now on the accidents of sleep which charge man with a double life. . . . Shouldn't there be a double science in this phenomenon? . . . It indicates at least the frequent disharmony between our two natures." But we must not look for some presentiment of the Freudian *Interpretation of Dreams* in this text, since Balzac adds: "I have thus found at last a testimony to the superiority that distinguishes our latent senses from our apparent senses." The dream, for Louis Lambert, is really a means of access to the supernatural. To the contrary, the nightmares described by Flaubert are bitterly realistic and explicitly given as the effects of his nervous troubles and his anguish.
10. I add that the word *castration* is for me merely the expression of facts *in a certain discourse*.
11. *Souvenirs*, 108.

CHAPTER NINE

1. Ibid., 63.
2. *Correspondance*, Supplement, 1:49.
3. *Souvenirs*, 46.

4. *Correspondance* 1:405, 23 November 1846. We note the flagrant contrast of this passage with others of the same period; with this one, for example (9 August 1846, *Correspondance* 1:231): "I had seen things and myself too clearly. . . . I had understood everything in me, separated it, classified it (before seeing you—therefore before August 1846)." Flaubert never entirely makes up his mind either to know himself or not to know himself.
5. *Correspondance* l: 37. The context indicates—we shall return to it—that he has since fallen back into stagnation because of the difficulties of *execution*.
6. The "bouncing back" will calm his rage but not his fits of rancor. In the same letter and in the one following, Louise will pay: she had sent him a comedy, which he tears to pieces. As for Gautier, he loses nothing by waiting. On 24 April of the same year, Flaubert writes to Louise: "Good old Gautier, he was yet a man born and made to be an exquisite artist. But journalism, the common course, poverty (no, let us not curse the milk of the strong), the prostitution of mind rather, for it is that, have often lowered him to the level of his contemporaries."
7. To Louise, 27 December 1852.
8. *Journal*, 2 November 1863.
9. To Louise, 8 August 1846.

CHAPTER TEN

1. Caroline's letter informs us that at this date, Madame Hamard lay dying.
2. This would not be the only one. For example, the letter that Caroline says she received on the 17th at five o'clock in the evening—which might allow a better understanding of Gustave's mental state at this date—has been lost or destroyed.
3. He writes "Pont-Audemer."
4. 9 February 1844, to the same Ernest: "[I am following] a stupid regimen." We shall return to this point.
5. But his submission prevents him from making the pleasure last: after one day or, at the most, two, he sends a note to Caroline.
6. Letter of 17 January 1844.
7. It goes without saying that I do not mean to deny the *truth* of such suffering. I am saying only that this biologically *rational* fact, the death of the other, is lived *in irrationality* because it is unrealizable and that, for this reason, all our acts are transformed into gestures. To cite only one example, to carry out the last wishes of a dying man can lead to real and difficult endeavors. But they are derealized from the outset because they are born of the futile decision to keep him alive, to institute him as living by claiming that he is at the source of acts which are in fact born of our personal options. The carrying out is *in principle* incommensurate with the *intention* one claims to realize; the results will be always *other* than what the dead man had foreseen, and we cannot help being aware of it.

CHAPTER ELEVEN

1. {Editor's Note: Sartre's *exis* is a misprint of the Greek word *Hexis*, a term in Aristotle's philosophy which Sartre repeats from his earlier works, meaning a relatively stable arrangement or disposition.}
2. G. Flaubert, *Pléiade* ed., 1:644. It will be observed that he has already sought

death "by saving . . . children from the depths. The abyss rejected him." *Madame Bovary*, vol. 1 of *Oeuvres*, text established and translated by A. Thibaudet and R. Dumesnil. Pleiade Edition. Paris.

3. My italics.
4. Which Madame Flaubert certainly had not had in 1821.

CHAPTER TWELVE

1. To Ernest, 11 November 1944, *Correspondance*, 1:157.
2. To Maxime, April 1946, *Correspondance*, 1:204.
3. To Louise, 2 September 1953, 9 o'clock, *Correspondance*, 1:331.
4. To Louise, 2 September 1953.
5. *On the surface*; deep down, there is a counterpart to which we shall return.
6. It is unlikely that the referential attacks arise spontaneously, without external provocation, like certain organic disorders that periodically reproduce themselves. It must be supposed, on the contrary, that Gustave, while maintaining his hysterical disposition to repeat the attack at Pont-l'Évêque, does not become convulsive unless family events more or less faithfully reconstitute the situation of January 1944—or at the very least dispose him to relive it. One surmises that such occasions are not lacking: the activism of the paterfamilias is perpetual provocation, as are, to a lesser degree, the presence or the words of the two "Achilles" when they come to the Hôtel-Dieu, the projects they are involved in, the future they imagine. We must take into account as well "Caroline's betrayal" and her engagement, the visits of Hamard, the friendship Flaubert is compelled to show him. When all these givens, in one way or another, converge, when his present state is *put in question*, when he feels observed, spied upon, when allusions to his comrades, to his future life reawaken dormant frustrations, in short, when the pond is disturbed and the slime rises to the surface, he reacts by becoming convulsive.
7. Obviously, to *situate* things is not the equivalent of an idealist designation: one discovers them as they are and in their real relations, but insofar as this set of relations is grasped as a practical environment by the agent. The discovery of an oil deposit immediately *situates* this stratum in relation to other strata (possessed by others), to means of transport, to drilling instruments, to the costs of exploitation (which result in great part from the above-mentioned determinations), to available capital, to economic conditions, etc. Be that as it may, the stratum has not awaited this discovery for its *being-there*.
8. None of this can be understood if we forget that praxis necessarily comprises a moment in which man (and beast) is turned back toward his own inertia (for the living being is inertia surpassed but preserved) in order to make it the unique means of working the inert (I have described that moment of praxis in the *Critique of Dialectical Reason*). Inertia is a certain structure of the living and consequently of action. Thus the inversion of transcendence—a typical but deviant moment of the pithiatic option in Flaubert—does not have to *invent* the inert. It restricts itself to making it an end when it was merely a means. We shall see further on, once again, how Flaubert *utilizes* this inertia. Not to gain leverage or to shoulder a weight, but—this is the positive aspect of the option—to free the imaginary from its practical matrix and to construct the unreal adventure of the artist. What I want to emphasize here is that, while the crisis of '44 is in

itself derealization, its real elements are given in the very structure of praxis. Gustave, being a passive agent, exploits his inertia to other ends, that's all. {Editor's Note: Sartre makes a distinction between action and praxis. Action is a happening that does not involve us with our general outlook on life, our project, nor with the historical context of our lives. That Gustave was a second son is a simple happening to him; but the complex meaning of this is a praxis. I developed this in my *Commentary on Jean-Paul Sartre's "Critique of Dialectical Reason, Volume 1: Theory of Practical Ensembles,"* 57, 65, 87, 221–22, 237–38.}

9. Obviously this is untrue: the inheritance will be divided into three equivalent portions. It is true that Gustave does not own Croisset, but he has other properties from which—until Commanville's ruin—he draws a comfortable income.

CHAPTER THIRTEEN

1. In contrast to Kafka's *Letter to Father*, which was never received by its addressee.
2. Jules is not made for action. But Henry, who seduces a woman, carries her off, and leaves for the Americas with her, is in fact led by chance every bit as much as his friend. Cf. above.
3. To Ernest, 9 February 1844.

CHAPTER FOURTEEN

1. That is, to destroy or conceal the relation of reciprocity.
2. A novel that Maxime didn't much like or didn't understand—though he thought it worthy of appearing in the *Revue de Paris*.
3. But the appraisal of the works is an underlying assumption, the point of departure, and the final term of the estimate of Gustave's behavior which is denigrated in the name of what it *might have been*. An absurd proposal: How can we know what it might have been without the crisis? But Maxime is too shrewd to show his hand: he claims to have us judge the works on the basis of their author's behavior. How could this woolgatherer, this enervated, abnormal fellow reach the heights in his works?
4. {Joseph Catalano, "Crafting Marks into Meanings and Things," *Philosophy and Literature* 20, no. 1 (April 1996): 47–60.}

CHAPTER FIFTEEN

1. Because that *other thought* designates, beyond rationalizations, *their own—which* is, in each of us, at once other and the same.
2. Still, if you like, communication continues to exist, misunderstood and indirectly intended; in effect, the neurosis attempts to infiltrate the very consistency of the words, but that consistency and otherness of language come naturally from the fact that language came to him through others and he remains *spoken* by them. The neurotic does not connect this *consequence* to its primary cause.
3. This is not a matter of organicism, as you might think. I shall clarify my views on this subject further on. {Editor's Note: Sartre rejects what he terms "hyperorganism"—namely, the notion that historical unities, such as cities and na-

tions, have an ontological status that is not reducible to individuals and their behaviors. Unities that are larger than individuals do exist; but they are parasitical, deriving and sustaining their unification from individual praxis and the "mediations" arising from these praxis.}

CHAPTER SIXTEEN

1. Edmond de Goncourt: "Imagine, our work—and perhaps this is its originality—is dependent upon nervous illness." Cited by Bourget, *Essais de psychologie contemporaine*, vol. 2, p. 162.

EDITOR'S CONCLUSION

1. Sartre, *Saint Genet*, 356.

Index